D1557418

The Lady Penelope

PASSION AND INTRIGUE
AT THE HEART OF THE ELIZABETHAN COURT

Sally Varlow

ANDRE
DEUTSCH

This edition published in 2014 by
André Deutsch
An imprint of the
Carlton Publishing Group
20 Mortimer Street
London W1T 3JW

First published in 2007

2 4 6 8 10 9 7 5 3 1

A CIP catalogue record for this book is available
from the British Library

ISBN 978 0 233 00407 5

Typeset in Liverpool by E-Type
Printed and bound in Great Britain by CPI Group (UK) Ltd,
Croydon CR0 4YY

For Grandpa, E. L. Mann,
author of *Unknown Warriors*, *The Chislehurst Mystery* and
The Battle of Lewes

They are gone. Their names unknown
No fair marble shrines display.
— F. W. Bockett

PICTURE CREDITS

Contents

Penelopy b. 1563 d 1607 age 44

Preface

"*T*he last request I will now impart to you, shall be to hold me in your memory," wrote Lady Penelope Rich to Secretary of State Sir Robert Cecil. It was July 1595 and she was at the height of her power and beauty.

Twelve years later, when she died, ironically it was Cecil who probably did most to blacken her memory and remove the real Penelope from history. Reduced to a stereotype – brazen adulteress, power seeker, heroine of the Court rat-pack – she joined the ranks of the "Unknown Warriors" whose lives are lost to us. Theirs were the tales that formed my favourite bedtime stories, written by my grandfather in his children's history book, *Unknown Warriors*. Ever since, I have relished piecing together lost lives and loves; and around The Lady Penelope there are enough scattered fragments to suggest that she was much more than a romantic beauty.

Four hundred years on from her death, it is time to look again at what is said and what is known about her. We should challenge the footnotes to famous men's lives, which cast her as merely a glittering Court figure who flaunted her beauty in brazen love affairs. We must move on from academic debates: "did she or didn't she" have an affair with Sir Philip Sidney, soldier-poet hero of the age, who wrote her more than a hundred love sonnets? We need to search among the records of Court intrigues and ask what political significance she held. Why did her brother, the Earl of Essex, point her out as a chief influence in the coup that cost him his life? What lay behind the special affection and tolerance the queen always showed her?

Since previous studies of Penelope – and there are only three – fresh facts have been revealed about her family and friends. Discoveries have been made about Catholic sympathies; about the underworld of Sir Francis Walsingham's spy network; and not least my own about her grandmother's paternity. Inside the Latin dictionary that belonged to Penelope's grandfather, Sir Francis Knollys, are details which put it beyond reasonable doubt that Lady Katherine Knollys was an illegitimate daughter of King Henry VIII. It adds new meaning to Elizabeth's extraordinary indulgence towards both

Penelope and her brother, and to their role in the politics of Elizabeth's dying years.

The task of gathering together slivers of information has been revolutionized by online data and catalogues, in particular the updated *Oxford Dictionary of National Biography*. No less visionary is the decision by some county library services, mine in East Sussex included, to give ticket holders free, home access to *ODNB* on line. And there are the British Library's brilliant on-line catalogues, free to all users.

It is access to myriad facts and sources that enables one to reconstruct a lost life. One element only is missing and has to be imagined – Penelope's emotions. Beyond her thirty-three brief letters we can only make informed assumptions about them. The rest is real.

Acknowledgements

*F*irst in my list of thanks must come Dr Simon Adams, whose encouragement and help since the start of my research into Lady Katherine and Lady Penelope have been invaluable; and Dr Michele Margetts, whose scholarship is inspiring and who could not have been more generous with time and discussions. I am also indebted to Richard Knollys for his kind interest in my research; to Hugh Knollys for informing me of the Latin dictionary's existence; and to its owner, Hugo Brunner, for readily making it available, and arranging for Magnus Brunner to photograph it. John Wood was also kind enough to share with me his knowledge of Knollys family history and portraits.

The rest of my research has been aided by countless acts of generosity. Philippa Gregory kindly talked me through her research into Mary Boleyn. Professor Gordon R. Batho was immediately helpful over queries on the Percy family. Dr Grace Ioppolo allowed me sight of her paper on Penelope's letters, when I had almost ended my study. Ylva French helped me with her encyclopedic knowledge of London; and Mara Prengler Hogg translated Antonio Pérez's Spanish letters. I used my own faulty French on some of Penelope's letters to the Hotmans, so the mistakes on those, and elsewhere, are entirely mine – as is the interpretation.

At libraries, county record offices and historic houses I have received fast and friendly help from: Dr Andrea Clarke and Dr Frances Harris, at the British Library; Christine Reynolds, Westminster Abbey Library; Dr Kate Harris, Longleat House; Richard Pailthorpe and Shirley Guest, Syon House; Terry John, Lamphey Palace; Josephine Barry, Petworth House; Dr Heather Wolfe, Folger Shakespeare Library; Mary Robertson, Huntington Library; Jackie Hogg, Warwickshire Record Office; Michael Carter, Centre for Kentish Studies; Matthew Blake and Joanne Cartwright, Staffordshire Record Office; Lesley Akeroyd, Huntingdon Record Office; Alison McCann, West Sussex Record Office. And on portraits: Katherine Coombs, V&A; Karen Hearn, Tate Britain; and Karen E. Denavit MLS, Yale Center for British Art, New Haven.

Reference to, and quotation from, original documents is made by kind permission of: the British Library; the Folger Shakespeare Library; the Bodleian Library, University of Oxford; the Trustees of Lambeth Palace Library; the Marquess of Bath, Longleat House, owner of the Devereux and Dudley Papers; the Earl of Aylesford, owner of the Essex Letter Book; the Marquess of Salisbury, owner of the Cecil Papers; and Viscount De L'Isle, owner of the De L'Isle Manuscripts.

At André Deutsch I have been blessed with Penny Phillips as my editor, and her predecessor Miranda West.

From the years that I have spent with The Lady Penelope, two images stay with me always. One is the great, sadly late, Elizabethan scholar Jasper Ridley, who replied to my questions, eyes twinkling beneath his pure white hair: "In my experience there is almost always some truth, somewhere, in a rumour." The other is Marjorie L. Davies, gently encouraging me each day to finish what is now her 101st birthday present.

My thanks to all of you, and especially to my husband, Peter.

Prologue

*I*t is an evening early in July four hundred years ago. In a large London house not far – let us say – from the royal palace of Whitehall the candles are already alight. There is a log fire freshly lit in the stone hearth even though it is high summer, for the woman seated beside the fire feels a little feverish.

Her pale, slim hands lie folded in her lap while she watches the flames grow stronger. Soon her jewels begin to shine and the pearls on her gown give off their soft milky glow. But they do not match the gleam of her large, dark eyes. No matter how many tears she has shed, her eyes still sparkle in the fire-light. The few strands of grey that mark her forty-four years have not dimmed her glorious red-gold hair.

There is a faint sound by the door and she looks up. Is it one of her children come to visit? Or her sister, my Lady Northumberland? Perhaps it is a messenger from her mother, the countess? But no, it is nothing. No one is there.

Penelope Devereux is alone. In days gone by she was surrounded by the most powerful people in the capital. In days gone by she was known as Lady Rich, the Countess of Devonshire, even "Stella" – the brightest star that shone in Queen Elizabeth's Court. Now she has no right to any title except The Lady Penelope, and she has only her thoughts for company.

She shivers a little and moves her feet closer to the hearth. Perhaps she knows this fever is serious. Perhaps not. Maybe she has guessed her life is drawing to its close. Her heart has known such pain – and joy – how can it bear any more? Her beloved Mountjoy has been dead full fifteen months, yet still her sorrow deepens at every dawning. Still, when she sleeps she sees again his dear head lying on its last pillow, eyes closed for ever. How cruelly the whisperers treated him, when he had served his country so well.

The Lady Penelope is accustomed to malice and rumour. Court gossip spreads like a summer breeze across a barley field, heads nodding as each ear bends to catch what is passing. The Court has been her life ever since she came to London, so many years ago, to be a maid of honour to her godmother, Queen Elizabeth. When King James followed to the throne and she enjoyed fresh royal favour, no slander could touch her. But now that the king has turned against her, the slurs and insults will grow. Few, if any, courtiers and ministers who once begged her attention will seek her company any more.

It is strange, she thinks, watching the fire flicker, that James banished her from Court for her second marriage, which he called illegal, just as Elizabeth banished her mother, Lettice, for secretly marrying Robert Dudley, Lord Leicester. Elizabeth favoured her "Sweet Robin" like a lover, and considered him her own, though she would not make him her husband. She forgave him the marriage, but she carried her hatred of Lettice to the grave. No doubt James would do the same. Such a faithless king. Had he forgotten how Penelope and her brother, Robert, Earl of Essex, backed his claim to the throne while he waited in Scotland for Elizabeth to die? The Lady Penelope permits herself a slight, satisfied smile, deepening the tiny lines that circle her full, red mouth. But her smile fades fast as she remembers the whispering campaign that began after Essex's rebellion six years ago.

Only a witch, some said, could have charmed Elizabeth's ministers into believing that Lady Rich intended no treason. Essex went to his death on the block claiming Penelope had urged him to raise London against the government. Yet she talked her way out of danger. Surely, they said, such influence comes only with magic or immoral power.

She did indeed have power. Lord Mountjoy, her lover, was commander-in-chief of her majesty's army. Even Elizabeth dared not raise her hand against the mother of Mountjoy's children while he campaigned so successfully in Ireland. But all that is passed. There is no one to protect her now. In years to come, when the smears and ribald jests are repeated, who will set the record straight? Who will ride out to be her champion, as Mountjoy did on that cold November day? Was it really sixteen years ago?

In the firelight she sees again the handsome figure riding bare-headed into the tiltyard on Accession Day, blue and yellow colours like sunshine on his armour, declaring to the world that he is her knight, her champion. She hears again the little gasps from the ladies near her as they read the meaning of his colours. Their eyes dart left and right, searching among the onlookers for her – and for her husband, Lord Rich. Mountjoy never pauses. He bows his head to the queen and rides on across the yard to take his place among the mounted challengers.

Penelope stretches her hand to the fire and feels the warmth of his body pressed against hers. She feels the weight of his head in her lap and the softness of his dark, curly hair. She remembers the long, blissful nights they first spent together – lying tired and sleepy in each other's arms. And the short, sad hours before daybreak when he had to depart on campaign again, leaving her and the children alone. She remembers – oh, so many more scenes and faces – as she stares into the flames. Lord Rich, her first husband, forced on her too young. Earl Walter, her father, dead these many years but never forgotten. Lettice, her devoted mother, and Lord Leicester, her powerful stepfather. Lady Katherine Knollys, the grandmother whose story held such meaning for them all. Sir Philip Sidney, who died a hero's death in battle far away, leaving all those love lyrics to her. Robert, Earl of Essex, her rash, adorable, moody brother – and the men who ruined him, crooked Robert Cecil and villainous Walter Ralegh.

She shudders and grips the chair, pressing her nails hard into the wood. She hears the sickening sound of the axe striking once, twice, three times into Essex's soft white neck. She sees the blood spurting over his fine linen – and falls back in her chair, head pounding, struggling not to vomit. Merciful God, will the nightmares never cease?

In days to come, who will understand the web of love, honour and intrigue that bound them all together? How soon will memories fade or be falsified? She did her best to set out the truth when she was summoned to Star Chamber to defend her marriage to Mountjoy and save their children's inheritance. Yet there was much she could not, would not, tell in court. It would be well, perhaps, to write a true account of what happened and leave it for her children.

Not tonight, though. Her eyes are hot and tired. The light is too dim. Only lovers, spies and politicians need write by candlelight, and she is none of those. Not now. Tomorrow, maybe, if she feels stronger, she might begin to set it down.

PART I

Childhood and Ancestry

1563–1580

Chapter One

> "An harlot, adulteress, concubine and whore"
>
> – Court of Star Chamber, 1607

*P*enelope Devereux died on 6 July 1607. If she wrote any memoirs they have long since been lost. Few of her letters survive and no details of her last hours are certain. No one even knows for sure where she is buried.

Yet Penelope was a legend in her lifetime. She was the most beautiful woman at the Court of Queen Elizabeth. Her charm and grace, her large dark eyes and red-gold hair, her sweet voice and skill at languages inspired some of the most famous love poems ever written. And her devotion to her brother, the Earl of Essex, led her to become the only female conspirator in his plot to bring down Elizabeth's government in the dying years of the reign.

From the day Penelope came to Court at the age of eighteen to be a lady-in-waiting to her godmother, the queen, she lived and loved at the centre of power. While the Spanish Armada was scattered, while Drake circled the world, Mary Queen of Scots was executed and Shakespeare came to London, Penelope knew everyone of note in government, in society, in the playhouses – and in hiding for their Catholic faith.

Her close family was a roll-call of the great and sometimes good. "Sweet Robin", Earl of Leicester, Elizabeth's supreme favourite, was her stepfather. Robert, Earl of Essex, said by some to be the queen's young lover, was Penelope's adored brother. Lord Mountjoy, the last and greatest Elizabethan general, was her lover and second husband. Her mother was Lettice Knollys, the red-haired "She-wolf" loathed by Elizabeth for marrying Lord Leicester. Her father, Sir Walter Devereux, was head of one of the most ancient noble families. Her grandmother was Katherine, Lady Knollys, Elizabeth's dearest "cousin" and daughter of "the other Boleyn girl". Her grandfather, Sir Francis Knollys, was the queen's trusted minister for more than forty years. Her sister Dorothy married "the Wizard Earl" of Northumberland. And Shakespeare's patron, the charismatic young Earl of Southampton, was Penelope's close friend and husband of her favourite cousin, Elizabeth Vernon.

When King James came to the throne in 1603, two years after Essex's failed coup, Penelope and her lover Lord Mountjoy rose instantly to royal favour. She was one of the grand ladies who rode north to welcome the new queen, Anna, and she was soon one of Anna's chosen companions. While Mountjoy was made Earl of Devonshire as a reward for his military successes in Ireland, Penelope was raised to the rank of one of the premier peeresses. Even in her forties she was beautiful and accomplished enough to take lead roles in Anna's elaborate Court masques.

But her role as Stuart royal favourite and political hostess lasted only three years. By the time Penelope died she was an outcast from Court, scorned by the king, stripped of all her titles and permitted only to sign herself The Lady Penelope. Soon that name would also be forgotten, along with the details of her death. Whatever her last illness was, it was brief. She had spent the previous few months chiefly in London. Since Lord Mountjoy's death in April 1606, his distant kinsmen had repeatedly challenged his will, and she was summoned by the Court of Star Chamber to answer charges of forgery to secure her children's inheritance.

The stakes were high. Mountjoy died a very wealthy man and his relations pursued his estate, and Penelope, through every court open to them. She was not, they insisted, his "lawful wife but an harlot, adulteress, concubine and whore", and she had obtained his lands "by devices and deceits". Mountjoy realized that living with her "dishonoured him with the king's majesty", they said, and his distress led to his death. In fact, it wasn't *living* with Penelope that was the problem, nor fathering five of her nine surviving children. James, and probably every member of the small group who made up high society, knew about their long-term love affair, their children and their home at Wanstead. Yet the king and queen still showered them with favours.

The real cause of the scandal and Penelope's banishment from Court was their marriage in December 1605. Under the terms of the divorce she had just obtained from her first husband, Lord Rich – father of her eldest four children – she was forbidden to remarry in Rich's lifetime. By deliberately flouting the law, James considered Penelope had challenged his divine authority. Fearful of powerful women, James warned Mountjoy that she had "a black soul", and her scandalous reputation would ruin his career. Mountjoy himself was too valuable to James to be dismissed. Given time, he might have softened the king's opinion and brought Penelope back into favour, but within four months of their marriage Mountjoy was dead. Penelope's disgrace was confirmed when he was buried in Westminster Abbey with the pomp and ceremony due to a national hero, but without her Devereux coat of arms quartered with his, as befitted his wife.

The subsequent scramble for Mountjoy's money unleashed all the censure and abuse against Penelope that her adultery had escaped. With her enemies circling like vultures to pick over her life, and none of her family left in power to defend her, she was easy prey. The allegations in court that she was immoral, shameless, unscrupulous and money-seeking soon leaked to listeners outside, and the humiliation was intense. Fifteen months after Mountjoy's death, and before the legal cases were concluded, Penelope also died. Few now paid tribute to the face and charm that launched so many sonnets and songs. Instead there were scurrilous rhymes about her:

> Here lies fair Penelope or my Lady Rich
> Or the Countess of Devonshire, I know not which.

Her removal from Court had been a bonus for Robert Cecil, secretary of state to Queen Elizabeth and King James. However cordial relations between him and Penelope appeared on the surface, they both knew he was her brother's bitterest enemy. When Essex had been alive James had no time for Cecil and his father, Lord Burghley. It was only after Essex's execution that James grew to trust Cecil, and Cecil could never be comfortable while Penelope was close to James and Anna. Each time her name was blackened, his short, hunch-backed figure could sit more easily in its fur-lined robes; and it was not difficult for him to manipulate the way history remembered her.

For years Cecil and his father had control of the paper trail that chroniclers would use to record the reigns of Elizabeth and James. It was Burghley's nominee, William Camden, who wrote the official biography of Elizabeth, using files the Cecils had filleted and archives they had arranged. In the aftermath of Essex's revolt, Cecil's agents had raided the homes of every conspirator, including Penelope, and removed every shred of paper they fancied.

Within a few years the facts of her life and loves were buried beneath slander and spin, or lost, along with most of her letters and portraits. The real Penelope Devereux disappeared. When the Protestant establishment rushed to create iconic heroes out of Sir Philip Sidney and Lord Mountjoy, the least said about Penelope the better: she was a stain on both soldiers' escutcheons. Victorian historians, faced with few facts and strong stories about her love life, fell back on moralizing and stereotyped her as a scarlet woman, "the scandal of her age". One of her descendants, the Duke of Manchester, would clearly have liked to horsewhip Essex for condoning her affair with Mountjoy.

Twentieth-century historians were often no more enlightened. If they remembered her at all it was as a two-timing wife who inspired Sidney's many sonnets about *Astrophil and Stella*; and the true daughter of a mother who "flaunted her beauty shamelessly, first to capture Walter Devereux, but soon after her marriage to capture other lovers". Penelope is branded as "false, sly, arrogant, and alternating between insolence and cringing"; an "emotional cripple" who gave herself "without love to the prosperous Lord Rich" and then began an affair with Sidney. Her long and loyal relationship with Mountjoy is described as "philanderings", during which she "bore her husband children". She even gets sole credit for starting the sex revolution in Elizabethan England, when: "Adultery seized the public imagination ... because of the unshackled behaviour of one woman, an inspirational beauty of huge vitality and sexual allure ... the poets who acclaimed Penelope Rich could not avoid knowing of her adultery."

Just a handful of biographers, writing about the most famous figures of the day, have wondered in passing what Penelope's real role was in Essex's revolt. Was she "perhaps a main instigator"? Maybe she was "a politician and a dangerous one", and her role "was probably crucial". But none has stopped long enough to consider why she was so swiftly air-brushed from history. Why did no one step forward and rescue her reputation? Were there more reasons for her to fall victim to the Protestant propaganda machine? Why did she plot against Elizabeth? And what was her real relationship to the crown?

Penelope Devereux had everything Queen Elizabeth longed for: youth, beauty, charm, unquestionably noble birth, a close and devoted family, a nursery full of children and a handsome lover. But if Elizabeth had cause to be jealous of Penelope, Penelope had every reason to loathe the querulous old woman who lingered on the throne.

Elizabeth ruined Penelope's father financially in a hopeless venture that led to his death in Ireland when Penelope was thirteen. Elizabeth humiliated her mother after Lettice's subsequent marriage to Lord Leicester. She refused to receive her sister after Dorothy's runaway marriage. And Elizabeth ensured her brother's ruin. First she failed to back him in his power struggle against Robert Cecil, and then she signed his death warrant.

There was one more potent factor in Penelope's relationship with Elizabeth. She had more royal blood than the queen. Through her Devereux ancestors, Penelope and her brother could claim direct descent from more medieval royalty than Elizabeth. And through her mother, Penelope had a blood tie to the Tudors that was too close to be admitted. Elizabeth never spoke of it, yet many a hand that rocked Penelope's cradle, many a grand lady who watched the pretty child grow up, knew the stories of forty years ago when Penelope's grandmother, Lady Katherine Knollys, was born to Mary Boleyn.

Chapter Two

1523–1563

"A perfect model of manly beauty"
– Venetian ambassador, 1529

King Henry VIII was in his prime when the Boleyn sisters began to make their mark at Court in the 1520s. Anne became his wife but it was "the other Boleyn girl", Mary, who first caught his eye.

Henry was strikingly powerful and vigorous, nothing like the bloated figure he became in later years. From boyhood he was seen as the most perfect prince in Christendom. His tutors called him quick-witted and quick-tempered. His fellows called him fearless. He could match any one of them at jousting, hunting, hawking, running and tennis. Foreign diplomats were awed by this six-foot Adonis. "Nature could not have done more for him – very fair and his whole frame admirably proportioned," enthused the Venetian ambassador. "His Majesty is the handsomest potentate I ever set eyes on," reported another, adding, "his complexion very fair and bright, with auburn hair combed straight and short in the French fashion, and a round face so very beautiful that it would become a pretty woman."

The ladies at Court may not quite have agreed about his face. To them he looked the ultimate thirtysomething alpha male: handsome, powerful and charming. He danced like a dream and he could strum "Greensleeves" sweetly on a lute (even if he didn't compose it).

In 1509, shortly before he was eighteen, he had inherited the crown from his father, Henry VII, and promptly married the Spanish princess Katherine of Aragon, widow of his late brother, Arthur. Katherine claimed Arthur never consummated their marriage and there was thus no problem in her marrying his brother. Ten years on, however, Katherine and Henry had no surviving son, though the king had a base-born son by his mistress Bessie Blount, one of the queen's ladies. Baptized Harry Fitzroy, the child's birth seems to have marked the end of Bessie's royal affair. She was married off to a country gentleman and Mary Boleyn slipped into her place in the king's bed.

Henry enjoys the reputation of a king who spared no woman in his lust. Mary has gone down in history as the greatest whore of her day. Both ideas are exaggerated, thanks to single-source stories. Mary's is particularly suspect, being an English account of an Italian report of a comment made in French at the very time her sister, Anne, was falling from favour.

Mary and Anne were the daughters of an ambitious diplomat and courtier, Sir Thomas Boleyn. Through Sir Thomas and their mother, Elizabeth Howard, Mary and Anne traced their ancestry back three centuries to King Henry III through both his sons King Edward I and Edmund, Earl of Lancaster. In the small world of medieval nobility such a connection was not exceptional, but ancestry was fast becoming an obsession among the nobility and it was enough to give the Boleyns some status at Court. On Saturday 4 February 1520 Mary made a good marriage, to Will Carey, one of the king's elite "squires of the body". They were Henry's chosen companions in the tiltyard and the tennis court, and wherever else he took his pleasures. Will was distantly related to the king, being a descendant of John of Gaunt, and at the wedding of Will and Mary, in the chapel at Greenwich Palace, Henry was their chief guest.

Shortly before or after that date, Mary began an affair with Henry which ended when he transferred his affections to Anne some time near the end of 1525. Anne held out several years before becoming his mistress and second wife in 1533, shortly before the birth of her daughter, the future Queen Elizabeth. Mary's two children, Henry and Katherine, were officially recognized as Will Carey's offspring and Will was amply rewarded by Henry with royal offices and leases. Mary's father was similarly recompensed for turning a blind eye to her royal affair, though Sir Thomas also earned his titles and properties with loyal service to the king. Mary's son Henry was born on 4 March 1526 and history has never been sure whether the king had stopped bedding Mary before or after the boy's conception. Contemporary rumour said Master Carey looked very much like the king, and one man found spreading the story was executed.

For Mary's daughter Katherine – Penelope Devereux's grandmother – there is no birth record, and she has been overlooked or assumed to be younger than her brother and therefore definitely Will Carey's daughter. But fresh evidence came to light in 2005 confirming that Katherine was born in the years when Mary was the king's mistress.

⁓

Hidden in a Latin dictionary owned by Sir Francis Knollys, Penelope's grandfather, are the dates of his marriage to Katherine Carey and the births of their fourteen children.

Some time between 1555 and 1558, during the Catholic regime of Queen Mary when Sir Francis was abroad as a Protestant exile, he decided to record his large and still growing family. Opening the first volume, A to E, of his dictionary, he wrote neatly inside the front cover: "Here followeth in order the names, with the times of the birth of the children of Francis Knollys and Katherine his wife that were married ye 26th day of April, anno 1540." Beneath, in his clear script, crossing through and correcting as he went along, Sir Francis entered the names and dates of his first eleven children, starting with "Harry", born "the Tuesday before Easter day", 1541.

Katherine was old enough, then, to be married as a cohabiting wife, not a betrothed juvenile. So she was not younger than her brother Henry. She was Mary's elder child, born before April 1525. But when? Again Sir Francis's dictionary holds the answer. It proves for the first time that the details on Katherine's splendidly pregnant portrait are correct. The inscription states that it was painted in 1562 when she was aged thirty-eight, or in her thirty-eighth year; and the dictionary shows she was indeed pregnant that year. Her eighth son, Dudley, was born "1562 – the 9th day of May, half a quarter of an hour before 2 of the clock at afternoon". Since the portrait was evidently painted in March or April, Katherine herself must have been born between March 1523 and April 1525 – the years when Mary's affair with Henry VIII was in full swing.

Knowing Henry as a ruthless despot – and no one knew it better than the families of his executed wives Anne Boleyn and Katherine Howard – it is little wonder that his courtiers assumed he was not happily sharing his mistress, even with her husband. There was only one conclusion: Mary's children were Henry's bastards.

It was not a claim that any sensible person would push in public. The Duke of Buckingham had lost his head in 1521 after openly boasting his descent from King Edward III, and it was not a mistake Mary's children would repeat. At court Henry Carey and Katherine claimed only that they were cousins of Elizabeth, and that was enough to explain their privileged position in her household. No one need remark that in fact they were the queen's half-sister and half-brother, and Elizabeth never did. The legality of her mother's marriage and her kinship to the Careys were subjects Elizabeth studiously avoided. And even if she wasn't *sure*, the possibility that they were her half-siblings was enough to keep her mute on the matter.

∽

Mary was by all accounts very pretty, more so than her sister Anne though probably not so striking as her granddaughter, Lettice, nor as beautiful as her great-granddaughter Penelope. And Mary set the pace for her female descendants, with her spirited behaviour and determination to follow her heart. Her daughter was the exception: Katherine lived a blameless, conventional, scandal-free life. Lettice and her daughters Penelope and Dorothy followed Mary's example faithfully.

A few years after Will Carey died of the "sweating sickness", Mary fell in love with a courtier named Sir William Stafford and, already pregnant, secretly married him in 1534. Anne, briefly riding high as King Henry's queen, was furious at not being consulted. She banished Mary and Stafford from Court and persuaded their father to cut off Mary's allowance. Anne underestimated her sister. Mary was "not going quietly" – as others have said when dismissed from royal circles. Mary wrote an impassioned plea to the king's chief minister, begging help to get her allowance reinstated and Stafford out of disgrace.

"Love overcame reason; and for my part I saw so much honesty in him, that I loved him as well as he did me, and was in bondage," she explained; "I had rather beg my bread with him than to be the greatest queen christened." Dorothy could not have put it better, fifty years later, when she wrote to Elizabeth's chief minister, Lord Burghley, with a similar request. Mary was never fully forgiven but she persuaded her father to let her live with Stafford at one of the Boleyn properties, Rochford Hall in Essex. Her daughter, however, was not tainted by Mary's disgrace, nor by the fallout from Anne's spectacular downfall and execution in 1536.

Katherine was quietly leading a charmed life, enjoying modest but significant marks of royal favour. Aged ten when the Princess Elizabeth was born, Katherine probably spent the next six years in the household of her young "cousin", whose great fondness for her in later life was obvious to everyone. Then, in November 1539, with the arrival of Henry VIII's fourth wife, Katherine was given the coveted job of maid of honour to Anne of Cleves. Since the six maids to an adult queen were usually aged fifteen or over, and two of the new maids were eighteen, it is further evidence that Katherine was older than her brother. Sadly for Anne of Cleves her reign was even shorter than her predecessors'. Within six months her household was reduced as Henry prepared to dismiss her, but it hardly mattered to Katherine. She was about to marry Francis Knollys, another of the young courtiers who had been sent to escort the new queen on her inauspicious entry to London. Soon after their marriage, legislation was passed assuring Katherine and Francis the joint right to inherit the Knollys family's manor, Grey's Court in Oxfordshire, underlining once again royal favour to the daughter of "the other Boleyn girl".

The Knollys family were "new" gentry. They had risen under Henry VIII's father, Henry VII, acquiring property and jobs from the king. Francis continued their upward mobility at Court, and by the end of Henry VIII's reign he had earned a knighthood and the post of master of horse to Henry's son, Edward VI. Francis also entered parliament, becoming prominent among the Protestant party, and accumulated more valuable offices and leases, such as Wallingford Castle and Ewelme Park.

In 1553, after thirteen years of marriage, Sir Francis and Lady Katherine had ten children. Harry, their firstborn, was followed by Mary in October 1542, Lettice in November 1543 and William (who would eventually be Sir Francis's heir) in 1545. Then came Edward, Maud, Elizabeth, Robert, Richard and Francis. It was an amazingly successful pregnancy record. In all Katherine produced sixteen children, for soon there were Anne, Thomas, Katherine, Dudley and two more who probably died at birth since they are not named in the dictionary. And at least eleven of them lived well into adulthood.

Sir Francis's role as a leading Protestant meant that the accession of Edward VI's elder and Catholic sister, Queen Mary, put a temporary break on his career – and on Katherine's pregnancies. Sir Francis made several trips to Protestant Europe and later in Mary's reign Lady Katherine joined him to live in Frankfurt, taking five of their children. When she departed, Elizabeth sent her a fond farewell letter, signing herself "*cor rotto*" (broken-heart) and promising "when your need shall be most you shall find my friendship greatest". For the rest of her life Elizabeth would treat Katherine as a much-loved older sister.

Which five children Lady Katherine took with her to Frankfurt is not known. Lettice was thirteen in November 1556 and may well have been left in the care of Princess Elizabeth. Nearly eighty years later it would be recorded on her tomb that Lettice "in her youth had been, Darling to the maiden Queen". Elizabeth, now aged twenty-three, had won the battle with her sister, Mary, for freedom to live away from Court at Hatfield palace in Hertfordshire, where she was carefully ignoring Mary's orders to follow the Catholic faith. At Hatfield, Elizabeth was also discreetly gathering her future household, including William Cecil, later Lord Burghley, and Robert Dudley, future Earl of Leicester. Both would play a powerful part in the lives of Lettice and Penelope.

When Elizabeth came to the throne in November 1558, she immediately promoted the "old flock of Hatfield" to be her advisers and attendants. Katherine and Francis quickly returned from the Continent and with Lettice were given salaried posts in the new queen's inner circle. Katherine became one of the four most senior ladies of the bedchamber, Lettice became a maid of the privy chamber and Sir Francis was made vice-chamberlain.

As Lettice grew up, few could have failed to notice her resemblance to Elizabeth. Her portraits show the alluring dark eyes of the Boleyn sisters, as well as the pale skin and striking red hair that Elizabeth proudly claimed came from her father. And when Lettice married a rising young courtier named Walter Devereux, Viscount Hereford, their first child was another dark-eyed beauty with glorious red-gold hair.

Chapter Three

1563–1568

"The christening of Viscount Hereford his child"

– New Year Gift Roll, 1562–3

*P*enelope's father, Walter Devereux, Viscount Hereford, was impeccably noble, with a lineage and ancestry that gave him instant access to Elizabeth's Court. In September 1558, the day after his nineteenth birthday, he inherited the title and estates of one of the most ancient families in the country.

The Devereux had come from Normandy and settled in Herefordshire soon after 1066. Down the centuries the family built up vast estates in the Marches, Wales and Staffordshire, which they ruled as proud and powerful feudal lords, wielding almost royal power over all who lived on their lands. At Carmarthen, then the busiest town in Wales, they made their power base in the massive castle that still dominates the town today, and there Walter was born on 16 September 1539. The early death of his father left Walter heir to his grandfather, Walter senior, who in 1550 became Viscount Hereford and a councillor to the boy-king Edward VI.

Walter senior could raise the largest private army in the country and he held a long list of titles even before he was made viscount. Through his father John he was Lord Ferrers of Chartley and from his mother Cecily he held the lordships of Bourchier and Lovaine. Although technically the Devereux did not come in the top tier of nobility, they had made impressive marriages and they could claim descent many times over from medieval kings of England. Cecily's grandparents, Isobel of York and Henry Bourchier, Earl of Essex, were direct descendants of three of Edward III's sons – Lionel, Duke of Clarence, Edmund, Duke of York, and Thomas, Duke of Gloucester. Furthermore, Thomas's wife Eleanor de Bohun was descended from Elizabeth Plantagenet, sister of Edward II, so their royal blood line doubled to Edward I and his father Henry III. Perhaps a little more imaginatively, the Bourchiers looked back to Charlemagne, the Bohuns to ancient Scottish kings and the Devereux to Irish royalty. But their descent from the English throne was unquestionable.

In 1536 young Walter's father added yet more royal connections when he married Lady Dorothy Hastings, daughter of the Earl of Huntingdon and Lady Anne Stafford, for the Staffords were also descended from Edward III's son Thomas and his wife Eleanor, *and* from the Beaufort offspring of John, Duke of Lancaster, yet another son of Edward III. The lineage young Walter would pass on to his children was therefore considerably more than a "trickle" of royal blood and it flowed not, as is usually claimed, from two or three but from *four* of the sons of Edward III.

Generations of Devereux had gathered stewardships and leases on royal lands and important jobs at Court. But with the accession of Queen Mary, Walter senior lost his place at the centre of affairs, retired to his Staffordshire estate, Chartley, and when he died on 17 September 1558 he was buried in the church at Stowe-by-Chartley. If his grandfather's loss of office under Mary gave the new Viscount Hereford any doubts about a Court career, they were dispelled when Mary died two months later. Soon young Walter was on his way to London to join the bright young things who circled the new queen, Elizabeth.

~

Walter Devereux decided to splash out on new clothes for his entry to Elizabeth's Court. His "reckoning" between October 1559 and May 1561 shows his tailor's bill totalled £158.9s.9d. (about the cost of a mid-range sports car at today's prices). It was tastefully spent: a black cloak, white doublet and black jerkin in satins and velvet, two more jerkins of best Spanish leather, all trimmed with gold and silver lace and dozens of tiny silk and silver buttons. The effect was well up to courtier standards. Walter intended to make his way in the world – and a good marriage.

Still a minor when he came into his inheritance, Walter had much to sort out in London, as well as paying homage to the queen. His wardship, the income from his estates, permission to marry and confirmation of his rights to inherit all needed royal approval, and it took until February 1561 for the legalities to be concluded. By then Walter was an adult and married.

In late summer 1560, before he turned twenty-one in September, "our beloved and faithful Walter Devereux Viscount Hereford and Lord Ferrers of Chartley" was married to Lettice Knollys, who reached her seventeenth birthday in November. The match benefited them both. Lettice was marrying into the old nobility; Walter was allying himself to the new professional class, a family of royal administrators who were closer than any other to the queen. And close to the queen was the only place to get leases, jobs, trading rights and support in any dispute that might arise with other landowners and courtiers.

Lettice was the first of Katherine's children to marry and Elizabeth was particularly fond of her. Before long her husband was receiving greater favour too. In December Walter was asked to stand in for an absent foreign dignitary due to be invested with the Order of the Garter at Windsor. For a time the newlyweds stayed at Court, but by early summer 1561 they were on their way to Walter's family and estates. The new Viscountess Hereford needed to be presented to the people of Carmarthen. From there they carried on thirty miles south-westward, heading for Pembroke. Just outside stood the former bishop's palace of Lamphey, Walter's childhood home, where his widowed mother, Lady Dorothy, lived with his brother and sisters, George, Elizabeth and Anne. His eldest sister Mary had died very young, and there is one record of a younger sister, Penelope, born shortly before their father died, though nothing further is known of her.

From south-west Wales, Walter and Lettice made their way back, perhaps through Herefordshire and the Devereux estates around Bodenham, Lyonshall, Thornbury and Weobley, to Staffordshire. Chartley, nine miles north-east of Stafford on the road to Uttoxeter, was the Devereux' principal seat in England and here Walter and Lettice made their home. It was more convenient for London, only half the distance between Lamphey and the capital, and the road was better. North of Chartley it ran on to Chester and Holyhead, the route that Walter and, years later, his son Robert would take to Ireland. South of Chartley were Warwick and the great estates of the Dudley family and the Earl of Leicester.

The manor of Chartley and its great stone castle had been in the Ferrers family for centuries before Walter's great-grandfather inherited it from his mother, Agnes de Ferrers. It stood on the uplands midway between two rivers, the Trent and the Blithe. Little of it now remains, but enough to show it was a warlords' stronghold. Huge half-round towers, battlements, a turreted gatehouse, arrow slits and three-metre-thick walls rose high on a man-made mound. Before the end of the fifteenth century it was already outdated. Walter senior and his father left it to crumble and built a modern house "a good flight shot" downhill from the keep.

Lettice's new home was a half-timbered mansion, high-gabled and ornately carved, built round a large courtyard, and surrounded by a wide moat. The grounds had now matured and the house and garden seemed to float on a lake, overlooked by the castle's romantic ruins.

~

For the first few years of their marriage, Viscount Hereford and his wife lived chiefly at Chartley, though they were not cut off from Court. Lettice remained on the list of the queen's gentlewomen, an unwaged, extra lady-in-waiting, and the couple paid occasional visits to London. But Chartley was the birthplace of most of their five children.

Penelope was the eldest, born soon after New Year 1563, and Walter was at home for her arrival. Instead of taking his seat in the Lords when parliament met on 12 January he sent a proxy. Elizabeth graciously agreed to be her godmother and sent a stand-in to represent her at "the christening of Viscount Hereford his child" on 3 February. It was usual for a girl to be christened Elizabeth when the queen stood godmother, but her godchild's name didn't deter her from sending a handsome christening present: a "gilt cup with a cover bought of the goldsmiths", weighing forty-five ounces.

In Penelope's pedigree were all the medieval queens of England from Eleanor of Provençe and Eleanor of Castile to Isabella of France and Philippa of Hainault; not to mention John of Gaunt's lovely mistress Katherine Swynford. She could also list the daughters of every great family: Anne Mortimer, Elizabeth Woodville, Cecily Neville and Margaret Beaufort. Now she had the current queen for her godmother and it was a duty Elizabeth took seriously. Godchildren held a special place in her heart even if, like that "witty fellow" Sir John Harington, they sometimes annoyed her.

Before Penelope was seven years old there were four more Devereux children: her sister Dorothy and her brothers Robert, Walter – known as Wat – and Francis, who died soon after his birth. Robert is the only one whose birth date is certain: 10 November 1565. Family tradition says that Dorothy, named for her Devereux grandmother, was born on 17 September, probably in 1564; and Wat on 31 October 1569. Whether or not they were born at Chartley, they spent their childhood there and for Penelope and Robert it would remain a treasured place, somewhere to return to for long summer visits, enjoying again the country where they learnt to ride, hawk, hunt and shoot with bows and arrows.

Beyond the moat were acres of park and orchards and beyond that lay open country, thick woodlands, bracken-covered moors and deep valleys, where deer and long-horned cattle roamed, and wild pansies and rock roses bloomed. Buzzards circled high overhead while warblers and chiffchaffs sang from broom and holly trees.

Barely half a mile east of the castle mound the ground fell away to Stoney Brook and Chartley Moss, an ancient floating peat bog, with wild orchids and fritillaries and countless dragonflies darting over the swampy grasslands.

A couple of miles further south-east stood Blithfield, ancestral home of the Bagot family. It was another moated manor house built round a courtyard, but smaller than Chartley. The Bagots were leading county gentry and though they were not on the Devereux' social level the two families became good friends. Richard Bagot was about nine years older than Walter. He married nearly a decade earlier, named his eldest son for Walter in 1557, and when the new Viscount Hereford took over Chartley, Richard continued to manage his estates. The Bagots' lawyer in London, Richard Broughton, a barrister at the Inner Temple, handled Walter's legal affairs, and most of Bagot's children became paid companions to Walter's. The Bagot girls were a little older than Penelope, but Anne in particular remained one of her life-long confidantes and formed a cherished link with Penelope's roots.

Two other youngsters were also drawn into the family while Penelope was growing up. One was Thomas White, son of a government official in Ireland; the other was Gabriel, son of the French Protestant leader, the Count Montgomery, who was executed in France in 1574. Both boys spent several years at Chartley before going to Cambridge with Robert and both owed their place in the household to Walter's personal interests. Penelope's father was a strong, scholarly and very present influence on his children's early years. Though Lettice would always be remembered as a dominating, red-haired beauty, it was Walter who set the cultural tone and Protestant atmosphere for Penelope's education. She was still in the nursery when Walter took on to his staff an ardent Protestant scholar from Cambridge, Mathias Holmes, and he would be her tutor from the time she "began first to learn" until she was fifteen.

Walter's patronage of reformist theologians produced numerous books of prayers and Protestant piety. He also appointed as his sons' tutors two leading educationists and scholars, Thomas Ashton, sometime headmaster of Shrewsbury School, and Robert Wright, fellow of Trinity College, Cambridge. But it was not all bible study that occupied Penelope's child-hood. The skills she was praised for in later life began with her parents' influence and lessons at Chartley. Her languages included "perfect" French, fluent Spanish and some Italian. Her intellect, letters and handwriting were admired by King James of Scotland, himself no mean scholar. Her love of literature and music, both shared with her father, led her to patronize numerous poets, to play the lute "divinely", dance gracefully and sing like a nightingale. Above all she learnt from Walter the importance of family history and genealogy.

Viscount Devereux was following the fashionable obsession with ancestry when he taught his children pride in their lineage. It was their duty to under-stand their links to the grandest families in the land and their royal descent, albeit often through the female line. At his death, Penelope's father was claiming alliances to all but five of the sixty noble families in England and he quartered their coats of arms in his. His son and heir's destiny was to be a great leader, and he looked to his daughters to defend the family honour. In the great hall at Chartley Penelope could see all the richly coloured coats of arms woven into tapestries hanging down the walls, watch as sunlight filtered through them in the stained-glass windows, and feel the symbols carved on oak timbers. They were a constant reminder of the Devereux' connections to people who held power and posts at Elizabeth's Court.

~

Local tradition has it that Penelope's parents took their young family to Lamphey in Wales each summer, though there is no evidence to prove it. Walter's father bought it in 1546, when it ceased to be a bishop's palace during the Reformation, and Walter lived there, for maybe a decade, after his father died. Some of the buildings round the large courtyard were centuries old, but under Walter's godfather, Bishop Barlow of St David's, it had become a luxury residence. It had a fine library, a parlour to dine in away from the public great hall and a private garden outside the courtyard. There were fishponds and mills and beyond them fields and woods running down to the sea.

It would have been a long slow journey from Chartley, by dusty roads or boats and barges down the Severn and round the coast to Pembroke. Neither route would have been comfortable for Lettice when she was pregnant, and both would finish with a bumpy ride downhill following cart tracks to the palace. Today tall sycamores still sway overhead. Warm summer winds blow in from the sea. Bright ox-eye daisies and pink willowherb flower beside the fields, and swallows swoop among the palace ruins. It seems an easy place to enjoy life. In later years Robert loved it as a retreat, somewhere to celebrate Christmastide, filling the great hall with friends, huge log fires and the sound of Welsh harps and singing. By then Dorothy was also in Wales, married to Thomas Perrot, whose family owned neighbouring Carew Castle. But for Walter's family of little children it was a long, long way to come from Staffordshire, and if Penelope did it once or twice that is probably all.

There were closer homes and families to visit when Chartley needed to be emptied and cleansed. There was Netherwood, near Bromyard, sometimes said to be Robert's birthplace. At Hodnet in Shropshire, thirty miles west of Stafford, Penelope's Devereux grandmother, Lady Dorothy, had moved in with her daughter Elizabeth, married to John Vernon, and mother of Penelope's favourite cousin, Elizabeth. And there was the Knollys family home, Grey's Court, near Henley-on-Thames, to visit.

Penelope's grandparents were still producing children when she was born. Their eighth son, Dudley, arrived and died only six months before Penelope's birth; and their younger children, Francis, Anne, Thomas and Katherine, were all less than ten years Penelope's senior. The elder ones had followed Lettice to Court, sharing the royal favour Sir Francis and Lady Katherine enjoyed; and in July 1565 Elizabeth gave permission for a tournament to celebrate the wedding of Penelope's uncle "Harry" to Margaret Cave, daughter of another leading courtier.

It was a rare honour. Only three wedding "tourneys" are recorded during the reign, and the other two were for earls. Elizabeth herself attended "the rejoicings" and the programme included "a supper, a ball, a tourney and two masques, the feast ending at half past one". Naturally there was a full family turnout, including Lettice and Walter. So many foreign diplomats decided to be present that there were problems over precedence that threatened to prevent Elizabeth's own attendance – until she cooled it, explaining to the Spanish ambassador, Guzman de Silva, that "she would be very sorry if she had to refrain from honouring these people of hers".

Behind the scenes during Harry's wedding there was another problem rumbling which had more lasting implications for Penelope's family. The on-off romantic friendship between Elizabeth and her "Sweet Robin", Lord Robert Dudley, on whom she had recently conferred the title Earl of Leicester, had run into a sticky patch. He seemed to be losing out to another royal favourite.

"The queen's majesty is fallen into some misliking of my lord of Leicester, and he therewith much dismayed," William Cecil noted in August, with a private smile. In September stories reached ambassador de Silva that Leicester had been trying to make Elizabeth jealous by flirting with "the Viscountess of Hereford, who is one of the best-looking ladies of the Court and daughter of a first cousin to the queen, with whom she is a favourite". The queen "was in a great temper and upbraided him with ... his flirting with the Viscountess in very bitter words".

There *was* a mysterious row between Leicester and Elizabeth in the late summer but whether it had anything to do with Lettice, and whether or not Leicester and Lettice were genuinely carrying on or pretending, is anyone's guess. Lettice was nearly six months pregnant at the time of Harry's wedding. Besides, she and Leicester had known each other for years, at least since Elizabeth's Hatfield days, and Leicester had struck up a friendship with her husband. In November, when Lettice's baby was born, Walter invited Leicester to be his godfather and name the little boy Robert.

But de Silva's story, true or not, did the rounds and a few years later, when Walter went off to Ireland and died suddenly, every scandalous old story was dragged up against Leicester and Lettice. One thing the story certainly proves: Lettice and Walter had not cut themselves off from Court life. No one could afford to do that. And since de Silva thought the story worth sending to Spain, it said a lot for life at Elizabeth's Court.

Chapter Four

1565–1569

"The Queen of love, and Prince of peace"

– Edmund Spenser, *The Faerie Queen*, 1590

*Q*ueen Elizabeth I was in her thirties when Penelope was growing up at Chartley. She was a striking figure, if not exactly beautiful, with her pale skin and red hair. On her long, fine fingers flashed priceless rings. Her gorgeous silk and satin gowns were crusted with pearls and jewels, heavily embroidered with gold and silver thread. More gems sparkled in her hair, more pearls hung from her neck and ears.

She was a mirage of wealth and power and her Court was a glittering, moving house party, travelling in stately procession between her palaces, Whitehall, Richmond, Greenwich, St James's, Nonsuch and Hampton Court, the most modern and impressive. It rose beside the Thames in a forest of turrets, topped with flags and gilded weathervanes. The finest chambers were hung with tapestries "garnished with gold, pearls and precious stones", and Elizabeth's throne was "studded" with large diamonds, rubies and sapphires. Sometimes through the spring or summer Elizabeth would progress between the grand country houses of her subjects. Wherever she went, the business of government went with her, but there was always time for hunting and dancing, masques and music.

Hovering around the queen was a group of gilded butterflies, her chosen courtiers, ruled by her vanity and jealousy. It was *her* party and they were privileged to attend. She could invite who she liked. Their role was to serve and amuse her, and play out the fantasy of adoration of the Virgin Queen: the men were her lovers, the women her handmaidens. On the surface it was a splendid spectacle of pageantry, jousting and merrymaking. There were water parties, fireworks and set-piece parades for St George's Day in April and her Accession Day, 17 November. When she travelled through London from Richmond to Greenwich, gliding downriver on her gilded barge, gun salutes sounded across the water. The finest poets, painters and musicians made their way to her palaces, adding to the image of grandeur.

But the cult of Gloriana and the Virgin Queen was a stately quadrille that would turn into a grisly dance of death. Beneath the romance and chivalry, the picture of a gracious monarch and her adoring Court, there was desperate rivalry and poisonous backbiting as courtiers fought for preferment, power and money.

Everyone needed money. The wealth of the nobility was shrinking fast compared with the incomes of the gentry, and the cost of keeping up appearances at Court was phenomenal. Official posts in Elizabeth's household included rooms and food, but there was an endless drain of rewards and bribes: to the boys in the kitchens, the stable hands, the boatmen on the Thames "taxis", torch-bearers, messengers who delivered gifts, the poor woman who presented a gillyflower in February. There was the cost of repairs to dented armour, "roses and other flowers for your lordship's chamber", and extra servants' lodgings. And there was no way out of the debt trap except by obtaining jobs, licences, monopolies, leases and wardships, which all came from Elizabeth and her administrators. Keeping close to the crown was essential and courtiers were therefore an intimate group who had known each other, or about each other, all their lives. They were drawn from a small group of intermarried families at the top of a population of only three million; and London held 200,000 of them, no more than Harrow does now.

Elizabeth's Court represented an extraordinary concentration of influence. Sir William Cecil, her chief minister, soon to be Lord Burghley, reckoned only about one hundred people were politically significant. And within that ruling elite Penelope's family formed an even tighter circle around Elizabeth. In the queen's privy chamber Penelope's grandmother, aunts and cousins were her majesty's intimate companions. Daughters followed mothers helping to care for her person, her gowns and jewels. Sons followed fathers managing her household. At the council table sat Penelope's grandfather, her great-uncle and the man who would be her stepfather.

~

No one was closer to Elizabeth in the late 1560s than Penelope's grandmother, Lady Katherine Knollys. Officially recognized as her cousin and leading lady-in-waiting, Lady Katherine – and her brother, Henry Carey, now Lord Hunsdon – have often been called Elizabeth's only blood relations when she came to the throne. In fact, Elizabeth still had two first cousins on her father's side. Both were unquestionably royal and both had forfeited her trust long ago.

One was the Countess of Lennox, daughter of Henry VIII's eldest sister, Margaret. She had been a favourite of Elizabeth's sister Queen Mary, and her household was awash with Catholic plotters and priests. The other was the Duchess of Suffolk, only surviving child of Henry VIII's younger sister Mary. She had sanctioned the abortive efforts to crown her own daughter, Lady Jane Grey, after Henry VIII's son Edward VI died, thus bypassing Henry's daughters Mary and Elizabeth herself. There was no chance Elizabeth would want the countess or the duchess among her close attendants.

Lady Katherine, on the other hand, was on Elizabeth's staff until she died. It was no easy job. There were long hours and royal tantrums to endure and despite her many children she was in almost constant attendance, especially after Kat Ashley died in 1565. Kat had been the queen's governess since she was three, but her meddling in politics and marriage plans for Elizabeth occasionally landed her in jail. Lady Katherine outranked Kat socially, kept her influence low key, and received some of the most expensive presents Elizabeth ever gave. At New Year 1562, Katherine's "three gilt bolls with a cover, per oz. 65 ½" were heavier than anyone else's. After Lettice, Katherine's younger daughters were all taken into royal service, and Elizabeth Knollys, another lookalike for the queen, was a particular favourite.

Penelope's grandfather, Sir Francis, remained one of Elizabeth's leading councillors for almost forty years and, although he was on the radical wing of the Protestant movement, which Elizabeth disliked, he carried great weight in council.

Lord Hunsdon, Penelope's famously plain-speaking great-uncle Henry, spent years waging war on Elizabeth's behalf in the Scottish Borders, but he too was a privy councillor before Penelope came to Court. He had almost as many children as Lady Katherine – seven sons and three daughters – and their Court nickname, "the Tribe of Dan", carried biblical hints of Hunsdon's royal paternity as well as of their privileged position. They were "*noli me tangeres*" – people not to be meddled with or opposed, according to one courtier, and they held numerous posts in the royal household. Hunsdon's eldest daughter Catherine, known as Kate, later Countess of Nottingham, took over from Lady Katherine as Elizabeth's closest confidante, and her sister Philadelphia, later Lady Scrope, was one of the ladies with Elizabeth when she died.

The combined presence of Carey and Knollys children in the royal household was formidable. And then there were Penelope's Devereux connections.

Her father's cousin, Henry Hastings, third Earl of Huntingdon, was the most senior member of the family and he was tied to another great dynasty. His wife Catherine was the youngest sister of Robert Dudley, Earl of Leicester. Regardless of Leicester's frequent philanderings he was never seriously challenged in Elizabeth's affections. Her fondness for him made him the most powerful man at Court, and his sisters, Catherine, Countess of Huntingdon, and Mary, Lady Sidney, were both prominent among the queen's ladies. Their standing at Court would become doubly important to Penelope after the Huntingdons became her guardians, and when Leicester became her stepfather.

It was not the Dudley connection, however, that put the political spotlight on Huntingdon; it was his royal ancestry. Like Walter he was descended from Edward III, and when Elizabeth nearly died of smallpox, in October 1562, Huntingdon was named among her possible successors. Elizabeth's illness showed how precarious were both her life and the country's stability. Treachery and plots would thrive all the time she remained single and without a named heir.

The name Elizabeth suggested, whispering through her smallpox fever, was Robert Dudley. But that did not appeal to her council at all. Her romance with "Sweet Robin" had been a scandal since she first wore the crown. The mysterious death of his wife, Amy Robsart, found dead at the foot of the stairs in 1560, led one foreign diplomat to believe Elizabeth was about to be taken to the Tower and replaced on the throne by Huntingdon's father, the second earl.

If Elizabeth *had* married Robert Dudley, the ambassador might have been right. But she didn't and she survived the scandal. Now in 1562 she survived again, devotedly nursed by Lady Mary Sidney. But she was unnerved by the strength of support for Huntingdon, especially from the growing Protestant party. Consequently she kept him out of high office and London for some time. When she gave him a big job, ten years later, it was president of the Council of the North based in York and Newcastle.

Penelope's father was not named in succession matters in the 1560s because he was not yet an earl and he made no claims on his royal lineage. The crown and the ruling elite had intermarried so often that most families had some royal ancestors. But few could boast so many as Walter Devereux's children, and they also had their unspoken royal inheritance from Mary, "the other Boleyn girl".

~

Elizabeth's marriage and the succession was one of two issues that dominated her reign. The other was religion. In Mary Queen of Scots those two problems came together: she was Catholic and a chief claimant to be Elizabeth's successor. Mary's Scottish birth, according to Henry VIII's will, made her ineligible to wear the crown of England. Yet there was no denying she was Elizabeth's most senior kinswoman. She was descended from Henry's eldest sister, and she was the focus for Catholic hopes that England might return to the "old faith", perhaps with the help of England's old enemy, Spain.

When some of Mary's own countrymen ousted her from the Scottish throne and she fled to England, one May evening in 1568, she mistakenly thought her "sister" queen would help restore her. Instead, Elizabeth imprisoned her and played for time. Mary's Scottish enemies and Elizabeth's ministers jointly prepared a show trial and a dodgy dossier known as the Casket Letters, which "proved" that Mary had plotted to murder her husband. Elizabeth, meanwhile, sent Sir Francis Knollys and Lord Scrope to supervise Mary's captivity at Bolton Castle in the north Yorkshire dales.

Minder to Mary Stuart was not a job Sir Francis liked and he begged Elizabeth and William Cecil to move her south for safety, and let him return to London. He particularly wanted to get back to Lady Katherine, who had fallen "into a fever" soon after he went north.

"I would to god I were so dispatched hence that I might only attend and care for your good recovery," he wrote to Katherine, suggesting she could use her influence with the queen to get him recalled. Elizabeth refused. When Lady Katherine improved a little she urged Elizabeth to let her join Sir Francis in the north instead. Again Elizabeth refused. She liked to keep Katherine near her and, she claimed, the "journey might be to her danger or discommodity". In that case, Francis wrote tartly to Cecil, as Elizabeth would not let him look after his wife, hopefully "her Majesty will comfort her with her benign clemency and gracious courtesy". It was the same tone Penelope would use one day with Cecil's son, masking her real feelings.

Cecil was, in fact, doing his best for them and Sir Francis was genuinely grateful for his sympathy and the news that Katherine was "well amended". But Francis had had enough of Court life and Elizabeth. On New Year's Eve he sat down in Bolton Castle and poured out his feelings to Katherine, "an other myself". The queen never granted what they wanted or rewarded them much, and "for the outward love that her majesty bears you, she makes you often weep for unkindness to the great danger of your health". Wouldn't they be happier if they retired and lived "a country poor life", he wondered: "Whereunto I thank god I am ready to prepare myself for my part if you shall like thereof." He would leave the decision to her.

Lady Katherine never answered. Soon after Christmas, still with the queen at Hampton Court while the feasting and music went on, she fell ill again. Elizabeth ordered her to be nursed close to her own chamber and sat with her often. As Katherine's condition deteriorated, the queen demanded hourly reports. On Saturday 15 January Katherine died, and Elizabeth was overwhelmed with grief and remorse. Only the day before she had written to Sir Francis without mentioning that his wife was ill. Now she issued instructions for Mary to be brought south with all haste and handed over to the Earl of Shrewsbury at Tutbury Castle, near Burton-on-Trent.

Francis was "distracted with sorrow for his great loss". The partnership that began back in Anne of Cleves's household, thirty years ago, had been intensely loving and supportive. "My case is pitiful," Francis wrote. Katherine had been the centre of the family, managed their large household, and "disburdened" him of many cares. She was the bookkeeper of his "public charges" and his "private accounts". Without her, "my children, my servants and all other things are loosely left without good order".

After the cold, slow journey south, on Friday 5 February Francis handed Mary over at Tutbury Castle, a dozen miles east of Chartley. Before he reached London three days later there was time for a brief visit to his daughter Lettice and her family. Penelope, his eldest grandchild, had just passed her sixth birthday and already showed promise of being a great beauty. Dorothy was four and Robert three the previous November. Sir Francis needed their support now, knowing that when he reached London Katherine would not be there to welcome him.

Lady Katherine's expensive funeral in Westminster Abbey and her brother Hunsdon's years later were both paid for by Elizabeth, once again suggesting their special kinship to the queen. Elizabeth was not noted for generosity, and her £640.2s.11d. payment for Katherine's burial was considerably more than she spent on the Duchess of Suffolk and the Countess of Lennox. A printed epitaph for Lady Knollys praised her "wit and counsel sound, a mind so clean devoid of guile", and pointed out that she had been "In favour with our noble queen, above the common sort". After her funeral, the valuable canopied hearse with its silk and velvet trappings, usually a perk for the abbey, was grabbed by the College of Heralds, provoking a row for months.

Even if Sir Francis did not blame Elizabeth for Katherine's death, others did. At Tutbury, Mary Stuart showed little sympathy that Elizabeth's grief had made her so "forgetful of her own health, she took cold, wherewith she was much troubled". It was Elizabeth's fault, Mary said, for making Sir Francis stay in the north. His family couldn't possibly comment: there were too many careers at stake.

∼

Penelope's father's career had been progressing nicely, partly thanks to Leicester. The relationship between Walter, Viscount Hereford, and the queen's favourite had not suffered at all from any rumours of Lettice and Leicester flirting, and sometimes Lettice attended Court without Walter. After Mary Stuart was installed at Tutbury, Walter and his cousin Huntingdon were made responsible for her security. They were ordered to keep a troupe of mounted soldiers ready in case of Catholic attempts to spring her from the castle, and it was Walter's job to oversee the county muster of men and arms.

When problems arose they were further north, as Sir Francis and Cecil had feared. The Duke of Norfolk had a plan to marry Mary which was supported by some northern Catholic magnates, and secretly by some privy councillors as well. Leicester was one of them. He was anxious to head off a proposal by Elizabeth that he himself should marry Mary. Elizabeth was furious when she was belatedly told about Norfolk's plan, and sent him to the Tower. But the Northern Earls were already in rebel mode. On 14 November they marched on Durham, entered the cathedral, tore up the Protestant prayer books and called on everyone to return to God's "true and Catholic religion". Nearly 6,000 men joined their army and large crowds attended mass in Durham and around the county.

It was the worst crisis Elizabeth had yet faced. The rebels were moving south fast and for all she knew an army from Catholic Spain might land and help free Mary. At once she sent orders for the Earl of Huntingdon and Viscount Hereford to move Mary from Tutbury to Coventry, place her under extra guard, and then assemble troops and head north.

It was late on a November afternoon when Elizabeth's messenger reached Chartley. Penelope's father was at home with the family, celebrating the birth of her youngest brother. Little Walter – Wat – born on All-Hallows Eve, would grow up to inherit the Devereux charm and good looks and some said he was their father's favourite. But the family's pleasure in his arrival was cut short. Walter must join Huntingdon and the rest of their kinsmen, Hunsdon, his son George Carey and Lettice's brother William Knollys, and face the rebels.

From the day Walter rode away his life was increasingly absorbed by matters of state. There would be little time with his family and no more pregnancies for Lettice. Mary Stuart's arrival in England had brought great changes in Penelope's family, and indeed no future national crisis would leave her life unmarked.

Chapter Five

1569–1575

"Beware of the Gypsy, for he will be too hard for you all"

– the Earl of Sussex, 1583

*T*he rebellion of the Northern Earls was a bungled affair and it was put down with unnecessary savagery. Although the earls' rallying cry was religion, the real motivation was loss of power by the old nobility. The Neville and Percy families felt their voices were no longer heard at Court and they resented the rising power of William Cecil. But loyalty to the crown and the English preference for not getting involved proved more popular than Catholicism and the pope. Elizabeth's lieutenants in the counties had no trouble raising troops to march north, and the rebels were crushed by overwhelming odds.

The list of lords lieutenant is a roll-call of the men in Penelope's life. Her father Viscount Hereford was responsible for Staffordshire; her grandfather Knollys for Oxfordshire; and her future guardian Huntingdon for the counties of Leicestershire and Rutland. In Worcestershire it was Lord Leicester's duty. His brother Ambrose had the job in Warwickshire. And in Essex and Dorset respectively, the men responsible for the musters were Lord Rich and Lord Mountjoy – the fathers of her future husband and lover.

It was her own father, however, who won the most glowing mentions in dispatches. Walter mustered 3,000 soldiers at Lichfield and showed himself a born leader. Lord Leicester recommended he be appointed lord marshal of the field, and Ambrose, Earl of Warwick, told the privy council: "I never saw nobleman in all my life more willing to serve his prince and country."

When the rebel earls fled back to the Scottish borders on 20 December reprisals began, and they were horrific. Nearly 800 men were executed, allegedly at William Cecil's instigation. In his eyes Catholics were traitors,

Protestants were loyalists and all the time Mary was alive there would be trouble. Soon after she reached England Sir Francis Walsingham's spy network had picked up news that France and Spain were planning a Catholic crusade against England, and "the advancement of the Queen of Scots to the throne". Walsingham, officially Elizabeth's principal secretary of state but more usefully described as her spymaster, had set up a counter-espionage team that infiltrated deep inside foreign embassies in London, and into cells of discontented Catholics. There was treason afoot throughout the kingdom and wherever Elizabeth's subjects were gathered abroad. The pope's declaration in April 1570, the bull *Regnans in excelsis*, stating that Elizabeth was excommunicate and her subjects no longer owed her loyalty, seemed to justify Cecil's opinion and it was shared by many of Elizabeth's advisers. "There is less danger in fearing too much than too little," Walsingham warned. It would be wise to keep England on the alert and reward loyalist leaders like Walter Devereux, Viscount Hereford.

For the moment Walter's job was done and before Lent he was back at Chartley. He had learnt some ruthless tactics and proved his worth. Over the next three years Penelope saw her father's rewards roll in and, with continuing political tension, his duties increase. In the summer of 1571 the queen accepted his claim to the title Earl of Essex, left vacant by the death of a distant Bourchier relation.

The following January, Walter was summoned to be one of twenty-five peers who tried the Duke of Norfolk for treason. He had a lot to do in London that spring, and Elizabeth allowed him lodgings in Durham House, one of the former bishops' palaces on the Strand that had passed to the crown. Penelope and Dorothy were old enough now to come to London with their parents, and children were occasionally allowed at Court.

At Greenwich Palace on 4 May the queen ceremonially conferred on Walter the title Earl of Essex and within the week, after the Court moved to Westminster, he took his seat as an earl in the House of Lords for the first time. A few days later, during elaborate Court celebrations for a newly arrived French embassy, Earl Walter led the charge in a mock night-time battle to entertain the queen and her visitors. And at Windsor on 17 June he was formally installed as a Knight of the Garter – "Being one of the few peers of the old blood who, during the conspiracy of the Duke of Norfolk, had remained faithful throughout to the queen."

Accession Day, in November, found Earl Walter and Lettice at Court again, but a riding accident caused the earl to cancel a trip to France in December to represent Elizabeth at the christening of the French king's daughter. Instead he, and probably his family, travelled to Herefordshire for Christmas. The following spring he was planning a longer, more dangerous journey. At Court in April he negotiated an ambitious project with Elizabeth that would take him to Ireland for two years.

~

Ireland was as big a danger zone for Elizabeth as Scotland. When the feuding Ulster chieftains were not fighting each other and the Scottish mercenaries in the Antrim glens, they were attacking the English settlement, the Pale, in and around Dublin and threatening to push England out of Ireland altogether. In addition, Spain or France might use Ireland as a launch pad for invading England. Until Ireland was subdued and colonized, Elizabeth's ministers warned, she would have no security.

Several "Ulster projects" had been put forward to settle Englishmen along the coasts of Antrim and Down. But "None will come from home," declared Sir Henry Sidney, who did two terms of duty as lord deputy of Ireland, sometimes accompanied by his wife Mary, Leicester's sister. Lack of army protection was the problem and Elizabeth, always short of money, never fond of war, would not commit enough resources to any plan in Ireland.

In 1573, however, she agreed to back Earl Walter's proposal. It was a profit-sharing scheme and he mortgaged one-third of his properties to her in order to raise his own £10,000 investment. Elizabeth would cover half the cost of 1,000 soldiers and grant him lucrative rights over the whole of Antrim. Through the early summer, Sir William Cecil, now Lord Burghley, slowly checked over the proposal for Elizabeth, and Earl Walter hovered around Court and Durham House, itching to get away and start campaigning before winter. "I have very great business to do in the country after I have done here," he wrote to Burghley on 22 June. Eventually he took leave of Elizabeth on 19 July, and while she signed his letters patent as governor and captain general of the northern parts of Ireland, he set off to drum up volunteers, adventurers and soldiers from his tenants around Hereford and Brecon. Then he headed north to stay at Chartley before he embarked at Liverpool. He wanted to see his family and sort out his will. There were dowries to fix for Penelope and Dorothy, £1,500 each, and some changes to the lands his "right well beloved wife" would receive as her widow's "jointure".

Penelope, at ten years old, could understand the importance of his visit. She was only six when he left hurriedly to fight the Northern Earls. This time was different. As his eldest child she had a special relationship with him. Besides, he was now an earl and a Knight of the Garter; his staff and servants paid him more formal respect. He had become a leader. Several of her Knollys uncles and two of Hunsdon's sons were volunteering to go with him.

For nearly a fortnight her handsome father stayed at home, busy about the estate and his affairs. They would be her best memories of him, in those high summer days at Chartley, with his neatly trimmed beard and moustaches, his long, thoughtful face and dark brows – not yet worn by two winters soldiering in the mists and bogs of Ireland. Planning his children's future occupied much of his thoughts and time at Chartley, and he continued after he left and landed in Ireland. In November he wrote to Burghley to propose a marriage between Robert and Burghley's daughter Anne. The following April he wrote again asking if Robert could now join the young gentlemen living in Burghley's household. It was time, Earl Walter explained, to remove Robert "from his mother's wing". Neither plan came to anything immediately, but the news filtering back to Chartley let his children know he was thinking of them.

One thing Penelope probably did not know was her father's fears, from the start, that Elizabeth would fail to support him adequately. Twice he mentioned to Burghley: "I am, my lord, departed from the Court with many good and fair promises; but of the performance of them, I know not what assurance I may make."

The problems began as soon as Earl Walter sailed from Liverpool on 16 August. Storms scattered his ships along the Irish coast from Belfast Lough to Cork. His army was badly equipped, the local loyalist forces were unreliable and his supply lines were uncertain. At the beginning of November he sent his secretary, Edward Waterhouse, back to London to explain that Elizabeth's present lord deputy, Sir William Fitzwilliam, was not cooperating. Plague and sickness were spreading through the camp. Harry Knollys, for one, would need to go home, and the gentlemen adventurers and volunteers were departing in droves. Lord Rich of Essex was among the first to go, anxious to avoid an Irish winter and making empty promises to return in the spring.

At best the projected colony has been called overambitious, at worst ridiculous. Grabbing huge swathes of Irish land and giving them to Englishmen to fill with settlers stirred up lasting local resentment. Earl Walter underestimated the difficulties he would face from the Irish rebels and their guerrilla warfare tactics; from the harsh conditions; and most of all from Elizabeth's viceroy, Fitzwilliam. Early in 1574 Elizabeth agreed to send more money, victuals and soldiers, but the problems worsened, and with them Earl Walter's reactions.

Convinced he was justified by the "deceit" of the Ulster chieftains, whom he viewed as barbarians, he committed appalling atrocities. His execution of the Irish chief Sir Brian macPhelim, his wife, brother and followers, and his massacre of hundreds of men, women and children on Rathlin Island, were repulsive acts of butchery that breached every code of decency.

It was some little comfort to his Irish enemies to know that his own English ones were having a field day. Earl Walter's absence from Court inevitably left him open to the endemic back-biting, scandal and rumour. His friends talked up his small successes, but his bigger failures were eagerly recounted. Elizabeth, never prepared to admit that her policy and spending on Ireland were inconsistent and inadequate, decided to abandon the enterprise – and then changed her mind. When he resigned, she ordered him to continue. When he planned to visit Court in December 1574 to explain what he was doing, he was asked to stay put. And when it was suggested he could replace Fitzwilliam as viceroy, Leicester vetoed the idea and Elizabeth agreed.

Leicester, Walter began to realize, was not his friend, and when he returned to England at the end of 1575 he found, if he did not know already, that stories had spread about Lettice and Leicester. Walter's trip to Ireland, some said, was "by the advice of those who desired his absence here under colour of doing him honour". And while Earl Walter was away Lettice had been visiting London, staying at Durham House, attending Court, and receiving New Year gifts from Elizabeth. She had also received gifts of venison from Leicester's Kenilworth estate, and joined hunting parties in Kenilworth's splendid deer parks.

Leicester was a dashing, dark-haired, roving-eyed chancer whose life was littered with scandals. Six months into Elizabeth's reign one foreign observer reported: "Lord Robert has come so much into favour ... it is even said that her majesty visits him in his chamber day and night." But the strange death of his wife, fifteen years earlier, continued to haunt him. Whenever someone he knew died, including Lady Douglas's husband, Leicester was rumoured to have had a hand in it. His ambition and his influence with Elizabeth earned him enemies everywhere and his nickname, "the Gypsy", was not a compliment. It had been in use for years when the Earl of Sussex issued his dark, deathbed warning: "Beware of the Gypsy, for he will be too hard for you all. You know not the beast as I do." Foreign diplomats reported he was "*giovane bellissimo*" but they could see that he was "generally detested" by Elizabeth's councillors. Elizabeth, however, shared a long and genuine affection with him. If it remained platonic it nonetheless satisfied something in them both, and Elizabeth wanted the emotional security of first claim on his companionship.

How far the relationship between Lettice and Leicester had reached in 1575 is impossible to tell. But when Walter set off for Ireland, allegedly encouraged by Leicester to get him out of the way, Leicester was still having a stormy affair with the widowed Lady Douglas Sheffield. It had been going on for two or three years and on 7 August 1574 she gave birth to a son. Leicester acknowledged the boy and named him Robert Dudley, but the affair was coming to an end. He rejected claims that he had secretly married her and wrote to say he never would, because marriage would put an end to his influence with the queen.

"Sweet Robin" was still Elizabeth's uncrowned consort after sixteen years on the throne and when she visited his Kenilworth Castle during her summer progress in 1575 he threw the biggest garden party of the century.

~

"The princely pleasures at the court at Kenilworth" went on for nineteen days and nights. From the moment Elizabeth arrived on Saturday evening, 9 July, it was a non-stop programme of pageants, plays, mock battles, music, dancing and fireworks – "the noise and flame of which were heard and seen twenty miles off". Giant figures of heralds with outsize trumpets greeted her arrival at the gatehouse. The Lady of the Lake announced that the castle was Elizabeth's to command, and gunfire saluted the queen as she rode into the inner courtyard.

Elizabeth had given Leicester the magnificent castle in the Midlands in 1563 and he had recently added a large range of modern apartments where the queen would be more comfortable than the draughty old fortress. When the days were hot she stayed indoors, listening to musicians and poets. In the cool of the evening she rode out and hunted in Kenilworth's park and forests. As she returned, savages and wild animals emerged from the trees and swooned at her beauty. Nymphs glided on floating islands across an artificial lake. Mermaids and dolphins rose out of the water. There were morris dancers, tumblers and more fireworks that seemed to fall into the lake and flare up again.

The illusions were magical and the cost fantastic. Everyone wanted to be there and the roads to Kenilworth were blocked for days with horses and carts bringing food and supplies, fresh groups of entertainers, and visitors. Among the many grandees who came with the queen were Leicester's sister, Lady Mary Sidney, her husband Sir Henry, their daughter Mary and their eldest son. Philip Sidney was one of Elizabeth's most promising young courtiers and he had just returned from a diplomatic mission abroad. It is unlikely that Lady Douglas was invited, but Lettice was there despite her husband's absence in Ireland. The Kenilworth gala looked to some observers like Leicester's last bid to marry the queen. To others it seems more a parting tribute to their lengthy romance, and the start of a new phase in his life.

The Devereux family's own nineteenth-century historian hotly denies that Lettice was Leicester's mistress while Earl Walter was away fighting for his queen and a large chunk of Ireland. But from 1575 they were often in each other's company. Once the party was over at Kenilworth, Elizabeth continued her Midlands progress to Lichfield and by 6 August she arrived at Chartley.

It was a quiet interlude after the extravaganza at Kenilworth. Chartley had too few chambers for Elizabeth and all her retinue, and her ushers and managers scoured surrounding estates for extra bedrooms. It is probable that Penelope and her brothers and sister were billeted with their friends the Bagots, three miles away at Blithfield. Yet they would still have come to Chartley during the queen's visit.

Elizabeth expected to see her godchildren wherever she went. She never lost her liking for the idea of marriage and children, even though it became an empty dream, and Lady Katherine Knollys's grandchildren were especially dear to her. Like Hunsdon's offspring, they were the nearest Elizabeth would have to grandchildren of her own, and the tolerance she showed to Penelope and Robert in later years spoke clearly of a special relationship. Lettice would be expected to present her pretty eldest daughter to the queen, to be admired and marked down as a future maid of honour. Now that there was only one royal household (no consort's establishment, no mini-courts for royal children) the paid posts at Court, with board and lodging guaranteed, were rare. Getting a girl's name down early was vital.

The Court visit to Chartley was also a chance for Leicester to see his godson, Penelope's brother Robert, and when the Devereux children came to the house, in all probability they met Leicester's heir and nephew, Philip Sidney.

Philip was already well liked by their father. During the 1560s the Sidney family were often in residence at Ludlow Castle, close to the Devereux estates; and when Philip was a schoolboy at Shrewsbury he was delighted to receive a present of a horse from Walter. Since then Penelope's father had followed his protégé's career closely; and though relations between the earl and Philip's father, Sir Henry, were not entirely smooth, Walter had his eye on Philip as a future husband for Penelope.

At the time of the Chartley visit, Philip was almost twenty-one. Penelope was twelve. He could see she was a pretty girl with reddish-golden hair and large, dark eyes. She could see he was a badly pock-marked young man with a lot of ambition, contacts and continental polish. What they thought of each other no one knows. Judging by the poems Philip wrote about Penelope six years later, immortalizing her as his heroine Stella, the love that blossomed at Court had not been love at first sight.

Earl Walter would have been pleased by a meeting between them, but he was waiting impatiently for Sir Henry to arrive in Ireland and begin his second term as lord deputy. There was an overlap in their respective roles which did not make for harmony and Walter wanted to get back to England and sort things out with Elizabeth. His efforts in Ireland had been a failure, and a financial disaster.

Chapter Six

1575–1576

"Some evil received in my drink"

– Walter Devereux, Earl of Essex, 1576

The first news Penelope heard of her father's return was not good. Sick and weary from a stormy crossing that forced him to land in south-west Wales, he went straight to Lamphey to recuperate before attempting the journey to London. When he reached Court at Windsor he could hardly avoid the rumours about Lettice and Leicester, and over Christmas there was obvious anger between the two men.

"As the thing is publicly talked about in the streets there is no objection to my writing openly about the great enmity which exists between the Earl of Leicester and the Earl of Essex," the Spanish agent Antonio de Guaras reported gleefully early in December. He went on to recount the spiciest gossip at Court: that Lettice had produced two children by Leicester while Earl Walter was in Ireland. It was a classic case of a spiced-up report, common among foreign agents in London, who were often fed fake material to send home. But there were enough rumours to suggest that Leicester *was* philandering with the Countess of Essex.

Walter was not in the mood for Christmas. He joined Lettice to attend Elizabeth and present her with New Year gifts at Hampton Court, but on the whole he kept out of things and stayed at Durham House in the Strand. "Because I know this Christmas time [is] altogether dedicated to pastimes, and, therefore, unapt for such as be suitors, I thought it a most convenient season for me to withdraw myself hither," he explained to the privy council, late in December. He needed time "to think upon mine own estate, by conference with such of my officers as have had dealings for me in mine absence, by whom I find how heavy mine Ireland service hath been to me".

He was facing ruin. His Irish enterprise had been a disastrous drain on his

46

assets and his debts had soared to more than £25,000, besides the £10,000 he owed Elizabeth. He needed to know if and how much Elizabeth would compensate him, and he was increasingly bitter at the way she prevaricated over Irish affairs. "I am come to that pass as, my land being entangled to her [majesty], no man will give me credit for any money," he told Walsingham in February. He had considered retiring to the country, but the only way out of his financial mess was to sell land in England, return to Ireland and make a success of the plantation he originally intended.

There were, in fact, considerable benefits to Elizabeth in sending him back. He had shown himself a ruthless army leader and she believed she needed one. She gave him the title earl marshal of Ireland, but his financial demands were too high. Behind the scenes Leicester in London, and Sir Henry Sidney in Dublin, were working on a compromise that would ensure Walter's return. But whether Leicester was doing it for Elizabeth's sake or because he wanted Walter out of the way, who could say?

There was one bright aspect to Walter's months in London. Philip Sidney was staying at Lord Leicester's town house a few yards along the Strand, and their mutual friendship continued. Tentatively, Walter informed Sir Henry he would like to see Penelope married to Philip, and though the response was evasive he continued to plan.

On 9 May, after months of angry arguments with Burghley, the council and Elizabeth, the terms of Walter's appointment were agreed and he was granted Farney and Island Magee in Ireland to compensate for the loss of his estates in England. Quickly he left London, heading north again by the old post road via Lichfield to spend a while at Chartley before embarking for Dublin.

He had aged a lot since Penelope watched him prepare to set off for Ireland three years before. He was still only thirty-six, but two winters in camp, fierce fighting and the strain of his financial problems had taken their toll. His severe illness the previous autumn indicated his health was broken, and he was no longer the vigorous figure his children once knew. He was with them nearly a month, finalizing more property sales to cover his debts and making changes to his will, including raising the dowries for Penelope and Dorothy to £2,000 each.

While Walter was settling his affairs, Philip Sidney was preparing to join his father in Dublin and it has been suggested that he travelled with Walter. If he did, he joined him at the dockside, not at Chartley. Philip was still in London on 21 June and by then the earl had left home. Having signed his will on 14 June, a few days later he bid his children goodbye and rode away. It is unlikely Penelope knew about her father's dreams and the premonitions of death that he confided to his chaplain, and she certainly did not know it was the last time she would see him.

For nearly a month Walter waited for "an easterly wind", trying to embark from different ports. On 28 June he was at Chester, on 12 July at Holyhead. Six days later he was still on the Anglesey coast, footing the bill for his soldiers because they had no money while they were hanging around. At last he wrote to Walsingham: "The master of my ship calls for me away ... I commit you to God ... In haste at Holyhead, the 18th July 1576." In fact, it was another four days before he left.

It seems unlikely that Lettice took any part in Walter's farewells. If she *was* at Chartley when he rode away, she hurried straight back to Court. Elizabeth was being as indecisive as usual about her summer progress. Leicester, however, had fixed his holiday. On 6 July Gilbert Talbot sent the latest gossip to his father, the Earl of Shrewsbury: "The physicians have fully resolved that wheresoever my lord of Leicester be, he must drink and use the Buxton water twenty days together." Three ladies were also heading for Buxton, Gilbert went on. One of them was "my lady Essex".

~

What happened to Earl Walter in Ireland will probably never be resolved.

He was in Dublin with Sir Henry and Philip Sidney for a while, but at the end of August he received certain letters from London which caused him to change his plans. Writing to lawyer Broughton on 13 September, Walter explained that the letters had prompted him to return to Court "with speed". What was in them he didn't say, nor who sent them. His departure, however, was delayed when "a disease took me and Hunnings my boy [page] and a third person to whom I drank, which maketh me suspect of some evil received in my drink for ever since I have been greatly troubled with a flux and vomits". Walter intended "presently, God willing, [to] embark for Milford and repose myself at my house at Lamphey". His secretary Edward Waterhouse wrote to the earl's doctor the same day directing him to go to Lamphey with all speed; "and let me see yourself there also," Walter added to Broughton.

In Dublin Castle five days later, weakened by ceaseless dysentery, he knew he was dying. To his "loving servants" he wrote: "My general request to you all is to be loving to my children." He urged them to make the annual maintenance payments laid down in his will "for my daughters and for Wat my boy. I have assigned them to [the Earl and Countess of Huntingdon] and do assure myself they will not refuse them ... And so to the Lord I commit you all." There was no mention of his wife.

He dictated a letter to Elizabeth on 20 September, bidding her farewell and begging on behalf of "my poor children that since God doth now make them fatherless, yet it would please your majesty to be as a mother unto them". Several times he asked if Philip could come to him, but there is no record that he made it in time. Sending him messages via Sir Henry, Walter said: "tell him I send him nothing, but I wish him well, and so well, that if God do move both their hearts, I wish that he might match with my daughter. I call him son; he so wise, so virtuous, and godly; and if he go on in the course he hath begun, he will be as famous and worthy a gentleman as ever England bred." To Burghley, Walter sent a letter repeating his wish that his ten-year-old heir, Robert, should be placed in his household, and still he made no reference to Lettice. It was his last, dictated on 21 September.

Richard Broughton was then on his way to Lamphey. He paused at Hereford on 25 September to write to Richard Bagot, "I ride in haste to see his lordship." He had come from Reading, "where the Court stayeth this fortnight". It was common knowledge there "that my lord is sick and cometh over into England". They had yet to learn that Earl Walter was already dead. After three weeks of intolerable discomfort and pain he died shortly before noon on Saturday 22 September.

They did know there were suspicions of poison. Waterhouse's letter to Dr Peny on 13 September hinted at the possibility and rumours spread rapidly. Why had Walter suddenly decided to rush back to London just before he was struck down? If it was official business at Court someone would have said so. Was it coincidence that there was so much gossip about Leicester and Lettice? Sir Henry Sidney, absent from Dublin during Walter's sickness and death, was put in charge of an investigation. Ignoring reports that Walter was certain "he had been poisoned by reason of the violent evacuation which he had", Sir Henry concluded there was no evidence of foul play and the earl had died of dysentery. No surprises there. The chief suspect in the poison rumours was Lord Leicester – Sir Henry's brother-in-law and the most powerful man in the country.

Leicester's alleged motive was naturally assumed to be Lettice, and their marriage two years later, almost to the day, seemed to prove it. More than half a century later, Lettice was still alive when Robert Naunton, secretary of state and husband of her granddaughter Penelope (Dorothy's eldest daughter), wrote his famous gossipy memoirs *Fragmenta Regalia.* "I am not bound to give credit to all vulgar relations," he pointed out, "but that which leads me to think him [Leicester] no good man" was Earl Walter's "death in Ireland, and the marriage of his lady, yet living, which I forbear to press". Others were less discreet, and numerous libels against Leicester rehashed the tale that he poisoned Earl Walter. True or not, they show what sort of reputation Leicester enjoyed.

Slowly the earl's body was brought back by boat from Dublin to Pwllheli in North Wales, and overland from there to South Wales, "with most painful labour of his servants in extreme tempestuous weather upon their backs, where horses with litter could not go". In the first week of October the sad little cavalcade finally brought him back to his birthplace, Carmarthen Castle, to await burial in St Peter's Church.

~

Penelope and her brothers and sister were at Chartley when they heard of their father's death. Edward Waterhouse, his secretary, who had accompanied the earl's body to Carmarthen, joined them in Staffordshire and gave them his account of his master's last days. Waterhouse also took charge of the funeral arrangements, ordering mourning black for the family and servants. Earl Walter's crippling debts were the immediate problem for him, Broughton and Bagot. But Waterhouse was also anxious to carry out his late master's deathbed wishes concerning Penelope.

She was now nearly fourteen and she had been much on Walter's mind. Ideally he saw her future linked to Philip's and he would have liked to speak to Philip before he died. Sadly he reflected on "the frailness of women" in these "vain and ungodly" times, and lamented lest his daughters should learn the ways of "the vile world". He prayed: "God defend them and bless them and make them to fear thy names. The Lord give them grace to live a virtuous and godly life." Penelope's best protection, he believed, would lie in her marriage, and Waterhouse did his best to bring it about.

In the midst of the funeral and financial arrangements Waterhouse wrote to Sir Henry Sidney from Chartley, on 14 November, stressing how much sympathy and support there was for the young Devereux from the queen and "the lords". All of them, he wrote,

> do expect what will become of the treaty between Mr Philip and my lady Penelope. Truly my lord, I must say to your lordship, as I have said to my lord of Leicester and Mr Philip, the breaking off from this match, if the defaults be on your parts, will turn to more dishonour than can be repaired with any other marriage in England. And I protest unto your lordship, I do not think that there is at this day so strong a man in England of friends, as the little Earl of Essex, nor any man more lamented than his father.

Waterhouse's appeal to the Sidneys' sense of honour fell on deaf ears. Sir Henry privately informed Leicester, as if he didn't already know, that he could not stand the late earl. "I take God to record, I could brook neither of them both," he wrote, referring to the Earl of Ormond as well as Walter. The marriage plan had never been formalized and he was not going to proceed with it now that the Devereux finances were in such a bad way.

The chance that the estate could come up with Penelope's £2,000 dowry looked remote, and Lettice was making things worse. Whatever Walter felt about her in the later years of his life, his will bequeathed a quantity of jewels, plate and properties to "my right well beloved wife". But there was also a clause cutting her off without a penny if she objected to the amount of the legacy. Legally she was entitled to a life interest in one-third of the estate, and Lettice decided to risk it, challenge the will and request an extra £60 a year, starting a legal wrangle that kept her short of money for months.

Meanwhile, Earl Walter was laid to rest in the chancel of St Peter's Church in the centre of Carmarthen. The new "little earl" had written to Burghley begging to be excused attending the ceremony and doing "my lord and father the last service". He would have been glad to, Robert explained, "if that my weak body could bear this journey". Waterhouse confirmed to Burghley that Robert was "weak and tender" and it would be better if he did not accompany Waterhouse "in this extreme cold weather to so long a journey". So the funeral went ahead on 26 November with Walter's brother George as chief mourner but with none of his immediate family present.

In his funeral sermon Walter was hailed as a hero of enormous valour and pious character. When it was printed and circulated, together with Waterhouse's account of his last hours, it began the myth-making process that turned him into a Protestant icon. In fact, at the time of his death Walter was ruthlessly engaged in trying to carve out an empire in Ireland for his own profit.

The memories Penelope cherished of him were doubtless closer to the romanticized figure in the sermon, and in years to come she would realize that he was the first of the three most important men in her life who all owed their untimely deaths to Ireland.

~

Earl Walter had placed Robert under the guardianship of Lord Burghley, and Penelope, Dorothy and Wat in the care of his cousin, the Earl of Huntingdon and his wife, Leicester's younger sister Catherine. Before long they would have to leave Chartley but early in December Robert wrote to Burghley again and obtained "leave to tarry here till after Christmas".

It was not going to be a happy Christmas season, but at least Chartley was not yet shut up and the servants knew they would be paid until April. Lettice may have spent the whole festival at Court. She was there for New Year, giving and receiving gifts from Elizabeth; and it has been suggested that Penelope and Dorothy were in London with her. But it would have been strange to leave Robert on his own at Chartley and the likelihood is Penelope, Dorothy and Wat stayed there with him to celebrate Christmas, New Year and Twelfth Night. On 12 January, however, it was time to go. The young Earl of Essex was summoned to pay his respects to the queen at Hampton Court and the four children probably travelled to London together. From Court, Essex would move on to Burghley's household at Cecil House in London and Theobalds, their country estate in Hertfordshire.

Burghley and his wife were running something akin to a small boarding school for a handful of young noblemen. Among them was their own second son, Robert. He was two years older than Essex but the earl, though not sturdy, was taller and stronger. Robert Cecil was crippled by a humped back, short legs and twisted foot, and his head turned awkwardly to one side. He confessed later to being miserably teased as a child, and some said the loathing that developed between the two Roberts began as schoolboys. But there was a class divide as well. Only fifty years back the Cecils were Welsh farmers, while the Devereux were ancient nobility, dripping with blue blood and titles; and the new earl was proud of his royal ancestry. For three months Essex lived with the Cecils, sometimes attending Court with Lady Burghley, and staying at Theobalds. From there on 10 May he set off to begin his student days at Trinity College, Cambridge.

Penelope's stay in London in January 1577 was equally brief, and it was followed by a year travelling around with Lettice and Dorothy. For a while Wat was with them, but he seems to have gone to the Huntingdons in York before his sisters. With the Chartley household soon to be disbanded, Lettice and her children no longer had a home of their own. In mid-January they went with a small band of servants to stay at the Knollys family manor, Grey's Court in Oxfordshire. It was a pleasant rural spot, like Chartley, and although Penelope's grandfather, Sir Francis, and her aunts and uncles spent most of their time at Court, Grey's served as a family retreat, and Lettice would continue to use it for some years. Now she settled in with her children, and Penelope and Dorothy got down to lessons with their tutor, Mathias Holmes. Lettice kept up a determined correspondence with Burghley, as her son's guardian, about her widow's inheritance and her need to increase her income. There had been talk of Elizabeth cancelling Walter's debts but it was wishful thinking.

In April a compromise was reached and Lettice, Lady Essex, accepted the Bennington estate on the borders of Hertfordshire and Essex as part of her settlement. For the moment, however, she was planning to move in with the Digby family at Coleshill in Warwickshire. Sir George was a former ward of Sir Francis Knollys and he had become prominent among the Dudley family's supporters in the West Midlands. As Colonel Digby he would rise to be one of Leicester's army chiefs in the Netherlands in the 1580s, and he was already proving a trustworthy ally. Coleshill was just ten miles from Leicester's

Kenilworth Castle and the authors of a famous libel on Leicester, published in 1584, were remarkably well informed when they pin-pointed Coleshill as the house Lady Essex and Lord Leicester used as their secret love nest.

Penelope was old enough to ride over from Coleshill to Kenilworth and join the hunting parties with her mother. While Earl Walter was in Ireland, Lettice had become a regular member of the groups that gathered in Lord Leicester's deer parks. Occasionally the deer were hunted with guns and hounds but mostly they were brought down with bows and arrows, and Lettice was an excellent shot. One year her tally was seven bucks, though the gamekeepers awarded a few of them jointly to "Lady Essex and Mrs West", her sister Anne. This year, 1577, Lettice went hunting often enough to bring her score up to nine, including three stags. Her brother William and his wife Dorothy were sometimes in the hunting parties. So were Penelope and the Digbys, and Penelope proved as good a shot as her uncle William when she killed a buck in a clearing in the woods.

It would not have escaped Penelope's notice that the gamekeeper now took orders from her mother about dispatching gifts of venison to her friends, and sending deer to be cooked in the castle kitchen. Leicester spent a fortnight at Kenilworth that June, on his way to take the waters at Buxton. It was the fashionable place among high society. Mary Queen of Scots was fond of it and Lettice had been before, while Earl Walter was in Ireland. It would be natural to go again this summer, taking Penelope and Dorothy.

Despite such pleasures, Lettice was keen for Penelope and Dorothy's education to continue. Mathias Holmes had been their tutor "since they began first to learn" and Earl Walter had granted him an annuity of £10 a year. Given the difficulties of getting money out of the estate, Holmes was anxious to see it paid and Lettice wrote urging Burghley to "give order it may be paid for he [Holmes] is one that teacheth my daughters". Holmes would have liked to visit Burghley in person but Lettice vetoed the idea because "I would be loath he should be so long absent".

There may have been another break from lessons in the summer. On 30 July Penelope's friend Anne Bagot was married at Blithfield to lawyer Broughton. The Bagots and Broughton were so important in the lives of the Devereux that it is hard to imagine Lettice and her daughters *not* attending Anne's wedding. In later years Penelope made a point of attending the weddings and baptisms of her friends and servants; and from Coleshill it was only twenty-five miles to Blithfield.

As autumn approached, Lettice wanted to be at Court ready for Accession Day, and in October she took Penelope and Dorothy back to London. "My lady of Essex came to Hackney a week past," Richard Broughton wrote to his father-in-law Richard Bagot on 5 November. Hackney was a small hamlet within the Stepney area which had become fashionable with the nobility. Several grandees had houses there including the Earl of Northumberland, and the likeliest hostess for Lettice and her daughters was Elizabeth's elderly cousin, the widowed Countess of Lennox. Lady Lennox, ambitious, scheming and Catholic, had outlived her husband and two sons and was now grandmother to both the main claimants to Elizabeth's throne. Her elder son, the murdered husband of Mary Queen of Scots, had fathered the present young King James of Scotland. Her second son had died recently of tuberculosis, leaving a baby daughter, Arbella Stuart, who currently lived with her grandmother in Hackney.

Lady Lennox, being an ardent Catholic, had been particularly close to Elizabeth's sister Queen Mary, and Elizabeth was rightly wary of her intrigues. In her youth Lady Lennox was herself heiress presumptive to the throne, and she knew the strength of Arbella's place in the succession stakes. She also knew the value of influential friends, like Lord Leicester; and her grip on current gossip would have told her about Leicester and Lady Essex, even if he didn't. When Lady Lennox died the following spring, two days after Leicester dined with her, it brought the usual flurry of poison rumours, though she had been in "a languishing decline" for some time.

From Hackney, Lettice and her daughters moved on to stay with the Russell family at "my Lady of Bedford's house in London". Broughton added: "I understand my young ladies shall go shortly, or at least against Candlemas, to York." For Penelope and Dorothy the year of travelling around with their mother was coming to an end. In February at the latest they must go north, but it would be hard to send them off before Christmas and all the Court revels. Leicester was there, inviting lawyer Broughton "to be bold to trouble him in anything" the young Earl of Essex needed; and Lettice was there, exchanging gifts again with Elizabeth. But after Twelfth Night it would be time for Penelope and Dorothy to be on their way, travelling north to live with the Earl and Countess of Huntingdon.

Chapter Seven

1578–1581

"How to breed and govern young gentlewomen"
– Catherine, Countess of Huntingdon, 1618

*T*he Earl of Huntingdon was the most powerful man in northern England. Appointed president of the Council of the North in 1572, he was the queen's viceroy everywhere north of the River Trent, except the royal duchy of Lancaster. He was a plain-speaking man of action and his wife had to remind her brother Leicester "he useth not such flattering behaviour as many will do". He had done a remarkable job imposing royal authority on the region, ensuring there would be no repeat of the Northern Earls' rebellion. And his obvious loyalty had wiped out Elizabeth's worries that he might act on his royal ancestry and bid for the throne.

Huntingdon was also the most senior member of Walter's family and a natural choice as guardian for Penelope, Dorothy and Wat, not least because he shared the radical Protestant views of their father and grandfather. Huntingdon would go down in history as "the Puritan Earl" and his countess, Lady Catherine, matched him prayer for prayer in religious zeal. Placing Penelope in their care looked like a good move in Earl Walter's plan for her to marry Philip: Lady Catherine was sister to his mother, Lady Mary Sidney, as well as Leicester and Ambrose, Earl of Warwick.

Earl Walter could not have picked a more suitable home for his children than the Huntingdons' sober, upright and godly household. It was run, like Burghley's, as an exclusive boarding school. Lady Catherine, Ambrose and Leicester (for many years) were childless, and the countess made a business of obtaining wardships, the legal rights to raise wealthy orphans and manage their estates. Her speciality was girls and she was proud to claim, "I know how to breed and govern young gentlewomen."

Huntingdon's family seat was Ashby-de-la-Zouche Castle, less than a morning's ride east of Chartley. His job as lord president, however, meant that he and the countess lived chiefly at the council's headquarters, King's Manor in York. Penelope, Dorothy and Wat were not, therefore, being packed off to some remote backwater to live in a draughty, old-fashioned fortress.

York was the capital of the northern provinces, the second most flourishing city in England. It was packed with rich merchants' town houses, thriving shops and markets. Around the magnificent minster a strong cultural tradition had grown up and the citizens were proud of their Mystery plays acted through the streets. There were strolling musicians, pedlars and ballad sellers. When the circuit judges and justices arrived for the assizes and quarter sessions, the streets and inns were crowded with visitors and horses. Just outside the city walls, but only yards from the bustle of the city and the minster, stood King's Manor. Its gardens ran down to the river and Huntingdon was upgrading the old brick house, once part of an abbey, to a splendid vice-regal residence.

York could supply all the language tutors, music and drawing masters Penelope was used to. Lady Catherine had received an excellent humanist education, including courtly accomplishments, and she continued to oversee the Devereux girls' lessons. But the Huntingdons' Protestantism placed new emphasis on religious instruction and the virtues of industry, self-discipline, obedience and submissiveness. Lady Catherine was determined that her girls should understand how to manage a large house, especially their duty to teach everyone within it the Protestant way of life. And to help her Catherine employed a series of militant Protestant ministers.

It was a form of religion Penelope was familiar with, but now it took on greater intensity. Daily life revolved around morning and evening family prayers, examining her conscience, studying scriptures, listening to sermons. It was a pattern of instruction designed to develop inner piety. On Margaret Dakins, who would briefly become Wat Devereux's wife, it worked well. She came to the countess as a young child and, judging by her diary (published under her last name, Lady Margaret Hoby), she followed Lady Catherine's training for the rest of her life. Earthly happiness and heavenly bliss were to be found in religious faith and honest industry.

Penelope would find bliss in other ways. She was fifteen and Dorothy nearly fourteen when they arrived in York in February 1578. They had had a taste of adult life and Court society and they were old enough to prepare for marriage. At Chartley they had naturally picked up the ways of a large household, but it was useful to learn more from Lady Catherine about their role in running one. They could expect stewards and ushers to carry out daily management, yet they needed to know how the kitchen, plate store, still room, wardrobes, ale house, fishponds and farms worked, not to mention midwifery, healing and accounting. Their grandmother's bookkeeping had been invaluable to Sir Francis, professionally and privately.

Penelope's tastes and independent character, however, were already fairly well formed; she was less open to Lady Catherine's influence than was little Margaret. In the Devereux family Penelope jokingly came to be known as "the idle wench" or "the idle housewife". To the Huntingdons, idleness was a mortal sin, not something to joke about: the soul's salvation depended on avoiding it. In the Devereux family religion was important, but there were other ways of occupying time than praying and examining one's conscience. Nothing in their later lives suggests that Penelope, Dorothy or Wat left the Huntingdons with great affection for them, or with pious plans to follow the Puritan path. Their brother Robert felt differently, about the earl at least, and grieved at his death; but Robert did not have to live with them until he had left Cambridge.

~

Robert had been at Trinity College, Cambridge, almost a year when Penelope reached York. His companion-cum-servant was Anthony Bagot, youngest of the Blithfield family but seven years his senior. Anthony had instructions from his father and Broughton to keep close faith and friendship with the young earl, steer him wisely and report back everything the "little lordship" was up to.

The friendship was no problem. Essex had the Devereux charm as well as the looks. He was exceptionally generous and loyal and his companions and servants stayed with him for life. Steering him wisely was more difficult. Essex soon established the habits of his lifetime: wildly overspending and going absent without leave. When he *did* have permission to take a break and go to London it was difficult to get him back to his studies. On one occasion Broughton had to threaten to ride with him all the way. Given the glamour at Court it is hardly surprising, and at Christmas 1578 excitement reached a peak.

Elizabeth was awaiting two important visitors: a French envoy, Jean de Simier, and the German prince John Casimir, Count Palatine. Casimir wanted money and soldiers for a Protestant campaign in the Netherlands. Simier's mission was more delicate. He was coming to negotiate a marriage between Elizabeth and the crown prince of France, a young man she had never met. The idea had been put forward years ago, when the prince was third in line to the French throne and known as the Duc d'Alençon. Since the death of his eldest brother, the king, he had become heir presumptive with the title Duc d'Anjou. He was more than twenty years Elizabeth's junior, notoriously short and ugly, and Catholic. The thought of Elizabeth marrying a French Catholic and making him king of England was a horrifying thought to many of her councillors, and the Court was in a state of tension and discord.

Elizabeth, nonetheless, ordered gala revels over Christmastide including hospitality for Casimir at Hampton Court, Windsor and Leicester's country house, Wanstead, in Essex. After that everyone returned to Whitehall. "This first of February there was such a show of noble men and gentlemen in the tilt yard at Whitehall as the like (by every man's report) hath not been seen this forty years," Anthony Bagot reported to his father. He was making excuses for Essex remaining in London. After the jousting there would be hawks and harriers and then they would, definitely, be off to Cambridge. It was actually the end of the month before they left.

Jean de Simier, meanwhile, a master of flattery whom Elizabeth fondly nicknamed her "Monkey", was having more success wooing her than was good for him. The second time gunshots narrowly missed him it was obviously not just an unhappy accident, except to the person who hired the assassin. Simier thought that was probably Leicester. He knew Leicester was deeply opposed to the French marriage, and Simier tried every trick in the book to destroy the earl's influence with Elizabeth. Simier's scoop, some said, was revealing to her later in 1579 the "secret" of Leicester's "recent" marriage to Lettice.

~

Penelope's mother had, in fact, married Elizabeth's favourite the previous September, six months after Penelope and Dorothy left London for York. How the news got out is a mystery, but the facts about the wedding are certain. Three and a half years later three witnesses to the wedding, including Penelope's grandfather Sir Francis, gave signed depositions under oath that Lettice, Countess of Essex, was married to Robert, Earl of Leicester, on 21 September 1578 at Wanstead. Two days later Elizabeth dined there at the end of her summer progress, oblivious to her soulmate's ceremony.

Elizabeth enjoyed staying at Wanstead and the September visit was her second in 1578. During a mini-progress in the spring she spent several days there. Arriving on Tuesday 13 May, "to see my lord of Leicester, who hath been there sick this fortnight", she stayed till Friday and then returned by barge across the Thames to Greenwich.

Wanstead moves in and out of Penelope's story like the players' favourite backcloth: setting the scene again and again for different episodes. Henry VIII granted it to Mary Boleyn's husband Will Carey in June 1524; and it is usually assumed to be a reward for complicity in Henry's affair with Mary, which led to the birth of Penelope's grandmother. Some years later it was acquired by Lord Rich, who hosted Elizabeth during her 1561 progress. It was then a relatively modest, twenty-bedroom house with a central quadrangle and two extra wings leading off the front. It had a hall, great chamber and gallery, a chapel, and a little gallery that gave on to the gardens. What probably most appealed to Elizabeth was the stabling for fifty-eight horses, plus the first-rate hunting in Waltham Forest.

In 1577 Leicester began leasing it from Lord Rich and a few months later he bought it and began turning it into a luxury country retreat. For Elizabeth's visit in May 1578 Philip Sidney wrote a dramatic masque, *The Lady of May*, which paid flattering tribute to her beauty and wisdom. In September, however, the drama was over before Elizabeth arrived. Her summer progress had been a lengthy journey through Essex, Suffolk and Norfolk, stopping at more than a dozen houses. With her as usual were Lord Leicester; Penelope's grandfather, Sir Francis; Lettice's cousin Kate, Lady Howard; and Leicester's brother Ambrose, Earl of Warwick. For much of the trip Lord Burghley was also present, as was Roger, Lord North, a good friend of both Elizabeth and Leicester. Privy council meetings were held wherever the queen happened to be, though she didn't normally attend. But when the council convened at "Mr Stonar's house", Luxborough Hall, on 21 September it had shrunk to three members. Leicester, Warwick, Sir Francis and Lord North were elsewhere.

The previous day, Leicester had taken leave of the queen to prepare Wanstead, he said, for her arrival on Tuesday the 23rd. Lord North also made some excuse and left, as did Sir Francis and Warwick. By nightfall they had gathered at Wanstead for supper. With them round the table were the Earl of Pembroke (recently married to Philip's sister, young Mary Sidney); Lettice's brother Richard Knollys; and Lettice. Summoning his private chaplain, Humphrey Tyndall, Leicester explained that "for the better quieting of his own conscience" he intended to marry "the right honourable Countess of Essex". He wanted, however, to do it secretly, so please would Master Tyndall be ready at seven o'clock the next morning. Duly on Sunday before eight o'clock Tyndall was escorted by Lord North into the "little gallery of Wanstead house opening upon the garden". There they were joined by Leicester, Warwick, Pembroke and Sir Francis, and "within a little after, the Countess of Essex herself, attired … in a loose gown". Tyndall married them "in such manner and form as is prescribed by the communion book", and "did pronounce them lawful man and wife". On Tuesday Elizabeth arrived for the last dinner of her progress, a celebration banquet organized by Leicester, and no one said a word about weddings.

Later it was claimed that Leicester and Lettice had been secretly married earlier in the year at Kenilworth, and the second ceremony at Wanstead in front of witnesses was demanded by Sir Francis because of Leicester's wicked reputation. The real reason for the Wanstead ceremony was more likely Leicester's wish to ensure the child Lettice was carrying under her "loose gown" was his legitimate heir, if it survived. But it didn't. And the witness statements were not taken for another three years, when Lettice reached the sixth month of another pregnancy. Three months after the Wanstead wedding, Lettice was back at Court and evidently still in royal favour. For New Year Elizabeth gave Lettice a gilt cup and cover; Lettice gave Elizabeth an amber chain with gold and small pearl decorations.

To Penelope her mother's marriage could not have been a surprise. But something about it took the queen unawares. Who told Elizabeth her "Sweet Robin" had married, and when, is the subject of endless speculation. Simier usually gets the credit for dropping the bombshell on the queen in the summer of 1579 because William Camden said so in his official and contemporary history of the reign. But it is probably a myth. The French ambassador knew about the marriage early in November 1578 and Elizabeth's fury at Leicester does not emerge till July 1579. At that point Mary Queen of Scots knew that Elizabeth was angry with Leicester (and with Sir Christopher Hatton, another favourite) for secretly marrying. But which of Leicester's secret marriages was Mary referring to? The one with Lady Douglas or with Lady Essex?

The chances are that Elizabeth knew about Leicester's marriage to Lettice, possibly from Leicester himself, before "the Monkey" started stirring things. The secret Simier revealed to Elizabeth in July, sending her into storms of anger and Leicester into temporary disgrace, was the fact that Leicester was already married to Lady Douglas, and Lettice had knowingly enticed him into a bigamous marriage. The more she aged the more allergic Elizabeth became to marriages among her inner circle. Sir Walter Ralegh, Sir Philip Sidney, the earls of Essex and Southampton, to name but four, were reduced to clandestine weddings for fear of her foul temper, and when she found them out they all fell from favour, albeit temporarily.

The marriage of her special partner Leicester was far more complex. The fraught triangle between Elizabeth, Leicester and Lettice has been called the "central enigma of her reign". Elizabeth had no intention of marrying Leicester herself, but that didn't mean anyone else could. And since Elizabeth could not face his absence from her side for long, Lettice took the full force of her anger. It was the start of Elizabeth's hate campaign against her. From now onwards Lettice was "that She-wolf" and her Court career was ruined.

But not her children's careers. Penelope was about to enter a small, competitive circle where the queen's loathing for her mother was common knowledge; and if she had not already heard the sordid rumours that swirled about her parents and her new stepfather, she would doubtless come across them. Yet while Elizabeth indulged her dislike of Lettice, she treated Penelope and Essex with extraordinary tolerance and partiality. It is as if, out of spite against their mother, she wanted to bind them to her with generosity, vying with Lettice for their affection.

Within a year of the fuss about the marriage, Elizabeth was offering to do something for the Devereux girls. She gave the Huntingdons permission "to put her highness in mind of these young ladies". Now that Penelope was old enough, the queen would consider finding her pretty god-daughter a post among her ladies, perhaps even as one of the six elite maids of honour. And when the countess took Penelope to London she could also try and wring more funding for her husband from the queen. Huntingdon was finding it increasingly difficult to finance his job as president of the Council of the North.

It was agreed that Lady Huntingdon would travel to London and present Penelope at Court in January 1581, soon after Penelope's eighteenth birthday. Before then, perhaps Essex should come and spend Christmas with them all at York. Huntingdon wrote to Burghley for permission; but Essex had been absent too long from his studies during 1580. Leicester, now formally his stepfather, was known to be "much grieved thereat", and would probably frown on him taking time out at Christmas.

By December Essex knew the plan had fallen through. Writing to Richard Bagot to thank him for some venison sent across to Cambridge from Chartley, Essex added: "I think I shall be in Cambridge this Christmas. If it fall out so" – Bagot could guess what was coming – "I look for more provisions." Robert's final request was more unusual. He wanted Bagot to check the identity of a new friend he had made at college: a Welshman named Gelly Meyrick. While Robert celebrated the first of many Christmases with Anthony Bagot, Gelly Meyrick and probably some venison, Penelope spent her last Christmas at York, preparing for a new life at Court.

Part II

Marriage and Politics

1581–November 1590

Chapter Eight

1581

"Toward Aurora's Court a nymph doth dwell,
Rich in all beauties which man's eye can see"

– Philip Sidney, *Astrophil and Stella*, 1582–3

*P*enelope's eighteenth birthday had just passed when she set out for London with the Countess of Huntingdon. Leaving York and the earl to his affairs in Newcastle, they travelled south, probably pausing at the Huntingdons' castle at Ashby-de-la-Zouche, and reached London on Sunday 29 January 1581. Wasting no time, they attended Court the following day and on Tuesday Sir Francis Walsingham was able to report to Huntingdon that his wife had been "very graciously received and welcomed by her majesty". There wasn't a vacancy among the maids of honour, but there was a good chance the queen would soon find a position for her pretty godchild.

Elizabeth was at Whitehall Palace, one of her favourites. Every inch of it breathed power and wealth. Its many chambers and galleries were treasure chests of priceless pictures, books and "cunningly wrought clocks in all sizes". Ceilings shone with gold paint and gilded carvings and the walls were hung with huge tapestries and royal portraits. When Penelope arrived everyone was still talking about the New Year festivities and the spectacular tournament in the tiltyard on 22 January. Philip Sidney had appeared as the Blue Knight, and the Earl of Oxford, Lord Burghley's son-in-law, stole the show as the Knight of the Tree, with an elaborate pavilion of brown and silver taffeta and an artificial tree, the "stock, branches and leaves whereof were all gilded over".

Philip was back at Court after months in disgrace with Elizabeth for openly opposing her plan to marry the young Duc d'Anjou. At New Year Philip presented her with a small gold whip set with diamonds and seed pearls, a token of submission to her. It was charming and ingenious, the sort of symbolism she loved, but it did not restore him to favour and the French marriage plan continued.

In the wake of Simier's wooing, Anjou had made a secret visit to Elizabeth eighteen months ago, and to the Court's astonishment the queen fell for him. Despite his youth and Catholic faith, his short legs and badly pock-marked face, Elizabeth became genuinely fond of him, calling him her "dearest Frog". He had recently led a Protestant campaign to support the Dutch rebels against their Spanish rulers and he wanted the marriage and money, so a grand group of French commissioners was on its way to finalize the treaty.

The Court Penelope came to was feverish with gossip and plans for more than the usual feasting, dancing and entertainment. There would be plays, music, bear-baiting, hawking and another spectacular tilt. The Countess of Huntingdon gave the queen a jewelled pendant in the shape of a frog hung on a gold chain and set with green emeralds. But most of Elizabeth's council was less than encouraging about the union. In two years' time Elizabeth would be fifty. Was she really contemplating marriage? Since there was no chance of an heir, surely she was just playing at political alliances.

Nonetheless elaborate preparations went on for the visitors, who were rumoured to number 500. For a time Elizabeth moved into the Palace of St James's while Whitehall was fumigated, purged with fires and spruced up. The large wooden banqueting hall, built in the Whitehall gardens ten years before, was redecorated like the richest May bower ever seen. On the ceiling there were stars, clouds and a beaming sun; greenery trailed from the rafters; holly and ivy seemed to grow on the canvas hangings, with "bay, rue and all manner of strange flowers"; and cloth of silver and gold hung down the walls.

Into this glittering world stepped a young woman whose beauty, charm and grace would become legendary. Her impact on a Court already thronged with celebrities – sophisticated, talented, rich and beautiful people – was extraordinary. Her large, dark eyes and golden hair, her sweet voice and lute playing, her dancing, languages, and her good nature captivated them. Poets, painters and musicians fell over themselves to portray her, and more than a few fell in love with her.

William Byrd, greatest of all Tudor composers, wrote songs about her "face as fair as silver, Not wanting rose nor lily white to paint it":

> Her beauty great had diverse gods enchanted,
> Among the which Love was the first transformed.

Philip Sidney, second only to Shakespeare among Elizabethan sonneteers, immortalized her as the heroine of his *Astrophil and Stella* poems. To him she seemed "Perfection's heir", and as he gazed at her beauty he wondered

When nature made her chief work, Stella's eyes,
In colour black why wrapt she beams so bright?

He praised her "joyful face", "fair skin", "chaste mind" and "lips so sweetly swelling". John Dowland wrote dances for her. Charles Tessier, the great French lutenist, dedicated his first book of songs to her, knowing that she was fluent in French and excelled at music. And the poet Henry Constable sat enchanted while she strummed

A lute of senseless wood by nature dumb
Touched by thy hand doth speak divinely well
And from thy lips and breast sweet tunes do come
To my dead heart, the which new life do give.

As well as music and poetry, Court life offered pleasures that Penelope had not been allowed at York. Gambling was endemic. Everyone played cards, chess, dice and backgammon. It helped to pass the idle hours waiting on the queen, and betting added spice to the games. Elizabeth liked cards, especially primero, but she was a notoriously bad loser. It was best to let her win and she happily took money off everyone, even good friends like Lord North, who lost £32 (nearly £6,000 nowadays) to her at a sitting. Often there was cockfighting to bet on, and sometimes bull- and bear-baiting.

Court etiquette was rigid and formal, yet nothing like the Puritan piety Penelope had known for the past three years. Above all it was an amorous atmosphere: flirting was everyone's default mode. The keynotes were courtly love and chivalry, played out in love songs, romantic poetry, chasing games, dancing and disguising. It was titillating fantasy and make-believe, which inevitably strayed further than fiction. With the French commissioners due any day, the Court was shocked to a standstill in March when Anne Vavasour, one of the queen's maids of honour, "was brought to bed of a son in the maidens' chamber". The scandal grew worse when it turned out the baby's father was the flashy, untrustworthy Earl of Oxford. True to form, he tried to skip the country, but all ports were immediately sealed and before long he was in the Tower with Anne and "others that have been found anyway party to the cause". The maids who shared her room must have noticed Anne was missing her monthly courses and growing somewhat rounder. It was a salutary lesson for the parents and guardians of every young lady at Court, and it may partly explain the Huntingdons' plans for Penelope. She was the most alluring of all: aristocratic, accomplished, witty, charming, beautiful, and stepdaughter to the queen's favourite.

Anne's departure left a vacancy among the maids which Penelope was ideally placed to fill. She may not have taken the oath of loyalty needed from Elizabeth's staff, but she certainly became part of the household, enjoying perks such as guaranteed rooms wherever the queen was staying, the best of the food and drink Elizabeth did not want, servants and stabling for horses; and, of course, access to the queen. Maids of honour, all dressed in white, were there to provide glamour around the queen, entertain her, help look after her and her clothes, and conduct the nightly search of the royal bedchamber. It could be mind-numbingly tedious waiting for Elizabeth to wake and dress, make her mind up and change it again about what she would do; and the service rota meant there was little time off. The bonus was that they were in the best marriage market in the country. The downside was the tyranny Elizabeth exercised over their lives. They needed her permission to be absent from Court; and to marry.

As Elizabeth aged, her vanity increased. So did her sexual jealousy. Since *she* was single there was no need for any of her maids to marry and her male favourites were supposed to be in love with her, not her ladies. Again and again she refused permission. Penelope's sister, Dorothy, and her kinsman Robert Carey were both forced into runaway and secret marriages, apart from the high-profile cases of her brother and her mother.

≈

Elizabeth's refusal to receive Leicester's wife at Court meant that Lettice could not watch Penelope's triumph there. But many others in the family were present to support her and see the admiration she drew. On the Knollys side there was her grandfather, Sir Francis; his sons Henry and William and several more of Penelope's uncles, about to take part in the tournaments and junkets for the French embassy; and her aunt Elizabeth, who waited years for permission to marry Sir Thomas Leighton.

Among the Careys there was Penelope's great-uncle, Lord Hunsdon; his son and daughter George and Kate; and Kate's husband Charles, Lord Howard of Effingham, soon to be lord high admiral. The Howards' daughter Frances, later Countess of Kildare, would grow up to be another Court beauty, though without Penelope's charm. Her reputation for gossip and ambitious scheming led Essex to call her "the spider of the Court".

And then there was Penelope's stepfather. Opinions vary about Leicester's relationship with her brother – some say his antipathy to Essex was notorious – but to Penelope and Dorothy he was kindly, thoughtful and generous. He set aside rooms especially for Penelope at Leicester House in the Strand, and at Wanstead. Her chamber and "outer chamber" in his London mansion were furnished in a red and green colour scheme, with embroidered "hangings with flowers and leaves" and "carpets of turkey stuff" at the windows. Her four-poster bed, made of "walnuttree", had a canopy "and curtains of scarlet all laid down with old gold lace". There was a white rug, "a green velvet chair" and another upholstered in "crimson wrought velvet", a square walnut table, a "carpet of green wrought velvet", a court cupboard and another cupboard in the outer chamber. It was a refuge whenever she needed it, or wanted to be near her mother.

Lettice was not a social exile hidden away in distant countryside. While Leicester lived she divided her time between his London home, Wanstead, and her own Bennington estate, less than twenty-five miles north of the city. Penelope's sister Dorothy may have been in London, too. It would be easier for the Countess of Huntingdon to bring Dorothy south rather than leave her behind, and if there wasn't room for her at Court, where beds were always in short supply, Dorothy could stay with Lettice. It was probably during 1581 that the pretty double portrait of Penelope and her sister was painted, and hung in Leicester House. Listed a few years later as "two ladies in one picture, my Lady Rich and my Lady Dorothy", it shows the sisters in matching red gowns and both with beautiful, large, dark eyes. Their golden hair hangs down about their shoulders showing they were unmarried, but the title on the family inventory suggests Penelope's marriage had already been agreed, while Dorothy's had not. It was one of the precious items that was not sold off after Leicester's death, and it remained "in the high gallery" at Leicester House "now in use and to remain for my lady's [Lettice's] service".

No amount of kindness from Leicester could make up for the absence of Penelope's father, Earl Walter. It was barely five years since he left Court to make his last, fateful journey to Ireland. Those who had watched him leave now watched Penelope arrive and at least some of them knew that Elizabeth's irresolute policy had contributed to his failure. One of them was Francis Drake, who had joined Earl Walter's Ulster enterprise. Since then Drake, a short, stocky, sea-worn figure, had perfected his prowess as a pirate. In September the previous year, having circled the globe, he returned to Plymouth loaded with loot from Spanish ships and colonies. Philip Sidney observed: "I know not the secret points; but about the world he hath been, and rich he is returned." Quite how much silver Drake brought back was a secret Elizabeth insisted he must share only with her, and she kept him talking privately all day while they went through his spoils. The Spanish ambassador reckoned it was a million and a half pesos, possibly more. But ignoring Spanish protests about "El Drago", Elizabeth led her Court down-river to Deptford early in April to honour him.

After dining on board his ship the *Pelican*, renamed the *Golden Hind*, Elizabeth picked up the gold sword she had brought and teasingly told him it was to cut off his head, as the Spaniards wished. Instead, adding insult to

Spanish injury, she passed it to the French envoy and gave him the honour of knighting Sir Francis Drake. During her play-acting Elizabeth managed to lose her ornate purple garter, which the Frenchman scooped up, claiming it as a token for Anjou. It was all very suggestive and, like Anne Vavasour's indiscretion, it was unfamiliar territory to Penelope, coming from the Countess of Huntingdon's strictly Puritan household.

Two weeks later, on Sunday 16 April, the French commissioners landed at Dover. They were the cream of the French diplomatic corps and aristocracy. As they made their way to London speculation was rife. The awful bloody massacre in Paris nine years before on St Bartholomew's Eve, when rioting Catholics started slaughtering Protestants, was still raw in many minds. Philip Sidney had been there at the English embassy, with Walsingham and his family, frightened for their lives. There was no certainty this large band of French Catholics would be welcomed by Londoners and Elizabeth put out a proclamation that they must be treated with due honour. Coming upriver in a fleet of barges from Gravesend to their lodgings at Somerset House, they were given a 200-gun salute, followed by days of official hospitality.

Penelope's brother Essex was also there to witness their arrival, and the St George's Day gala on 23 April. When Burghley gave him permission to come down from Cambridge, Essex ordered a new satin doublet, velvet hose and a crimson jerkin laid over with silver lace, blowing his student budget as usual.

On Monday 24 April, cousin Kate's husband, Lord Howard, escorted the Frenchmen to Court for an audience with the queen. The following day they dined with Elizabeth in the beautiful banqueting hall. On Wednesday negotiations formally opened with the privy council. And the next day Penelope's stepfather threw a grand dinner for them at Leicester House "where her Majesty was present and used some long speeches to them". Elizabeth would not want Lettice present, but that was no excuse for Penelope not to attend. Elizabeth would expect her ladies, Penelope included, to take their seats with her in the flotilla of boats that glided downriver from Whitehall to Leicester House for dinner. And Essex, presumably not rushing back to Cambridge, would be somewhere in the crowd, listening to Elizabeth's speeches – and wondering what she meant by them.

Elizabeth was brilliant at disguising her real intentions. The negotiations dragged on for weeks. After the usual May Day revels, mumming, dancing and a bear-baiting, there were more eye-wateringly expensive entertainments for everyone at Court to attend. Whitsun week brought one of the grandest pageants and tournaments of the reign. For two days the jousting, speeches and songs went on, devised by Philip Sidney and his fellow knights. Together they rode in as the "Four Foster Children of Desire", each followed by pages, ushers, trumpeters and gentlemen in colourful liveries. Their object was to besiege "The Fortress of Perfect Beauty" – Elizabeth herself in the gallery overlooking the tiltyard, watching with her guests and ladies.

To Penelope it looked like another family turnout: four of her Knollys uncles, Henry, William, Robert and Francis, took part in matching armour, their horses uniformly caparisoned. The effect was stunning, but underlying the chivalry there was political meaning. The Latin motto Philip had devised to wear with his blue and gold armour and on his followers' sashes – "a band of silver which came scarf-wise over the shoulder" – read "*Sic nos non nobis*", "Thus ours but not with us". Tournament mottos always had multiple meanings directed at Elizabeth, and sometimes to one of the ladies. Few watchers would have missed the hint that union with France was not welcome.

After six weeks' talking and feasting, however, the marriage treaty was signed on 11 June, and three days later the French delegation departed. Whatever it had achieved, for Penelope it had been an extraordinary introduction to Court life.

~

As the visitors left, the queen's ladies began packing her gowns and jewels, face paints and perfumes, and the personal treasures she liked to have by her. On 20 June Elizabeth was moving to Greenwich. It was not a full progress this summer; instead she planned to stay at her own palaces near London. There was less work for Leicester, organizing the horses and baggage wagons that moved slowly cross country with her army of servants, and late in June he paid a visit to Oxford. The grooms knew from long experience what to do, going on ahead to prepare each palace, fix hangings around the chambers and set up beds.

It was a busy time and a happy one. Elizabeth loved Greenwich in spring and summer. Built by her grandfather, Henry VII, it was her birthplace. The "delightfulness of its situation" beside the river, fanned by breezes, made it a place for pleasure. Behind the long river frontage and the tall watergate tower, the main apartments were grouped round three courtyards, and beyond them stood a tiltyard, armour shops and a covered tennis court. Away from the river there were orchards, gardens and archery fields sweeping uphill to the wooded deer park and an old hunting tower. Looking down from the hill, one could see how the fast-flowing Thames looped round the palace in a great bow. Eastwards the river went winding away to the sea. Westwards lay London; and north, across the river, fields and woods spread away to Wanstead and Waltham Forest, where Elizabeth loved to hunt.

After a fortnight at Greenwich Elizabeth decided to spend a few days at "Mr Stonar's". It was a pleasant journey across the river in the royal barge, with its crimson canopy and liveried oarsmen, and then a short ride.

Elizabeth had been a guest at the family's Loughton Hall and Luxborough before. This time she spent three days with them and on Saturday 8 July she went back to Greenwich for the rest of the summer. Early in September there were reports of plague in the city. It was not one of the worst outbreaks but bad enough to delay the autumn law term, and on 22 September Elizabeth moved further from London to Nonsuch Palace at Ewell. It was only a dozen miles by road, but for her ladies it meant hurriedly packing up ready for the baggage wagons to rumble away south-westwards into Surrey.

While Elizabeth was there, her ministers took a break to check on their own estates. On 28 September, Leicester was at Kenilworth, Burghley was briefly at Theobalds and Walsingham was at Barn Elms. Early in October Elizabeth moved again, and as her cavalcade made the seven-mile journey to Richmond Palace, crowds cheered and all seemed well. But beneath the spectacle and ceremony, the artificial adoration of the Virgin Queen, there was increasing tension. Elizabeth had been on the throne twenty-two years. Her government had grown repressive. Rigid state control was enforced: on the clothing that different classes could wear; on how citizens must clean the streets; and – highly unpopular – when the playhouses must close. The two great matters that had exercised Elizabeth's ministers and parliament for twenty years, religion and the succession, were more pressing than ever, and there were more extreme measures against Catholics.

Years ago the pope had called Elizabeth "old, probably barren and a heretic", and foreign diplomats realised she meant to "befool the world" with her marriage plans. Surely Anjou could not seriously be wooing her now? In truth, he was only desperate for money and troops for his Netherlands campaigns, but he was about to pay another visit to clinch the marriage and exchange rings. Penelope, caught up in the excitement, listening to the gossip about Elizabeth and her "Frog" prince, certainly had no wish for her own marriage to be arranged.

Chapter Nine

1581

"In years very fit for my Lady Penelope"

– Henry, Earl of Huntingdon, 1581

*P*enelope had been at Court less than a month when her guardians began planning her marriage. Her father, on his deathbed in Ireland, had made it clear he wanted her to marry Philip Sidney, "if God so move both their hearts". Whatever God had or hadn't done to Penelope's heart, and whether or not Philip was madly in love with her, the Earl and Countess of Huntingdon had other plans.

At Court Lady Huntingdon soon picked up rumours that the very rich Baron Rich of Leighs in Essex was dying and his young heir would be one of the leading landowners in the region. Quickly she passed on the news to her husband in Newcastle. On 27 February Lord Rich duly died, having signed his will two days earlier, and on 10 March the Earl of Huntingdon wrote to Lord Burghley to ask his help in fixing the marriage. "God hath taken to his mercy my Lord Rich who hath left to his heir a proper gentleman," Huntingdon explained, in his large scrawling script, making several blots and crossings out. Rich's son and heir was "in years very fit for my Lady Penelope", he added. Penelope's marriage needed the queen's permission and Huntingdon wanted Burghley to persuade Elizabeth to give it. To be on the safe side, he wrote to Walsingham with a similar request.

History has few words to say about the Rich family and fewer still are good ones. They were not so far outside the Court circle as is sometimes implied and they had several connections to Lord Leicester. The late Lord Rich's sister, Winifred, was first married to Leicester's eldest brother, and on his death she married Elizabeth and Leicester's friend Roger, Lord North. The late Baron Rich and his wife both attended Court occasionally and at New Year 1581 the baroness gave Elizabeth "a bodkin", or small dagger, made

72

of gold "with a pendant of gold, being a wreath set with pearl and a hart in the midst".

The Rich family had risen to eminence only fifty years before, when Sir Richard Rich, a successful lawyer from the landed gentry, became solicitor general to Henry VIII. Part of his job was to sell the vast estates Henry acquired through the dissolution of the monasteries. Under Henry's son, Edward VI, Sir Richard was ennobled as Baron Rich and appointed lord chancellor. But on his way up he acquired a consistent reputation for corruption, treachery, disloyalty and greed.

"He is full of dissimulation," one contemporary claimed: "he passeth all that ever I sued unto." Most infamous of his deeds was giving evidence against Bishop Fisher and Sir Thomas More, alleging they had denied Henry VIII's supremacy of the Church and were guilty of treason. Rich's testimony brought Fisher and the saintly Thomas More to the block, and More's description of Sir Richard as a liar and gambler "of no commendable fame" stuck to the family for generations. Three centuries after Sir Richard's perjury, one historian, using papers passed down by Penelope's granddaughter, declared Richard Rich was "the legal murderer of Sir Thomas More". Penelope's future husband, he said, was "one of the most sordid and vulgar scamps", though, intriguingly, he gave no evidence.

Selling off the former monastery lands for Henry VIII gave Sir Richard a golden opportunity to pick up whatever plums he fancied. The king gave him Leighs Priory, north of Chelmsford, and Sir Richard added many more manors in Essex. Wanstead, Rochford and Shelley Hall, to name a few, made him the second largest landowner in the county. He also took over as his London home the prior's lodgings at St Bartholomew's in Smithfield. The former priory was famed for its ancient hospital and vast church, and it held the rights to the annual Bartholomew Fair three-day cloth market in August. Over the years it had expanded into London's biggest carnival, a noisy motley of food stalls, musicians, jugglers, tumblers, puppet booths, pickpockets, pimps and prostitutes.

Sir Richard's son, the second baron, did little to improve the family reputation. He went with Penelope's father to Ireland in 1573, taking troops to swell the earl's army. And he was one of the first to give up when winter set in, leaving Earl Walter complaining to Burghley how badly he'd been left in the lurch. Self-preservation and ambition were family traits. Like the Cecils, what they lacked in nobility they made up in astute management, accumulating land, contracting canny marriages and hosting Elizabeth's costly summer visits. Elizabeth loved nothing better than hunting deer in their forests, and the expense of having her as a house guest, which nearly ruined some courtiers, was no problem for the Rich barons. She particularly liked

Leighs and Wanstead, which they had recently sold to Lord Leicester, and she stayed at Leighs several times while the new Lord Rich was growing up. Even if he was billeted with neighbours to make room for her, he would have been presented to the queen, and doubtless she remembered the nineteen-year-old when he was picked as a husband for Penelope.

~

In the eyes of Penelope's guardians, Robert Rich had much to commend him. Born late in December 1559, he was three years older than Penelope. At least she was spared the fate of poor Mary Sidney, Philip's sister, who was only fifteen when she was married off to the fortysomething Earl of Pembroke.

When Lord Rich was baptized in January 1560, with Lord Leicester as his godfather, he had an elder brother. Robert, as a second son, missed out on a university education, and at eighteen went straight to Gray's Inn. He was destined to be the family's legal expert, handling their many property deals and attending local courts. But his brother died in 1580, leaving him as the heir. His father's death at the beginning of 1581 must also have been unexpected, since Robert fought a by-election and took his seat in the House of Commons three weeks before he inherited his father's seat in the House of Lords.

At twenty-one Robert Rich owned land worth £5,000 a year (three times the Devereux estates' revenue) and controlled the appointment of dozens of parish clergy. After his father was buried at Felsted on 4 April, he could address himself to the matter of his marriage. His education was not up to Penelope's standard. Whereas she had mastered French, Spanish and some Italian, he was by his own account "a poor man of no language". He did not share her love of literature and word games, nor her skill at music.

It was his religion that Penelope's guardians found so appealing. The late Lord Rich had been well out on the Puritan wing of the Church and with the assistance of his half-brother Dick he tried to fill the parishes in his control with extreme Protestant clergymen, much to the annoyance of the Bishop of London, John Aylmer. Now the new Lord Rich and his uncle Dick continued to fight the good fight for radical Protestantism, appointing more ministers who would oppose play-going, dancing, gambling, music and similar sinful pleasures. In September the two men paid a visit to Bishop Aylmer which became so heated that he claimed Dick "did shake him up" and abuse him more violently than any man had ever done. Dick ended up in jail and Penelope's future husband was lucky to get off with a stiff warning. It did not, however, stop him trying to eject the conformist vicar of Felsted the following year. These were not necessarily tactics the Huntingdons endorsed, yet the young baron's Puritanism chimed perfectly with their own wish to see religious reform and the removal of all church ritual. Lord Rich seemed just the man for Penelope.

It is easy to picture the Huntingdons as an uncaring couple who cynically arranged a hasty marriage because the Devereux finances were in dire straits; who ignored Earl Walter's deathbed wishes; and who passed Philip over because Lord Rich was the highest bidder and they liked his religion. In fact, Lord Rich may have been a very astute choice. He was devoid of royal ancestry. His lineage added to Penelope's would *not* push her children closer to the throne. Elizabeth was acutely sensitive to marriages by anyone with royal ancestry and she withheld consent as long as possible. If they were foolish enough to marry in secret she invariably sent them to the Tower, sometimes for life.

Penelope's guardians had cause to be wary about the succession issue, since Huntingdon had already appeared on illicit lists of possible claimants. Some contemporary chroniclers ruled him out because he was descended from the Yorkist royal family, and might reignite the Wars of the Roses if he wore the crown. But while Penelope and Essex shared his Yorkist ancestry, they also had a blood line to the Tudors, who had carefully linked the warring houses of York and Lancaster. Marrying Penelope to Lord Rich pushed her children further away from royalty and in the nervy, final decades of Elizabeth's reign that was a wise move. Elizabeth could relax. This union would create no threats to the throne and it was being arranged with her full knowledge. The queen could continue to smile on her god-daughter, and she did. Royal approval for the marriage was granted unusually swiftly.

Yet a marriage between Penelope and Philip Sidney would also have distanced her children from the succession stakes. What was so wrong with Philip that his aunt ignored him?

~

Money was an obvious problem. At the time Earl Walter first suggested the marriage to Philip's father, Sir Henry was struggling to finance Philip's grand tour of the Continent. This was no cheap, student's year abroad: his equipment and entourage were expensive. To set Philip up in a married household in suitable style was more than Sir Henry could manage. He'd been forced to turn to Leicester for a dowry for his daughter Mary to ensure her wedding to Pembroke went ahead in 1577; and thereafter Philip turned for lodgings to Pembroke's residence in Baynard's Castle, because Sidney funds did not run to a town house.

To secure Philip, Sir Henry needed more than the £2,000 dowry Earl Walter was offering with Penelope, and Sir Henry didn't like the earl anyway. True, Philip had been a very desirable bachelor. He was a budding diplomat, soldier and poet and he seemed to have every prospect of reaching the top of the Court ladder. He was also the heir to two of the most eminent men in the country. His mother's brothers, Ambrose Dudley, Earl of Warwick, and Robert Dudley, Earl of Leicester, had no legitimate children. But by the time the Huntingdons brought Penelope to Court things had changed. Philip's character had developed and his prospects had not.

The Sidneys were Kentish gentry who rose, like the Cecils, through service to Henry VIII and his children. They were not aristocracy, certainly not ancient noblesse like the Devereux, and Elizabeth maintained a cautious, ungenerous attitude to them. She never properly repaid Sir Henry for years of hard work in Ireland and Wales, and the Sidneys struggled to keep a footing at Court, often edged out of their rooms. In 1562, while Sir Henry was absent, Lady Mary selflessly nursed Elizabeth through the smallpox, inevitably contracting it herself. "I left her a full fair lady, in mine eyes at least," he said, recalling her horribly scarred face; "when I returned I found her as foul a lady as the small-pox could make." And notwithstanding Philip's success in the tiltyard, his courteous manner and brilliant writing, Elizabeth did not take to him. She never flirted with him as she did with Sir Christopher Hatton or Sir Walter Ralegh.

Philip could be violently short-tempered. He was not joking when he wrote to his father's secretary: "I assure you before God that if ever I know you do so much as read any letter I write to my father, without his command-ment or my consent, I will thrust my dagger into you. And trust to it, for I speak it in earnest." Philip was equally forthright in opposing Elizabeth's policy, especially her marriage to Anjou. During lengthy travels in Germany and France he had built up a good diplomatic reputation, but that did not endear him to Elizabeth either. She was suspicious of anyone who was too popular abroad or on the streets of London, as Essex would learn.

To Penelope's guardians there may have been another downside to Philip: his position on Catholicism was changeable. His iconic status as the "crown prince" of Protestant England, defender of the reformed faith, hero of the age, is largely a posthumous invention; and it owes much to his memorable death. While he lived, however, he was friendly with a number of prominent Catholics and his admiration for the Jesuit Fr Edmund Campion was no secret. The Huntingdons would have been wary of anyone suspected, even briefly, of being a Catholic fellow-traveller. But the reason they passed Philip over lies equally in what Lord Leicester was up to.

Within weeks of Penelope's arrival at Court, Leicester obtained signed statements from the witnesses at his wedding to Lettice which proved they had been legally married in September 1578. Lettice seems to have suffered at least two failed pregnancies or infant deaths since then. She was probably carrying Leicester's child when they married, and according to the French ambassador she was pregnant in February 1580 while staying with her father at Grey's Court. The following autumn she was pregnant for a third time (and back at Grey's in October). Now in March 1581 it looked as though her pregnancy would go to term and Leicester was determined there would be no doubts about the baby's legitimacy; for if it were a boy, he would be heir to both Leicester and Ambrose.

On 6 June, at Leicester House, Lettice *did* give birth to a boy. Baptized Robert Dudley, with Lord North as godfather, the child took Leicester's courtesy title, Baron Denbigh, and became known in the family as "the Noble Imp". Philip immediately lost two large inheritances and Penelope and her brothers and sister took a step back in Leicester's life. Generous he might be but his own son would naturally take priority and Lettice, aged thirty-seven, might have more children. All Penelope could expect was what Earl Walter had promised in his will, and with Essex's regular overspending the Devereux estates would struggle to provide it.

The birth of "the Noble Imp" confirmed that the Huntingdons' plan was a wise step, and arrangements for Penelope's wedding moved forward.

~

To Lord Rich, Penelope seemed an ideal partner. He had more than enough money to make up for her shortage. She had all the class needed to make up for his lack of noble ancestry. Her contacts were unbeatable and in the run-up to the wedding Lord Rich did his best to get on with them. Soon after her brother received his MA at Cambridge in July, Lord Rich rode up to visit him and suggested they set off for a couple of weeks of "*voluptatis honestae*" – honest pleasures.

Essex gladly went along, though without prior permission from Burghley. Later, sending a written apology, Essex told his guardian that Rich was "*charissimus*", most dear to him, for many reasons which Burghley was aware of. Lord Rich was even dearer to him after he sent Essex a gift of a gelding. It was the start of an amicable relationship that survived till the earl's death, and Essex began eagerly preparing for the wedding. He had spent heavily on clothes for St George's Day and May Day, yet now he bought more. Between his jaunt with Lord Rich and a visit to Kenilworth and Chartley with Lord Leicester, Essex found time to splash out another £40 on two sets of clothes for Penelope's big day, and to order specially embroidered Devereux badges for his servants to wear when they accompanied him to London.

The Earl of Huntingdon was out of London for most of the summer while the Devereux managers struggled to raise Penelope's £2,000 dowry out of the estate. But Penelope's grandfather, Sir Francis, solved the problem by advancing the first £500 payment due to Lord Rich. By mid-September, while Elizabeth and her ladies were at Greenwich, the wedding date was fixed. Richard Brakinbury, a gentleman usher at Court who looked after the maids of honour, wrote to the Earl of Rutland with the latest London news. Plague deaths had reached seventy-five in the past week, and Lady Penelope Devereux "will be married about Allhallow-tide to Lord Rich. Though your lordship is mindless of beauty, our maids are very fair."

Penelope, taking a last ride up the hill through Greenwich Park before the Court moved to Nonsuch, could look out across the Thames into Essex. Somewhere over there were the huge estates that would soon be hers. It was not something she wanted to think about. She was enjoying the excitement and entertainments at Court.

The Countess of Huntingdon, having fixed the wedding for early November, went to Wilton House near Salisbury to see her niece Mary, Philip's sister. Mary's dutiful submission to her arranged marriage with the elderly Earl of Pembroke was what Lady Huntingdon expected of Penelope. On 15 October Mary gave birth to a daughter and the countess stood godmother, before returning to London.

Gradually the family gathered. The Earl of Huntingdon had reached London in the autumn. Roger, Lord North, took delivery of the wedding present he had ordered: "a cup to give my lady Penelope to her marriage" costing around £12. It was three years since the death of his wife, Lord Rich's aunt, yet he still played the generous uncle. And in Cambridge, Essex, with nearly twenty servants wearing their new Devereux badges, prepared to ride to London for the ceremony. One person who seems to have been absent was Philip Sidney. He took leave of Elizabeth on 9 October, wrote to Burghley the following day before he left London and stayed away nearly a month.

The teenage bride, meanwhile, was not anticipating the event with pleasure. Years later, in the only surviving record of the wedding, Penelope's second husband claimed that she was "married against her will unto one, against whom she did protest at the very solemnity, and ever after". The author had everything to gain by exaggerating her objections, yet it was soon common knowledge that Penelope was not happy about her marriage.

Penelope had just begun to enjoy Court life. It was her natural orbit and she knew she sparkled there. For three years she had lived with her strait-laced guardians waiting to come to London, and now her carefree pleasures had ended almost as soon as they started. Once married she would cease to be a maid to the queen and even if she was given a place as a lady-in-waiting, like cousin Kate and her aunt Lady Leighton, the flirting and flattery she had enjoyed would never be the same again. The glorious party was over. There was no point in a wedding feast, and there probably wasn't one. It was not part of the Puritan way of doing things which her husband and guardians preferred.

Why didn't she withhold consent? Refusing to say the words was pointless. It was her guardians' duty to choose her husband and they had done what they thought best. If she held out against their choice she would bring disgrace on her family and possibly lose her inheritance. Having made her point, she went ahead with the ceremony. It was essential to maintain the family honour and her wealthy marriage at least meant she was no longer a burden on the Devereux estate. Restoring the family fortunes, furthering her brother's ambitions, would rule Penelope's life.

Chapter Ten

1581–1583

"You teach my tongue with one sweet kiss"
– Philip Sidney, *Astrophil and Stella*, 1582–3

Coping with a marriage Penelope did not want was not easy, and Lord Rich was not the man to change the mind of a vivacious eighteen-year-old beauty. Staying at Court for a time made it easier to bear, and made sense to her husband. Lord Rich had a trophy wife and it was pointless carrying her off immediately to the country. The benefits were at Court, making contacts and adding to his influence. Besides, the Duc d'Anjou had reached Elizabeth at Richmond on 2 November. Everyone wanted to be there and to enjoy the celebrations, including the Accession Day tilt on 17 November. Not that Lord Rich had any desire to take part, but it was the place to see and be seen.

Essex also remained in London, and time spent with Penelope would suit both of them. They had been parted soon after Earl Walter's death but throughout their adult lives they kept up fond and frequent contact. Essex's latest extravagance at her wedding meant Richard Broughton had to advance him another £18 in November, and it brought to a head plans to curb his spending. "By reason of the great expenses of the Earl of Essex" his guardians obtained Elizabeth's consent (needed because he was a minor) for him to be "committed to the charge of Sir Francis Knollys his grandfather from November 22 until February 20". After that he would be sent to York to live "under the oversight of the Earl of Huntingdon". Three months under Sir Francis's puritanical supervision would be a trial for Essex, and Penelope's company would certainly improve things. It is tempting to think Shakespeare had Sir Francis in mind, sermonizing to his spendthrift grandson, when he invented the tedious figure of old Polonius, as well as Essex for his flawed hero in *Hamlet*.

The Accession Day tilt brought Philip Sidney back to London. Shortly before he went away in October he told Burghley he was disenchanted with Court life, frustrated at not rising more rapidly and needed a well-paid job. Meeting and greeting Elizabeth's guests and political exiles, as he had been doing, was not enough. He knew greater things were expected of him. He was still at Gravesend on 10 November, but four days later he was back in town.

The November tournament at Whitehall was probably the one where Philip wore the ambiguous motto "*Speravi*" – "I had hoped" – crossed through and meaning that his hopes were dashed. It is unlikely he was referring to his lost inheritances. It would have been unchivalrous to whinge about that in public when Leicester had been blessed with a son. Philip's message probably had political, personal and romantic meanings, referring to his dashed hopes of preventing the "Frog" marriage, rising at Court and winning Penelope.

Early in December Philip left Court again to stay with Mary at Wilton, while Elizabeth continued dancing and play-acting with Anjou about marriage. Eventually, in February, Elizabeth sent her "Frog" away with £10,000 and pretty promises – but with no intention of marrying him. She went with him as far as Canterbury and sent a noble escort, 600-strong, to see him safely to Flushing – or to make sure he did not come back. Philip was among them and after he returned to England, still without a job and with time on his hands, he wrote some of the loveliest love poems of all time. In a sequence of 108 sonnets and eleven songs, he told the story of Astrophil's passion for a beautiful married lady named Stella.

∼

That Stella was Penelope was settled long ago. Penelope was Philip's muse and his model for the divine Stella. But was the story just a fantasy? How deeply Philip had fallen in love with Penelope, or she with him, is one of the great mysteries of English literature.

The *Astrophil and Stella* poems were read at first by only a very small group of friends. They were not printed until after Sidney's death, and only one manuscript copy contained the telltale sonnet which virtually names the heroine:

> Rich in all beauties which man's eye can see;
> Beauties so far from reach of words that we
> Abase her praise saying she doeth excel;
> Rich in the treasures of deserved renown,
> Rich in the riches of a royal heart,
> Rich in those gifts which give the eternal crown;
> Who, though most rich in these and every part
> Which make the patents of true worldly bliss,
> Hath no misfortune but that Rich she is.

Yet there were plenty of other puns and pointers to Penelope's identity. "Hath this world aught so fair as Stella is?" Astrophil demanded, repeatedly describing her golden hair and unusually dark eyes:

> That whereas black seems beauty's contrary,
> She even in black doth make all beauties flow?

Further clues lay in coded references to the Devereux coat of arms, "Where roses gules are borne in silver field". There were additional puns on "rich, meaning my Stella's name". And comments about her husband:

> ... that rich fool who by blind Fortune's lot
> The richest gem of love and life enjoys.

There may also be an allusion to Penelope's pedigree in the line "Rich in the riches of a royal heart", which more recent readers have overlooked. Unaware of Penelope's descent from Henry VIII and Mary Boleyn, they have missed a double meaning that would have been well known to anyone as close to the Devereux as Philip. And it must be significant that Philip describes her as "royal" in the sonnet where he is at pains to identify her.

Astrophil, meaning star-lover, was obviously another wordplay on his own name, and references to the Sidneys' coat of arms and his father as governor of Ireland left no doubt that Philip himself was the melancholy lover who sighed and watched

> With how sad steps, O moon, thou climbst the skies!
> How silently, and with how wan a face.

Vivid, erotic, sensual, full of desire and ultimately despair, the poems have numerous details which date them to 1582, and which Penelope would remember. There was Astrophil taking part in a tournament attended by the French ambassadors, while

> Stella looked on, and from her heavenly face
> Sent forth the beams, which made so fair my race.

Astrophil cursing "the coachman that did drive so fast" when she passed him one night. And Stella gliding downriver on a boat "While wanton winds ... in her golden hair ... did themselves, oh sweetest prison, twine".

Philip had made a name for himself as the creator of Court pageants, plays and amusements, weaving images out of words. *Astrophil and Stella* may be a dream world invented to satisfy his sexual desires, or a complex fairy tale written to flatter and amuse the most beautiful young woman he knew. And certainly Stella stands for more than Penelope: she is immortal beauty. But it is impossible to believe the poems are purely imaginary. The lines that make his sonnets soar are too fresh and sincere; they break the old conventions of love lyrics. He admits he did *not* fall in love with her at first sight: maybe as a child at Chartley, or hunting at Kenilworth, or even when she arrived at Court.

"I saw, and liked; I liked, but loved not," he explains. Cursing himself for not pursuing her before she was married or promised to another, he wishes: "That I had been more foolish or more wise." When he finds her asleep and steals a kiss, again he misses his chance and sighs

> Oh, sweet kiss! But ah, she's waking!
> Lowring beauty chastens me.
> Now will I for fear hence flee:
> Fool, more fool, for no more taking!

And when he takes another kiss from her "sweet-swelling lip" he hurriedly promises:

> I will but kiss, I never more will bite.

It doesn't read like someone faking it. And it sounds as though Stella is responding when he writes:

> Sweet lip, you teach my tongue with one sweet kiss.

Yet the poems do not prove, as one of Penelope's modern critics claims, that she "had just given herself without love to the prosperous but spineless Lord Rich, whom she was openly to cuckold first with Sir Philip Sidney". In fact, Astrophil is frustrated and angry because she *won't* commit adultery. "Is it not evil that such a devil wants horns?" he asks, referring to Stella's husband. Philip uses "wants" in its old meaning: Stella's husband *lacks* the horns that were traditionally the sign of a cuckold. Each time Astrophil sings the refrain "Take me to thee, and thee to me", Stella replies "No, no, no, no, my dear, let be"; though there is a twist in the last verse, when she denies his death will please her. But the conclusion leaves Astrophil despairing and lovelorn.

If Philip and Penelope *were* an item, they covered their tracks remarkably well. The usual gossips give no hint of an affair between them. In a Court where reputations were lost faster than a game of primero against Elizabeth, everyone knew what Penelope's brother was up to with his mistresses. And everyone close to Lord Leicester got smeared in the libels published against him. There is no way the scandal-sheet writers would have passed over a juicy story about Penelope and Philip, if there had been one.

Philip's so-called confession to an illicit relationship with Penelope, made on his deathbed five years later, has been shown to be unreliable and "doctored", but there is no reason why he should not have remembered her in his last hours. Penelope had been his muse, the cause of his finest poems. And they remain a tender record of her early months at Court, her beauty and her bewitching charm.

When Philip's fame spread and he was idolized as the most perfect courtier-soldier-poet, it was gratifying for Penelope to know that "her" poems had sparked a craze for love sonnets. Soon the *Astrophil and Stella* songs were set to music by the best Court composers, William Byrd, John Dowland, Thomas Morley and Robert Jones, and within a decade William Shakespeare was following Philip's lead and writing sonnets.

~

Had Penelope's marriage been blissfully happy she would not have welcomed the many dedications that later linked her to Philip's work. And Philip could not have written about her "misfortune" that "Rich she is". But was Lord Rich as odious as history makes out? The opinions of Philip and of Penelope's second husband, Lord Mountjoy, cannot be taken at face value. Philip's claim that Lord Rich treated her with "foul abuse", and Mountjoy's assertion that "he did study in all things to torment her", were both special pleading, using Rich as a whipping boy. And history has gone on, calling him "rough and uncourtly in manners and conversation, dull and uneducated"; and "a little man ... willing to sacrifice self-respect for advantage".

Judging by Penelope's choice of lover in years to come, Robert Rich was not the sort of man she liked. His education had been different from hers and her tastes became increasingly sophisticated, not to say decadent, as she grew older. They occupied different levels of society; her rank was not his; and he did not excel at the things she liked. Not for him the tiltyard, the lute, languages and literature. Yet to write him off, saying he "did not make his mark in any career or enterprise", is wrong.

Lord Rich was one of the most powerful people in the region, and his impact on the rise of extreme Protestantism in Essex was considerable. It was far too forceful for many people's liking. In December 1581 the privy council had to order him to show charitable consideration rather than harassing some of his tenants, and his bullying tactics in ejecting the vicar of Felsted in favour of a reformist minister also reached the courts. He continued to annoy

Bishop Aylmer of London with his systematic attempts to put Puritan clergy in as many parishes as he could; and his vote-rigging and election-fixing to get "godly party" candidates into parliament upset Elizabeth and her ministers, who were worried by the rise of religious radicals in East Anglia. As a Justice of the Peace Lord Rich's attendance at the twice-yearly assize courts and the quarter sessions, usually held in Chelmsford, was spasmodic and some of his judgments came in for criticism. But whose didn't?

Penelope kept clear of Lord Rich's county crusade for Protestantism, but at Leighs she could not avoid the effects. If she breathed a sigh of relief when she left the Huntingdons, her heart must have sunk when Lord Rich employed Ezekiel Culverwell as his family chaplain at Leighs later in 1586. Ezekiel was an outstanding member of a remarkable family of religious radicals. Penelope's favourite pastimes, music, play-going, cards and "pestiferous dancing", were loathsome to him. His extreme views and fame as "the preacher of Felsted" soon drew the attention of Bishop Aylmer, who kept him under scrutiny and suspended him for a while for nonconformist practices.

There were compensations at Leighs, however, especially in the early years when Penelope found herself in charge of her first large household. Lord Rich's widowed mother lived at Rochford Hall, twenty miles south-east of Leighs, near the sea. By curious coincidence, Rochford was once the Boleyns' house, where Penelope's great-grandmother, Mary, lived after her secret marriage to Stafford. Mary eventually inherited all the Boleyn properties that remained after Anne's downfall, and passed them to her children, Lady Katherine Knollys and Lord Hunsdon; and in time Rochford was bought by the rising Rich family. It was distant enough from Leighs and large enough to keep Penelope's mother-in-law occupied, and it was her responsibility. When there was a problem with the trees at Rochford not being properly lopped, "Lady Rich widow" was named at the quarter sessions, not her son.

Leighs, once an Augustinian priory, was a delight. Lord Rich's grandfather had converted it into a "worldly paradise, a heaven on earth". The large outer courtyard, entered through a tall brick gatehouse, contained the stables, stores, a brew house and dairy. On its eastern side another towering gatehouse led to a pretty inner quadrangle, once the monks' cloisters. Ranged around it were the principal chambers and guest rooms; the great hall, formerly the nave of the priory church, still lit by high, pointed windows; and the chapter house, now the family chapel. The first Lord Rich had also had some of the old stone walls refaced in fashionable new red brick, and added large windows, pointed gables, and tall, fantastically ornate chimneys.

In the grounds, where stew ponds once fed the monks with fish, there were gardens with summer houses, streams, a bowling green, banqueting house and walled private garden. Beyond lay a wilderness, huge kitchen gardens and three parks. "My lord," one visitor remarked to the second baron, "you had needs make sure of heaven, or else when you die you'll be a great loser."

Among Penelope's servants at Leighs was her much-loved lady-in-waiting, Jeanne de Saint-Martin, one of the many French Huguenots who had fled to England. Penelope was on good terms with all her staff, but Jeanne held a special place in her affections, and Penelope's letters to her, in French, are full of love and friendship. "Since I first knew you I have borne you such affection that neither time nor absence will ever blot out the recollection of your great merits," she wrote. There is "no fault in the world that I hate more than inconstancy and I assure you that you will never find it in me but on the contrary a friendship unchangeable and perfect that will last all my life." It was not an idle boast. Half of her surviving letters were written to request help and favours for her servants, neighbours, family and friends.

In her warm-hearted correspondence Penelope echoes her mother. Lettice's letters to her children are brimming with love and concern. The idea that her behaviour turned her children into "emotional cripples" belies all the evidence. Penelope was deeply attached to her mother and one of the benefits of Leighs was the short distance, less than thirty miles, to Wanstead. Lettice and Leicester often spent time there with their baby son, "the Noble Imp", and at Wanstead Penelope had her own rooms, just as she did at Leicester House. Penelope seems never to have blamed Lettice for not preventing her marriage to Lord Rich. And in truth Lettice could have done little. The queen had given permission for her godchild to marry according to the Huntingdons' plans, and that was that.

~

Rather than cause a rift, the bond between Penelope and Lettice deepened over the years, and when Penelope's first baby was born she named the child Lettice. It was done in defiance of Elizabeth's hostility to her mother, and it showed Penelope would always put family loyalty above the queen's displeasure.

Between her marriage in November 1581 and early summer 1586, when Penelope conceived her first son, she produced only two children, both girls; and there is no evidence until later that she suffered miscarriages or infant deaths. Little Lettice, probably born late in 1582 or early 1583, came to be known in the family as Lucy. Her second daughter was given the unusual Christian name Essex, which started a family tradition, and was again chosen from Penelope's relations, not Lord Rich's.

In the first five years of marriage Penelope's grandmother produced five children and Lettice had at least three. Penelope's pregnancy rate gives the impression she kept Lord Rich at arm's length as much as possible. And if she did, it was not because she disliked children. Penelope's fondness for her sons and daughters would become a family joke.

One evening after Penelope's brother failed to show up at a family gathering, Lettice told him: "if you had come this night you had found a knot of good company here together, and the idle housewife your sister in one of her worst humours solemnly disposed in doubt that her best beloved daughter should be a little sick." It was obvious to outsiders, too, how much Penelope adored her offspring. Dedicating a book to her, John Florio, the famous translator, teased her that when "invited to show your richest jewels", Penelope "would stay till your sweet images (your dear-sweet children) came from school".

It has been suggested that Penelope's absence from Elizabeth's New Year gift lists for January 1584 indicates the imminent birth of one of her daughters. Lord Rich alone is noted as giving the queen a pink satin jacket that year, but the lists, compiled by Elizabeth's staff, are incomplete and gifts were sometimes presented on behalf of absent courtiers. If Lord Rich did attend Court then, he didn't stay for the full season. He was back home by 9 January, doing his duty as a Justice of the Peace in the quarter sessions at Chelmsford.

As a senior magnate in the county, Lord Rich was also responsible for government hospitality, and in April 1583 he was under orders to welcome the Polish prince Count Laski, who arrived at Colchester. Accompanied by a few other gentlemen, including Arthur Throckmorton, Lord Rich met the prince outside the town, took him to dine with Sir Thomas Lucas at his Colchester home, the former abbey of St John's, and delivered Laski to his official lodgings in London. It was a particularly memorable trip for Arthur. At Sir Thomas's house he met his future wife, and when they set up home with her parents three years later they became country neighbours of Lord and Lady Rich. Arthur already knew many of Penelope's family, including her aunt Lady Vernon. His late father, Sir Nicholas Throckmorton, had been one of Elizabeth's ministers and a keen Protestant, like Sir Francis Knollys.

Penelope's role as a country hostess, supporting her husband as a local landowner, was never going to content her. However much she loved her children, managing a large household and hunting in the local forests, her ambitions for her family ranged wider than Lord Rich's Essex estates.

Chapter Eleven

1583–1585

"Your sister that most infinitely loves you"

– Penelope Rich, c. 1589

*P*enelope had been married little more than a year when her sister Dorothy decided it was time she did something about her own marriage. In June 1583 Sir Thomas Perrot wrote to Penelope formally asking her to recommend his "service, zeal and love unto my lady your sister". Thomas was in no doubt that Dorothy was in love with him and Penelope had already, informally, given him her approval.

Having seen what had happened to Penelope, Dorothy was choosing her own husband, a man she loved, though he was almost twice her age. Sir Thomas Perrot was the son of the Devereux' neighbour in South Wales, Sir John Perrot, owner of Carew Castle. Father and son were buccaneering types and rumour said (on virtually no evidence) that Sir John was an illegitimate son of Henry VIII, though it was not a claim Sir Thomas pushed. The main obstacles for Thomas and Dorothy were the difference in their rank, the Perrots' lack of money and Lord Leicester's efforts to marry her to someone else.

Within three months of Penelope's marriage, Leicester drew up a new will promising "my well beloved nephew Philip Sidney and Lady Dorothy Devereux" the sum of £2,000 if "such love and liking might be between them as might bring a marriage". It didn't. Dorothy may not have found the pockmarked, earnest, unflirtatious Philip attractive, and she would certainly have been aware of his love for her sister. Her opposition to the plan could explain why one historian said Leicester banished her to Broxbourne in Hertfordshire. But Leicester did not give up. In 1583 there were reports that he aimed to marry Dorothy to King James of Scotland. True or not, Dorothy had to move quickly, without the consent of Elizabeth or her guardian, Huntingdon, and she must have known it was safe to involve Penelope.

Broxbourne was the home of Sir Henry Cock and his family and it stood on the edge of Hatfield Heath and Epping Forest, less than fifteen miles easy riding from both Wanstead and Lettice's Bennington estate. If Penelope had alerted their mother, it would have been simple to intervene. But she didn't. Penelope was not going to spoil her sister's chance of happiness, and Dorothy's plan went ahead. On 17 July Thomas obtained a marriage licence from the Bishop of London's court without revealing Dorothy's real rank.

Two days later, while Thomas was visiting Broxbourne, Dorothy got up early, dressed "with great labour of trimming herself", and told her host's daughter she was expecting a visit from her guardian, Huntingdon. The household went into overdrive preparing for the earl's arrival, which gave Dorothy a chance to slip out for "a stroll" with Thomas, some friends and her lute. Reaching the church they summoned the vicar and showed him their licence, but he smelt a rat and refused to conduct the ceremony. Thomas, however, had brought a "strange minister" and with "two men guarding the church door with their swords and daggers under their cloaks", the said minister went ahead with the ceremony, "minus surplice, in his cloak with his riding boots and spurs and despatched it hastily".

Such a truly cloak-and-dagger business could not escape investigation, and at Court it "gave great offence" because of the inequality of the match. Dorothy was "of right noble and ancient blood". Bishop Aylmer, called before the privy council to explain why his office had been lax about issuing the licence, must have thought he'd heard enough about the Devereux girls, and wondered what he had done to be plagued by their husbands.

Elizabeth was furious. Her anger may have been sharpened by the rumours that both bride and groom were illegitimate descendants of her father. Sir Thomas was sent to the Fleet prison and his father, wisely keeping below the parapet, refused to help them unless the queen gave him permission. Thomas was released after a couple of months, but they were in dire financial straits and Dorothy begged Burghley to help. Having married without her guardians' consent she was not entitled to her dowry or maintenance money. In November they received some of it, though they were forced to live with the Perrots in South Wales, and four years later Elizabeth would still refuse to admit Dorothy to her presence.

Before September was over Elizabeth was enraged by yet another unexpected wedding. It was Philip Sidney's turn and his wife was Frances, fifteen-year-old daughter of the queen's spymaster. Foreign diplomats rated Sir Francis Walsingham better informed on foreign affairs than anyone in government. Whether Philip was marrying Frances on the rebound from Penelope or to gain a useful ally in government is open to question. There is no sign he felt as passionately about Frances as he had about "Stella", and there *is* evidence that the marriage sorted out his financial problems. The pre-nuptial settlement included Walsingham's generous and unusual agreement "to pay or discharge the debts of the said Philip". He also allowed the couple and their servants to live under his roof, sparing them the cost of a town house.

Elizabeth did not consider it a great match and it did nothing to improve her views on Philip, partly because she disliked Walsingham's radical Protestantism. But her anger was unreasonable: neither Frances nor Philip needed her permission to marry. At times Elizabeth's capricious judgement bordered on being unbalanced. She could be as ruthlessly cruel as her father, and equally callous in executing people close to her. The picture of a benign monarch adored by her subjects is largely "spin" by her ministers. Her need for flattery was insatiable and the convention that all male courtiers were her lovers became grotesque. Mary Queen of Scots said Bess of Hardwick privately considered it "beyond all reason" (though Mary was good at stirring, so she may have fibbed about Bess's comment). Leicester, for one, was beginning to tire of it, and the time would come when Essex would refuse to dance to Elizabeth's tune, to play surrogate son and "lover" to the aged queen.

~

For the moment Essex was still living under the shared supervision of the earls of Huntingdon and Leicester. In February 1582 he had left London to spend eighteen months chiefly in York with Huntingdon, trying to keep within his annual £210 "ordinary allowance", and getting to know his younger brother. Wat was a boy of seven when Essex left home for Cambridge; now he was a teenager, getting ready to go to university, and the friendship that formed between them would last until Wat's untimely death. Around the end of 1583, Essex was also getting better acquainted with Dorothy and her husband in South Wales, and enjoying life on his Lamphey estate, which his uncle Sir George Devereux had managed since Earl Walter's death.

In May 1584 Essex was still enjoying life in the country, though he had shifted to Chartley. There he proudly played host to Lord Leicester, at a cost of £45.7s.9d., before they set off on a summer tour of Leicester's extensive properties in the Midlands, Denbigh and Chester. Penelope and Lettice remained in the south with their young children; but soon after her stepfather and brother returned, Penelope's half-brother, Lord Denbigh, "the Noble Imp", fell ill.

Little Denbigh's brief life was spent partly at Leicester House, where he broke and "quite defaced" at least one important picture, and partly at Wanstead, where Lettice was with him in the summer of 1584. At some time after his third birthday early in June, he became unwell. By mid-July there was no hope of recovery. Leicester summoned his lawyers and altered his will, revoking the settlements he had made in favour of his legitimate "heirs of his body". The idea that Denbigh was born a sickly child comes from a libellous attack on Leicester, titled *Leicester's Commonwealth*, written before the boy's death and distributed soon afterwards. It claimed the child was cursed with the "strange calamity of the falling sickness" as a punishment for his parents' adultery, "sin and wickedness".

The libel recycles buckets of old gossip and most of it has a grain of truth. There is no basis, however, for assuming that Denbigh's nickname means he was deformed or undersized. Infants were often termed "imp" and "manikin". Huntingdon's heir, for example, was called "a noble imp of great virtue and towardness". Whatever ailed Lord Denbigh, his death on Sunday 19 July seems to have come more suddenly than his parents expected.

Leicester was away at Court. After his summer tour he joined Elizabeth at Richmond and moved with her a few miles south to Nonsuch Palace. There the messenger from Wanstead gave him the sad news. Leicester left immediately, pausing only to ask Sir Christopher Hatton to make his excuses to the queen. He couldn't wait for Elizabeth's permission; he wanted "to comfort my sorrowful wife". Leicester had "received many afflictions within these few years," he told Hatton, "but not a greater" than the death of his son.

It was touching how many old politicians and peers expressed their sorrow, realizing Denbigh was Leicester's last hope of a legitimate heir. Walsingham wrote to George Talbot, Earl of Shrewsbury, husband of the indomitable Bess of Hardwick, explaining that Leicester was absent from Court "upon the late death of his son which is no small grief unto his lordship". Shrewsbury, who was currently Mary Queen of Scots's captor, was not the most tactful of men and at that moment he was hard pressed trying to get Elizabeth to cover Mary's maintenance costs. Yet as soon as he heard the news he found time and sympathy to send his condolences.

Leicester replied, broken-hearted: "I do thank you for the care you take for the loss of my young son which was indeed, my good lord, great to me for that I have no more and more unlike to have, my growing now old." Lettice was over forty, but it was not her advancing years that Leicester blamed. It was his own, and though he was little past fifty himself he writes as a defeated old man, resigned that "the will of God must be obeyed in all things whatsoever, for He doth all for the best".

A few days later Lettice and Leicester left Wanstead, rather than stay and attend the funeral. Lettice wanted to get away to Grey's. *En route* they made an unscheduled stop at Burghley's magnificent country house, Theobalds, near Enfield. Burghley was at Court but he gave his household orders to treat the earl and countess well. On 31 July Leicester wrote thanking him for his hospitality, and for his efforts to soften Elizabeth's attitude to Lettice. He was grateful "that it pleased you so friendly and honourably to deal in the behalf of my poor wife. For truly, my lord, in all reason she is hardly dealt with." Burghley's civility to Lettice contrasted sharply with Elizabeth's abiding dislike.

At any other time Leicester and Lettice would have enjoyed hunting in the deer parks at Theobalds. On this occasion, Leicester explained, though they scared a few stags they had not killed any. Leicester and Burghley had their differences in council but they had a genuine regard for each other. In years to come, while Penelope and Essex retained a lingering respect for Burghley, relations with his son Robert would be very different.

Denbigh's funeral took place at Wanstead on 1 August and a few weeks later he was laid to rest near the altar of the Beauchamp Chapel in St Mary's Church, Warwick. Leicester had chosen the chapel, built a hundred years earlier for the great "King Maker", Richard Beauchamp, Earl of Warwick, as the place for his own burial. He was devastated that his infant son should lie there before him. Denbigh's death changed the future for the Dudley and Devereux families. Since Leicester's illegitimate son by Lady Douglas Sheffield could not inherit his lands and titles, Philip Sidney again became heir apparent to Leicester and Ambrose, Earl of Warwick. But Leicester was in no rush to rewrite his will naming Philip, nor publicly to embrace him as his chosen successor. Philip's lack of favour with Elizabeth made him less than ideal to take over Leicester's roles at Court. Besides, the earl had an alternative. He could groom his stepson, the young Earl of Essex, now almost nineteen, to step into his place beside the queen.

It was a transfer of power that would suit Leicester very well. Essex was exactly the sort of handsome young man Elizabeth liked to have around. He had not yet made his Court entry; had not yet blotted his copybook with the queen; and he came from more noble stock than Philip Sidney. Essex could become the next royal favourite, if he could be persuaded to give up country life and come to Court.

It was Philip, however, as the best writer in the family, who took on the task of defending Leicester from the recent libellous attacks in *Leicester's Commonwealth*. Written to destroy Leicester's character and influence (and through him Elizabeth's) it smeared everyone in Leicester's circle. The earl himself, it said, was a lecherous old liar, poisoner, traitor, adulterer, atheist and murderer. Lettice was a scarlet woman and probably just as good at poisoning. The Digbys were bawds because Lettice and Leicester had used their home, Coleshill, as a "love nest". But it contains no mention of Penelope. Had there been the faintest whiff of an affair between her and Philip, it would surely have been dragged in.

The authors of *Leicester's Commonwealth* were a bunch of disaffected, pro-Catholic exiles living on the Continent; members of the conservative aristocracy who loathed Leicester's closeness to Elizabeth and feared his growing influence as leader of the Protestant party. Skilfully weaving together well-known facts, reports from foreign ambassadors, old rumours and exaggerated gossip, they made a compelling case against him. They raked over his first wife's death and his affairs with Douglas and Lettice, accusing him of murdering both ladies' husbands and various political opponents. His ultimate plan, they insisted, was to remove all claimants to the crown before polishing off Elizabeth. Written before Denbigh's death, it went on to declare that Leicester would marry the boy to Arbella Stuart, heiress to the Scottish throne.

What guaranteed its popularity were the salacious details of Leicester's alleged Viagra-type treatments. They included an Italian ointment, "whereby he is able to move his flesh at all times", because "his inability be otherwise for performance". There was also a special tonic which "his lordship had a bottle for his bedhead of ten pounds the pint to the same effect". It made irresistible reading, and Elizabeth had to issue a proclamation against anyone found with it. The biggest threat to the queen lay in the document's subversive content: her right to sit on the throne. If Leicester was the most devious, libidinous devil on earth, then she was immoral for relying on him, and since she was not fit to be on the throne the next best person was Mary Queen of Scots. Mary was a problem who had already touched Penelope's family keenly and she would do so again before long.

∾

While Philip and Leicester were busy with damage limitation, Essex set off again. He wasn't ready to come to Court. His trips to the country were becoming a habit and it worried his family. To fulfil his destiny as the head of the Devereux he must take his place at Court, but Essex would always be torn between his political ambitions and his inner life – his desire to play "the monk".

His absence from London led to sharp exchanges with his mother. After Denbigh's funeral Essex was away for the best part of a year. At Michaelmas he and "his honourable friends … did repair to his house at Lamphey, in the county of Pembroke, and there did very honourably and bountifully keep house with many servants in livery and the repair of most gentlemen of those parts to attend his lordship". The party went on over Christmas well into January, and among the local gentry happy to keep him company were Dorothy and Sir Thomas, still rusticated for their runaway marriage, and living on the Perrot estates.

On 30 January 1585 Essex told Richard Bagot he would be leaving Lamphey before the end of Lent. Yet on 12 April he was still there, and getting stiff letters from Lettice. In his reply he vigorously denies her charges "of undutifulness as a son", and "carelessness of mine own estate". If, "in your ladyship's wise censure I be thought inconsiderate, I plead as a young man pardon for that fault whereto of all others our age is most subject". Despite begging her pardon and signing himself "Your ladyship's most obedient son R Essex", he set off again for York, and it was autumn before he was back in London.

From Penelope there would be no ticking off; Essex knew he could count on a sympathetic hearing. They understood each other. They shared the same humours and flights of fantasy, playing on words, twisting ideas. Penelope was the sister he looked up to and confided in. In turn, Essex was the brother who could judge her moods exactly.

"Your sister threatens revenge on you for hitting her humours so right," Lettice wrote to him. It was an easy-going, teasing relationship, mutually supportive, caring and understanding. Essex could admit to Penelope his weaknesses, his frequent splitting headaches brought on by anxiety, his fits of depression, despair and sense of futility.

"I have such a humour fallen down into one side of my head as I dare not look out of my chamber," he wrote. It was the start of what he called "a fantastical letter", one of two he sent to her at Leighs. "Hope for that which I have not, is a naive expectation, so delight in that which I have is a deceiving pleasure," he explained; and "to wish the return of that which is gone from me is womanish unconstancy."

At times he writes like the little brother Penelope knew at Chartley: "I will neither brag of my good hap [fortune] nor complain of my ill for secrecy makes joys more sweet, and I am then most unhappy when another knows that I am unhappy." She could almost picture him, proud and determined while their brother Wat walked off with his bow and arrow: "I do not cry, because I will do no man that honour to think he hath that which I want." Yet elsewhere he echoes the lyrical lines of sonneteers and metaphysical poets: "Those things that fly me, I will not lose labour to follow." Essex's letters to Penelope, like his moods, swing between fanciful and trite, revealing and guarded, but never less than intimate.

They are letters between a "brother that loves you dearly" and "Your sister that most infinitely loves you".

Naming her second baby girl Essex underlined Penelope's great love for him. Whether he attended the christening, or sent a stand-in godfather, is unknown. Nor is there a record of the baby's birth date, though it was probably in 1585, for in June the following year Penelope became pregnant with her third child.

~

At New Year 1585 Elizabeth again received a gift from Lord Rich but not his wife, possibly showing that he attended Court while Penelope was confined at home; and once more the present was something for her wardrobe: "a forepart of a kirtle" – the decorative panel behind the front of an open gown – made of "white satin richly embroidered".

The rest of that year proved unusually fine. By the end of July good weather had brought the hay and corn harvests on together and the summer muster of soldiers was delayed while men saw to the crops. Leicester took Lettice to Kenilworth, which greatly annoyed Elizabeth, and early in September Essex, now approaching twenty, at last came to Court.

Elizabeth was at Nonsuch when Leicester introduced his stepson and, though Essex was the handsome young head of an ancient family, it seems his arrival did not attract much notice at first. Two things were occupying Elizabeth's attention: Sir Walter Ralegh and war with Spain. Ralegh, knighted in January that year, was the queen's latest favourite. He was six feet tall and handsome, with dark, curly hair, glittering eyes, a taste for gorgeous clothes and a nice line in poetry. He could name the oldest West Country families – Carew, Grenville, Champernowne and Gilbert – among his relations, and his aunt Kat Ashley had been Elizabeth's governess until she died. That endeared him to the queen, but his buccaneering background didn't impress the ancient noblesse. He lacked the class of Leicester or Essex and he was never considered "one of us" by other courtiers. Leicester in particular was opposed to him, and Ralegh had numerous run-ins with the earl's supporters, including a brawl with Thomas Perrot that sent them both to the Fleet prison in 1580.

More serious than the constant Court in-fighting was England's conflict with Catholic Spain. After years of uneasy peace, Elizabeth agreed to Leicester's requests to lead an expeditionary force to help the Protestant Dutch rebels against their Spanish overlords. It was tantamount to open war on Spain and she had delayed sending troops in hopes that France would do it and spare her the cost. But since France was not taking the initiative she reluctantly agreed to Leicester's expedition to the Netherlands, which occupied him for the next two years.

To Essex it looked like a golden opportunity to win his spurs and spend lots more money equipping himself and his retainers with expensive armour, horses and liveries. Grandfather Knollys, also at Court at Richmond in November, angrily reminded him: "Your father hath not left you sufficient lands for to maintain the state of the poorest earl in England." Like Polonius, he had no effect.

The first wave of troops left for the Netherlands in October under Sir John Norris and included a young gentleman who had recently arrived at Court named Charles Blount, the younger brother of Lord Mountjoy. By the middle of November Sir Philip Sidney and his brother Robert were on their way. Elizabeth had come round to Philip sufficiently to make him governor of Flushing. She also agreed to be godmother to his first child, baptized Elizabeth on 15 November, a few hours before Philip departed. There was talk of Lord Rich going to the Netherlands, too, in charge of a troop of fifty lances, but it came to nothing. Finally, in December, Leicester and Essex were ready to sail, taking Sir Thomas Perrot, Sir Christopher Blount, who was Leicester's master of horse, and Jean Hotman, Leicester's French secretary.

Jean, son of an eminent French Huguenot scholar and jurist, had arrived in England in 1581 to study at Oxford. The following year he became one of Leicester's private secretaries, and Penelope's visits to Leicester House and Wanstead brought him into company with her much-loved lady companion, Jeanne de Saint-Martin. Both French and Huguenot, they fell in love, and some time in the autumn, perhaps prompted by the war, to Penelope's delight they married. In December, Penelope, Jeanne and Dorothy shared their fears as they watched Essex, Jean and Thomas leave for the Netherlands.

Chapter Twelve

1585–1588

"The world was never so dangerous"
— Robert Dudley, Earl of Leicester, 1587

*C*hartley and the Staffordshire countryside that she had known as a child never lost their hold on Penelope. Many a time she returned, taking family and friends with her on summer visits. After her mother retired to Drayton Bassett, twenty miles south of Chartley, Penelope would stay with Lettice and on impulse ride over to Chartley, or to Blithfield to see the Bagots, who still managed the Chartley estate. They were her lifeline. Anne Bagot's marriage to lawyer Broughton in July 1577 meant Anne lived chiefly in London, and after Penelope's marriage the two remained close. Penelope relied on Anne to come to Leighs when she needed her help and companionship. Round and round their tight-knit circle the Devereux, Bagot and Broughton households passed gossip and gifts, food and horses, household goods, and above all love and friendship. Anthony Bagot, having been Essex's student minder, stayed in the earl's service till his death. Margaret Bagot and her husband William Trew managed Essex's domestic affairs at Chartley and later in London. They were all Penelope's extended family and she looked to them for support and news.

The news that came from Chartley almost as soon as Leicester and Essex sailed for the Netherlands was not good. The house had been requisitioned as a prison for Mary Queen of Scots and she would be moved there from Tutbury Castle, ten miles away, before New Year. The idea had been mooted months earlier and Essex did his best to prevent it. He sent instructions to Richard Bagot to "remove all the bedding, hangings, and such like stuffs" to Blithfield for a while. When that failed he wrote, "To the honourable, my very good grandfather, Sir Francis Knollys ... I am so much moved to think my poor and only house should be used against my will ... the spoil of my wood, the marring of my little furniture, the miserable undoing of my poor tenants."

Sir Francis sent the letter to Walsingham with a subtle hint: "I pray you move her majesty to have some compassion … it is no policy for her majesty to lodge the Queen of Scots in so young a man's house." Any contact between Mary and Essex could turn into a romantic one. Everyone knew Mary had helped wreck the Shrewsburys' marriage. But the matter was settled. Chartley fitted the bill for Mary's next prison. The moat made it easy to secure and it did not have a brew house. Ale was delivered regularly in barrels from a brewery in Burton-on-Trent.

On Christmas Eve 1585, Mary was taken to Chartley under armed escort, and over the next nine months the Babington Plot was played out there with the help of the "brewer of Chartley". It was the final phase in Burghley and Walsingham's plan to trap Mary, and Richard Bagot helped them set up the scam that led Mary to incriminate herself in a plot to murder Elizabeth.

For fifteen years Mary had been imprisoned as a "house guest" of the Earl and Countess of Shrewsbury, chiefly at Sheffield Castle and Sheffield Lodge. She had been replaced on the throne of Scotland by her young son James, who ruled with the help of regents and the leaders of the ultra-Protestant church; but she remained the focus for disaffected Catholics. While she lived, Walsingham and Burghley believed, plots against Elizabeth would continue. For a time she was held at Tutbury, which was damp and disease-ridden, while Walsingham's men made contact with a double agent in another local family, the Giffords. Gilbert Gifford was an enthusiastic young Catholic but ultimately a loyalist to Elizabeth. He was known to the Catholic community in Paris, in particular to Thomas Morgan, Mary's key agent abroad. Morgan, believing Gilbert trustworthy in Mary's cause, sent him to England to set up a secret mail service to Mary. But when Gilbert was picked up by Walsingham's agents he agreed to help them instead; and jointly with code-breaker Thomas Phelippes he devised a means of monitoring Mary's secret letters. Walsingham knew she had a constant feed of documents from Catholic supporters in Europe, some via the French embassy in London. It was not difficult to plant his men among her friends and the embassy staff – though who was spying on whom is almost impossible to unravel.

"The world was never so dangerous, nor never so full of treasons and treacheries as at this day," wrote Leicester to Elizabeth from the Netherlands. He never said a truer word. The persuasive powers of torture and bribery meant double agents were two a penny and some, like the infamous Robert Poley, turned more often than a hanged man twisting in the wind on the end of a rope. Poley was allegedly working for Walsingham and was placed in Philip Sidney's household as a secretary. At the same time he was gaining the confidence of Mary's friends, and liaising between her and Christopher Blount, one of Leicester's staff trusted by Mary's friends, who was also allegedly working for Walsingham. In the bungled Babington affair, however, Poley and Christopher look suspiciously like Catholic plotters.

Gilbert Gifford was now sticking to Walsingham's side, though Mary's friends believed he was a trusty go-between carrying her letters to and from the French embassy and passing them to "the brewer of Chartley" to be hidden in the ale kegs that went in and out of Chartley. In fact, Gifford was routing them via Phelippes to be copied, deciphered and cunningly resealed. Like Poley, Gifford kept in touch with the naive Anthony Babington, ostensibly the chief conspirator, and encouraged him further into treason whenever he looked like giving up. And at Chartley it was Richard Bagot who facilitated Gifford's part in the plot by enabling him to lodge with the Chartley steward whenever necessary.

It is a mystery how far it was all a stitch-up by Walsingham and Burghley to frighten Elizabeth into agreeing to Mary's execution. They certainly fostered it once it was moving, and Babington was too incompetent to be a lead player without their "help". Mary's own letters didn't totally implicate her in Babington's plans for a Spanish invasion and Elizabeth's murder, but Walsingham nonetheless prepared to move in. On 25 July Phelippes wrote cryptically to Richard Bagot about "hunting afoot" at Chartley. On 9 August Mary was tricked into leaving Chartley for a day's hunting and she was then forced to ride to Tixall, a house three miles away. Chartley was strip-searched and every scrap of paper removed. The plotters were rounded up and after a fortnight Mary was returned to Chartley.

Walsingham had "found" what he needed: the letters and ciphers that "proved" Mary was complicit in Elizabeth's murder. On 21 September Mary was taken on her last journey, from Chartley to Fotheringhay Castle. Her so-called trial in October took two days, though the "guilty" verdict was a foregone conclusion, and parliament demanded her death. Only Elizabeth held back: Mary was an anointed queen as well as her cousin. Executing her did not set a good example, but Mary's custodians refused to fix her murder. That left Elizabeth no choice and on 1 February she signed the death warrant. When told a week later that it had been carried out, she made out that she was furious, insisting she never gave permission for the warrant to be used.

What Elizabeth never knew was how far Walsingham's *agents provocateurs* were involved in the plot. Richard Bagot knew, and for years Phelippes and Bagot went on corresponding about Gilbert Gifford's valuable part "in that secret negotiation" they had "with the brewer of Chartley". Part of Gilbert's pay-off was lenient treatment from the authorities for his Catholic family, and four years later their immunity was causing local jealousy. "It may now more frankly be said that the son rendered service of prime importance," Phelippes advised Bagot. In fact, to cover his back in such uncertain times, Bagot would have needed to tell Broughton about it from the start.

Everything Richard Bagot did at Chartley was in his professional role as manager for the young Earl of Essex. Common sense told him to keep the family lawyer informed. The Bagot–Broughton archives show the two men shared complete confidence over Devereux affairs. And the chances are that at least something of what Broughton knew found its way back to his wife – and to Penelope.

~

The day after Mary left Chartley for Fotheringhay, Sir Philip Sidney was wounded fighting in the Netherlands. In less than a month he was dead. His remarkable talents as a poet and a soldier, and his final heroism, were the stuff of legends. In a masterpiece of mythology he was raised to the level of a Protestant martyr, and only one story spoilt his messianic image: the tale of a deathbed confession about "my Lady Rich".

From the start the Netherlands campaign had been botched. Elizabeth kept changing her mind about objectives and management. "There is never a man here who will believe her majesty will do anything," Leicester wrote to Burghley. There were money problems, delays in supplies, confusing chains of command and personality clashes. Leicester's tactless decision to accept the title Governor General from the Netherlanders themselves, without consulting Elizabeth, made things worse. She was alarmed by the thought that he, and particularly Lettice, might set up their own Court there.

Elizabeth's crooked government fed on secret agents, wheeling and dealing in information and "spin", and Walsingham had several spies keeping tabs on Leicester. But while he believed he was running Christopher Blount, Mary Queen of Scots's friends were equally certain he was working for her. According to one of Mary's informers: "You may assure yourself, Blount is a gentleman, and will be faithful unto you, and may perhaps draw others, worth the having, to serve your majesty." When gossip spread that Christopher's kinsman Charles Blount "is installed in the good grace of her of England", they began to wonder if Christopher might be more use back in England. "I hear she [Elizabeth] hath now entertained one Blount, brother of the Lord Mountjoy, being a young gentleman whose grandmother she may be for her age and his," Mary was told.

From another friendly Catholic Mary heard that Robert Poley was in a good position to send her information, being "servant to Sir Philip Sidney, and thereby remaining with his lady" at Walsingham's house in London. Sidney's wife, Frances, was in fact about to join Philip in the Netherlands, taking their baby daughter. She was pregnant again when he was wounded.

In early morning mist outside the Spanish garrison at Zutphen, the English forces were surprised by enemy soldiers. Philip, hurrying to arm, left off his thigh plates and rode in to a fierce attack. When one horse was killed beneath him he mounted another and rode to rescue a fellow knight who was surrounded. At that moment a musket shot shattered his left leg above the knee. At first it seemed he would recover, but by 8 October it was obvious he was dying. Stinking gangrene had set in. The fever and pain were intolerable, yet he stayed cogent almost till the end, surrounded by doctors, clergymen and secretaries.

During those agonizing nine days Philip was said to have made a deathbed confession about Penelope. One of the many ministers and physicians who attended him claimed that in clearing his conscience Philip said: "There came to my remembrance a vanity wherein I had taken delight, whereof I had not rid myself. It was my Lady Rich." Scholars doubt the authenticity of the two manuscripts that report the story. There seem to be words added or missing, and if he said it at all it is not necessarily a confession of adultery. Why should Philip *not* recall "Stella" during his dying days? She had inspired his love and his sweetest poetry, and he may well have said something about her. He had, after all, just bequeathed his "best sword" to "my beloved and much honoured lord, the Earl of Essex", and Essex was there to pay his last respects to the man who had been his hero.

With Frances beside him, Philip died on 17 October. "Your sorrowful daughter," Leicester wrote to Walsingham, "is here with me at Utrecht till she may recover some strength, for she is wonderfully overthrown through her long care since the beginning of her husband's hurt, and I am the more careful that she should be in some strength ere she take her journey into England, for that she is with child."

Essex and Thomas Perrot returned to England almost at once. Philip's remains were shipped back early in November and Leicester followed days later. On 17 November the Accession Day tilt went ahead at Whitehall. Not quite as usual: a riderless horse was led in, caparisoned in black in Philip's honour, and Essex made his debut in the tiltyard wearing the motto "Nothing can represent [my] sorrow". On Christmas Eve Walsingham wrote to Leicester, "I thank my god for it I am now in good hope of the recovery of both my daughter and her child." Sadly, Frances suffered a miscarriage soon afterwards.

Philip's funeral was delayed due to his vast debts and problems with his will, which was complicated by the death of both his parents a few months before his own. Walsingham was bowed down with grief for Sidney, "who was my chief worldly comfort". He was worried about Frances, and nearly bankrupted by the debts, but he was still determined to give Philip a hero's farewell. When it finally took place, on 16 February at St Paul's, it was magnificent, a state funeral in all but name. Everyone attended. Sir Robert Sidney, Philip's brother, was chief mourner. Behind him rode the earls of Huntingdon, Leicester and Essex, Lord Rich and Lord North. Sir William Knollys, Sir Thomas Perrot and Sir Francis Drake walked shoulder to shoulder. Vast crowds watched and wept as 700 mourners – scholars, gentlemen, citizens, and soldiers, their muskets reversed and pikestaffs lowered – marched past to the slow beat of fifes and drums.

It may or may not have been deliberate, but the great show of grief for Sir Philip Sidney displaced any mourning for Mary Queen of Scots, who had been quietly executed eight days earlier, well away from public gaze at Fotheringhay.

~

Penelope's reaction to Philip's death is not on record, and the love he felt for her seems to have been a distant memory when he died. But his passing was not the end of the connection. Before long his widow Frances and his brother Sir Robert Sidney became two of her close companions. And whatever grief Penelope felt for Philip was tempered by relief: for Essex's safe return from the war, and for the safe arrival of her first son.

Penelope's third child, Lord Rich's long-awaited heir, was born in the spring of 1587. She had been married nearly six years and at last she had done her duty. It was fortunate that her husband and her brother shared the same name and the baby could be baptized Robert without argument. Penelope's love for all her children was well known, but she must have given special thanks for her son, probably born at Leighs, and everything augured well for the child's future. For the moment, however, it was Essex's future that occupied the family. He returned from the Netherlands with a knighthood and his rise to royal favour was astonishing. At New Year he presented Elizabeth with "a fair jewel of gold, like a rainbow, garnished with rubies", diamonds and opals. By May he was constantly in her company.

"When she is abroad nobody near her but my lord of Essex, and at night, my lord is at cards, or one game or another, with her, that he cometh not to his own lodging till birds sing in the morning," Anthony Bagot wrote excitedly to his father. As for Sir Walter Ralegh, "he is the hated man of the world". Anthony was exaggerating out of loyalty to Essex, but Ralegh was temporarily out of favour and Essex was occupying the rooms he usually had at Nonsuch.

Essex is said to have shot to favour with a woman thirty-two years his senior because he appealed to her "lewd cravings" and "intruded himself by a straight-forward appeal to the queen's susceptibilities – as Dudley, Ralegh and Hatton had done before him". Essex's appeal was anything but straight-forward. He had the virility, sophisticated wit and gallantry Elizabeth loved, and in the Netherlands he had won his spurs and proved himself brave and chivalrous. But his relationship with her was more complex than that of any other favourite. He did not need to intrude himself into her circle: he was born into it. He was old nobility. He was brought up believing he was destined to play a lead role within a ruling elite. He was more nearly related to Elizabeth than any of the others. Even if Elizabeth refused publicly to call Lady Knollys and Lord Hunsdon more than cousins; even if she preferred to doubt that they were her father's children, she could never be sure. She could never escape a certain maternal feeling for Essex and Penelope, and, though "the She-wolf" had forfeited her good opinion, the family connection and Elizabeth's fondness for Lady Knollys inclined her to treat Penelope and Essex with special indulgence. In the end, it was an indulgence that saved Penelope but which could not save her brother.

Essex's first step up came on May Day when he learnt he was to take over Leicester's role as master of the horse, responsible for arranging the supply and stabling of the hundreds of mounts, dogs and carriage horses Elizabeth and her household used for travelling, hunting and ceremonial occasions. It was the job that had kept Leicester by Elizabeth's side since she came to the throne thirty years ago. Now Leicester was moving aside, anxious to transfer power to his own nominee, knowing he was ageing. He also knew he had to return to the Netherlands for a while. When he left in June, Elizabeth insisted Essex stay with her at Court.

But the relationship between Elizabeth and Essex already had its stormy moments. Essex's loyalty and pride in his Devereux family boiled over the following month when Elizabeth refused to receive Dorothy, four years after her runaway marriage. Dorothy was already staying at North Hall, home of Leicester's brother Ambrose, Earl of Warwick, when Elizabeth arrived and ordered Dorothy to remain in her room. Convinced Ralegh was behind it, Essex got into a shouting match with Elizabeth which grew worse when she insulted Lettice. Essex felt acutely "this disgrace both to me and my sister; which was only to please that knave Ralegh". He sent Dorothy away in the night, and set off as if to go abroad and join Leicester. But he paused long enough to write a lengthy letter about the row, allowing Elizabeth's messenger to catch him with her orders to return to Court. Elizabeth soon forgave him, and it was a pattern they repeated several times.

The other side of Essex's Devereux charm was a moody, wayward, quarrelsome character, often involved in spats in the fiercely competitive atmosphere at Court. Elizabeth tried to ban duelling, but it was a rite of passage, proof of testosterone, and Essex had a go at various young men, most notably Charles Blount. Charles had caught Elizabeth's eye before he set off for the Netherlands with Sir John Norris and apart from a spell of sick leave he stayed fighting there until Elizabeth recalled him in October 1587, when he too returned with a knighthood conferred by Leicester.

In mid-December Leicester himself returned, for good, and Elizabeth could enjoy Christmastide with her two chief favourites beside her (Ralegh wisely decided to absent himself). At New Year, Penelope, Lord Rich and his mother were among those who presented her with gifts. This year it was Penelope who gave her something for her wardrobe, a "forepart of white cloth of silver" heavily embroidered, while Lord Rich gave her £10. Enjoying the pleasures of Court life together evidently created some harmony between Lord and Lady Rich, for in March, Penelope, now aged twenty-five, was pregnant again.

Hovering over the feasting and gaiety, however, was the threat of war with Spain, and early in 1588 rumours of a massive Spanish Armada grew louder.

~

Leicester's campaign in the Netherlands had prompted Philip of Spain to plan a counter-attack on England with a large fleet and an invasion army. Drake's daring raid on Cadiz in April 1587, when he "singed the King of Spain's beard" and destroyed nearly thirty ships, was good for national morale, but it merely delayed the inevitable. A year later reports flooded in from Walsingham's agents that Philip's forces were ready. In June a cargo ship bound for Hamburg put in at Plymouth with news that the Armada was on the high seas. King Philip's 130-strong fleet, commanded by the Duke of Medina Sidonia, was made up of heavy-gunned galleons, oar-and-sail galleasses, merchants' carracks forced into service, small sailing barques, lightly armed caravels, fast feluccas and pinnaces. Their plan was to link up with Spain's army of Flanders, led by the Duke of Parma, which would embark in 200 flat-bottom barges and cross the Channel to the Thames Estuary.

Shudders went through everyone in and around London, and fears ran wild when government propaganda, aiming to put vim and vigour into the local militia, spread stories about the things invading Spaniards did to women and children. Robert Sidney sent his young family away from the capital to stay with his sister Mary at Wilton. Lord Rich's estates in Essex looked particularly vulnerable, never mind that official wisdom said Kent was the likeliest landing place. Leighs was only twenty miles inland and at

Rochford Hall, overlooking Maplin Sands, Penelope's mother-in-law could practically eavesdrop on shipping in the river mouth. Earlier in the year a defensive chain was quickly positioned across the lower Thames, and as quickly swept away. There were few castles and fortifications along the northern shoreline of the estuary and the local militia were no match for Parma's men. To the relief of the county, Lord Leicester, commander-in-chief of the anti-invasion army, placed his 5,000 soldiers and several hundred horses on the north bank, and camped at Tilbury Fort.

Elizabeth, declaring a national emergency, summoned her peers, including Lord Rich, to attend her at Court. But he was also needed to help turn out the militia in Essex. "Though he be no man of war," Leicester wrote to Walsingham, "I find the country doth much respect and love him, especially that he is a true, faithful subject to her majesty and known to be zealous in religion." If the queen would please send Lord Rich back to the county, "his presence with me would do much good".

Steadily the Armada advanced up the Channel and invasion fears peaked when the vast fleet anchored off Calais, expecting to escort Parma's barges out of Dunkirk and across to England. Only Parma wasn't ready. While the Spanish ships sat waiting for his invasion force off Gravelines, the lord admiral, Charles Howard, sent eight "hell-burner" fireships loaded with explosives in among them, under cover of darkness. Throughout the following day, 28 July, the stricken Spaniards were pounded by gunfire and scattered. Damaged almost beyond repair, demoralized and in danger of being driven on to the sandbanks, the Armada was blown northwards, chased and harried by Howard in gale-force winds as far as the Firth of Forth. Only hindsight could see that the battle of Gravelines ended the threat.

At Tilbury it was far from certain the danger was over and ten days later Elizabeth paid her famous visit to the camp. On 8 August she arrived and dined there with Leicester and his officers, among them Lord Rich who had temporarily been made captain of a company of lances. And while they ate invasion rumours continued. "The queen being at dinner," reported one of Leicester's staff, there was news "that the prince of Parma was embarked with 50 thousand men foot and 6000 horse, and that he put to sea yesterday, and it was surely expected he would land here or somewhere upon this island tomorrow." That night Elizabeth slept at Arderne Hall at Horndon, home of one of Penelope's in-laws, Edward Rich. The following day Elizabeth returned to the camp and delivered her speech with the ringing phrases: "I am come amongst you"; and "in the midst and heat of the battle, to live or die amongst you all."

"I know I have the body of a weak and feeble woman, but I have the heart and stomach of a king, and a king of England, too," she went on, looking magnificent in her red wig, huge pearls and diamonds, her white velvet gown and shining silver breastplate. In front of her was carried her sword of state and silver helmet. Either side of her white horse, as she rode through ranks of cheering troops, walked grey-haired Lord Leicester and the dashing young Earl of Essex.

It was a brilliantly stage-managed scene. Everyone watching could see that Essex would follow Leicester as the queen's principal favourite. No one realized how soon that would be.

~

The queen returned to St James's Palace and preparations began for a triumphal thanksgiving at St Paul's. Essex was now constantly with her, but Leicester felt too ill to stay. At Tilbury he had picked up "camp fever", a form of malaria. Begging leave of Elizabeth, he went back to Wanstead and on 27 August set off with Lettice for Kenilworth and Buxton spa, meaning to rest and take the waters.

Penelope hurriedly contacted Leicester on his way out of London and asked him to write to Burghley, in his role as master of the court of wards. She wanted to remind them about her request for the wardship of a friend's child. However rich Lord Rich was, it made sense to increase her income by bidding for the right to manage wealthy orphans' lives and property. That evening Leicester duly wrote to Burghley that "a great bellied lady" had asked "her uncle your true servant" to pursue the matter for her. He didn't need to explain who he meant. Burghley would have seen Penelope around Court often enough to know she was at least six months pregnant; and he knew she looked on Leicester as her kindly old counsellor, her "uncle".

Leicester travelled on slowly to Warwickshire, and paused again on 29 August to write to Elizabeth. He wanted to ask about her health, thank her for the medicine she had sent from her own physicians to "your poor old servant"; and he prayed "for your majesty's most happy preservation". He reached Cornbury House, his lodge in Oxfordshire, but could travel no further, and with his "well beloved wife" beside him Leicester died on 4 September. Fifteen years later his letter was found beside Elizabeth's bed, marked "his last letter".

Leicester had expressly stated that he was to be buried at Warwick and, at his grand funeral there on 10 October, Essex was chief mourner assisted by Sir Robert Sidney. Almost every male member of Penelope's family, including Lord Rich, joined the hundreds in the procession; and one of the six pallbearers was Sir Charles Blount. Elizabeth's grief was intense, but it didn't stop her swiftly taking steps to secure Leicester's massive £25,000 debt to the crown.

And Penelope continued angling for the wardship she wanted. On 10 September she wrote to Burghley following up Leicester's letter. "I would have been glad to have waited on your lordship myself, if I might have done you any service, but my burden is such as I am fitter to keep the house," she explained. Her tone is courteous, yet there is more than a little pressure as she reminds him she is still "hoping only in your lordship's favour, which is the means to accomplish my desire", and urges him "to set it so forward as that I may shortly hope to see an end of it".

Penelope was writing from York House, which Elizabeth had granted to Essex at the beginning of 1588. It was another of the grand mansions on the river side of the Strand owned by the crown, and Essex now allowed Penelope to lodge there as well. She had relatively little space in York House, but it was much closer to Whitehall Palace than Lord Rich's town house at St Bartholomew's; and she could be certain she wouldn't have to endure the likes of Lord Rich's chaplain Ezekiel Culverwell.

Two months later, Penelope's "burden" was delivered. At Leighs, one Friday early in November, she gave birth to another daughter. Queen Elizabeth graciously agreed to be godmother and sent her staff to prepare the chamber for the christening. She also sent 100 shillings for Penelope's nurse and midwife. On the christening day, 26 November, one of Elizabeth's senior ladies arrived to represent her, bringing the royal christening gift: a splendid silver-gilt bowl with a cover weighing more than fifty ounces, twice the weight of the queen's regular New Year gifts.

Penelope and her baby received another pretty tribute, from a gentleman poet named Henry Constable. He predicted the baby would grow up a beauty and "many hosts of hearts thy face shall slay"; although Penelope's beauty had cornered the market in slain hearts:

> Thy mother so shall thee of praise bereave.
> So many hearts she hath already slain,
> As few behind to conquer do remain.

Constable was employed as a political messenger in and around Court, sometimes on missions overseas. He was part of Essex's circle and he was at least a little in love with Penelope. In a letter to Jean Hotman she sent her remembrances to Constable and advised him to be "amorous no more". His forecast for the baby, however, proved wrong. The child died soon after birth and Constable's poem on her death is not one of his best. Nonetheless he went on to write dozens of sonnets to Penelope and to act as her messenger on an important assignment to Scotland.

Penelope's baby did not keep her out of circulation long. At Christmastide she was back at Court with Lord Rich, anxious perhaps to keep an eye on Essex. Ralegh had returned to Court after Leicester's death and the running battle between Ralegh and Essex was getting worse. By Christmas it was so intense that Elizabeth reportedly made a special journey from Greenwich to Richmond to insist they calm down. But they secretly planned a duel, which the privy council "repressed … and buried in silence" so that Elizabeth heard nothing about it. At New Year, both men were dropped from her gift list but Penelope was there, at Richmond, presenting the queen with another richly embroidered "forepart" for her wardrobe. Lord Rich and Penelope's mother-in-law were also in attendance and each gave "in gold £10". Elizabeth responded with gifts of gilt plate to each of them, and Penelope's was the heaviest.

Lettice, of course, was not present. She was busy elsewhere. Like Elizabeth, her grief at Leicester's death did not prevent her taking decisive action. And early the following year Penelope found she had a new stepfather – Sir Christopher Blount.

Chapter Thirteen

1589–1590

"The fineness of her wit, the invention, and well writing"
— King James VI of Scotland, 1589

Sir Christopher Blount was a curious choice of husband for Lettice, who had twice been married to an earl. He was openly Catholic, twelve years younger, relatively poor and without a position at Court. He was, on the other hand, tall, dark-haired and valiant. For several years he had served Leicester as master of the horse, a job that put him above servant level, yet still way below Lettice.

"There is a good deal to be told about Blount which has escaped his professional biographers," wrote the Victorian historian George Craik. His research into the Babington Plot led him to conclude that Blount "had a short time before his marriage with the countess of Leicester been deeply involved in proceedings of a treasonable nature; unless, indeed, he was a spy in the pay of Walsingham." Blount, he added, "is a very questionable character" about whom there had been a 300-year cover-up.

Born around 1555, Christopher was the second son of Thomas Blount of Kidderminster, Leicester's chief administrator until his death in 1568. Christopher's mother was Margaret, or Marjery, Poley, an ardent Catholic, and thanks to her he was educated by Catholic tutors and spent time in the Catholic college at Douai. In Paris he got to know the Catholic exiles plotting for Mary Queen of Scots's release but he followed his father and brother into Leicester's service. During the Netherlands campaign he fought at Zutphen, became lieutenant to Sir Thomas Perrot, remained at the front when Leicester went back to England, and received a knighthood shortly before he too returned in January 1589.

The speed of Lettice's marriage to him inevitably sparked stories. One said they were having an affair before Leicester died, and Lettice poisoned the earl when he found out. A later tale claimed Leicester tried to poison her but she turned the tables and gave it to him. Penelope and her siblings were used to it. It was the same sort of story they had heard about their father. Nonetheless, the remarriage was a surprise. Leicester's will suggests nothing but fondness for Lettice and she was generously provided for, with Wanstead, Leicester House and Drayton Bassett. Added to the estates she inherited from Earl Walter, she had an income of £3,000 a year and nearly £6,000 worth of possessions. On the downside, Leicester's debts were a formidable problem, and Elizabeth's temporary seizure of Wanstead and Leicester House made things worse. At Drayton Bassett, Lettice needed Richard Bagot's help to forcibly evict a gentleman squatter who claimed he was the rightful owner. And in November she lost £8,000 when Leicester's agent, Thomas Fowler, fled to Scotland pocketing every penny he'd collected from Leicester's debtors.

It is hard, however, to see Lettice as a defenceless widow who needed a husband's help. Given her strength of character and influential family, what could Sir Christopher fix that her son, father and brothers could not? So it was either a love match, or Sir Christopher deliberately worked his way into Lettice's heart and the Devereux circle. Lettice always referred to him as "my best friend" and there is no reason to believe they were unhappy. But evidence of how her children reacted to him is conflicting. Essex once called it an "unhappy choice", yet Sir Christopher was his right-hand man in all his campaigns for the next ten years, and played a lead role in the rebellion that cost them both their lives in 1601.

However strange Lettice's choice of new husband looked then, he looks far odder now that he is known to be part of a spy ring that included Robert Poley. Poley was "no fool", according to Robert Cecil, and he reached the peak of his unsavoury career a few years later with the murder of the brilliant young playwright Christopher – "Kind Kit" – Marlowe. Walsingham had recruited Marlowe, Shakespeare's greatest rival, as a spy at Cambridge. His plays and poetry were pure magic and his mighty *Tamburlaine* was a sensation. But his homosexual friendships, his links with Ralegh's so-called "atheists", and his suspected contacts with the Scottish court, were making Marlowe too hot to handle. In a private room in a house in Deptford, "Kind Kit" died with a dagger through his eye. And Poley was the most senior of the three men he had gone to meet. The murderers said it was a drunken brawl over the dinner bill, but it was almost certainly a contract killing to silence Marlowe.

Sir Christopher and Poley were undoubtedly working together in 1586, and Walsingham believed they were working for Elizabeth. Mary Queen of Scots, however, believed they were good Catholics scheming for her, and that their jobs on the staff of prominent men like Leicester, Walsingham and

Philip Sidney gave them good cover. But was Sir Christopher still working for Walsingham, keeping an eye on Essex, when he married Lettice and got inside the family circle? And if Sir Christopher was *not* Walsingham's agent in 1586, he *was* working for Mary Queen of Scots. And that makes his entry into the family particularly strange in view of the secret correspondence Penelope, Essex and Lord Rich began a few months later.

∼

The year 1589 had started with Penelope and Lord Rich at Court together. It went on with them both working on Essex's affairs, and it marks perhaps the most harmonious period of their marriage. It certainly marks the start of Penelope's active politicking. Now that Leicester was gone, Penelope assumed a more senior role in Essex's life and her husband followed her involvement in his affairs. It is another reason to wonder whether Lord Rich was as awful as history makes out. If Penelope and Essex couldn't stand him, they didn't need to involve him. And if he was a reluctant partner, as sometimes claimed, he could have refused: he was a grown man, nearing thirty, who could be a bully when he wanted.

Essex had been Elizabeth's constant companion for a year now. He escorted her to the Armada thanksgiving at St Paul's, and he moved into Leicester's old rooms close to hers at Court. But those who knew him best were aware he resented being controlled by an ageing queen who did not share his love of warfare. Her "unconstancy" infuriated him. It was typical of women, he complained to Penelope, and "the time wherein we live, [is] more unconstant than women's thoughts". He evidently excluded Penelope from that criticism. It was her determination, he declared later, that caused his rebellion. In the spring of 1589 he was getting restless and in April, ignoring Elizabeth's orders, he slipped away from Court to join Drake and Norris's expedition to Portugal. It was another rite of passage, proving his boldness, courage and daring to disobey the queen.

The expedition was more than a reprisal raid on what remained of the Spanish Armada. It aimed to release Portugal from Spanish domination, storm Lisbon and place the would-be king Dom Antonio on the throne. Then it would head for the Azores to capture the Spanish treasure fleet. It was going to be bloody and dangerous and Elizabeth expressly forbade young aristocrats – Essex, the Earl of Northumberland and Charles Blount – from joining the fleet. Lord Rich considered going but thought better of it, and his presence at Court proved useful. Essex's previous effort to do a runner, from North Hall, had been a half-hearted impulse. This time he was prepared and determined. He needed to profit from the trip, as well as gain military glory. His debts had now spiralled to £22,000.

The Court was at Whitehall on Thursday 3 April while the fleet was at Plymouth, 220 miles away. Essex, having asked Lord Rich to come and sup with him in his chamber, disappeared at dusk and put ninety miles behind him before he sent back any explanation. Anthony Bagot, Essex's comrade-cum-servant, described to his father how Essex "took horse in St James's park" and "is gone to Plymouth and I fear away with the fleet to Portingale". The groom who returned with Essex's horses brought a letter for Lord Rich and the keys of Essex's desk, "wherein there was letters above 40 of my lord [in] his own hand writing to the queen, the council, and other of his friends in Court, and his servants". Clearly miffed, Anthony went on: "he neither sought nor spake any word of me, but referred all to my Lord Rich."

Essex knew the repercussions for disobeying royal orders would be dire and he had thrust his brother-in-law into an awkward position. Yet he evidently knew he could rely on Rich to take charge of his affairs and handle them as well as possible. Elizabeth, as expected, sent numerous messengers post-haste to bring Essex back, but he had reached the fleet in a day and a half. Secretly he joined brother Wat on board the *Swiftsure* and sailed to Falmouth to lie low till Drake left Plymouth. Then the *Swiftsure* followed, reaching Portugal in time to attack Lisbon.

The expedition proved a failure on all fronts, especially the financial one, and when Essex returned early in July the fallout was indeed dire. For months Elizabeth refused to be mollified by his safe return and it seemed to his family that all hope of a successful Court career had been "strangled almost in the very cradle". Tales of his heroism, jumping into shoulder-high water to lead the troops against the enemy on the beach, pleased the crowds in London but not the queen. Essex never did learn the dangers of courting popular favour. But her fury fell on the captain of the *Swiftsure*, Sir Roger Williams, who was a good friend of the Devereux. He was so scared by Elizabeth's anger that he made his will, leaving "my great ruby unto my lady Rich".

Lord Rich escaped Elizabeth's wrath and the experience did not wipe out his willingness to be involved in another risky escapade with Essex. This time, however, it was Penelope making the running, and it was treason.

~

In October Lord Burghley received a tip-off from Thomas Fowler in Edinburgh. King James of Scotland was receiving secret messages from "Rialta, Ernestus and Richardo".

Burghley knew that Fowler had robbed Lettice of £8,000: he signed the warrant to search Fowler's house just after Fowler had made off to Scotland. Yet Burghley was content to employ him as an agent and Fowler was feeding him excellent information. Lady Rich, he reported, had devised "a nickname for everyone that is partaker in this matter"; and "a long scroll as an alphabet of cypher to understand them by". She was Rialta, Essex was Ernestus, Lord Rich was Richardo. Their letters and messages were overtures of friendship to James, code name Victor. Elizabeth's days were numbered and James could count on them to support him as her successor; they were not backing his English-born kinswoman, Arbella Stuart.

Fowler knew what was in the letters because his informer was the very person Penelope's emissary, Jean Hotman, was dealing with at James's Court. Hotman had moved on to Penelope's payroll after Leicester's death and he carried her first consignment of letters and messages to Edinburgh late in July. He gained an audience with James and, once the coded parts of Penelope's letter were explained to him, the king "commended much the fineness of her wit, the invention, and well writing".

It was the content that bothered Burghley, not Penelope's style. In Fowler's words, Penelope and Essex were giving "the poor king to hope for hap shortly, and that her majesty could not live above a year or two". Their offers of friendship and support for James were designed to establish Essex in pole position with the next monarch, and show him how much they disliked the current regime. Penelope made it clear, Fowler said, that her brother "the weary knight" considered it "a thrall he lives now in and wishes the change". At best their sentiments were unfriendly to Elizabeth and at worst they were interfering in the succession, which Elizabeth still banned from discussion.

Various letters and responses followed Hotman's first visit. Penelope sent at least one from Leighs in September, enclosed with a note to Jeanne Hotman in London. Writing in French as usual to Jeanne, Penelope explained that her enclosed letter was unaddressed but it was *"une reponse pour le prince câche"* – a reply for the disguised prince. Jeanne needed no further instruction, and Penelope's letter moved on to other matters. Hotman, however, was soon taking a trip to France and in mid-October Penelope used another courier for the messages to Scotland: her poetic admirer, Henry Constable.

Burghley and Walsingham knew everything about Constable's movements. They had been keeping an eye on him for a while, and a couple of years hence he would confirm their suspicions by converting to Catholicism. In Edinburgh, Fowler informed Burghley, Constable had "secret conference sundry times with Victor". And with the messages he had brought a fashionable gift for James: a portrait miniature of Penelope by Nicholas Hilliard, the finest "limner" of the day.

Hilliard's exquisite little watercolours, "limnings", cased in gold and jewelled settings, were highly prized and it was a privilege to sit to Hilliard. He rarely took likenesses of anyone twice, except Elizabeth and Leicester, yet he produced at least two miniatures of Penelope, possibly three. Hilliard had a long-standing connection with her family. As a boy he knew her grand-father in Geneva when they were all living abroad as Protestant exiles in the 1550s; and after they returned to England at the start of Elizabeth's reign, the Knollys family were a valuable source of commissions for him. Through them Hilliard found his chief patron, Leicester, and Lettice and her children continued to be friends as well as benefactors to Nicholas and his wife Alice. In May 1583 Lettice was probably godmother to their daughter, named Lettice. And Penelope was godmother to their youngest daughter, her name-sake, on 31 October 1586 at St Vedast's Church, round the corner from Hilliard's home in Gutter Lane.

Some time in 1589 Penelope climbed the stairs to Hilliard's studio at the top of the house and sat for the portrait that would be given to King James. A first sitting for a miniature could take up to four hours and Hilliard thought it important to create a comfortable atmosphere, with "sweet odours" to "comfort the brain", or "discreet talk, or reading, quiet mirth or music". With Penelope he could while away time talking French, which Hilliard had learnt in Paris as well as in his boyhood years in Geneva. He enjoyed chatting about his work as he painted the tiny picture, placing minikin pearls in Penelope's hair, and burnishing each tiny dab of gold with the tip of a stoat's tooth bound to a stick.

He had already painted a full-length miniature of Essex as a "Young man among the roses", and he was enough of an insider to know Penelope's connection with Philip Sidney, who was one of Hilliard's heroes. There was no reason, however, for the artist to tell her about the portrait he had painted of Charles Blount. It was one of his best and it showed Charles's curly brown hair and handsome face capped with the words *"Amor Amoris Premium"* – "Love [is] the reward of love". Whatever they talked about, Hilliard must have enjoyed the sessions or he would not have painted Penelope again. And her letters prove he was working on a picture of her a year later.

The miniature that went to King James inspired Henry Constable to write another poem. It is addressed "To Mr Hilliard upon occasion of a picture he made of my Lady Rich", but Constable ended up praising Penelope more than Hilliard, carried away with the idea that it was her beauty not his skill that "Doth make the jewel which you paint seem Rich".

Thomas Fowler was delighted to report to Cecil that when the precious miniature was presented to the king, Constable could not persuade James to write back to Penelope. Constable "would have had Victor write to Rialta", but "he could not bring it to pass for Victor was troubled other ways", according to Fowler. James was increasingly preoccupied with his plans to marry a Danish princess named Anna, and in November the Rialta letters came to an end. Fowler smugly informed Burghley: "the best is Victor regards not their offers much." But Fowler was not quite right. Although James made little immediate response, and forecasts of Elizabeth's imminent death were over-optimistic, Penelope's friendly overtures paid off handsomely. Essex was James's most trusted ally for the next decade, and Penelope would continue to reap the benefits after James became king of England. But short term it was a high-risk strategy. Nothing in Fowler's accounts suggests this was intrigue for fun, or light-hearted social exchanges.

"There were many things, wrongs of her family, and wrongs of her own, to make [Penelope] feel vindictively towards Elizabeth," wrote one rare historian 150 years ago. Elizabeth's government had become corrupt and her policy was at odds with Essex's ambitions. The queen was at least partly responsible for the unhappy end of Lady Knollys, Penelope's grandmother; for the ruin and early death of Earl Walter, her father; and for the public disgrace of Lettice, her mother.

No wonder Penelope wanted to see the end of Elizabeth's rule, the power of the Cecils curbed and the honour of the Devereux restored. It was not power for herself that Penelope was after. Essex was the hope and pride of the family. Her objective was to position him in his rightful place among the new king's advisers. While Elizabeth reigned they had a duty to support her – so long as her rule was reasonable. But it would not be long before the playhouses aired the idea that a monarch had a duty to govern well, and one who did not might be replaced.

That way led rebellion, but to succeed it would have to be carefully planned. And there is something *Boys' Own* and amateurish about the Rialta affair that leaves question marks. Was this another set-up by the Cecils, fishing to see if they could trap James or Essex in a plot to remove Elizabeth? If James were implicated, his chance of Elizabeth naming him as her successor would be ruined. The Cecils would like that. They knew James loathed them. They would also like to get Essex out of the way. There is clear evidence they tried to link him to other plots, but implicating himself would be much better.

If the Rialta affair *was* a trap, it was a master stroke encouraging Penelope to be the ringleader. Anyone inside the Devereux circle – and plenty outside – could see her influence growing over Essex. In her letters she writes confidently on his behalf, promising and bestowing his favours. Whatever the origins of the Rialta affair, it seems Burghley and his son, Robert Cecil, did not tell Elizabeth everything they knew, which adds weight to the idea that they were using a mole. Penelope's part in the affair went unpunished and Essex was only ticked off for unauthorized correspondence with a foreign monarch.

Essex, however, seemed hell bent on ruining his favoured position with Elizabeth in 1589. First the dash to Portugal, then the Rialta letters, and by the end of the year he decided to marry Philip Sidney's widow, Frances. The date of their wedding is unknown. It was deliberately kept secret from Elizabeth and her response when she found out was predictably choleric. Tradition says they married shortly before Frances's father, Walsingham, died in April 1590; Elizabeth learnt of it in the autumn when Frances was visibly pregnant; and Essex's first son was baptized in January 1591. More significant than when, is why?

Essex had hero-worshipped Philip from childhood and could doubtless recall that summer day at Chartley when Elizabeth and her courtiers came to stay. Essex was then a puny lad of nine and Philip a debonair twenty-one-year-old. At Zutphen when Philip was fatally wounded Essex won his spurs and inherited Philip's "best sword". He watched his hero's pretty, pregnant, young wife grow pale by her husband's deathbed. Back in England, waiting for Philip's funeral, the Devereux–Dudley family stayed close to the Walsinghams while Frances struggled to regain her health but lost her baby. It could scarcely have been a more romantic introduction.

Essex's motive in marrying Frances is often said to be his wish to follow Philip as the champion of Protestantism. That probably reflects Protestant propaganda and it certainly underestimates the effect of a nubile twenty-two-year-old on a virile young man. Essex was earning a randy reputation around Court and he was arguably more hooked on sex, chivalry and heading up the anti-Spanish pro-war party than he was on religion. It is true he admired Frances's Protestant father, but Essex's focus on foreign affairs suggests he was equally interested in Walsingham's spy network.

Sad-eyed and weary, Walsingham spent years protecting Elizabeth through his secret service team, with precious little reward, chiefly because the queen disliked his extreme Puritan views. Frances did not follow the Protestant path so closely as her father. Her best friend at the time she married Philip was Marie Bochetel, the very Catholic wife of the French ambassador, and they spent much time together at the Walsinghams' house at Barn Elms. The ambassador, Seigneur de Mauvissière, was keeping open house at the embassy to every Catholic plotting to put Mary Queen of Scots on Elizabeth's throne. But Walsingham had perforated their network with so many double agents that it leaked news to him as fast as it reached the ambassador; and Mauvissière never knew that his eminent guest Giordano Bruno was moonlighting as Walsingham's spy, Mr Fagot. Somewhere, if not from Marie, Frances picked up Catholic sympathies (Philip himself was rumoured to share them) and she eventually married a Catholic and converted.

But it was Frances's lack of fortune and nobility, not her religion, that made Elizabeth think her unfit to be Essex's wife. Actually, Elizabeth would have been unhappy whoever Essex married, but she could have better borne it if he had made a more illustrious match. After a while Essex was readmitted to Court and Frances had the sense to keep away, and "live very retired in her mother's house" so that Elizabeth could monopolize her husband in public. Among contemporaries it seemed that Essex's marriage "had disparaged the dignity of the house of Essex", and Penelope could say "amen" to that. She stayed good friends with Frances till her death, yet her hopes must have been set higher. Essex's marriage could not fulfil her ambitions for him and her Devereux pride. Wat's marriage was different. By the spring of 1589 he too had a wife and at least she had money.

～

Penelope's younger brother Wat was nineteen and still in the Huntingdons' care when his marriage was arranged. He had left York in June 1584 to go to Christ Church College, Oxford, and he was too young to join Essex and Leicester in the Netherlands later the following year. In 1588, however, it was his turn to begin soldiering, under the watchful eye of Sir Roger Williams in France; and in April 1589 he was with Sir Roger again when Essex joined them on board the *Swiftsure*, heading for Portugal.

Before they sailed, however, Wat was married to his former "school-mate", eighteen-year-old Margaret Dakins (later the diarist Lady Margaret Hoby). Margaret was heiress to a huge estate in Yorkshire and her parents had sent her to the Huntingdons' "school" to acquire courtly manners and an aristocratic husband. Wat, some eighteen months older than Margaret, was still there when Margaret arrived. Penelope and Dorothy probably left just before, or soon after; and Lady Huntingdon's lessons in the Puritan way of life doubtless had more effect without them around. For the rest of Margaret's life her daily routine began and ended with prayer and devotion. The countess could pride herself on turning out an obedient, submissive and pious wife.

Considering Penelope's response to her guardians' choice of husband, Dorothy's runaway wedding and Essex's independent character, the Huntingdons might have realized Wat was a marriage risk. He had all the Devereux charm and high spirits and Margaret's quiet piety was unlikely to appeal to him. But the Huntingdons were not concerned with character mismatch. Margaret had money and was in their care to make a noble alliance. Wat needed a fortune and had all the breeding the Dakins could wish for. It was a guardian's duty to negotiate their union, and it had recently taken place when Wat sailed to Portugal, not returning till the summer.

Penelope, meanwhile, was experiencing a hiccup in Lord Rich's spirit of cooperation: he was making difficulties about the Hotmans. When Penelope made Jean her secretary, after Leicester's death left him jobless, she also gave him and Jeanne lodgings in London, probably in St Bartholomew's. And Lord Rich was not happy.

Penelope wrote to Jeanne on 11 September to reassure her they could stay there for the moment. She knew Jeanne well enough to admit she was furious with Lord Rich. "I assure you I have never been so cross with him as I am now for your sake," she told Jeanne. She had gone to Leighs to have it out with him, but she hoped to return to London within a fortnight "because I do nothing all day long except quarrel with Lord Rich about this matter". Between domestic arrangements and gossip, Penelope slipped in a one-line instruction for Jean to deliver a message to King James, but most of the letter is devoted to a new hairpiece Jeanne could make for her.

Jeanne's growing family meant she was no longer in attendance on Penelope, but her mistress still found work for her. She was good at making headdresses and her ladyship wanted, as soon as possible, a hair support that was close fitting over the ears, with a point at the front. If Jeanne could not find blonde hair to cover it, Penelope would do so after she received it, presumably using her own. It was typical of Penelope to remain concerned and helpful to her old servants. She might be busy, ill or pregnant, yet they could rely on her to write letters for them, plead their case to important people about lawsuits, find them new jobs, attend their weddings and be godmother to their children. She accumulated a small army of godchildren, including: Dorothy's daughter, Penelope Perrot; two of Essex's children; her cousin Elizabeth Vernon's daughter, Penelope; Sir Robert Sidney's son; Hilliard's daughter; at least one of her Knollys cousins; and various offspring of her country neighbours and French diplomats in London. And her own family continued to grow.

Despite her quarrels with Lord Rich, by the end of 1589 Penelope was pregnant again. The following spring, while she awaited the birth of her baby, Lettice was in town, staying at Leicester House. Lettice was still sorting out Leicester's debts and Essex tackled her on the subject of Wanstead. Elizabeth, acknowledging Lettice's rights to the properties Leicester left her, was encouraging Essex to take over Wanstead. It was a fitting country estate for the queen's favourite, somewhere he could entertain foreign royalty and diplomats on Elizabeth's behalf. From Court at Greenwich, Essex wrote to Lettice in March to enquire about obtaining her outstanding lease on the property: "Though I confess I do greatly affect it, yet I will not desire it so as your ladyship shall lose one penny profit or one hour of pleasure that you may have there."

The queen was pressing Essex to sort it out so that he could entertain her at Wanstead on May Day. He knew he was rushing the deal but he was anxious to be fair to his mother and added: "Whatsoever you ask I will agree unto it." The one thing he couldn't agree to was visiting her: "The queen hath stayed me here this day, but tomorrow I will see you if I can."

Elizabeth was playing power games with Lettice's son. She knew Lettice was in town and there was sweet revenge in making it difficult for Essex to keep appointments with her. It flattered Elizabeth's vanity to have a handsome young courtier dancing to her tune. She was approaching sixty and her face would soon look "wrinkled; her eyes small yet pleasant; her nose a little hooked, her lips narrow and her teeth black". Treating Essex like a younger lover was part of the fantasy she had built up around the "Virgin Queen". Yet beneath the obscene charade Elizabeth also felt genuine fondness for Essex and Penelope. Again and again she behaved like a fairy godmother, treating them with the love and indulgence that flows from family ties – and that only families understand.

The Wanstead deal did not go smoothly, and months would pass with sharp letters between Essex and Lettice before it was his. But there were happier family matters to attend to. In June Essex wrote to the new king of France inviting him to be godfather to Penelope's baby. Henri of Navarre had succeeded to the French throne as Henri IV the previous summer and Essex was convinced France was now "the theatre and stage whereon the greatest actions are acted". He had long admired Henri and supported him against the French Catholic faction and threats of Spanish aggression. Now he wanted to be seen as Henri's chief supporter, and Penelope shared his political ambition. Their interest in French affairs went back to childhood days at Chartley when young Gabriel Montgomery lived with them. Now in London, Penelope cultivated the friendship of French diplomats and émigrés, and Jeanne and Jean Hotman were her link to them.

Early in 1590, she sent greetings via Jean to Monsieur de Buzanval, one of Henri's representatives in London. She also arranged for Nicholas Hilliard to paint another miniature of her. It was to be a gift for the French ambassador, Seigneur de Beauvoir la Nocle, and whether it was a fresh likeness or a copy of her gift to King James, there is no knowing. The evidence for it exists in Penelope's letters, and for years it has been assumed that none of the Hilliard pictures of her survive. But there is a miniature in the present royal collection at Windsor traditionally titled "Possibly Lady Rich" and experts say there is no reason to doubt it.

Writing to Jeanne, probably from Leighs, Penelope enclosed a letter for Hilliard and instructions for Jean. Hotman was to hand Hilliard his letter, collect the portrait, present it to the ambassador and give him her apologies for not writing or presenting it personally. She had been ill again with a heavy cold, and her pregnancy was well advanced. The good news, Penelope went on, was that her mother-in-law "has promised me her house in Stepney, which will be ready for me ere long". Jeanne was too much in Penelope's confidence to need further explanation, but evidently Penelope wanted a lodging on the outskirts of town, and there she gave birth to her second son, early in August. On 19 August the child was baptized at Stratford-le-Bow and named Henry for his French godfather. By early September Penelope was sufficiently recovered to leave the house and on 6 September she was "churched" after her safe delivery.

Penelope had provided Lord Rich with a second sturdy boy and he joined Lucy, Essex and Robert in the nursery at Leighs. Now she could separate herself from her husband knowing she had given him an "heir and spare". She spent the next month in the country, not at Leighs but "a hundred miles from my house". Her children and Lord Rich's demands for her help would always draw her back to Leighs for long and frequent visits, but in future her life would be her own and her duties at Leighs would only be part of it. Her brother was coming to the height of his power. Supporting his political ambitions was of paramount importance to her. There were other changes in her life with Lord Rich, too. Her future children would not be his.

Three months after the birth of her second son, the Accession Day tilt marked the start of a new relationship for Penelope.

PART III

Love at Last

NOVEMBER 1590–MARCH 1601

Chapter Fourteen

NOVEMBER 1590–JUNE 1591

"Comes Sir Charles Blount … Rich in his colours"

– George Peele, 1590

The Accession Day tilt on 17 November 1590 was to be even more spectacular than usual. For weeks the Earl of Essex had been planning to upstage all challengers in the joust with his costume and speeches. But another knight, who would go down in history as the greatest Elizabethan general, was also making special plans, though his were more subtle.

Accession Day marked the glorious moment in 1558 when Elizabeth inherited the crown from her Catholic sister Queen Mary. It also signalled the start of the Court winter season and the run-up to Christmastide. Summer was over, Elizabeth was back in her capital after her progress; and her councillors had returned from their country estates to their freshly fumigated town houses, hoping the summer plague was over.

Londoners turned out in thousands, church bells rang, cannons fired, trumpets sounded, choristers sang, bonfires blazed, and from the raised pulpit outside St Paul's the Bishop of London preached his Accession Day sermon. Anyone day-dreaming in the large crowd, shuffling and listening in the open air, could be forgiven for wondering whether they were marking the day when the Virgin Mary ascended the throne of England, or praying to Elizabeth, the Virgin Queen in heaven.

The best entertainment was in the tiltyard at Whitehall Palace where more than twenty knights jousted on horseback. The main palace stood on the river side of King Street and its gardens ran down to the Thames. On the opposite side of the road were tennis courts, a cock-pit, bowling alleys, a permanent tiltyard with space for 12,000 spectators, and viewing stands, entry price twelve pence. Along one side of the yard was a gallery, lined with colourful shields from previous tournaments, where the queen and her guests gathered to look down on the tournament. Beneath them the crowd roared encouragement and gasped with fear as the heavy horses thundered past along the barriers. At each end the knights would rein in, horses snorting and stamping, turn and lower their lances once more, and charge again. For hours the tiltyard rang with the thud of hooves, the clash of weapons and the shouts of the crowd. And as each new pair of knights entered, mottoes and colours brightly painted on their shields, they paraded their servants and followers in matching liveries and embroidered sashes, repeating their mottoes and themes.

With drums beating, trumpets playing and flags flying against grey November skies, it was a fantasy of chivalry and of days nearly past, but not quite. The dangers were real – there were always injuries and wounds, sometimes fatal. It needed skill, energy and courage to survive, let alone to win, and it was chiefly a young man's sport. The phallic symbols of the lances and swords were lost on no one, certainly not on Elizabeth and her ladies.

For Penelope the tournament was, as usual, a family affair. Three of her Knollys uncles were taking part, Lettice's brothers William, Robert and Thomas, as well as her uncle by marriage, Sir Philip Boteler, husband of Lettice's youngest sister, Katherine. Then came rash Robert Carey, son of Lord Hunsdon; Thomas Sidney, youngest of the Sidney brothers; and Everard Digby, kinsman to the Coleshill Digbys.

When her brother Essex entered, he stole the show. Dressed head to toe in black armour, standing in a black chariot drawn by "coal black steeds", with plumes "black as raven's wing", he paraded round the yard with "all his company in funeral black". It was awesome. Court poet George Peele, describing the event in his poem *Polyhymnia*, said Essex was still mourning "Sweet Sidney". Others wondered if he was really grieving for Elizabeth's favour, which he had not yet fully recovered since his marriage.

Up in the gallery the queen and her guests smiled and watched, applauding the winners as they rode back and bowed to her. Essex, of course, rode more recklessly and shattered more lances than anyone. But it was the next two knights who captured Penelope's gaze. One was Thomas Vavasour, brother of Anne, who caused such a scandal when Penelope first came to Court. The other was Sir Charles Blount, a handsome, dark-haired man whom Penelope had known for some years. His family had long been courtiers, though with little power or wealth. As he rode into the yard she could see that his armour and liveries were "or and azure", gold and blue.

They were colours Philip had often used. The Sidney crest was a gold arrowhead on a blue background, and who could forget him in his blue and gold armour at the Whitsun tilt almost ten years ago? Philip's poems were still only in manuscript but his death had started a craze for the sonnets and it was no state secret that Penelope had been his heroine. Was Charles signalling that *he* was now her champion; that he worshipped her beauty and would fight for her honour?

As the light failed on that November afternoon, Elizabeth led her guests down from the gallery and into the palace for supper, masquing and music. By the end of the evening the whisperers could be in little doubt that Lady Rich had an admirer. And to make it abundantly clear, Peele's *Polyhymnia* soon spelt it out:

> Comes Sir Charles Blount in or and azure dight [dressed]
> Rich in his colours, richer in his thoughts,
> Rich in his fortune, honour, arms and art.

It was an obvious echo of Philip's lines:

> Toward Aurora's court a nymph doth dwell,
> Rich in all beauties which man's eye can see …
> Rich in the treasure of deserved renown …

~

The one thing in which Sir Charles Blount was not rich was money. His father James, sixth Baron Mountjoy, had squandered his fortune on studying alchemy, "the search for the philosopher's stone", hoping to turn base metals into silver and gold, and speculating in mining ventures. When James died in 1581, Charles's elder brother William inherited the title and carried on ruining the family "with untimely prodigality".

Once upon a time the Blounts had been wealthy and powerful. Like the Devereux they came from noble stock, originally Norman, and though not quite so illustrious as Penelope's family, they had served the country well, often close to the crown. Sometimes exceptionally close. There were two main branches of the Blounts, both descended from Lady Isolda and Sir John Blount, who died in 1358. Their elder son, Sir John Blount of Soddington, built up estates in Shropshire and Worcestershire, and from him descended the Blounts of Kidderminster and Kinlet. Most famous among them was Bessie Blount, who occupied Henry VIII's bed shortly before Mary Boleyn, Penelope's great-grandmother. Bessie's son, Harry Fitzroy, was the only bastard acknowledged by the king, who treated Harry as a possible heir until the birth of his legitimate son, the future Edward VI.

The other branch of the family came from the third son of Lady Isolda and Sir John, whose descendants acquired the title Baron Mountjoy and numerous estates in Derbyshire and Dorset. William, fourth Baron

Mountjoy, was chamberlain to Henry VIII's first wife, Katherine, and held various offices for Henry. His daughter Gertrude married the king's cousin, Henry Courtenay, and for a time she was the first peeress of the realm. In the Shrove Tuesday revels of 1522 she joined Mary and Anne Boleyn among the select group of young ladies who defended the mock castle, "Château Vert", against a hail of sweetmeats and fruit from the king and his squires.

William Blount, the fourth baron, began the family reputation for bookishness and theology. He was a leading patron of the Dutch humanist Erasmus, and a friend of Sir Thomas More. His offspring inherited his humanist interests and love of scholarship, together with the Dorset estates of Hooke and Canford Magna. Unfortunately, their ownership and mining rights to the estates had been disputed for years by Penelope's guardian Lord Huntingdon, and Charles's brother was continuing the long and costly lawsuits. Being a second son, Charles knew he must live by his wits or his sword; and the motto he adopted in childhood, "*Ad reaedificandam antiquam domum*", "To restore the family fortunes", suggests he intended to do more than earn his own living.

Born in 1563, the same year as Penelope, Charles went to Oxford; left without taking a degree; moved to London to study law at Clifford's Inn; and in June 1579 transferred to the more prestigious Middle Temple, next door to Leicester's town house. From the Temple gardens the students and lawyers could watch boats taxiing to and from the river steps at Leicester House, and the earl's horses and carriages coming to the yard doors in the Strand, opposite St Clement Danes Church. On summer nights music and merrymaking drifted across from open windows, and at Christmastide the residents in Leicester House were guests of honour at the Temple revels.

Charles's connection with Leicester went back generations. His Midlands kinsmen, the Kidderminster and Kinlet Blounts, formed a network of staff and supporters for Leicester and the Dudley family. Sir Thomas Blount was the most senior member of Leicester's household for years and he was related by marriage to Leicester's mother. When Thomas's sons followed his career path, Edward minded Leicester's affairs in and around Kenilworth; and Christopher, Penelope's future stepfather, became Leicester's master of horse and went with him to war in the Netherlands.

Charles was "about twenty years of age, of a brown hair, a sweet face, a most neat composure, and tall in his person" when his brother William took him to Court to see the queen at dinner. But Charles was not a typical courtier. As one contemporary put it, "there was in his nature a kind of backwardness which did not befriend him, nor suit with the humour of the Court". He was shy, scholarly, modest and reserved. When Elizabeth caught sight of him, so the story goes, and summoned him to kiss her hand, he was overcome with confusion. Ignoring his blushes, she assured him, "fail you not to come to Court, and I will bethink myself how to do you good". Charles, however, wanted to make his mark before lounging around at Court gambling the hours away. In 1584 he entered parliament and in the summer of 1585 he became captain of a company in Sir John Norris's army heading for the Netherlands.

Sir John had learnt soldiering in the brutal school of Irish warfare, serving under Penelope's father who praised him highly. Since then Norris had become the finest leader in Elizabeth's army and he would remain Charles's mentor till his death. At the request of the Protestant rebels in the Netherlands, Elizabeth put Sir John in charge of the first troops she sent there, and Charles went with him. But during a skirmish in October Charles received a bullet wound in the thigh. Norris praised him in dispatches to the privy council and sent him home for a while, reporting: "The bullets are taken out and he is in no danger." The following year, 1586, after Leicester took over supreme command, Charles returned to the front and was involved in the skirmish at Zutphen where Philip Sidney was fatally wounded. Unlike Essex, however, Charles stayed in the Netherlands until Elizabeth ordered him home, and he returned to Court with a knighthood late in 1587.

During the Armada crisis the following year some accounts put Charles on board Lord Henry Seymour's flagship, the *Rainbow*, one of the queen's newest and largest warships. Another claims he was in command of a man-of-war named the *Lion*. And a contemporary Spanish account says he was on Drake's *Revenge* with the Earl of Northumberland, both in Drake's cabin when a bullet went clean through it. At Leicester's funeral soon afterwards, the Midlands branch of the Blount family was strongly represented, but from the Mountjoy side it was Charles not his elder brother who attended and had the honour to be one of the six pall-bearers.

Charles was now twenty-five. Service abroad had matured him. His "forehead was broad and high; his eyes great, black and lovely; his nose something low and short, and a little blunt in the end; his chin round; his cheeks full, round and ruddy; his countenance cheerful". The description, written later by his devoted secretary, Fynes Moryson, was indubitably biased, though it was honest enough to point out that he "had little hair on his body" and what he had was "blackish" and thin:

The crown of his head was in his latter days something bald, as the forepart naturally curled; he only used the barber for his head, for the hair on his chin (growing slowly) and that on his cheeks and throat, he used almost daily to cut it with his scissors, keeping it so low with his own hand that it could scarce be discerned, as likewise himself kept the hair of his upper lip something short, only suffering that under his nether lip to grow at length and full.

In 1587, newly knighted, Sir Charles began to climb the Court ladder. He still drew his pay as an army captain though Elizabeth, anxious to keep him out of the firing line, handed him several salaried positions. By the end of 1589 he was keeper of the New Forest and a gentleman pensioner – one of the handpicked soldiers who stood near her at all times. It was probably about this time that he aroused Essex's jealousy. After Elizabeth presented Charles with a gold queen from her chess set "in token of her favour", Essex acidly remarked: "now I perceive every fool must have a favour." Charles was not going to ignore an insult like that and challenged him to a duel. Under Elizabeth's orders duelling was banned, yet they went ahead and Essex lost, "hurt in the thigh, and disarmed". According to the story, recorded later by Penelope's nephew-in-law, Elizabeth heard about it and "swore by God's death it was fit that some one or other should take him [Essex] down and teach him better manners, otherwise there would be no rule with him".

It was Essex and Charles's only recorded quarrel. Essex soon realized Charles was not challenging him as the queen's chief favourite. Charles was not a ladies' man and he never played the flattering lover to Elizabeth. He was not a mirror image of Essex, as has been claimed. Charles was a reflection of Penelope's father: a complex man, quiet and serious, a listener rather than a talker. "He loved private retiredness with good fare and some few choice friends." His indulgences were books, fine wine, good food, and, unfortunately, the new fashion for smoking tobacco. And there would be only one woman in his life.

On Accession Day 1590 when Sir Charles Blount rode into the tiltyard he was one of the queen's favourites, but it was Lady Rich who ruled his heart.

≈

Penelope was twenty-seven, radiant and confident. She was beautiful, she had four lovely children, a delightful country home, a very rich husband, a powerful brother and an eminent circle of friends and relations. She had known Sir Charles for at least five years. How far she was already in love with him, only she could tell. She had done her best with an arranged marriage to an apparently suitable, but incompatible, husband. If she had been in love with Charles for long, she had at least waited until she had given Lord Rich an heir and spare before she began a clandestine affair.

Over Christmastide and New Year, Penelope had much to occupy her apart from thoughts of Charles. Her baby Henry was growing well, so were his brother and sisters. She had no need to be anxious for them, but Essex's wife was expecting their first child soon, and Frances had had problems with her pregnancies before. Everyone was hoping for a son and heir for Essex, and Lettice was in London while Frances was lying in at Walsingham House in Seething Lane. Frances was always happiest at her mother's homes, in the city and at Barn Elms, and Penelope was a frequent visitor. She knew the Walsinghams' household so well she purposely delayed leaving town in order to attend the wedding of one of Frances's ladies.

On New Year's Day Broughton, keeping his father-in-law up to date with news from London, wrote to Richard Bagot: "The Countess of Essex doth within eight days expect her time, and the good Lady Rich is with her." Essex's marriage could have caused problems for Bagot's daughter Margaret and her husband William Trew. Frances might not have wanted them to continue managing Essex's households. It was a relief that Broughton could report: "The countess maketh much of my sister Trew." As for Broughton's wife, Anne, she always got on well with Lady Rich; and after the Hotmans left England for France in the autumn of 1590, Penelope needed her company.

On New Year's Day Lady Rich had just sent word that she would have supper with Anne the next day, Broughton continued. She had also told Anne "that she doth not greatly care how extraordinarily she be used". The problem was significant enough for Anne to mention to her husband, and Broughton repeated it to Bagot without explanation. Someone was saying something against Lady Rich, and Broughton assumed Bagot already knew about it. If the whisperers around Court were spreading stories that Penelope and Charles were lovers, Penelope did not care. How true it might be was another matter, and at that date it probably wasn't.

Over the following ten years Penelope and Charles took considerable care to shield their relationship from general scrutiny: not living together, not mentioning each other in letters and preserving the semblance of Penelope's marriage. It seems unlikely then that Charles intended his tiltyard appearance to announce to the world that they were lovers. If he was already sleeping with her, it would be foolhardy to publish the fact: and Charles was never that. Elizabeth took a dim view of flagrant extra-marital activities, but within the fantasy world of the tournament, and the conventions of chivalry, it was all right for him to declare his passion for Penelope's charm and beauty. Charles's appearance on the tiltyard meant only that Lady Rich had won his heart, and possibly that he had captured hers.

A few days after Broughton's letter, Frances's baby arrived, and the whole family gave thanks for Essex's first son and heir, naturally named Robert. On his tiny shoulders rested all the royal ancestry, hopes and honour that fuelled his father's ambitions. At his baptism on 22 January, recorded at St Olave's

Church on the corner of Seething Lane, Lettice was his godmother. His two godfathers were his great-grandfather, Sir Francis Knollys, and Lord Rich, still playing an important part in family affairs.

As winter gave way to spring, "When birds do sing", there was more time for love and light hearts. Charles was under instructions from Elizabeth not to go abroad with Sir John Norris's army, which had been drafted to Brittany to assist the Protestant French, under siege from Spanish forces. For a while he was with them at Dover, but from now onwards he was largely an absentee captain, on full pay.

At Wanstead, April was a heady month. On Elizabeth's behalf, Essex entertained the French ambassador who had come to summon help against the Spaniards. For two days Wanstead was awash with music and feasting. The visitors arrived on Friday afternoon, 9 April, stayed for supper and overnight and on Saturday they enjoyed everything that Wanstead and money could offer. Having dined royally, at the end of Saturday afternoon they returned to London. Catering for them was a major operation and Essex's steward had to call in extra supplies: sixteen pounds of bread from the bakers at Stratford a few miles away, and another twelve pounds plus quantities of flour, from Lady Rich's bakers at Leighs.

They were probably not the only things Essex called on Penelope to provide. Frances was not cut out for official entertaining. She never seemed keen to be part of Essex's public life, and at times he paid her little attention. Penelope was a natural political hostess and with the help of the Hotmans she had developed good contact with the French diplomatic corps in London. Over supper at Wanstead she could talk easily in fluent French, her dark eyes and her beauty shining in the candlelight. When the tables were cleared for music and dancing, it was Penelope who sang to the lutes and stepped out to dance the galliards and corrantos written for her. And as the bucks were driven through the forests around Wanstead, Penelope was there aiming a bow with the best of them, and riding fast with the wind in her golden hair.

When the French embassy left, there was no reason to shut up Wanstead. The hunting was superb in Waltham Forest fringing the estate, and a little northwards lay Epping, where Elizabeth had her own hunting lodge. On 21 May Arthur Throckmorton was part of the Wanstead house party. Since his trip with Lord Rich and Count Laski, his Court career had not run entirely smoothly, and he was no great fan of the Cecils, which made him a useful ally for Essex. Soon after his stay at Wanstead he sent Essex an expensive pair of pistols. Penelope was also at Wanstead in May, staying in her own rooms and hunting in Waltham Forest, where she killed a buck. Soon after midsummer, while the days were long and evening light lingered over Wanstead's gardens, Penelope became pregnant with Charles's first child. In days to come when they could risk, and afford, a home of their own, it would be Wanstead.

Wanstead held their happiest memories. It was the house Lord Leicester bought from Lord Rich's father shortly before he married Lettice, and it stood in forty acres of walled grounds and gardens, surrounded by fields and forests. By the time Leicester had finished improving it there were twin lodges widely spaced at the front, a broad sweep to the door and splendid guest chambers round the quadrangle. At first Lettice loved it, but after "the Noble Imp" died there she tended to use her other home, Bennington, north of Hatfield. Settling Leicester's estates took years and Wanstead was not formally transferred to Essex until 1593. Since 1590, however, he'd been using it to entertain government guests and close friends. And now that Essex no longer feared Sir Charles Blount as a rival for Elizabeth's favour, he was a welcome addition to Essex's inner circle.

It could not have taken Penelope long to be sure she was pregnant again: she had already given birth to five children. And if anyone else had doubts about whose baby she was carrying, Charles did not. The child was the first he named in his will, and all of Penelope's subsequent children were his beneficiaries. But that lay years ahead. In the summer of 1591 the future was uncertain for this baby. Charles was the love of her life, yet she could not know that he would be hers till he died. And she could not know how Lord Rich would react. Legally Penelope was his wife and property.

Chapter Fifteen

AUGUST 1591–MAY 1593

"O mistress mine! where are you roaming?"
— William Shakespeare, *Twelfth Night*, c. 1599

ord Rich knew quite a lot about bastards. As a Justice of the Peace he heard numerous cases of illegitimate children dumped on the parish. Only a few months before there was a "bastard child born of the body of Helen Clarke in the parish of Felsted". William Chapman, Lord Rich decided, had until Christmas to prove the boy was not his, or else pay twelve pence a week to the parish until the lad could fend for himself. Then there was the man and woman guilty under the 1575 statute "concerning a child begotten and born out of lawful matrimony". The couple must be "together at one time tied to a cart and drawn twice through the town of Felsted and be well whipped upon their naked bodies", Lord Rich decreed. It was not the sort of treatment he would want anyone to sniggeringly suggest his wife should undergo.

In August Penelope was back at Leighs, and it was not in *her* best interests to go public on the paternity of her child. But why did Lord Rich agree to hush things up? He is always portrayed as a wimp and a cynic, not brave enough to confront Charles, and too keen on keeping in with Penelope's powerful brother. But he also had his own family honour to consider. To expose her would compromise his position in the county, let alone make him a laughing stock at Court. There is also the possibility that, in his own way, he loved her. Clearly she was unhappy with the marriage, but Charles's later claims that Rich treated her badly are a single-source story.

Lord Rich was not the most agreeable and intelligent of men, yet he could still appreciate that Penelope had given him his heir and spare. She had not gambled his fortune away. She had not tried to poison him, as other unhappy wives were known to do; nor hired assassins to waylay him on a dark night as he rode around his estates. She supported him in public, attending Court at

New Year together. She even got on well with his mother. And he could see how much Penelope loved Charles. Perhaps Lord Rich hoped it would pass. In the early months of her affair, when her first bastard child was born, he could not know that if he accepted this baby into his household there would be others; that her love for Charles would deepen as years went by. For the moment at least, what mattered was to preserve the protocols of their marriage.

His own four children must remain under the Rich family roof. Lucy, Essex, Robert and Henry were none of them yet ten years old. Robert and Henry were his heirs and there was no reason to separate them from their sisters. Later critics would brand Penelope a whore because she was often at Leighs. Of course she was: she adored her children. Lord Rich placed no bar on her visits and she was free to take her mother and sisters there with her. So long as Lord Rich permitted it, Penelope would want to spend time with them. To walk away from them was unthinkable. Anyway, to live in open adultery was out of the question. Charles had no establishment of his own and though he was technically heir to his brother, William might yet marry and produce a son. Penelope and Charles would have to conduct their affair discreetly, at Essex's town house and at Wanstead.

At Wanstead, however, the party was over for the summer. Essex was on his way to war in France. Elizabeth had agreed to send another army, as well as Norris's, to assist Henri IV against his Catholic and Spanish enemies. On 22 July she signed Essex's commission as "Captain General of the English forces sent into Normandy" and he set off, taking brother Wat with him. Wat's marriage was not going well. His high spirits didn't square with Margaret's piety. Since moving to their Yorkshire estate, Hackness, he seems to have preferred roistering with the young county squires, and Huntingdon had to lecture him for not spending more time with his wife.

Essex's marriage was in trouble, too, and he set sail without a word to Frances. He was used to women with wit and sparkle, like Penelope and his mother. Even Dorothy, relatively tactless, was a forceful character. Frances was different: submissive, obedient and pleading. She was deeply upset at "your going away without taking leave of me". When a messenger reached her with a letter from Essex, she replied promising to "strive to overcome those extreme passions which my affection hath brought me to, and I will have the more care of my self for your little one's sake". Marriage to Frances had not ended Essex's habit of bedding Elizabeth's ladies, and when he set off with Wat to besiege Rouen, both his current mistress, Elizabeth Southwell, and his wife were pregnant. Essex, now twenty-five, had become the leader of the fast-living younger courtiers who shared his quest for martial honour and excitement.

At Leighs, Penelope was enjoying the summer. The children were growing up. She was in love – with a passion that was returned – and she was expecting Charles's baby. One August weekend she had a visit from Arthur Throckmorton. He rode over from Colchester to stay at Leighs, and Penelope, knowing he was useful to Essex, treated him as a welcome guest. His sister Bess was one of Elizabeth's ladies, and she and Penelope had a lot in common. They were both strong-minded and beautiful, with high foreheads and pretty mouths, though Bess had a longer nose and chin. Both had been left fatherless at a young age and both had formidable mothers.

Lady Anne Throckmorton was determined to make a good marriage for her only daughter, Bess, yet she consistently supported her objections. One suitor was dismissed because Bess was too young at seventeen; another because of Bess's "unmeetness yet to marry: not for her age only but for the littleness of growth and the unaptness I do find in her to match with any". In fact, Lady Anne was waiting for a post in Elizabeth's household for Bess, to give her the best chance of making the best match; and in 1584, when Bess was nearly twenty, she became a gentlewoman of the privy chamber.

At that point Essex had not arrived at Court, and Sir Walter Ralegh was challenging Leicester as Elizabeth's new and younger favourite. His proud character and swashbuckling charm endeared him to Bess as well as Elizabeth, but to few others. Ralegh was not A-list and there was something dubious about him. His poetry and soaring imagination were admirable, but his sceptic views on religion and his interest in science and mathematics were a little unorthodox. When Essex did appear at Court, his meteoric rise eclipsed Ralegh and caused friction between them. But in 1591 Ralegh still carried weight with the queen and he needed to be handled carefully. He was a maverick who could easily swap sides. In the early months of the year their shared enthusiasm for war in France brought Ralegh and Essex together for a time.

While Essex kept on good terms with Ralegh, Penelope made friends with Bess; and Bess was flattered. Penelope, with her wit and intelligence, her wealth and beauty, and her closeness to Essex, wielded a lot of influence. Like her, Bess was particularly close to her brother. Quite close enough for Arthur to know in August that Bess was carrying Ralegh's baby.

Elizabeth was not going to like it. Bess needed her permission to marry, and Ralegh was supposed to be devoted to Elizabeth, not bed-hopping around her staff. Arthur knew that Essex had ridden out a storm when Elizabeth discovered his marriage to Frances: if anyone could help Bess, Penelope could. What Arthur didn't know during that weekend at Leighs was that Penelope was carrying Charles's baby. As well as helping Bess in order to keep Ralegh on Essex's side, Penelope could sympathize with Bess's predicament. When Bess and Ralegh needed it, they could count on Penelope and Essex for support. But before that time came, there was devastating news from Normandy.

On 8 September, outside Rouen, Wat was trapped in an ambush, shot in the face and killed. Essex went into a state of mental and physical collapse. His campaign was not going well anyway, and Elizabeth was fuming over her army's costly failures. Now even his enemies sent Essex their sympathy for "the late accident of your noble brother". Elizabeth, alarmed for his safety as well as the waste of money, instructed him to return. He made two brief trips to Court to keep her informed, and then ignored her advice to call off the campaign. Elizabeth was incensed. She wrote suggesting he must be "senseless" and ordering him "upon the sight hereof, to make your speedy return".

For a time Essex's family feared that he was indeed senseless with grief. Matters were made worse for them all when Wat's widow, Margaret, rushed back into the marriage market even before his body had been shipped home. It was a tactless move, though it was not entirely Margaret's fault. She was a very wealthy widow and under pressure from several suitors. Lawyer Broughton, writing to Bagot in Staffordshire on 12 November, alerted him that Mistress Walter Devereux had come to London with her mother and was staying with her former guardians. Within days it transpired that the Huntingdons were arranging to marry her to another of their wards, and on 22 December she became the wife of Thomas Sidney, Philip's youngest brother.

~

Penelope wisely kept clear of Margaret's wedding plans, perhaps because Sir Robert Sidney and his wife Barbara had become her good friends. But she did get involved in Bess and Ralegh's marriage. Like Penelope, Bess had passed the fourth month of her pregnancy and could be pretty sure it would proceed to term. On 19 November, Arthur noted in his diary, "*le jour quand je savoye le marriage de ma soeur* [sic]". He always defaulted to French when he was worried, and he was certainly worried about his sister's secret marriage. The best they could hope was to keep it from Elizabeth as long as possible.

While Penelope waited for Essex and Wat's body to return from France, there came another death that touched her closely. Lord Rich's mother was buried at St Gregory's Church, near St Paul's, on 21 December. Penelope had little in common with her mother-in-law, for the Dowager Lady Rich followed the Puritan faith, like her son. But she had treated Penelope fairly, despite the obvious failures of the marriage. She had remarried just over a year before, yet she was still known as Lady Rich at Court, where she attended and exchanged gifts with the queen. To Lord Rich it was doubtless something of a relief that his mother died before the birth of Penelope's next baby: she would have been seriously embarrassed by its paternity.

Elizabeth's Court was not a permissive society. Compared with the Catholic Church, the Church of England took a less dramatic approach to the seven deadly sins, yet the queen considered lechery at Court deadly serious. Illicit sex and unauthorized marriage were threats to the social hierarchy and property deals that she presided over. Besides, lax morals among her attendants were a stain on her princely image and Elizabeth did not want every foreign ambassador gleefully spreading the word that her Court harboured louche, layabout fornicators – even if it was sometimes true.

Obvious flirting and kissing were taboo. Some culprits got their ears boxed, others were banished from Court for a while. Giving birth to an illegitimate child was living dangerously – and Penelope knew it. When she first came to Court she had seen what happened to Anne Vavasour. Penelope might be in love and ecstatically happy about her baby but the future for an adulterous courtier was uncertain. Elizabeth was bound to be told by someone, some time, and it would damage Charles's career, at least temporarily.

Essex's libidinous habits were becoming a problem. Lettice mentioned his lady friends in her letters and Dorothy wrote to him hinting at similar concerns: "I infinitely long to hear that you were freed of your ill companion which is unworthy to be entertained by you." In January 1592, when Frances gave birth to their second son, she may not have known that Mistress Southwell had given him a son only weeks earlier, but she probably guessed he was unfaithful. Frances's baby, named Walter in honour of his dead uncle, was baptized at Walsingham House on 21 January, with Dorothy's husband Sir Thomas Perrot and Sir William Knollys as godfathers, and Frances's mother, Ursula, Lady Walsingham, as godmother. Briefly it seemed Frances had also given her husband a spare as well as an heir. But the baby lived less than a month and was buried at All Hallows Church, Barking, on 19 February. Nine days later Wat was finally laid to rest beside Earl Walter at St Peter's Church in Carmarthen.

Penelope, meanwhile, was awaiting the birth of Charles's baby at Leicester House, soon to be renamed Essex House, where she had gone for her lying-in. Her rooms had changed since Lord Leicester furnished them for her when she first came to Court. In 1590, after Elizabeth grabbed the house, most of the contents were sold off to settle Leicester's debts to the crown. But the house had been returned to Lettice and refitted partly with furnishings from Wanstead. Lady Rich's chambers now had a black and gold colour scheme. The great canopied bed was curtained in black and gold velvet, taffeta and damask, trimmed with gold lace. More black velvet covered the gold-framed chairs and stools, scattered with cushions of cloth of silver. In these regal rooms Penelope's baby was born and on 30 March, across the road at St Clement Danes Church, the baby was baptized Penelope, "the daughter of the honourable Lord Rich".

There is no knowing what it cost Charles Blount to have his child named

Rich, and to know she would grow up under Lord Rich's roof at Leighs. But there was no choice. Penelope and Charles had embarked on a way of life that could have spelt disaster: he was one of the queen's favourites; she was married to one of the wealthiest men in the country. And it was clear this was not to be a short-lived affair. To have one illegitimate child might be a misfortune, and forgiven; to have two – or more – was not careless, it was deliberate.

Just how dangerously they were living, Bess and Ralegh were about to find out. The day before baby Penelope was baptized, Bess gave birth to a son, and as promised the Devereux stood by them. On the last day of February, while Ralegh was with the queen's ships at Chatham, Bess went to her brother's house at Mile End, "to lie here", Arthur noted in his diary. Despite rumours about their marriage, Ralegh was denying everything. Early in March he assured Robert Cecil he would have told him "before any man living" if he was married. On 29 March Bess "was delivered of a boy between two and three in the afternoon", and Arthur sent the news to Ralegh. When the little boy was baptized Damerei, on Monday 10 April, the ceremony took place not at Mile End but at St Clement Danes Church again, suggesting Bess and her baby had moved to Essex House. In a show of solidarity, Essex stood godfather, together with Arthur, and Lady Anne Throckmorton was the boy's godmother.

Four weeks later Bess was back at her job at Court as if nothing had happened. A week later Ralegh put to sea. But soon after he returned Elizabeth learnt the truth, and early in August she ordered them both to the Tower. Throughout the sweltering late summer, the hottest anyone could remember, Elizabeth kept them there. In mid-September Ralegh was released, to undertake another naval expedition, but not Bess. In October the plague in London was so serious that Elizabeth withdrew to Hampton Court. Yet still Bess was detained in the Tower. When she was finally released three days before Christmas, she was alone. Damerei either succumbed to the plague in prison, or died somewhere far from her.

Penelope was not around when Bess was taken to the Tower. In June she went to see her mother and stay in Staffordshire. It was a pattern Penelope followed, off and on, for years. She loved to spend part of the summer back in the countryside where she was born. But this year there were special reasons to be with her mother. The tragedy of Wat's death hit Lettice even harder than it did Penelope and Essex; and though the state of Penelope's marriage to Lord Rich would be no surprise to Lettice, it would be good to reassure her about the new baby. Penelope's departure, however, was a last-minute decision. On 14 June Anne Broughton wrote hurriedly from London to warn her parents that Penelope was coming. Anne was preparing to travel there as well, she explained. But if Lady Rich visited the Bagots at Blithfield before Anne reached them, her mother could help herself to everything she needed from Anne's country home, in order to provide for Lady Rich and whoever was travelling with her.

~

Back in London in the autumn, in good time for the Court winter season to start, Essex had successfully covered his tracks about his mistress and Thomas Vavasour took the blame for what was euphemistically called Mistress Southwell's "lameness". Elizabeth was not told for years that the baby, also named Walter, was Essex's love child. For the moment, it was the best of times for Essex. Over Christmas he was with the queen at Hampton Court; and on Shrove Tuesday 1593 he was sworn in as a member of the privy council. It was the start of the statesman status that Essex longed for. His friends thought he had turned over a new leaf. Anthony Bagot wrote home to his father that the earl was "a new man, clean forsaking all his former youthful tricks, carrying himself with honourable gravity". The queen had granted him some lands to help pay off his debts, and his speeches in parliament and the council were going down well. But Essex had only been attending council meetings a short while when Court life was disrupted by the continuing plague.

Everyone expected the epidemic, which started in the summer while Bess was in the Tower, would fade as usual during the winter. But there was no let-up, and in the spring of 1593 Elizabeth retired the Court to Nonsuch. Others followed suit, fleeing London. Late in May lawyer Broughton informed Richard Bagot "The plague increaseth", and Lady Rich would soon leave London for Leighs. She was "desirous to have my partner [Anne] with her at Leighs", he added. Lettice was also in London and the group Penelope took with her to the safety of Leighs eventually included her mother, Dorothy, Anne Broughton, "as well as many good gossips", and Frances, who was pregnant again. The baby, born at the turn of the year, would be Essex's first daughter, another godchild for Penelope – another Penelope Devereux.

While Lady Rich was settling her party in at Leighs Priory, Essex was hosting more government guests at Wanstead. It was an even grander gala than before and it cost nearly four times as much. On "the 21st and 22nd of May and for many days before and after", Essex gave the foreign diplomats (sent by Henri of France) the full treatment: hunting, feasting and fishing for information. Special stands were built for the guests to shoot from, and the deer were driven past by packs of hounds. This time Penelope's fluent Spanish would have been useful, as well as her French. Among the visitors was an exiled Spaniard named Antonio Pérez, with whom Penelope formed her oddest friendship.

Chapter Sixteen

SUMMER 1593–SPRING 1594

"Your Ladyship's flayed dog"

– Antonio Pérez, c. 1593

*O*f all the colourful foreigners who arrived at Elizabeth's court on embassies from Spain, France, Italy and the Vatican, none was more exotic, extravagant and devious than Antonio Pérez. He stayed twice in England between 1593 and 1596, and soon after his arrival Shakespeare's audience was laughing at the fantastic character Don Adriano de Armado in *Love's Labour's Lost*. On stage the don is a comic braggart fond of flamboyant phrases. In real life Pérez had more sinister habits. His extravagances helped to ruin Essex and the blackmail threat he later made to Penelope was only half in jest.

Antonio Pérez was a scholar-secretary to King Philip II of Spain before he fell foul of the Inquisition and fled to France. He was wanted for every crime from sodomy to seducing the king's mistress, and his political double-dealing (with Philip's bastard brother Don John of Austria for one) was equally complex. In France he attached himself to King Henri IV's staff and in April 1593 he arrived in England with the official envoy, the Vidame de Chartres, son of the French ambassador in London. That gave Pérez an entrée at Court and in May he was wallowing in the expansive hospitality Essex laid on for the Vidame at Wanstead. When the French delegation was ready to go home in October, Pérez decided to stay put. He had got himself on to Essex's payroll and soon he was occupying a cosy chamber in Essex House.

Pérez was bewitched by Penelope. Her ladyship, he insisted, might try to hide the fact that she is an angel, but it cannot be done. Penelope was equally intrigued. Pérez was impossible to pin down. He was intellectually brilliant yet pretentious, mercurial yet diligent, perceptive yet superficial – and something of a hypochondriac. Two things she could be sure of: he was as old as her father and he was a rogue. He exchanged reams of Latin letters with Essex and his secretaries on politics, while showering Penelope with flowery compliments in Spanish. He knew her Spanish was so good that she could understand his erotic letters, and her husband and servants could not.

Penelope had taken up Spanish when she first came to Court and found Elizabeth and her ladies reading a Spanish book by Jorge de Montemayor, named *Diana*, after the goddess of the moon and hunting. It was a tangled tale of rustic romance among shepherds and shepherdesses, and it swiftly became the Mills & Boon of its day. In 1598, when it was published in English with a sequel, the translations were dedicated to Lady Rich.

Penelope was not alone among Court ladies in mastering a foreign language. Many spoke Spanish, Italian or French. Penelope was unusual in writing and speaking all three, and her skill was one reason she became Pérez's closest companion among the Court ladies. But she evidently enjoyed his company too, and recommended to her friends the potions and bezoar stones he carried everywhere in a small chest. He, in return, took every opportunity to be intimate and familiar with her.

Ordering several pairs of gloves for her from Spain, some in dog skin, gave him the perfect excuse for sexual wordplay. At first he wrote apologizing for their late arrival and offering: "to sacrifice myself for your service and flay a piece of my own skin from the most delicate part of my body, if such a coarse individual as me can have any delicate skin". "I often flay my soul for the one I love," he went on, signing himself, "Your Ladyship's flayed dog". When the gloves arrived, one pair for Lettice, he pointed out that they were made of dog, "not of me", and since dogs were renowned for loyalty he hoped the gloves would gain favour with their owner. He could not resist adding that he had "seen dogs in very favourite places of ladies". Penelope must have replied in similar style, for Pérez wrote again: "My Lady, Do not value the creatures so little."

Pérez had left a trail of crimes and enemies across the Continent that made him an assassin's target, but Penelope's favour, he assured her, was as powerful an antidote to poison as all the bezoar stones in the world. Unlikely though it sounds, he was more than an ageing flatterer who fancied her and amused her with his decadent tastes. He shared the Devereux' love of literature and literary games. He shared their humanist way of thinking, and – for a fee – he was prepared to share with Essex his chain of informers and his inside know-how of the French royal offices and the Escorial, King Philip's monastic headquarters in the mountains above Madrid.

∾

Essex was hungry for news: it was the route to power. If he could show Elizabeth his information about her enemies abroad was better than the

Cecils', she would have to give him a bigger say in government. Essex had learnt a lot from Walsingham and he inherited many of his agents. Steadily through the 1590s he expanded his team of spies and secretaries, recruiting the best brains from Oxford and Cambridge: Edward Reynolds, Anthony Bacon and the three Henrys – Cuffe, Savile and Wotton. By the end of 1593 he had added Anthony Standen, poached from Burghley's continental network, and Antonio Pérez.

Pérez helped Essex establish a clear lead in intelligence gathering but the extravagantly dressed foreigner was an odd addition to the studious secretariat in Essex House. The earl had given up York House in 1592 and moved into Leicester's former home in the Strand, renaming it Essex House, and fitting up six or eight rooms as offices and apartments for them. They didn't all appreciate Pérez's presence, especially when he was awarded the plum job of being Penelope's minder. Lady Rich, her rooms restored to her, was often at Essex House and she got on well with the secretaries, and with senior staff like William Downhall, an old family retainer inherited from Leicester's household. Whenever she wrote to Robert Cecil she was courteous and friendly, usually addressing her letters "To the right honourable Sir Robert Cecil". To Downhall and to Anthony Bacon she would mark her letters: "To my especial friend …"

Anthony Bacon, newly installed as bureau chief of the earl's secret intelligence service, occupied a particularly important post. Almost housebound with gout, he was the backbone of the service and, as Penelope well knew, he and his younger brother Francis enjoyed a special relationship with Essex. The Bacon brothers were nephews of Lord Burghley's wife and they were bitter that he blocked their careers in favour of his son Robert. In Essex they found a patron who admired their intelligence and learning and who could make good use of Francis's legal expertise (he would become the most skilful queen's counsel), and of Anthony's continental connections. During twelve years abroad Anthony had made friends with the Catholic double agent Standen, who also joined Essex's team.

Lady Bacon, Anthony and Francis's indomitable mother, was not happy about them joining Essex's circle. She may not have known about the suspicions of sodomy that hung over them, but their friendship with Pérez irritated her: "I would you were well rid of that old, doted, polling papist. He will use discourses out of season to hinder your health, the want whereof is your great hindrance."

Penelope, like her brother, valued Pérez and Anthony's talents. She dined with them and often wrote to them requesting and exchanging information. They in return treated her with the respect due to someone whom the earl regarded as a key player in his affairs. Within Essex House Penelope was free to come and go. She needed no chaperone while she dined with her brother's supporters. It was a freedom and stimulus she thrived on, a contrast to life in the country with her husband. At times Lord Rich was also at Essex House, still part of the Devereux circle, but it was quite usual to find her at supper with Pérez, the secretaries and her cousin, Sir Nicholas Clifford. If there were other ladies present, Anthony Standen didn't notice them. And when her brother arrived suddenly with Sir Robert Sidney it was Penelope who took charge, re-arranging his plans for the following day. Sir Robert and his wife Barbara were now among Penelope's closest friends – and they knew all about Charles.

Essex had come home that evening to tell Pérez to accompany him to Court early the following morning. Henri of France was about to send Elizabeth a summons for the return of the wandering Spaniard, who was technically still one of the king's agents. Essex was hoping to persuade the queen to let him stay. After Court, Essex explained, they would collect Anthony Bacon from his house in Bishopsgate Street and then dine at Walsingham House. When Penelope heard the plan she decided "she would go also to dine with them". Since they couldn't all fit in the one coach, she suggested Essex should get out at Bacon's house, while she carried on to Seething Lane with Sir Robert and the coach could then go back for Bacon and Essex and bring them to dinner. Somewhat wearily, Standen warned Bacon about the new plan, "to the end you be not taken unarmed". His conclusion, "Women's determinations being uncertain, it may be she will not dismount, and the contrary may also fall out," says more about Standen's attitude to women than it does about Penelope. Indecision was not part of her character.

Henri's demands for Pérez's return were staved off for a while. The reason, Standen snidely claimed, was that Essex had given Pérez "the same office those eunuchs … have in Turkey, which is to have the custody of the fairest dames". Essex, worried perhaps that Penelope was behaving too independently in public, had instructed the Spaniard to escort her. It meant she was often in Pérez's company, and she became genuinely concerned for his health and safety. When he fell ill at Essex House, the earl himself summoned Roger Giffard, physician to the queen, to attend Pérez urgently. That may, however, have been a tactical move in the sensational affair of Dr Roderigo Lopez, Elizabeth's physician-in-chief, who ended up being tortured and executed as a traitor.

~

It is difficult to determine how much real danger there was in the Lopez affair. Pérez was definitely on the Inquisition's hit list and their agents came to London to assist Lopez in his covert dealings. But Lopez was at least partly the victim of an entrapment scam by Essex, intended to give himself an intelligence victory over the Cecils. Essex claimed the foreigners' plot included poisoning the queen, and their "confessions", extracted under torture, suggest there was also a plot to kill Pérez. But since Pérez took a hand in "finding" the evidence, it is unreliable, to put it mildly.

Dr Lopez was a businessman, diplomat and spy, as well as physician to the rich. Born the son of Portuguese Jews, he moved to London and set himself up as a doctor, acquiring Elizabeth, Leicester, Walsingham and Essex as his patients. For Leicester, Lopez was rumoured to prescribe his famous Viagra-type ointment. For others he offered a potent range of poisons. For Walsingham it was Lopez's skills as an undercover agent that were most useful. But after Walsingham's death the doctor's continued and unauthorized secret contact with Spanish officials left him open to charges of treason by his enemies, who now included Essex. The earl was furious when Lopez let out that his illness – tactfully described by his staff as agues and indisposition – was something which did his lordship "dishonour". And Essex decided to investigate the doctor's dealings.

In January 1594, Essex wrote jubilantly to Anthony Bacon: "I have discovered a most dangerous and desperate treason. The point of the conspiracy was her majesty's death; the executioner should have been Dr Lopez, the manner by poison. This I have so followed as I shall make it appear as clear as noon-day." Lopez was examined and his house searched, but nothing was found and the Cecils insisted he was innocent. So did Elizabeth, and she could have saved him if she'd tried. But Essex had made it a test of strength against the Cecils. He was bent on proving Lopez's guilt and the superiority of his own information network. In February a commission, including Lord Rich, was summoned to the Guildhall to begin hearing the case, and under torture Lopez's two accomplices put the finger on him. All three were dragged to Tyburn Fields, hanged, drawn and quartered.

In Lopez's so-called trial the prosecution was led by the new attorney general, Sir Edward Coke. He had a reputation for savage cross-questioning and he was keen to show off in his new job. His attack on Lopez made great play on the doctor's Jewish background and stirred a wave of anti-Semitic feeling in London. Jews had been officially excluded for three centuries, though diplomatic visitors had immunity, and there was an undercurrent of antipathy to them which soon found voice in Shakespeare's character Shylock. But there was also a general, and growing, anti-immigrant attitude, bred by unease in the capital. These were uncertain times and there was increasing opposition to Elizabeth's government.

Corruption, cozening, cheating and discontent were everywhere. The poor were worse off than at any time for nearly 250 years. Riots were endemic. In 1592, the arrest of a felt-maker for debt in Blackfriars sparked a series of midsummer riots that spread to the apprentices in Southwark. At once the privy council ordered a night watch throughout London and shut the playhouses on Bankside. The lack of passengers heading for the plays and brothels threatened the watermen with bankruptcy, but despite their begging letters to the council the theatres stayed shut for months. In May 1593 there was a rash of anti-alien demonstrations. And there was plague.

The serious outbreak that drove Penelope away from London to Leighs went on into autumn. It was the worst epidemic in more than twenty years. In November Elizabeth celebrated her Accession Day at Windsor, the only time the tilt was not held at Whitehall. And still the plague spread, like a filthy tide seeping silently under every door, killing thousands. Where it paused, the pathetic sign "Lord have mercy upon us" could be seen scrawled on the door. In its wake it left orphans and widows, weak and penniless with no breadwinner to support them. Crime rose, thieves and cheats stalked the streets in daylight. By night there was violence. No one ambled through alleyways in a well-made cloak without a link boy to light the way and a servant swinging a stout staff. And on the throne sat an ageing queen who seemed determined not to die, and not to name her successor.

The following year things got worse; 1594 saw the start of a four-year run of wet summers and bad harvests. It sent bread prices rocketing. In an effort to defuse a situation that was becoming unstable, Elizabeth's government, always authoritarian, cracked down harder than ever on freedom of expression. And, naturally, stricter state control caused greater unrest and discontent. Against this background of tension and uncertainty, with the queen increasingly depressed and withdrawn, Essex was becoming embroiled in a bitter power struggle with Robert Cecil. In the Lopez affair Essex was the victor and the doctor was mostly an innocent victim caught in the crossfire. Essex had "proved" his superior team of informers could guarantee Elizabeth's safety. He was not just a decorative royal favourite; he was a force to be reckoned with in matters of state.

～

Unfortunately, Elizabeth did *not* see Essex as a statesman. She wanted him to stand at her side, amuse her, lead her into the dance, write sonnets to her. When he disappeared from Court in November 1593, frustrated at her attitude, Elizabeth didn't like it but she welcomed him back; and at Christmastide when the players came to perform at Court it was Essex who sat beside her. But he wanted more. He was manoeuvring to get old Burghley's job as chief adviser to the queen. But his rival was Burghley's son, Robert Cecil. And each time Essex and his nominees were refused top jobs (in particular when Robert was named secretary of state in 1596) Essex turned angry.

It was not only the power of the posts that mattered: it was the money. Debt was a problem for everyone at Court – the expenses were astronomic – and Essex was getting desperate. As a student he had indulged his extravagant tastes, and now as head of the family he handed out funds for his cousins' foreign travels, provided pensions and annuities, and kept open house with a large band of servants. His family knew how much he was spending, and worried. In just two years, 1589 and 1590, he ran up a bill of more than £1,305 with London's foremost jeweller and merchant, Peter Vanlore. Elizabeth's grant to Essex of the licence for "the farm of sweet wines" helped defray it a bit, but in less than four years his debts to Vanlore had more than doubled and out of future "sweet wines" profits £4,000 was secured to the jeweller. By 1598 Essex's total debts reached a dizzying £30,000. The gambling craze at Court did not help, with betting on everything from cock-fights to tennis matches. If the Earl of Rutland could lose more than £200 in a week, others had to keep up to keep in fashion.

Essex's secretariat and spy network was another spiralling cost. The £20 a month retainer he paid Pérez was only a basic consultancy fee. From November 1593 until July 1595, Essex spent £400 a month on the Spaniard's "entertainment" and picked up other bills that probably totalled £1,000. Extending the reach of his network was essential; he needed foreign intelligence to back up his case for a more aggressive foreign policy. Essex was the natural heir to the old pro-war, interventionist party that Leicester once led. He was for honour, war and national glory. Robert Cecil followed his father's peace programme, anxious to avoid the costs of war and to hide the desperate state of the national bank balance. Between Leicester and Burghley those opposing views had not led to personal bitterness, and both Essex and Penelope retained some regard for the old lord treasurer. Essex still looked up to him as his former guardian, and Penelope could recall Burghley's courtesy to Lettice after little Lord Denbigh died. But with Robert Cecil there was deep rivalry and the council was splitting into two camps: Cecil's bureaucrats and Essex's swordsmen.

Cecil's camp had one major weakness, and with Elizabeth's approaching death it was a crucial one. King James of Scotland was her likely successor and he loathed the Cecils; while Essex, he knew, was his leading supporter. In April 1594 James wrote to Essex to apologize that he had "this long time forborne the writing unto you". Over the next few years he made up for it, sending a torrent of letters, ignoring the dangers of them being intercepted, and frankly calling Burghley "my enemy, though undeserved as God knows".

Penelope's Rialta letters were paying off. Part of James's preference for Essex and Penelope stemmed from their ancestry and royal connections. James was a snob. He liked to hear his agents report "the whole nobility here speak honourably and seem well affected" to the Earl of Essex. Whereas Burghley, some said, was a covert democrat.

Together Essex and Penelope nursed the family honour, superiority and ambition, and they expected Elizabeth to back them against an upstart like Cecil. When Essex appeared at ceremonial occasions he came at the head of hundreds rigged out in his livery, like an old-fashioned grandee. And when he felt he had been denied his noble destiny he retired to his country estates to sulk. Not for long though. He was too far in debt to leave Court permanently and he assumed, rightly, that the Cecils would work against him behind his back.

∽

Was there "something of the night" about the Cecils?

Few courtiers made money in Elizabeth's service, yet Lord Burghley amassed enough wealth to found two great dynasties and build two of the most fabulous houses in the kingdom. Burghley House in Northamptonshire went to his elder son, Thomas. Robert, his younger son and political heir, got Theobalds, near Enfield. It was the largest non-royal palace in the country, and its sumptuous decorations were legendary before the paint was dry.

Burghley occupied the two most lucrative posts in government – lord treasurer and master of the Court of Wards. On top of his salary they produced a fast-flowing revenue stream of bribes and tips. Burghley did big business selling wardships – the right to manage the incomes and estates of wealthy minors – while Robert took backhanders from those who wanted him to persuade his father to push wardships their way. After Burghley's death Robert milked the system still harder.

And after Burghley's death Robert would turn into Essex and Penelope's nemesis. Already the family knew they could not trust him. In 1592 Essex wrote to Robert: "Whether you have mistaken the queen, or used cunning with me, I know not. I will not condemn you, but leave you to think, if it were your own case, whether you would not be jealous. Your friend, if I have cause, R Essex."

Uncle William Knollys, at Court observing Cecil's behaviour with Elizabeth, wrote to Essex: "If we lived not in a cunning world I should assure myself that Mr Secretary were wholly yours." Cecil seemed "to rejoice at every thing that may succeed well with you, and to be grieved at the contrary". "I pray God it have a good foundation," William went on. "Yet will I observe him as narrowly as I can, but your lordship knoweth best the humour both of the time and the person and so I leave him to your better judgement."

Cecil could easily hide his double-dealing behind Elizabeth's ambivalence, and sit quietly beside the throne while others went off campaigning.

Penelope's father had destroyed himself financially and physically in Ireland. Lords Leicester, Huntingdon and Hunsdon, her stepfather, guardian and great uncle, ruined their lives and fortunes on costly missions for the queen, in Ireland, northern England and on the Continent. Yet the Cecils went on increasing their power, staying safely at home, secure in their unspoken pact with the queen. She would not investigate too closely and she would support them down to the line, so long as they delivered her safety and took on jobs she did not like – such as ordering executions.

But there were doubts about Burghley's financial management. Waste and corruption in Elizabeth's government were on a massive scale and Burghley did virtually nothing to control them. If Elizabeth realized how bad things were, she chose not to notice. She went repeatedly to Theobalds, enjoyed the entertainment and hunting, and knighted Robert Cecil there in May 1591. Burghley was coming to the end of his life, a martyr to gout, and he wanted a seamless handover of power to his son so that his failing and corrupt practices would not be revealed. Anyone who stood in the way would have to go. Ruining a man, or woman, was all in a day's work to the Cecils.

Some said they were behind the death of the Earl of Derby, whose vomit came up "like soot or rusty iron" when he fell ill of a strange sickness. Penelope had little doubt they were behind the downfall of her sister's father-in-law, Sir John Perrot. In spring 1592, after a year in the Tower, he was tried for treason and making "irreverent speeches against the queen". He admitted he probably *had* called her a "base bastard pissing kitchen woman", but only privately; and the idea that he'd been endangering national security was rubbish. It was all piffling stuff and no one believed he deserved his death sentence. Elizabeth was about to issue a pardon, but on 3 November he was found dead in the Tower. It was strongly suspected that he had been poisoned by Burghley's fixers because of his involvement in Irish affairs. The Cecils were covering up for another administrator there, their incompetent relation Sir William Fitzwilliam, who had helped ruin Penelope's father. And they did not want their own part in Irish affairs exposed either. Racketeering and profiteering in Ireland were on a greater scale than in England, and it was Burghley who should have sorted it out.

Corruption walked hand in hand with the Cecils, but for the moment Essex's chief disagreements with them lay in policy. Steadily he and Robert Cecil were adopting polarized positions, especially on war and religion. If Robert was opposed to recusants – the Catholic refuseniks who paid fines rather than attend Church of England worship – then Essex would fly the flag for Catholic toleration.

Early in her reign Elizabeth tried not to outlaw ardent Catholics, but the number of Catholic-inspired plots against her, and ongoing fears of Spanish invasion, led to a crackdown on recusants. The pope's edict in 1570, excommunicating Elizabeth and absolving her subjects from obedience to her, enabled extremist Protestants to claim that all Catholics were subversives and enemies of the state. In fact, the majority wanted to remain loyal to Elizabeth. And there were many of them. As well as devout Catholics there were countless crypto-Catholics drawn to the "old faith" and fond of its practices. Not the papacy necessarily, but the ceremony and ritual that chimed with old customs and were part of daily life, like rent days and law terms linked to saints and feast days. Elderly Protestant ministers, such as Burghley and Penelope's grandfather, Sir Francis, pressed on with creating the Reformed Church, enthusiastically supported by younger Puritans like Lord Rich, anxious to sweep away all remaining signs of Catholic "idolatry". Yet at Court among the "fast" young set there was a vogue for Catholicism. They had not witnessed the persecution and exile of Protestants under Elizabeth's sister Queen Mary. Besides, who knew whether the next monarch might not reverse things again?

Robert Cecil was a dedicated Protestant like his father, whereas Essex, though some claimed him as the patron of Protestant hopes, was publicly promoting Catholic toleration. It also reflected his private attitude. His chaplain on his next expedition, to Cadiz, was Fr Alabaster (admittedly a shaky Catholic). At least one of his pages and his gentleman usher Edward Bushell followed the "old faith". He gave Sir Christopher Blount key jobs beside him on the Cadiz raid and all his subsequent campaigns; and in Ireland he appointed another Catholic as his colonel of the horse. Catholic sympathies were almost the norm among the young courtiers and gifted poets, playwrights and musicians who frequented Essex House, including Shakespeare's patron, the dazzling young Earl of Southampton. And many who backed Essex's rebellion in 1601 would appear again in the Gunpowder Plot (the Powder Treason) four years later.

Penelope had been instrumental in establishing Essex's link to King James. She made friends with his informer Antonio Pérez and his think-tank secretariat. She supported his French contacts, sending gifts and greetings to the ambassador and others in the French community. She had even tolerated a marriage which helped shore up the family finances that Essex was depleting. Now she began working in unison with her brother in religious matters. While Essex developed his pro-toleration public image, securing relief for well-known recusant Sir Thomas Tresham, Penelope was holding secret talks with Fr John Gerard – the most hunted Jesuit priest in England.

Chapter Seventeen

SPRING–DECEMBER 1594

"To lay bare what was deepest in her heart"

– Fr John Gerard, 1609

*F*ather John Gerard was the most charismatic priest in the Jesuit mission to England during the 1580s and 1590s. The son of a Catholic landowner in the north, he was tall, good-looking, approaching thirty and, like all priests in the Society of Jesus, highly intelligent, highly educated and highly motivated. He was trained to dispute faith with people who thought forcefully and clearly, and he relished the chance to do so. When he came to visit Penelope at Leighs, probably early in 1594, her affair with Charles had been going several years and Gerard was in no doubt that she was deeply in love. Yet, as he wrote years later: "Though she led a life of frivolity, she was brought to the point where she was ready to see a priest provided he could come without anyone knowing."

The Jesuits were ideally suited to the undercover job of bringing comfort to Catholics, and would-be Catholics, in Elizabeth's England. They were strong physically as well as mentally, honed on abstinence and meditation, and toughened up by the boot-camp mentality of their training devised by their founder, Ignatius Loyola, who had set up his new religious order in 1540 as part of the Counter Reformation movement in Europe to oppose Protestantism.

In England, since the papal edict of 1570 the Jesuits had taken on a special missionary role. By the time Fr Gerard landed on the Norfolk coast one night late in October 1588, numerous priests had made their way to England to sustain the Catholic faithful. Many were betrayed, smoked from their hiding places, imprisoned, tortured and executed. The most famous martyr among them, Fr Edmund Campion, a scholar admired by Elizabeth, was tracked down and arrested in the summer of 1581. He was held in the Tower for four months, racked and tortured, tried and taken to Tyburn Fields for the horrific ritual of a traitor's death. He was hanged, cut down while still alive, castrated and disembowelled. His entrails were thrown into a cauldron of boiling water, and the remains of his mutilated body were finally hacked into quarters. The crowds who watched, standing in the rain, were unusually silent. There was shock and horror at such a bloody death for such a brilliant, peaceful man.

No one at Court could be unmindful of his fate. Certainly not Penelope. It was the summer when her marriage was arranged to Lord Rich, an ardent Puritan like those who clamoured for Campion's death. Her grandfather, Sir Francis, was another; so were her guardians, the Earl and Countess of Huntingdon. Yet her stepfather, Leicester, had promised Campion when he was a student at Oxford: "the queen and I will provide for the future." Penelope was too young to have seen Protestants suffer equally under Queen Mary. Father Campion was proof of what the reformed faith could lead to, and she was not likely to forget what would happen to a captured Jesuit.

The luckier members of the Jesuit mission were passed from safe house to priest's hole until, disguised as a friend or servant, they could slip into the undercover post of resident chaplain in some wealthy household large enough to hide them and their vestments. In Norfolk and Suffolk Fr Gerard's job was to extend that network of safe houses into an "underground" route through Essex to London. In later years, living out his life in safety in Italy, he was criticized for his focus on families with wealth and power. But in truth, as he argued, if England were to return to the "old faith" the decision would be made by people with wealth and power. In any case, he was sure to be noticed if he lived among rustic people who knew each other's comings and goings. He was born of aristocratic stock and he was best disguised as a gentleman, ministering to people of his own class. He was proud of his converts and contacts, and the most illustrious among them was "one great lady … sister to the Earl of Essex (then at the height of his favour with the Queen) … married to the wealthiest lord in the whole country".

Lord Rich was not only the wealthiest, he was the most radical Protestant. His religious extremism no longer brought him to the attention of the council so often, but he was still a leader of the Puritan faction in a county notorious for reformist thinkers, and closely linked to the Protestant teachings of northern Europe by the ports of East Anglia. There were still some staunch Catholics, like William Wiseman's family, neighbours and relations by marriage to Lord Rich. Penelope was godmother to William's daughter Penelope, and William sometimes sat as a Justice of the Peace alongside Lord Rich. Their home, Broadoaks Manor, near Thaxted, was a handsome house less than fifteen miles from Leighs.

The Wisemans had an elderly resident priest, ordained under Queen Mary and therefore partly protected against Elizabeth's laws. Nonetheless, Fr Gerard considered William strayed "far from Christian perfection", because he outwardly conformed to the Church of England in order not to risk losing his Essex farmlands. His widowed mother Jane, however, who had a house of her own nearby at North End, was a "true" Catholic. Not realizing how closely Walsingham and Burghley were monitoring recusant activity in the area, or that the Wisemans were already under suspicion, Fr Gerard decided Broadoaks would be a useful base. It was large, with plenty of panelled rooms, high roofs and chimneys, and at the end of 1591 he moved in.

~

Twelve months later the Wisemans were raided. Their elderly priest was discovered, but not Fr Gerard, and the family was only charged with hearing mass. In December 1593, the day after Christmas, the family was raided again. This time it was North End, Widow Wiseman's house, that was ransacked, and though the searchers had a tip-off that another priest was also hidden in the house, they failed to find either Fr Brewster or Fr Gerard. As 1594 opened, it was obvious the net was closing. During the spring Jane Wiseman was taken to London and imprisoned, and Fr Gerard, on a visit to London, narrowly escaped capture in a house leased by Wiseman where he had planned to sleep. His servants were taken away for questioning, and William was brought to London and interrogated by the attorney general. While William and Jane were both under guard in London, Fr Gerard made his way back to Broadoaks to celebrate Easter with the remaining family. On Easter Monday, preparing to say mass, he was trapped when the house was surrounded at dawn and raided yet again. Unknown to the Wisemans their servant John Frank was the informer. Despite his secret help and the assiduous officers, who stripped and smashed every room, the search failed. For four days Fr Gerard lay in a tiny hole specially constructed beneath a grate, almost without food and water, until the raid was called off.

A fortnight later in London, however, thanks to further betrayals by Frank, Gerard was caught at another Wiseman property in the early hours of Wednesday 24 April. He spent the next three years in prison, periodically "interrogated", until he was transferred to the Tower and tortured, suspended by his wrists for hours. Six months later, in October 1597, still weak from torture, he escaped over the Tower roof, down a rope to a rowing boat, and was spirited away to spend another ten years in England, still ministering to Catholics and avoiding capture.

It was after the Christmas raid on North End that "old Mrs Wiseman" rode over to "Lord Rich's", John Frank claimed in May 1594. Spilling beans as hard as he could, Frank told the official investigators that, after the search was called off, "Suffield, William Wiseman's man" had taken Fr Brewster safely to Broadoaks before returning to North End to ride over to Lord Rich's home with Widow Wiseman. She was evidently close enough to the Richs to go to them when she needed help; and seeking shelter in a Puritan household would look good to the authorities. It was probably soon afterwards that she arranged with Penelope for Fr Gerard to visit Leighs.

Old Mrs Wiseman was "given up to all good works and full of zeal", and she doubtless felt it her Christian and moral duty to try to bring Penelope "to be reconciled" and make a full confession of her love affair with Sir Charles Blount. But she may have had an ulterior motive. The priest hunters were close on Fr Gerard's heels and her house was no longer safe. She may have realized she would soon be taken to London, and she needed to help him find another hostess with a large house. And where safer than under the roof of an arch Puritan? She must have been confident Penelope would not betray them, and she was right. Penelope agreed to Gerard's visit.

Accordingly, John Gerard rode up to Leighs "as though I were bringing her a message from another great lady, a relative of hers" – Dorothy. The man who presented himself to Penelope had dark features, a high forehead, short, dark, curly hair and a small, well-trimmed beard. He was expensively dressed in velvet and lace, carried a sword and dagger, and was clearly at ease in aristocratic company. His days of travelling and studying abroad had taught him the languages Penelope spoke. He loved gardens and orchards, like those at Leighs and Wanstead, as she did. And he was more than happy to indulge in hunting and hawking, cards and gambling, as she was. If he told her to her face that her life was one "of frivolity", she could be forgiven for slyly asking if he had to join in those pastimes *quite* so often to keep up his disguise. Many ladies who met him found it incredible that this hunting-gambling man was a priest; and it amused him to fool them.

Penelope could hardly help but like him. Their first meeting went well and he joined "all the gentlefolk in the house" for dinner. Sitting at the long tables in the great hall, once the nave of Leighs priory church, Penelope could watch his firm, steady gaze as he listened to her guests; hear his slight faltering lisp; and study the nose that some said was hawk-like and others called "wide and turning up" – like Charles's. There was much about Fr Gerard that would remind one of Charles and it went deeper than dark, curly hair and an upturned nose. They shared that quiet bookishness and love of theology that people would always recall about Charles. Maybe they had both learnt it at Oxford. There was an inner calm and stillness about them, an air of authority that was utterly dependable. Both men preferred to listen while they ate, rather than talk. Yet there was nothing monkish about the way they rode and hunted.

Dinner over, Penelope drew Fr Gerard into a quiet chamber where they could talk undisturbed. The others at dinner would expect her to spend time alone with a newly arrived visitor who brought a letter from her sister and messages from her family. Every messenger carried unwritten news, it was safer. For more than three hours Gerard debated with her "all the doubts she raised about the faith". His next step was "to stir her will" to come into the Catholic Church. Before he left, "she asked me to instruct her how to prepare for confession", and they arranged a day for him to come again.

Father Gerard's autobiography is a single-source record of what happened and he would naturally wish to add weight to his near-success in leading Penelope to confession. Some of his account sounds exaggerated, but the back story – Penelope's "deep and enduring love", Charles's success in Ireland and their final disgrace – is correct. Furthermore, Gerard's claim that there was "nothing in the world [Penelope] wanted more than to lay bare to me what was deepest in her heart" would be consistent with Penelope's essentially conservative nature. All her upbringing, from her father's chaplains as well as her guardians, argued against her love affair. If after confessing her sins, claiming she was truly penitent and receiving absolution, it was her duty to renounce Charles, maybe she should. For the children's sake? For his own? Perhaps if Charles were free to marry someone else he would have the legitimate son and heir he longed for.

Debating with Fr Gerard would be deeply disturbing for Penelope. He specialized in uncovering innermost feelings, bringing people to admit "the temptation of sin". She might claim she was not in this situation by choice. She never wanted to marry Lord Rich, and she was not – despite her critics – lightly abandoning her responsibilities to him and their children. Nor was she flaunting her life with her lover. Yet her childhood taught her that what mattered was the honour of the family. Maybe Fr Gerard had been sent as a turning point in her life?

～

Penelope's meetings with Gerard have been dismissed as a "mischievous escapade" to amuse herself while she was pregnant, bored and stuck in the country; or a ruse to annoy her Puritan husband. Catholicism was something people died for in screaming agony. Suspicion of harbouring priests meant their houses were ruined, with plaster stripped from the walls, brick chimneys torn down, panelling splintered, furniture smashed, chests and cupboards forced open. Since Fr Campion's death, new laws stated that anyone who did "receive, relieve, comfort, aid, or maintain any such Jesuit" or other priest would be "adjudged a felon". That was not so bad as a traitor, but it was still criminal. The dangers of receiving a disguised Jesuit were enormous and Penelope was too intelligent to be unaware of the risks, or to run them unless she wished to discuss serious matters of religion. If anyone recognized Gerard she might claim ignorance of his identity, but she would still be watched for years. There is no chance that she met him as a "diversion".

Father Gerard had probably never crossed Penelope's path before, but he was far from a stranger to her family and friends. He was born into the Lancashire landowning families who sheltered Shakespeare during his "lost years" in the 1580s, and when Shakespeare reached London, mixing with the creative spirits who gathered around the Devereux, his patron was the Earl of Southampton, a favourite intern at Essex House. Southampton's chaplain and cousin by marriage was Fr Robert Southwell, and Southwell was Gerard's friend and fellow Jesuit. Gerard shared other family ties with Penelope, too. His uncle, George Hastings, who took Gerard under his wing for a time, was brother to Penelope's guardian, the Earl of Huntingdon, and first cousin to her father. His mentor, who arranged for him to train abroad as a Jesuit, was Anthony Babington, well known to Sir Christopher Blount; and the "mole" Gilbert Gifford was Gerard's second cousin. In the small world of Elizabethan England, and the smaller community of Catholic activists, naturally the same names crop up. And their need for secrecy makes it difficult now to work out who was pulling whose strings. But the number of links between Fr Gerard and Penelope make it unlikely they were in the dark about each other – or the significance of their meeting.

Penelope considered the encounter so important that before she made a confession to Fr Gerard she wrote to the "nobleman in London who loved her with a deep and enduring love". She wanted to tell Charles "the step she proposed to take, intending perhaps to break with him". It was the logical thing to do: it affected him more than anyone. How far Penelope had gone in preparing herself and planning to break with him, only she ever knew. But Charles took it seriously enough to travel straight to Leighs. If she went ahead there could be no future for them. In Fr Gerard's version Charles threatened suicide. It doesn't sound like Charles, the rational, calm, bookish man fascinated by theology. Yet he had nothing to lose by telling Penelope that life without her would be a living death. He had never wanted to marry another woman, and he never would.

What Charles did next was typical of a tactician with charm and a soldier's instincts. He persuaded Penelope "to ask her 'guide' [Gerard] the answers to certain doubts he himself had about the faith". Charles promised that if the Jesuit's replies were convincing, he too would turn Catholic. Gerard had to admit it was clever: as though Charles had challenged Gerard to single combat for Penelope. They would fight it out on paper. Charles lacked a Jesuit's training but he had been well tutored in mathematics, cosmography, Latin and Italian; and his "chief delight was in the study of divinity". His secretary, Fynes Moryson, claimed he was "the best divine I ever heard argue", and in his youth Charles admitted he was "addicted to Popery".

Charles's questions for Gerard covered "two whole sheets of paper about the Pope, the worship of saints and that kind of thing". Penelope forwarded them with a note of her own to Gerard, "begging me to do her the kindness of answering, for it would be a great gain if we could convert him". Gerard replied with careful answers, "and long ones at that", but he guessed Charles was buying time. Charles was, in fact, urging Penelope to return to London and, though he failed, the crisis had passed. Her mind was made up. If being a confessed Catholic meant renouncing Charles, the price was too high.

By the end of April Gerard had been captured, and he and Penelope would never meet again. It was the closest Penelope came to openly embracing the "old faith" until she died, but it did not signal an end to her Catholic sympathies. During the Broadoaks raid in March another priest, Fr John Bolt, had been caught and threatened with torture. Bolt had been a popular Court musician until he turned Catholic, earned Elizabeth's anger and left Court. Many had admired him and his music, yet it was Penelope who intervened to stop his torture, secure his release and help him leave for the Continent. And when, the following year, Fr Southwell was facing death it was Charles who went to his aid.

Robert Southwell, who "won the hearts of all" with his wisdom and poetry, was picked up in 1592 and spent nearly three years being regularly tortured in the worst ways the sadistic priest hunters could invent. Finally, in February 1595, he was dragged to Tyburn for the same bloody end as Fr Campion. But when the hangmen moved to cut him down still conscious, the crowd grew angry and Charles stepped in to stop them, so at least the poor priest would be insensible while his broken body was hacked to pieces. It was also Charles who convinced Elizabeth that Southwell was innocent of any plots against her.

Little wonder that Charles has been called at least a "fellow-traveller" with the Catholic community. And he is only one of the many Catholic sympathizers who surrounded Penelope. If her early taste of Puritanism from her grandfather Sir Francis and the Huntingdons, followed by her forced marriage to an ardent reformer, all inclined her to the "old faith", Penelope had plenty of other connections who also pointed that way: the Treshams, Digbys and Sir Christopher Blount; her sister Dorothy, shortly to marry into England's greatest Catholic family, the Percys; her sister-in-law Frances – and who could tell where Sir Philip Sidney's heart lay? Some hailed him as the prince of Protestantism, yet there is ample evidence of his sympathy with Catholics.

Penelope, like Essex, appointed a Catholic, Mistress Deacon, among her personal servants (though it must be remembered the Hotmans were Huguenots) and after King James succeeded Elizabeth, his pro-Catholic wife Anna chose Penelope as one of her closest companions. It adds up to a web of Catholic contacts too densely woven to be coincidence.

~

In the weeks that followed Penelope's talks with Fr Gerard she had little time for reflection. In May Sir Robert Sidney picked up the news and wrote to tell Barbara that "My Lady Rich hath not gone out her time", but "I hear she is reasonable well again". If his letter is dated correctly, it was either old news of a miscarriage that happened a while back, or it was a false alarm, for the following January Penelope was safely delivered of another child.

Meanwhile, at midsummer Charles's brother William, Lord Mountjoy, died suddenly. He was not yet thirty-three years old and he was a bachelor. He was said to have "hastened his death by debauchery". He had certainly carried on ruining the family finances by the long-running legal battle with Lord Huntingdon over mineral rights to the Blounts' Dorset estates. So it was no surprise after William's funeral, on 23 July, when Charles became the proud possessor of an estate worth only 1,000 marks (£666.12s.8d.) a year. His new rank as a peer was gratifying and useful, but financially he would have to go on making his own way in the world. In January he had taken up the important job of governor of Portsmouth, but his poverty, he explained to Cecil, guaranteed he would do the job loyally: he could not afford to lose it by displeasing the queen.

There wasn't much chance of the new Lord Mountjoy displeasing Elizabeth. She rated his charm almost as highly as Penelope did, and she had already turned a blind eye to his extra-marital activities for several years. Elizabeth was also treating Penelope with an exceptional level of tolerance. Lady Rich was welcome at Court and Elizabeth could not have been more friendly and lenient to her. Given Elizabeth's antipathy to Lettice, her relationship with Penelope was remarkable. The Devereux were in high favour. They might match with the grandest families in the land. And Penelope's sister Dorothy did.

~

Dorothy's husband, Sir Thomas Perrot, lived barely a year after his father died in the Tower; and early in 1594 Dorothy became a widow. Her son, baptized Robert in March 1592, had not survived, but she had a daughter to share her grief. Penelope's niece and godchild Penelope Perrot was nearly six years old. Dorothy had married Thomas for love and, like Lettice, she discovered how hard Elizabeth could set her heart against a woman, while a man might work his way back into royal favour. So when Dorothy looked to marry again, like Penelope she married for position and the sake of the family. It would be a grand alliance, and husbands did not come any grander than Henry Percy, ninth Earl of Northumberland.

The Percys were one of the oldest, noblest and richest families in England. They were also Catholic. Henry had been deliberately tutored by an Anglican clergyman and in days ahead he would strongly deny that he was a practising Catholic. Yet two of his sisters were named by Fr Gerard as devoted Catholics, and many considered Henry the white hope of Catholic resistance. The French ambassador openly called him "*Catholique en son ame*" – Catholic at heart.

Henry Percy had inherited his vast estates in 1585 at the age of twenty-one, when his father died in mysterious circumstances in the Tower, where he was being held on suspicion of treason. The official verdict on his death said: "He laid violent hands upon his own life, by discharging a Dag with three bullets under his left pap, wherewith he pierced his heart." It was generally believed, however, that he was done to death for his Catholic faith. Yet it wasn't religion that earned his son Henry the nickname "the Wizard Earl". It was his interest in science, astronomy and mathematics, and his friendship with Ralegh's "School of Night".

After a wild and sometimes violent youth Henry was ready to settle down and during 1594 his marriage to Dorothy was settled. It would not have escaped some observers' notice that Elizabeth's mother, Anne Boleyn, had hoped to marry the Percys' heir (before she caught Henry VIII's eye) and was refused because of her lack of nobility. Yet now a daughter of the Devereux family was deemed fit to marry a Percy.

As the end of the year and Christmastide approached, the Earl of Essex and his sisters were at the height of their influence.

Chapter Eighteen

DECEMBER 1594–JANUARY 1596

"No man is more high and eminent"

"R. Doleman", 1595

The Christmas revels for 1594 had been worrying Lady Bacon for weeks. She shared Lord Rich's Puritan convictions and early in December she wrote to her son Anthony about the Gray's Inn students' plans: "I trust they will not mum nor mask nor sinfully revel."

Of course they would. The Inns of Court masques and plays, music and madrigals, dining and dancing were famously drunken, disorderly occasions. Lady Bacon's younger son, Francis, was a senior member of Gray's society of lawyers, and a shrewd guess told her Anthony and the Essex House residents would be among the lawyers' guests of honour. It was the most fashionable place to party. Elizabeth sometimes attended and rumour had it this year's revels would be better than ever.

A week before Christmas the students turned the great hall into their own kingdom, elected a prince and privy council, presented a parody of Elizabeth's Court, and summoned professional actors to perform for them, as Elizabeth did. On Saturday night, 28 December, Shakespeare's *A Comedy of Errors* proved so popular that the grand guests hardly had room to dine, and the students had to abandon their own plays in favour of "dancing and revelry with gentlewomen". The following night the students staged a mock trial, indicting a "sorcerer" for the crime of causing chaos in the revels.

There was another Grand Night on Friday 3 January 1595, when more "great persons" were invited to watch a comic ceremony: the installation of "The Honourable Order of the Knights of the Helmet". With the Bacon brothers on his payroll, and Elizabeth demanding Essex by her side, the earl and his family were bound to be in the audience; and some accounts say Lord Rich was among them, as well as Mountjoy and Penelope.

Plays were a pleasure that she shared with her lover. Both their fathers had supported troupes of players and Essex often hired actors to perform in his London home on special occasions. For Dorothy's wedding to "the Wizard Earl", he paid £10 for professional players to entertain the guests in Essex House. Many of those who watched must have wondered why Dorothy had taken Northumberland as her second husband. Henry Percy was notoriously difficult and anti-social, partly due to his deafness, with little appeal beyond wealth and power, but he did not realise Dorothy was equally determined. Before long he protested that she had misled him about her wealth, though it was Dorothy who held the lease on their principal home, Syon House, the riverside estate formerly granted to Sir Francis Knollys. Court gossips regularly reported their separations and stormy marriage, which was not helped by the death of two sons in 1597 before either was a year old.

~

Mountjoy's job as governor of Portsmouth kept him busy fortifying the town and defending the harbour against the constant threat of Spanish invasion, yet he evidently found time to join Penelope during the spring, and to discuss her meetings with Fr Gerard, for in January 1595, in "My Lady Rich's Chamber" at Essex House, Penelope gave birth to another daughter.

Mountjoy had inherited his title since the birth of their first child, yet their second daughter, christened Isabella on 30 January, was also registered as Lord Rich's child. Rich must now have abandoned any hopes that Penelope's affair would be short-lived, yet he agreed Isabella should join her sister and his four children at Leighs. Lucy and Essex, Robert and Henry were all growing strong and well and in years to come they would remain close to Mountjoy's children. What it cost Penelope and Mountjoy to go on hiding their family for discretion's sake, no one else would ever know. For the moment at least they had no option but to preserve the fiction of Penelope's family life with Lord Rich – though the inner circle at Court were aware that Lady Rich and Lord Mountjoy were more than casual lovers.

If Lord Rich was ever tempted to complain publicly that there were three people in his marriage and it felt a bit crowded, he resisted. For three days in February he went along with Lord Mountjoy on a trip arranged by Essex to Cambridge University. Essex still had many contacts from his student days at Trinity College, but this was not a jolly escapade to recapture misspent youth. It was a high-profile public relations tour to demonstrate Essex's intellect and high standing among scholars, his prestige and patronage. And so he rode off to Cambridge with a band of Devereux stalwarts: Penelope's husband and her lover; his cousin Sir Nicholas Clifford, soon to embark with Drake and Hawkins on their last, ill-fated voyage; Antonio Pérez, still pushing his luck staying in England; Lord Burgh, an Anglophile Irish noble whose son was living in Essex's household; and Sir Robert Sidney, currently in England to report on affairs in the Netherlands, where he had succeeded his late brother Philip as governor of Flushing.

Robert was desperate to obtain a post in London to be nearer his wife Barbara and their growing family. Barbara, three years older than Penelope, had inherited enough money to be able to marry for love, not caring that Robert was then a second son, and she joined him in Flushing. Returning to London with their first two children, she moved into Baynard's Castle (the London home of Robert's sister Mary Sidney and her husband, the Earl of Pembroke) and became firm friends with Penelope. They had both spiritedly chosen their own partners, and both had growing families with absentee fathers.

A few weeks after Essex returned from Cambridge his third son, Henry, was christened. Frances had again given birth at her mother's home in Seething Lane and the baptism, on 14 April, was recorded at St Olave's parish church. For the moment all seemed well and again the family hoped this was a "spare" for Essex. "The Wizard Earl", in the first flush of marriage to Dorothy, happily agreed to be godfather and to give the boy his name, while Penelope and Lord Burgh were his other two godparents.

Early that summer Penelope was out of town, but as usual she was busy writing letters on behalf of others to obtain jobs and favours for them. In June and July 1595 she sent a volley of requests to "Worthy Sir Robert" Cecil, always carefully preserving the niceties of courtly correspondence, sending greetings to Lady Cecil and begging Sir Robert to "hold me in your memory and to believe that I will be ever your most affectionate friend Penelope Rich". Mountjoy's career made it doubly important that she stay on good terms with Cecil, no matter what she thought of him and his attitude to Essex.

In July Antonio Pérez returned to France, finally summoned home by the French king. The night before he left, Essex gave a dinner for him at Gravesend, treating him well because Pérez, pen-named "Peregrino", "the Wandering Spaniard", had agreed to continue as his agent abroad. But Essex's feelings for Pérez had cooled by the time he returned to England during the Cadiz crisis, and Elizabeth decided he was a "Spanish traitor". Penelope, however, was still concerned to enquire if he minded his poor reception; and for the next few years she kept in touch with him. In her story he comes and goes: a shadowy figure in the candlelight, never quite revealing who he was working for. She need have no regrets about him. She had done her best to smooth his path and "Peregrino" would remain a colourful, amusing interlude in her life.

As the summer wore on, Penelope was in Staffordshire staying with her mother at Drayton. Mountjoy was busy in Portsmouth and Lord Rich was at home getting irritated. He guessed that Essex's messengers were carrying private letters to and from Penelope and her lover, and on 11 September he wrote to Essex about "your letters into Staffordshire, to your sister, and the other party". Trying to make a joke of it he insisted he did not dare intercept the letters "for fear of these troublesome times will bring forth shortly a parliament and so perhaps a law to make it treason to break open letters written to any my lords of the council, whereby they are freely privileged to receive writings for other men's wives without further question". It was a "wicked age" but he remained "Your lordship's poor brother to command in all honesty".

Penelope was still away in mid-September and she and Lettice were not expected back for some time. Lord Rich was out of town so Rowland Whyte had no news of either to pass on to Sir Robert Sidney. Whyte was invaluable to the Sidneys. He was their business manager in London, where he kept an eye on Barbara and the children, and he sent frequent bulletins to Sir Robert in Flushing. At present they were full of details about some tapestries Robert had agreed to buy for Lord Rich. He also sent news of Lady Huntingdon, Robert's aunt, who was beginning "again to mourn the death of your brother". Whyte advised Robert to send her a message of sympathy. It was nine years since Philip received his death wound and the anniversary of the battle of Zutphen would always be a time to mourn. The publication in 1591 of the *Astrophil and Stella* poems had raised Philip's profile still higher and during the 1590s Penelope received numerous dedications from other authors hinting at her role as Stella.

Rowland Whyte expected Lord Rich in London daily, though he had not arrived by 8 October and his letters were being dropped off at Essex House. Gradually everyone returned to the capital ready for Accession Day and on Friday night, 7 November, Whyte reported: "My Lady Leicester and Lady Rich are yesternight come to London, and my Lord Rich will write unto you about his hangings." Penelope was involved in the choice of the tapestries despite being out of London and she let Whyte and Robert know that if they were still available she would like a piece or two that showed the story of Cyrus, "and money will be sent to you".

Lord Rich, however, warned that if they were not like the details he had originally received, "they will not serve their turn". When the samples arrived a week later, Penelope sent word to Robert that she liked them, adding that Lord Rich had not yet seen them. At this point Lettice said she thought them expensive but wished "her friend Sir Christopher" had been sent some. Three days later Lord Rich pronounced that the border on them was not the right

Left:
Mary, "the other Boleyn girl", was Penelope's great-grandmother. It was no secret that she was Henry VIII's mistress before he fell in love with her sister, Anne, mother of the future Queen Elizabeth I.

Right:
...elope's grandmother, ...y Katherine Knollys, ...gnant with her fourteenth ...d, Dudley. She was ...abeth's principal lady-in-...ting for a further seven ...s until she died.

Above:
Penelope's father, Walter Devereux, the handsome 1st Earl of Essex, died in Ireland wondering if "some evil received in my drink" had caused his dreadful dysentery.

Left:
Lettice, Countess of Essex, dubbed by Elizabeth a "She-wolf", was Penelope' flame-haired mother. For marrying the queen's adored "Sweet Robin" she wa exiled from Court almost for life.

Above: Kenilworth Castle, where Elizabeth was entertained by the Earl of Leicester to nineteen days of "princely pleasures" – pageants, music, hunting, feasts and fireworks.

Right: "Sweet Robin", Earl of Leicester, Penelope's stepfather, was the love of Elizabeth's life. He had known her since childhood and when she died, fifteen years after him, his last letter was beside her bed.

Below: Lettice kneels at the front of her sisters in the line of "weepers" beside the grand tomb to Penelope's grandparents in St Nicholas' Church, Rotherfield Greys, Oxfordshire.

SERO, SED SERIO

Left:
Robert Cecil, principal
secretary of state to both
Queen Elizabeth and King
James. Short and hump-backed
he was Elizabeth's "Pygmy",
James's "little Beagle" – and
Essex's arch enemy.

Right:
Penelope's friend the Wandering
Spaniard, Antonio Pérez, was a
spy, diplomat and scoundrel. He
wrote her intimate letters signed
"your Ladyship's flayed dog", and
encouraged her taste for decadence.

Henry Percy, "the Wizard Earl" of Northumberland, spent years in the Tower after the Gunpowder Plot. Scientific interests led to his nickname, and his deafness and sarcasm led many to dislike him – including his wife, Penelope's sister Dorothy.

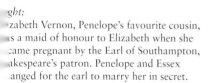

zabeth Vernon, Penelope's favourite cousin, s a maid of honour to Elizabeth when she ame pregnant by the Earl of Southampton, akespeare's patron. Penelope and Essex anged for the earl to marry her in secret.

As Queen Elizabeth aged, her clothes (like her attitude to courtiers' marriages) grew increasingly bizarre.

Above left: Sir Philip Sidney was the hero of the age, a brilliant soldi diplomat and poet who died in battle. He was inspired by Penelope write his passionate sonnets *Astrophil and Stella* in 1582–3, but how deeply he loved her is a mystery.

Above right: Penelope and her sister, "Two ladies in one picture, my Lady Rich and my Lady Dorothy", probably painted when Penelope came to Court in 1581.

Below: Leighs Priory and its large estate in Essex became Penelope's country home when she was married – against her will – to Lord Ri

THE WEST VIEW OF LEEZ-PRIORY, IN THE COUNTY OF ESSEX.

Right:

Penelope's brother Robert
Devereux, Earl of Essex, said to be
Elizabeth's young lover, was named
by Shakespeare as "the General of
our Gracious Empress". Twice he
appeared dramatically dressed in black
armour to tilt in a royal tournament.

Below:

The miniature portrait of Penelope by
Nicholas Hilliard, now in the Royal
Collection, is probably the picture she
sent in 1589 with her secret letters to
King James of Scotland.

Right:

Penelope's lover for fifteen years,
Lord Mountjoy (later Earl of
Devonshire), with his eyes "great,
black and lovely" and his nose
"a little blunt in the end", was
the father of her last five children.
Their marriage in 1605 was
officially deemed illegal.

Above:
Penelope's lover Charles Blount, Earl of Devonshire, sits in the centre of the English nobles on the right for the peace talks with Spain at Somerset House in 1604, sixteen years after the great Armada. At the front on the right is Robert Cecil.

Right:
Mountjoy Blount (later Earl of Newport), Penelope's eldest son by Devonshire, had his father's snub nose and curly hair. Despite his royalist background, he sided with the king's critics in the Civil War and danced with Cromwell's daughter when she married Penelope's great-grandson Robert Rich.

depth, and Lettice again queried the price. Caught in the middle, Whyte could only report to Robert that Penelope "liked the hangings very well". The matter rumbled on and it was January when Penelope let Robert know exactly how the hangings should be made.

Meanwhile, something more serious had arisen. Early in November Whyte wrote to Sir Robert: "My Lord of Essex, as I wrote unto you in my last, was infinitely troubled with a printed book the Queen showed him … yet doth he keep his chamber." The book was "dedicated to my Lord Essex and 'tis thought to be treason to have it".

∼

The book, smuggled in from Antwerp, was titled *A Conference about the next Succession to the Throne of England.* Queen Elizabeth was adamant, despite her advancing years, that the subject was banned while she breathed, and anyone who discussed it publicly was put in the Tower. Yet here was a book that blew the subject wide open, and it was dedicated to Essex because "no man is more high and eminent in place or dignity at this day in our realm than your self". Its Jesuit authors, using the single pseudonym R. Doleman, argued that a monarch must possess exceptional qualities. They rejected the Tudors' right to sit on the throne and dismissed all claimants descending from them, including King James of Scotland and his cousin Arbella Stuart. The best option, they insisted, was the Infanta of Spain, descended from John of Gaunt, Duke of Lancaster.

If such complicated and ancient claims as the Infanta's could be endorsed, how much greater was Essex's claim, descended from no fewer than *four* sons of Gaunt? Yet the authors did not mention Essex as a possible successor; instead they claimed that no one would "have a greater part or sway in deciding of this great affair than the Earl of Essex". Yet to everyone who knew the Devereux' multiple royal descent – and ancestry came before astronomy in aristocratic education – the next question had to be: why not Essex as king? He was the embodiment of ancient nobility, youth, chivalry and royal favour, and he was making it clear he had lofty ambitions. With his illegitimate descent from Henry VIII, how high was he aiming?

The book sent alarm bells clanging through the Devereux camp. Essex would choose how and when he furthered his ambitions, not the troublemakers behind this book. Elizabeth fumed at him at first, but after Essex went off "sick" for a few days she accepted his word that he knew nothing about it. The idea, however, that Essex might bid for the crown would not go away, and his next display did little to dispel his enemies' fears.

At the Accession Day tilt of 1595 Essex put on his most elaborate performance to prove he was back in royal favour and to draw a line between him and the Cecils. The tiltyard was a foreign country to Robert Cecil, and the place where Essex excelled. The previous year he had taken on fifteen challengers and shattered fifty-seven lances. This year, to raise the stakes and his reputation as the most chivalrous knight at Court, his script-writing staff prepared a pageant portraying him as Elizabeth's official favourite. The crowds who watched thought it wonderful – Essex was their hero. Others thought it was a send-up of the Cecils. Elizabeth thought it was too much about Essex. This was her day, she was supposed to be the centre of attention, and she went off to bed. If it didn't cross Penelope's mind that her brother was losing his powers of persuasion over Elizabeth, it certainly crossed Sir Robert Sidney's. Essex had achieved nothing in terms of getting royal permission for him to come home from Flushing.

~

While London was still buzzing about Essex's performance, Barbara Sidney decided to go to Court herself and press for Robert's leave. She was expecting another baby any day and the journey by carriage to Whitehall was not easy. Nonetheless on Monday 24 November she took her three eldest children, Mary, William and Catherine, with her, to help make the point that Robert's family needed him. At Court Lady Sidney spent a useful day lobbying everyone she knew, including the lord admiral, Charles Howard, and Burghley. They were, Rowland Whyte reported, "exceeding glad to see her", and the admiral "much pitied her journey, being so big and so near her time". Essex was too busy to come down from the council chamber and see her, though he sent a message of support; and the queen ordered one of her ladies to look after Lady Sidney and to see she had a private chamber in which to dine. The children were a big success. The admiral told Mistress Mary she was "already a fit maid for the queen", and assured Barbara that if the queen hadn't been so busy she would have come down to see them.

It was as well she did not. The Sidney children had recently had measles and by Friday Barbara had it, too. Whyte reported to Sir Robert that his wife was "full of the measles, had withall a great cough and a gentle fever", and the doctor warned "seeing my lady is so near her time, god willing it will not prove dangerous". The midwives and wet nurse were brought in straight away and on Monday 1 December Barbara was "safely brought to bed … of a goodly fat boy, but as full of the measles in the face as can be". Kept warm and given the wet nurse's milk and saffron, "which he suck out of a spoon", the baby thrived and the Sidneys arranged his christening.

Penelope and Mountjoy were at the top of their list of possible godparents and Rowland Whyte set off to tell them the good news. Penelope was delighted. If she had not been off to Epsom, she told him, she would have let

Lady Sidney know it herself. She was adamant she would attend the christening herself and not send a proxy, insisting she was not worried about the measles because "after eight days there was no danger to be feared". Whyte, wondering if she might regret being so impetuous, visited her again at Essex House that afternoon and found her just as determined. Penelope was also curious, Whyte reported, "who was thought upon to be the godfathers: I said my Lord Mountjoy for one, but I could not well tell who the other should be". Penelope probably didn't care who the other was, and instructed Whyte to tell Mountjoy that she wanted him to say yes.

Whyte duly hurried off to "my Lord Mountjoy at his house" in Holborn and got the same delighted response and an assurance that "whensover the day was appointed he would not fail to be there". Despite being ill in December, Mountjoy was in demand at Court, privately advising Elizabeth on military matters. Some wondered if she would make him a privy councillor, but she never did. Elizabeth knew about Mountjoy and Penelope, and adding a strong Essex supporter at her council table would unbalance it.

The date for the christening was left to Penelope to decide and at first she suggested three or four days before Christmas, as she was planning to be in the country until then. Barbara sent back word that "it should be then or when else she would please to appoint it". Then Penelope explained that as she would be away until Christmas Eve, she would name the day when she returned. Fortunately, Mountjoy and Lord Compton, now named as the second godfather, were happy to "attend her pleasure". Whyte, however, was anxious to see about provisions for the christening party. Lady Sidney had given away all the boar pies Sir Robert sent over for Christmas. Essex had one, Burghley had one and the two intended for the Sidney household had gone to Robert Cecil, in hopes he would persuade Elizabeth to let Sir Robert come home.

The next message from Penelope left Whyte resigned: "My lady Rich is not yet come, it will be Christmas Eve; she must appoint the day and time for it." When Christmas Eve arrived, it was Essex's wife Frances, not Penelope, who came to visit Barbara and her children. Walsingham House was less than a mile from Baynard's Castle and Frances stayed three hours. Doubtless she brought her own children, "Little Robin", Essex's five-year-old heir, and Elizabeth, Philip Sidney's ten-year-old daughter, first cousin to Barbara's children. It was a happy Christmas household: Barbara's baby had recovered well, little Philip was just walking – and could "go alone" since September – while Mary and Catherine were already able to read.

Penelope was, in fact, at Leighs for Christmas with Lord Rich and her six children, and though she returned to London the day after, the christening was put off till New Year's Eve. Rowland Whyte said her excuse was that Lord

Compton had urgent business in the country. But he privately thought it was because she had a spot on "her fair white forehead". Barbara was now getting anxious to have the christening done, yet she was fond enough of Penelope not to get cross. As Whyte put it, "my lady Rich's desires are obeyed as commandment", including her choice of name for the baby – Robert, for his father and her brother, not in honour of her husband.

The christening party was a major family bonding session and Lord Mountjoy was there in an important role. Surrounded by close family and friends – "my lady Cumberland, her daughter, my lady of Essex, her daughter and son" and "many other gentlewomen and gentlemen" – Mountjoy and Penelope were jointly acting as godparents, and together with Lord Compton they generously gave the little boy three matching plate bowls that Whyte thought "may be worth £20" each. Everything had gone well, he assured Sir Robert, and the family was praying for his "speedy return".

Sidney was indeed making a speedy return. The Earl of Huntingdon had died suddenly and Elizabeth wanted Sir Robert home to comfort his aunt. Lady Huntingdon was one of her oldest companions. She lived at Court now while her husband still worked as president of the Council of the North, and she was distraught. Her husband had died hugely in debt and Robert must sort things out. Huntingdon had been guardian to Penelope and Essex and their father's first cousin. His death left Essex distressed, perhaps more so than Penelope, and it removed one of Essex's most senior allies. His father and stepfather, Earl Walter and Lord Leicester, had been dead for years, and obviously his grandfather, Sir Francis Knollys, and great-uncle Henry, Lord Hunsdon, could not live much longer. As the "old guard" passed away, Essex found himself lacking heavyweight support in council – particularly with Mountjoy ruled out by his love life.

Chapter Nineteen

1590S

"Sweet Thames, run softly, till I end my song"
– Edmund Spenser, *Prothalamion*, 1596

The ties that bound the Devereux, Sidney and Dudley dynasties went beyond christenings and marriages. They shared a cultural and intellectual bond that Sir Philip Sidney cemented when he made Penelope his muse in the *Astrophil and Stella* sonnets. Philip was part of an important group of writers, artists and thinkers who enjoyed Lord Leicester's patronage and hospitality, including Edmund Spenser, "the Prince of Poets in his time", miniaturist Nicholas Hilliard and map-maker John Stow.

After Essex took over his stepfather's home in the Strand early in the 1590s and renamed it Essex House, the show went on. The great hall and the riverside gardens once again rang with revels, music and laughter. Like Leicester, Essex was a lavish host and a generous patron, and the Devereux' tastes ranged from poetry and private theatricals to metaphysical debates and madrigals. In 1596 Edmund Spenser, on leave from his job in Ireland, was back at Essex House and writing his best-loved lines. *Prothalamion* pictures the house with its tall brick tower, the lawyers' quarters next door in the Temple, two swans swimming slowly by, and each verse ends:

Sweet Thames, run softly, till I end my song.

The poem was written for the double wedding of the Earl of Worcester's daughters, celebrated at Essex House on 8 November. They too were part of the extended Devereux family. Their mother was Earl Walter's cousin and sister to Penelope's guardian, Huntingdon. Their father, Worcester, who was Catholic but a loyalist, was a close ally of Essex; and Spenser, after honouring the brides in his poem, paid fulsome tribute to Essex himself.

But it was Penelope who was usually the star of the Essex House show and by 1596 the cult of Lady Rich was firmly established. Poets and composers showered her with dedications and praises. The first printed dedication to "The right excellent and most beautiful lady, the Lady Penelope Rich" appeared in 1594 in Richard Barnfield's tale *The Affectionate Shepheard*, which portrayed her as "the fair Queen Gwendolen" who loved a "lusty youth, that now was dead", meaning Philip; and it was followed by countless allusions to her as Sidney's "inestimably Rich" heroine. In 1591 the first printed edition of *Astrophil and Stella* was issued and though it was swiftly withdrawn as unauthorized, Philip's sister, Mary, Countess of Pembroke, soon produced her own version. In 1598 the full sonnet sequence was in print and they were achieving best-seller status. Clearly Penelope liked the fame and tributes they brought, otherwise writers seeking her patronage would not have kept up the flow of puns and cryptic references to Sidney, Astrophil, Stella, stars and star lovers.

They praised her beauty, charm and talents. They wrote songs for her to sing, music for her to dance to, and even dances for her daughters. It would be naive to imagine they were driven purely by creative instinct, or even, less purely, by the need for meal tickets. The Earl of Essex was in great favour with Elizabeth, his sister was a key player in his affairs and the cult of Penelope carried political messages. Homage to Penelope showed allegiance to Essex's agenda – King James as Elizabeth's successor and toleration for the "old faith", goals that were naturally shared by Catholics.

William Byrd, openly Catholic and the finest composer of the Tudor age, was one of the first to set *Astrophil and Stella* songs to music, and his 1589 collection, *Songs of Sundry Natures*, included two new numbers about Lady Rich. *Weeping full sore* tells of an onlooker who asks why "so fair a dame" should "be so full of sorrow?"

> No wonder, quoth a nymph, she wanteth pleasure,
> Her tears and sighs ne cease from eve to morrow.
> This lady Rich is of the gifts to beauty,
> But unto her are gifts of fortune dainty [sparing].

In case anyone missed the pun, the following number began "Penelope that longed for the sight ...". Lady Rich had been married for nearly eight years and Byrd's melancholy air matched what everyone knew about the state of her marriage.

Byrd enjoyed the queen's personal protection, yet his Catholic faith, shared with his patron Worcester, brought problems, and he was frequently charged with recusancy. He was known to be in touch with the Catholic underground and he "made music with Jesuits". In 1594, while Penelope was meeting Fr Gerard at Leighs, less than a dozen miles away Byrd settled his family into a new home at Stondon Massey in order to become part of the local Catholic community that included both Fr Bolt and Fr Gerard.

Recent research has put Byrd's alignment with the Sidney–Devereux faction beyond question, and his satirical song *My mistress had a little dog, whose name was Pretty Royal* is said to be loaded with Essexian references. His pupil Thomas Morley, however, has long been seen as a political activist. With John Dowland, Thomas Campion and others, Morley formed a group of madrigal and lutenist composers who were overwhelmingly Essex sympathizers. Morley, best remembered for his settings for Shakespeare's songs *O mistress mine!* and *It was a lover and his lass*, is said to have made Penelope the "Diana" of his *Oriana* songs, and the connection with Diana became as clear and pronounced as the Stella link.

John Dowland, another of Elizabeth's favourite composers, wrote a song in praise of Wanstead Woods that clearly alludes to Penelope. Issued in 1600, when Essex was under arrest and Mountjoy and Penelope had taken over Wanstead, it begins with a couplet from one of Philip Sidney's poems and laments that the woods are a place of sorrow where

> … the fairest nymphs have walked.
> Nymphs at whose sight all hearts did yield to love.
> You woods, in whom dear lovers oft have walked.

In happier moments Dowland and others wrote dances for her including a lively *Lady Rich's Galliard* by Dowland; *Corranto Lady Rich*, composer unknown; and a short, high-stepping *La Volta Mistress Lettice Rich*, for her eldest daughter.

Around the end of 1596, as the cult of Penelope, her political stature and her patronage blossomed, the great French lutenist Charles Tessier arrived in London and made her the dedicatee of his *Premier Livre de Chansons et Airs*, as a tribute to both her musical and linguistic abilities. Two of the thirty-five French and Italian songs were specifically written for her, including *Câche toi, céleste soleil!*, Hide yourself, celestial sun! It is written for solo voice and lute, addressing Apollo, the sun god and patron of music and poetry, and telling him that his harp does not sound so sweet as Penelope's lute, his songs are less beautiful than hers, and

> Your fine golden hair is not as rich
> As that of the lovely Rich
> And Europe does not deserve
> As much as our Penelope.

Lady Rich, then, was more than a beautiful adornment to the Essex House circle. She was one of its most accomplished performers, and the range of her patronage and her correspondence reveal her intellect, education and sophisticated tastes. Her own letters, always fluent, often forceful, were praised by King James; and those addressed to her prove her pleasure in multi-layered meanings and wordplay. Her brother's "fantastical" letters are full of elaborate conceits, while Pérez's epistles reveal a taste for playful flirting and decadence.

Penelope may have owed some of her skill at Spanish, French and Italian to John Florio, the famous language tutor and translator who was part of the Devereux–Sidney circle. Soon after Penelope arrived at Court he was employed by the French ambassador and his wife (Frances's great friend Marie Bochetel) to give lessons to their daughter, and more recently he'd become tutor to Essex's friend Southampton. When, a few years later, Florio published his brilliant three-volume translation of Montaigne's French *Essays* he dedicated the second volume jointly to Lady Rich and to Frances's daughter, now the Countess of Rutland.

From Florio's preface it is obvious he knew Penelope well, including her intense affection for her children. She was "in riches of fortune not deficient", he said, "but of body incomparably richer" and "of mind most rich". The volume also contains a sonnet to "The honourably virtuous lady, Lady Penelope Rich", by Florio's friend and collaborator Dr Matthew Gwinne. Within the fourteen-line poem Gwinne manages to quote from seven *Astrophil and Stella* sonnets, including Philip's telling phrase, "Perfection's heir".

The writers who read Philip's poems in manuscript were familiar with another major work of translation: Bartholomew Yong's *The Diana of Jorge de Montemayor*, the Spanish story that was all the rage when Penelope came to Court. Yong translated it in 1582–3 while he was a law student at Middle Temple and when it was printed fifteen years later he dedicated it to the "magnificent mind" of Lady Rich – "so high and excellent a patroness". Yong recalled how she had sat among the great and good at the revels in Middle Temple, in "certain years past", when he acted "the part of a French orator". As he spoke his lines in French, he explained, "there was not any, whose mature judgement and censure in that language I feared and suspected more than your ladyship's". That night, "by your gracious aspect and mild countenance I flattered myself with your favourable applause". Now he hoped she would be similarly pleased with his *Diana*.

It is no coincidence that Henry Constable, the poet-cum-messenger who carried her Rialta letters and her portrait to King James, addressed at least some of his thirty-odd *Diana* poems to Penelope. His verses were in manuscript several years before they were printed in 1592, and they form the earliest sonnet sequence after *Astrophil and Stella*, which Constable read prepublication. Like Philip, Constable punned on the name Rich, and admired her "sparkling" black eyes and "waves of gold" hair. He listened, spellbound by her singing as well as her beauty:

> Seeing and hearing thee we see and hear
> Such voice such light as never sung nor shone …

How far he was genuinely in love with her, or mimicking Philip, or simply a devotee of her political agenda, is hard to tell. Certainly politics and religion came into it. After Constable converted to Catholicism he became a go-between for the pope and King James, and Penelope was one of the first to welcome him on his return to England, and Court, after Elizabeth's death.

The literary DNA that linked Constable and Philip Sidney's fellow writers and followers defies decoding. Yet one thread is easily discernible: at the heart of their mental and physical world sat Penelope, radiating star quality and celebrity status.

The poems, pictures and praise she received were, of course, partly the product of her brother's power, and the wealth that paid for portraits. At least three pictures of her hung in Essex House and Wanstead, apart from the pretty double portrait of her and Dorothy, and the Hilliard miniatures. But the cult of Penelope continued after Essex's downfall, reflecting her own influence and talents. In her forties she still danced and sang well enough to take prominent parts in Court masques; and after Mountjoy's death her voice and sorrow inspired John Coprario to compose some of the loveliest mourning songs ever written, *Funeral Tears*, knowing she could sing them perfectly, if not happily.

The tributes paid to Mountjoy by writers such as John Ford and Samuel Daniel brought more proof of Penelope's beauty, charm and skills. And before a posthumous silence closed around Penelope herself, there were moving testimonies to her, such as Thomas Campion's Latin *Umbra*, recalling "the star of Britain, Penelope" who "with her dulcet voice bewitched the ruler of the Irish" – Mountjoy.

Her vanishing act lay years ahead. In the 1590s there was a burgeoning industry in dedications to Penelope and authors queued up, as John Davies of Hereford put it, "To descant on thy name as many do". Even William Shakespeare followed the fashion for sonnets like *Astrophil and Stella* and puns on Lady Rich:

> Who is it that says most, which can say more
> Than this rich praise, that you alone are you?

When Shakespeare began to make his mark in London early in the 1590s, he naturally gravitated toward the Essex House circle. It was the most exciting and avant-garde group of aristocrats and intellectuals in London; and it ranged from the brilliant brains of the Bacon brothers to the beautiful – some said bisexual – Earl of Southampton, Shakespeare's first patron. Despite his youth, Southampton was the head of an ancient Catholic family. His confessor, and cousin, was the sweet-tempered Jesuit Fr Robert Southwell, whose dying agonies were eased by Mountjoy. Scholars will doubtless debate until the "last syllable of recorded time" whether or not Shakespeare was a Catholic. Whatever he was, he could not avoid the heavy scent of Catholic sympathy that hung about Essex House. It was almost as popular as punning on Penelope's name – and playgoing.

Everyone in London understood the power of plays and players to shape public opinion on current affairs. In the watershed years of the late sixteenth century, when the Rose, the Swan and the Globe theatres opened on Bankside, plays were the new black – sometimes very black; and in the Devereux circle plays were highly prized. Essex, Penelope and Mountjoy had grown up in households that patronized private troupes of actors; indeed the company that Shakespeare now joined, the Lord Chamberlain's Men, was backed by Penelope's great uncle Henry, Lord Hunsdon, and his son George Carey.

Shakespeare was bent on writing topical dramas with political bite for the Chamberlain's Men, and among the Devereux and their devotees he found themes and characters he could use. Montemayor's *Diana* (probably Yong's manuscript translation) gave him the plot for *Two Gentlemen of Verona*. For *Love's Labour's Lost* he took the political background and French gossip from Essex's agenda, recreated the diplomatic deer hunts at Wanstead and put Antonio Pérez on stage as Don Armado. The play's theme, that women triumph because they are stars, has also been claimed as Shakespeare's defence of Penelope's beauty against male-chauvinist attacks from Ralegh and his "scientific" friends.

Again and again Shakespeare and the Chamberlain's Men sided with Essex in his factional war with Cecil. When Cecil's supporter, Lord Cobham, found a connection between himself and Shakespeare's randy old "hero" Sir John Oldcastle in *Henry IV Part I*, Shakespeare hotly denied it. He renamed the character Sir John Falstaff in *The Merry Wives of Windsor*, but the connection stuck and Falstaff ended up as a national treasure as well as Cobham's nickname. It is easy to imagine, too, that Rosalind, Beatrice, Katherina, and maybe Helena and Olivia, owe something to Penelope's bright and forceful character.

Eventually the company's support for Essex would get them into serious trouble. *Henry V*, written soon after the earl led the army to Ireland in 1599, which compared him with the warrior-king, raised government fears about

Essex's ambitions. Performing *Richard II*, in which the king is deposed and murdered, on the eve of Essex's rebellion would prove a play too far. But for a while the Devereux' deeds lay just behind the curtain of Shakespeare's plays.

There was a war of minds and information to be won: at the theatres, in the back rooms of ale houses like the one where Kit Marlowe was murdered, at the council table, in whispered words floating across the Thames, and on the tiltyard. Culture and politics went hand in hand and manipulating public opinion was an art form. Elizabeth had been doing it for years with her summer progresses, St George's Day parades and tournaments.

Essex's performance at the Accession Day tournament in 1595 had been spectacular, yet it was only a curtain-raiser for the real thing. Through the winter he planned his greatest triumph – the raid on Cadiz in the summer of 1596.

Chapter Twenty

JANUARY–DECEMBER 1596

"With best forewinds guide the journey, speed the victory"
– Elizabeth I, 3 June 1596

*E*ssex's daring raid on the Spanish port of Cadiz in the summer of 1596 would be his finest hour. It brought back memories of Sir Francis Drake's brilliant attack nine years before, when he "singed the King of Spain's beard" by firing Philip's warships in the same harbour. And it showed, to Penelope's joy, that a Devereux was the queen's chief military commander.

Throughout the previous year Essex grew increasingly frustrated as Elizabeth ignored his intelligence that Spain was preparing a fresh invasion. Antonio Pérez in France had been intercepting letters and sending Essex warnings of war. Yet "Roberto il Diavolo", as Pérez nicknamed Cecil, encouraged Elizabeth to do nothing, and the queen and Essex were at loggerheads. Penelope, writing to Robert Cecil in July to obtain a favour for the bearer of her letter, explained, "my brother's own troubles make him unfit" to help secure a favour. Cecil knew about Essex's differences with Elizabeth and Penelope had no need to elaborate.

After the Spaniards mounted a small summer raid on Cornwall, the queen's views began to change and during the winter there was a flood of reports from Europe that Spain was gathering another armada. Even in Turkey Elizabeth's ambassador was aware of "a mighty army the King of Spain made against the Queen". Some of King Philip's growing fleet of galleons might be needed to escort the Spanish treasure fleets, loaded to the gunnels with gold and silver, sugar and spices, from the East and West Indies. They were sitting ducks for buccaneers like Drake and Ralegh. But Philip was mobilizing an army as well as ordering new vessels to be built with all haste. Some rumours said his target was Calais; others said Brittany and Ireland, where France and England were most vulnerable.

The Irish rebels, led by the Earl of Tyrone, were increasingly militant. The last thing Elizabeth wanted was Spain supporting them and she swiftly ordered her own armada and army to make ready. In March 1596 it was reported across the Continent that England was on stand-by for war. The Earl of Cumberland was sent to Ireland to prevent the Spaniards joining Tyrone's rebellion, and to bring Tyrone a prisoner to London. And on 18 March Elizabeth signed a joint commission to Essex and lord admiral Charles Howard to be "our Lieutenants General and Governors of our whole navy and army upon the sea at this present". In theory Lord Howard had authority at sea, while Essex was commander-in-chief on shore. English agents abroad were briefed to leak the story that one hundred ships were ready to sail for the West Indies to reinforce Drake's fleet, which had been causing havoc with Spanish ships and settlements around Havana and Puerto Rico.

In fact, "El Drago" was about to sleep in his last hammock "slung atween the round shot in Nombre de Dios bay". He would harry the Spaniards no more. After several maulings by superior Spanish forces, his tattered fleet had been wracked by fever and on 27 January 1596 he died of dysentery, to the undisguised glee of King Philip and the tears of every ballad-loving Briton.

Elizabeth's commanders were not bound for the West Indies. Their destination was Spain and they would not leave for weeks. Although Essex and Howard were impatient to strike before Philip's navy mustered its full strength, Elizabeth was undecided whether to let her warships go. She was especially uncertain about Essex's desire to establish a footing on Spanish soil and maintain an English presence in Europe's battle zones.

For Penelope the weeks of waiting were unbearable. Any day she might hear that the ships in Plymouth Sound had carried away both her brother and her husband. Not, praise be, her lover: Elizabeth had ordered Mountjoy to stay at his post in Portsmouth, though it was arguably the most dangerous job on the home front. If rumours were correct, the Spaniards would make straight for Portsmouth, the Isle of Wight and the Hampshire coast. And thanks to Elizabeth's cheapskate approach to defence procurement, Portsmouth was underfortified.

Penelope was in no doubt about the dangers Mountjoy and Essex faced. She was less certain about Lord Rich. He had advanced Essex £1,000 to help finance the expedition, and declared he would go to Cadiz, but he was not a born sailor. In April she wrote urgently to Robert Cecil asking him to help her messenger gain access to Essex. "Worthy Sir Robert," she wrote: "I must yield you many thanks for the often kindnesses you do me, and pray you now to procure if you can possibly that this bearer may ... give a farewell to my brother ... as I have committed some trust unto him of late when I thought my Lord Rich should have gone this voyage, and about that business would I fain have him confer with my brother."

On 3 May, writing to Anthony Bacon at Essex House, Penelope complained she was desperate to hear what was going on "while I am in this solitary place, where no sound of any news can come". She was probably at Leighs and nothing short of pregnancy or serious illness – her own, her sister's or her children's – would have kept her away from London.

"I must entreat you to let me hear something of the world from you, especially of my brother," she begged Anthony; "and then what you know of the French affairs, and whether there go any troops from hence to their aid." Penelope, tactical as ever, was exaggerating her lack of news to encourage Bacon to tell whatever he knew. She had already discovered that the war front had shifted to France. She had also picked up that Pérez was back in England, part of a mission to Elizabeth urging her to send troops to France. In a short, seemingly casual postscript to Bacon, Penelope added: "I would fain hear what becomes of your wandering neighbour." No one who knew Penelope would be fooled by a throwaway line like that, and Anthony knew who was calling his tune. Two days later a full briefing was on its way back to her.

In the first days of April, while the fleet awaited Elizabeth's permission to sail, a Spanish army from the Netherlands had marched on Calais, taken the town and laid siege to the garrison. It gave Spain a foothold on England's doorstep that was far too close for comfort. In the gardens at Greenwich, it was said, Elizabeth could even hear the guns at Calais. Nonetheless, a week went by before she put Essex in charge of a relief force to go from Dover to Calais, "at the importunate request of our good brother the French King". But more days drifted by before Essex was ordered to Calais and it was then too late to dislodge the Spanish force. The French garrison fell, leaving Calais in enemy hands, and Essex returned to Plymouth. It was not Essex's fault, but it reflected badly on him, since Elizabeth, true to form, hid behind conflicting orders. For a while in May she cancelled the whole expedition to Cadiz. Essex fumed to his secretary Ned Reynolds: "If this force were going to France, she would then fear as much the issue there as she doth our intended journey. I know I shall never do her service but against her will."

For Penelope the anxious waiting dragged on. She knew Essex was eager to be gone. She knew, too, that her stepfather, Sir Christopher, could look after himself. But if Lord Rich went with them, how would he fare at sea and under attack? If anything happened to him it had serious implications for her and the children. Their eldest son Robert was a fine lad, but still only nine years old in March. If his father died, whoever obtained her son's wardship, and control of his vast estates, might well close down Leighs Priory, just as the Chartley household had been disbanded after her father's death.

And if anything happened to Mountjoy, what would become of his two daughters? For the moment little Penelope, aged four, and Isabella, now eighteen months, were safe sheltering under Lord Rich's roof and his name, but their prospects would be bleak if Rich did not return, or Mountjoy was killed at Portsmouth.

And who could tell what the future held for the new baby Penelope was carrying? It was no secret that she was with child again. Antonio Pérez, writing to her shortly before the French crisis brought him to England, knew that Penelope, Dorothy and Frances, "three sisters and goddesses", were all expecting to "push forth" three "buds of those divine beauties". The sexual innuendos in Pérez's compliments were as obvious and as hollow as his jokey threat to blackmail Penelope: "Oh, what a book of secrets I have," he reminded her. The next time he came to England he would not need to earn his living; he would sell the secrets in his notebook. They both knew he wouldn't dare if he ever wanted to be employed by Essex again. Or would he? One could never be sure with Antonio.

More pressing than dubious threats were Frances's sufferings. She had a sad time of it between her dying babies and her philandering husband. A year earlier the queen had discovered that Essex, not Thomas Vavasour, was the father of Mistress Southwell's bastard boy, born at the end of 1591. Elizabeth was beside herself with rage when she realised she had sent an innocent man to jail. The humiliation for Frances was made worse by knowing that Southwell's son, also named Walter, was a healthy child (sent to live with Lettice in Staffordshire) while her own little Walter lived barely a month. And now, while the fleet prepared to sail to Cadiz, yet another of her children died. On 7 May her one-year-old, Penelope's godson Henry, was buried at All Hallows by the Tower.

Early in June Queen Elizabeth at last sent final dispatches to the fleet and nearly 120 vessels, including sixty great warships, sailed slowly out of Plymouth Sound heading for Cadiz. With them Elizabeth sent her prayer that God would "prosper the work and with best forewinds guide the journey, speed the victory, and make the return the advancement of thy fame and surety to the realm, with the least loss of English blood". No one would have echoed the last line more fervently than Penelope: "To these devout petitions, Lord, give thou thy blessed grant! Amen."

～

After three weeks at sea Elizabeth's fleet rounded the cape into the Bay of Cadiz and began demolishing the Spanish navy. Essex led the troops ashore and stormed the city. On Midsummer's Day it was all over. Ralegh and Howard held the high seas, Essex and his men occupied the town and the

Spaniards were forced to fire and scuttle their heavily loaded merchant ships trapped in the harbour.

Cadiz was the major port on the Andalusian coast, some forty miles from Seville. It had plenty of rich pickings and it made an ideal bridgehead for Essex's plan to establish a military presence in Europe, and force Elizabeth to back his hawkish foreign policy. But after a fortnight, Essex was compelled to leave: his fellow officers were pleased with their spoils of war and wanted to be off. Essex was nonetheless the hero of the hour and his bravery was the stuff of legend. Even the lord admiral, usually at loggerheads with Essex, had to admit to Lord Burghley: "There is not a braver man in the world than the Earl is; and I protest, in my poor judgment, a greater soldier, for what he doth is in great order and discipline performed."

Essex's enemies in England, however, were criticising his campaign and the small share of spoils that seemed to be coming Elizabeth's way. Penelope, still in the country, tried hard to dispel adverse comments. In mid-July she wrote to Cecil: "When you hear any more news of my brother, I pray you let me enjoy the sound of it." There was no need to ask for news of Lord Rich. He had left the expedition early and was at Wanstead in July.

While the fleet was still at sea, Penelope heard from Cecil and wrote back, briefly, with "infinite thanks" for "the happy news of my brother's safety, who I hope hath performed to his power, that which was fit for him, and his country". "How it is accepted in Court I would fain hear," she added, "for there are some already out of their own base envy seek to detract what they can from his honour, though their words return to their own disgrace, rather than his dispraise." His critics were having a field day behind his back and she intended to pursue the point when she returned to London. "When I see you I will let you understand what I know of this matter," she went on, unwilling to name names in a letter that could fall into the wrong hands.

There was another member of the family on Penelope's mind as well. With her grandfather's advancing years, his son Sir William Knollys was keen to take over his job as treasurer of the queen's household. Robert Cecil would have a large say in who got it, and twice in her letters to Cecil Penelope put in a word for her uncle William. It was vital to drop hints in the right ears, to obtain Court appointments. Heavy doses of flattery were the norm and Penelope offered "infinite thanks" to "Worthy Sir Robert" for "the grace you vouchsafe my uncle". William, she added, would be beholden to Cecil when the job was given to him, "as it is thought it will tomorrow".

It wasn't. It went to Lord North, who must long ago have decided his wedding gift to Penelope was a misplaced gesture. William had to be content with the job of comptroller of the household, though he became a privy councillor and got the post of treasurer a few years later.

Sir Francis's death on 19 July was a blow to the whole family. He was well over eighty and though his extreme Protestantism had left him sidelined in government, he was one of Elizabeth's most respected councillors. He never remarried after the death of Lady Katherine and it was probably fond memories of her that led Elizabeth to appreciate him more than other committed Protestants.

At Grey's Court, on a quiet hillside in the Thames Valley, where red kites now circle overhead once more, Sir Francis had dreamed of living a "country poor life" far from Court – the same dream that Essex often cherished. In August Sir Francis was buried nearby in St Nicholas's Church. Ten years later William raised a magnificent tomb to his parents in a side chapel of the church, where it remains beautifully kept, with effigies of their many children kneeling beside them.

Sir Francis was "the lamp and torch of truth", Thomas Churchyard wrote in his epitaph, and his death was a great loss. "In one year's course died many men of mark", Churchyard went on; for within a week Penelope's great uncle Henry, straight-talking Lord Hunsdon, also died. It was said in the family that Elizabeth paid him a last visit and offered him an earldom; only to be told that since she hadn't thought him worthy of it while he was living, he did not want it now that he was dying. If it wasn't strictly true, it underlined family anger against the queen. Neither Hunsdon nor his sister Lady Katherine claimed they were more than Elizabeth's cousins, but his funeral raised questions again. Like Katherine's it was a grand occasion in Westminster Abbey and it cost Elizabeth £800. So how nearly were they "the queen's near kindred", some wondered, looking at Hunsdon's large tomb, which does not name Will Carey as his father.

In council Hunsdon had often supported Essex, and it was another worrying sign when his job as lord chamberlain did not pass to his son George Carey. Instead it went to elderly Lord Cobham, whose son was Essex's sworn enemy and whose daughter was Cecil's wife. In quick succession two key posts had passed into enemy hands, albeit temporarily.

The passing of the "old guard" left Elizabeth increasingly forlorn and dependent on the Cecils. And for Penelope the loss of her grandfather was compounded by concern that, as the chairs changed round the council table, Essex's position looked a lot weaker. For the moment, though, he was returning in triumph.

~

Essex's conquest of Cadiz has been called "the most complete and dramatic victory of the war against Spain", and on the streets of London he received a hero's welcome. Edmund Spenser spoke for everyone when he called Essex:

Great England's glory and the world's wide wonder,
Whose dreadful name, late through all Spain did thunder.

The earl was everything the crowds loved: a lean, handsome, thirtysome-thing soldier with chivalry in his blood, a rough, square beard on his aristocratic chin, and all the charm and confidence born of success. Before they left Cadiz Penelope's stepfather, Sir Christopher, could not resist boasting how well they had done – and having a dig at Lord Rich. "I commend my duty unto you," he wrote to her, "and salute my lord your husband's absence with grief, who, I wish, had been a partaker of the glory." Courtly compliments could always hide a snigger.

Back in London, Anthony Bacon boasted how Essex "hath with the bright beams of his valour and virtue scattered the clouds ... that malicious envy had stirred up against his matchless merit; which hath made the Old Fox to crouch and whine". He was foolishly optimistic. Burghley was incapable of crouching and whining. The Cecils were fighting a public relations war with Essex, and though the earl was the capital's darling, winning the hearts and minds of the common people was a dangerous game. Shakespeare, musing on his next play and often at Court with the Lord Chamberlain's players, watched Essex's "courtship to the common people, how he did seem to dive into their hearts", and guessed it would prove his downfall. Elizabeth could not permit anyone to be more popular than the crown.

What bothered Elizabeth most in the immediate aftermath of Cadiz was money. Essex returned to Court in August and found her furious. She had heard accounts, probably exaggerated, of the booty brought back from Cadiz and it seemed that everyone but her had benefited from the trip. She sent a salvo of messages to Mountjoy, busy at Portsmouth improving defences in case Spain retaliated, and ordered him to impound any loot offloaded near him and keep it for her majesty. In particular, if the *Swan of London* docked at Portsmouth, the two bronze cannons the crew had captured were defi-nitely hers. Elizabeth held Essex personally responsible that her share of the spoils was so slight. Far from being a success, the trip had been badly handled, the Spanish fleet was damaged but not destroyed, and she had been made to look like the aggressor. It was not an image Elizabeth liked. She put the Cecils in charge of investigating Essex's conduct of the campaign, and published a justification for sending her forces against Spain.

Essex was cleared of incompetence, but the backwash from the Cadiz raid was lasting and bitter – and in his absence Elizabeth had given Robert Cecil the job of secretary of state. In reality Cecil had been doing it for seven years, without the title or the pay, but this made it official and guaranteed a seam-less transfer of authority when his father finally departed. Cecil's relationship with Elizabeth would go from strength to strength, at least on the surface, while Essex's never fully recovered.

Essex and Sir Christopher had returned safely and Penelope's concerns now turned to Mountjoy and their baby. When summer turned to autumn, rumours increased that King Philip would seek revenge by attacking Portsmouth, and as diplomatically as possible Mountjoy warned the privy council that Portsmouth's defences were too weak to repulse an invasion. In the end, stormy winds and seas saved England yet again, by blowing Philip's fleet off course. And to Penelope it must have seemed that God had answered her prayers again when her baby was born a healthy, handsome boy. This child would never inherit his father's title, but at least he could use Mountjoy as his Christian name. His surname, however, must still be Rich.

～

Lord Rich was busy with his own affairs that autumn. If he bailed out of the Cadiz trip to avoid getting seasick in the Bay of Biscay, he made a big mistake joining Lord Shrewsbury's diplomatic mission to France. He was not only ill at sea, he was ill at ease with men who knew him for a Puritan and a cuckold – one of the oldest comic characters: the unheroic husband who couldn't hold on to his beautiful wife.

The mission that Rich joined in September, heading for Rouen, was a charm offensive to get King Henri IV to join another war against Spain in the Netherlands and expel the Spaniards from Calais. The Earl of Shrewsbury led the embassy, but four days after leaving London on 11 September he had to admit he was still hunting near Canterbury. The wind was against them, he claimed. The following evening it turned fair and he embarked with Lord Rich on the *Antelope*, only to run into more storms. "All our gallants have been notably sick and some of them ready to make their will but that they wanted a scrivener," Shrewsbury wrote to Cecil. Lord Rich, he added, had twice been driven out of Shrewsbury's cabin "by knavish tales". How far the bawdy humour was directed at Lord Rich and who was telling the tales, Shrewsbury claimed he "knew not". But he endorsed the cover of his letter; "Sir, my Lord Rich and I are bold to send a badge of our profession of good husbands within your packet." The "badge" is lost to history, but any irony would not have been lost on Robert Cecil.

They spent several more days "tumbling and tossing on the seas" but in France things improved. The English visitors were thoroughly wined and dined for a fortnight, and "the health of everyone's mistress at the table was so often remembered in the cup as they could scarce call one another by their name". Shrewsbury and Lord Rich, waiting to see Henri's triumphal entry into Rouen, spent three hours seated opposite the king's mistress.

Shrewsbury, forgetting he was reporting matters of state back to London, speculated whether she employed "art to help her beauty", and what sort of hair colour her ladies used. Remembering to "crave pardon" of Cecil, he offered the lame excuse: "it is not amiss you should understand anything that is news."

At Rouen Lord Rich encountered Antonio Pérez. The wandering Spaniard had returned to France after his spring mission to England and he called on Shrewsbury and Lord Rich, as Rich diligently reported to Essex. Pérez had given him a letter for the earl, insisting it was "of great secrecy" and could only be entrusted to Lord Rich to forward to Essex.

After more than a month abroad Lord Rich came home and his experiences brought out the bawdy side of Penelope's humour. A few days before Christmas, while she and Rich were staying in the Barrett family's Essex home, Belhouse, at Aveley (where Elizabeth stayed the second night of her Tilbury visit), Penelope decided to "help" Lord Rich reply to a letter from her brother. Essex had recommended a French secretary to Lord Rich, whom Rich declined. His part in Shrewsbury's mission was over and he did not expect to undertake anything else like it. He offered Essex his "best prayers to bless you" and signed himself, as usual, "your lordship's poor brother to command". After Penelope intercepted and amended his reply it read as though Lord Rich had picked up a dose of the "French disease" (syphilis) but, having had intercourse once during the mission, he wasn't expecting to repeat the experience. For good measure she added a postscript: "You may imagine my Lord Rich hath no employment for a language secretary except he has gotten a mistress in France."

~

It was all very well Penelope making fun of Lord Rich and his sex life, or lack of it, but her brother's bed-hopping habits had become a real problem. Private adultery was one thing but brazen seduction was another, and everyone, including Essex's wife and mother, knew about his mistresses. As soon as he was back from Cadiz, gossip said he'd taken up with an old flame, "a nobleman's wife, and so near about her majesty".

Lady Bacon had often warned her sons about the louche lifestyle in Essex House – wine, women and lute songs, not to mention gambling. Now she gave Essex a thorough dressing down. The "unwifelike and unshamefaced demeanour" of his paramour was destroying "her ancient noble husband", she wrote at the beginning of December. The earl's "carnal dalliance" and "backsliding to the foul impudent" was especially reprehensible because his wife was pregnant. He had made "her heart sorrowful to the hindrance of her young fruit within her". It was widely believed "her last did not comfortably prosper", and died soon after birth, because Frances was upset. In full sermonizing flow, Lady Bacon used the Bible to back her argument. And in case Essex hadn't got his copy to hand, she quoted in full the First Epistle to the Thessalonians – "This is the will of God, that ye should be holy, and abstain from fornication."

Essex reeled under the attack. Just because Lady Bacon was Burghley's sister-in-law it did not mean she could ignore Court etiquette and write to him, an earl, in that tone. He did the only thing he could and replied immediately in a way that was impossible to tell if he was truly penitent or sending her up. Thanking her for letting him know what she had heard, he insisted he was innocent. He had only seen and spoken to the woman she was referring to in company with others "who if they would do me right could justify my behaviour. But I live in a place where I am hourly conspired against and practised upon." That was the crux of it. If his critics couldn't convince Elizabeth their accusations were true, "they give out to the world" instead.

At Court, during the Christmastide festivities, there were signs that Essex was right: his enemies used every means to disgrace him. When Shakespeare and the Lord Chamberlain's actors performed for the queen at Whitehall, one of Essex's secretaries, Edward Jones, caught the flak. Lord Cobham spotted him among the seats reserved for A-list courtiers. Before the secretary could explain that he was simply speaking to his pregnant wife, who *was* entitled to a seat, Cobham bawled him out as "a saucy fellow" and ordered him to the back of the hall. It was deeply embarrassing for Jones, only slightly less so for Essex; and it did not augur well.

Chapter Twenty-One

NEW YEAR 1597–SEPTEMBER 1599

'The General of our Gracious Empress'

– William Shakespeare, *Henry V*, 1599

On Twelfth Night 1597 Penelope attended the revels in Middle Temple, next door to Essex House. Like their colleagues at Gray's Inn, the lawyers at the Temple celebrated Christmastide and New Year with gusto and cheer, food and wine, music and masquing. It was years since Penelope had sat in the Temple watching a young Bartholomew Yong make his speech in French; but the same traditions and entertainments went on. In the flickering light of the great hall "many noble lords and fair ladies graced and beautified these sports", and the revelling continued into the small hours of the morning.

The festive season was soon forgotten at Court, however, when news came that Mr Secretary Cecil's wife had died following a miscarriage. It was a reminder to Penelope that pregnancy carried increasing risks as she grew older. Essex was also depressed and after a row with Elizabeth he took to his rooms, allegedly sick. Some said it was depression and "agues", others said syphilis. At the end of February, Rowland Whyte told Robert Sidney: "My lord of Essex kept his bed the most part of all yesterday, yet did one of his chamber tell me ... his lord was not sick. There is not a day passes that the queen sends not often to see him, and himself every day goeth privately unto her."

Penelope's attendance at Court was all the more important when Essex was keeping to his rooms; and she tried not to bother him with the many begging letters and petitioners who hung about hoping to enlist his help in their private troubles. Some cases, however, touched her sympathies and she felt compelled to pass them on. "Worthy Brother," she wrote in March, "I was so loath to importune you for this poor gentlewoman ... and yesterday I sent her word by her man that I would not trouble you with it." When the woman approached her a second time Penelope felt duty bound to forward her plea to Essex, adding "none will pity her misery, and her children if you do not".

Essex sought Elizabeth's permission to retire to Lamphey until after Easter, but she didn't like the idea. Nor did his supporters. It would give an "opportunity and advantage to the cunning plotters and practicers of the Court"; and the journey was "far, tedious, unpleasant, and soon after his indisposition". The real problem was Essex's attitude. "Truly I fear that his lordship is wearied, and scorneth the practices and dissembling courses of this place," one secretary observed. Penelope knew it, too. His "bookishness" was always threatening to take over. It was something he shared with Mountjoy, who "spent his vacant hours with scholars best able to direct him" and took "such pains in the search of natural philosophy".

The illness of Lord Cobham, leading to his death on 5 March, prompted Essex to postpone his trip and get back into Court politics. Cobham's job as lord chamberlain would go to George Carey, the new Lord Hunsdon, so at least that was back in the family. But Essex was anxious to stop Elizabeth and Cecil handing the office of lord warden of the Cinque Ports straight to the new Lord Cobham, Cecil's brother-in-law and Essex's enemy. For a time Essex considered going for it himself. Then Robert Sidney decided to apply, hoping for a job that would bring him home from the Netherlands. Barbara, meanwhile, was planning another christening. Her latest baby was to be named on 2 March, and it would be another gathering of the extended Sidney–Devereux family. "All the great ladies" – Penelope, Dorothy, Frances and her mother Lady Walsingham, Lady Warwick, Lady Bedford, Lady Sussex – were expected; and the young Earl of Southampton "most willingly" stood godfather.

Once that was over, and it was known that Elizabeth had refused Essex the lord wardenship (she pacified him with master of the Ordnance) Rowland Whyte began canvassing for Sidney. Penelope, often at Court, popular and with easy access to the queen, was a natural ally. Where her brother was "fickle" and still keeping to his rooms when he chose, Penelope could be relied on to make a case for a friend. Besides, she sympathized with Sidney's longing to be with Barbara and the children.

She had already pushed his name forward before Whyte bumped into her at Court and she offered to deliver Robert's letter of application. No one else was apparently willing to do it, but Penelope "put it in her bosom and assured [Whyte] that this night or to morrow morning" she would deliver it to the queen in person. Her efforts were wasted. It was already a done deal, and it went to Cobham.

When Penelope failed to appear at Court a few weeks later, unlike her brother she was not feigning sickness. She had smallpox. At first her fever and headaches did not cause undue anxiety, but once the dreaded rash appeared on her face and hands', and the tiny pink spots turned to blisters, there could be no doubt. Smallpox carried at least a one in five chance of death. The possibility of blindness or disfigurement was higher and at first it was feared "the small pox has much disfigured Lady Rich".

Elizabeth had almost died from it in 1562, as the Sidney family had reason to remember. When Robert's mother, Lady Mary, contracted the disease while devotedly nursing the queen, it left her face so disfigured she became almost a recluse.

For once Penelope was happy to withdraw to Lord Rich's town house at St Bartholomew's rather than Essex House, to avoid spreading infection, and Lord Rich stayed with her. On Saturday 16 April he wrote to Essex, "This banishment makes me that I cannot attend on you." To avoid the risk of Penelope writing directly to Essex, Lord Rich enclosed a letter from a girl who had asked Penelope's help. Lord Rich's jokes to Essex – about contracting the great pox (syphilis) rather than small pox, Penelope infecting the pretty young girl out of jealousy, and Penelope's need for a mask to cover her scarred face – were not in good taste at the time and they are almost unfathomable now. But beneath the misplaced humour he was trying to help her, and there is some concern in his parting line to Essex: "If you dare meet her I beseech you preacheth patience unto her."

Fortunately the fears for Penelope's looks were unfounded and on Tuesday Rowland Whyte reassured Robert and Barbara: "My Lady Rich is recovered of her small pox without any blemish to her beautiful face."

～

There was much to give thanks for by the end of April and it seemed the family's fortunes were mending. Essex was still at Court and despite his chagrin over Cobham's appointment he was patching up an alliance with Cecil. And, if Penelope did not know it before, she knew in May that she was again expecting Mountjoy's child. Mountjoy was reaping the rewards of his careful governorship of Portsmouth. On St George's Day 1598 he was nominated a knight of the Garter. It was a sign of Elizabeth's regard for him as well as a tribute to his discretion. Preserving the protocols of Penelope's marriage was paying dividends and Elizabeth was about to send another token of favour to "noble wise" and "faithful Mountjoy".

On 2 June Rowland Whyte – in his customary position, ear close to the ground – learnt that "Lord Mountjoy hath gotten leave and is lieutenant general and hath a regiment". Over the heads of older, more experienced campaigners, Mountjoy was to be deputy army commander in a major offensive against Spain. At last he had royal permission to leave Portsmouth; he would not have to watch Essex, Sir Christopher and even Lord Rich, sail off to glory.

Essex had brokered a deal with Cecil and Ralegh (back at Court after five years in disgrace for his marriage) to mount a full-scale attack on Spain. It was anyone's guess how long an accord between the three could last, but Spain was reported to be planning a fresh invasion and Essex convinced the other two that a pre-emptive strike was vital. In council Essex was increasingly criticized as a warmonger, and in vain his advisers told him to soft-pedal on military glory. Essex pressed on and agreed with Elizabeth that they would first demolish Philip's fleet in its home ports, then attack Spain's garrisons on the islands of the Azores, and finally intercept the Spanish treasure fleet on its way home.

The "Islands Voyage" was a fiasco. There were mutterings of mismanagement even before they left, and stormy weather immediately drove them back to Plymouth for repairs. At the end of July, before they could sail again, Lord Rich left for home, too seasick to continue. "I have enforced my brother Rich and your majesty's servant Carew Reynolds to stay," Essex told Elizabeth, "for if I had carried them to sea, they would have been dead in a week." The fleet that set off a second time, in the middle of August, was much smaller and most of the army had been dismissed. They hit more storms and Essex, ignoring Elizabeth's orders, sailed straight for the Azores.

Penelope knew about the expedition's problems and was doing what she could to limit criticism of the Devereux. Writing to Cecil on 24 September, while she stayed at Belhouse in Essex again, she told him that whatever "a lady and friend of yours did make known unto you", Cecil could take it from Penelope herself "that I was not changeable in the constant opinion I have of your virtues". She wanted to "commend my affection, to your noble and true judging mind". With Essex, Mountjoy and Sir Christopher away, someone at Court was speaking ill of her, and probably them, and it was crucial to counteract it. But Penelope was not about to send a letter and a messenger without soliciting news, and she begged Cecil to "let me hear from you, when you have any news of my brother, since I infinitely long to hear that all the troubles of this voyage were past, and some hope of his speedy return". Tactful to the last, she didn't mention Mountjoy.

The situation in the Azores was, in fact, deteriorating. Essex missed a vast Spanish treasure fleet carrying enough silver bullion to bankroll Spain for years and he failed to overcome the main Spanish garrison. In mid-October he called the expedition off and as his ships ran for home they were damaged and scattered by more storms.

If one man came out of it well, it was Mountjoy. Heading into Plymouth ahead of Essex, he encountered three Spanish frigates and realized that the ships Essex should have immobilized in their home ports were about to attack England. To Elizabeth's immense relief, Mountjoy began putting the south coast on invasion alert, though it was stormy weather that really saved England again. The Spaniards limped home without setting foot on English soil and Mountjoy got the credit.

Cecil was quick to compliment Mountjoy and make Elizabeth aware of his success. He could see the benefits of befriending a rising star like Mountjoy, especially if he could drive a wedge into Essex's circle. Mountjoy and Essex were inextricably linked by Penelope, and since the passing of the elder statesmen in their family her strong character and influence over Essex had increased. Yet her power would be weakened if Mountjoy owed some allegiance to Cecil. And if Penelope's letters showed she could keep up cordial relations, Cecil could play the same game.

Essex's sisters and mother were, as usual, overjoyed at his safe return. Lettice was at Drayton when she received a short letter from him and replied immediately: "You can hardly imagine my dear sweet son how joyful these lines of your hand hath made me." Despite the trip's failure, Essex was more popular than ever with the crowds in London. His bravery under fire led people to cheer him wherever he showed his tanned, handsome face. But that did not suit Elizabeth and at Court his reception was cooler. The safety net that had once been there for him had unravelled with the deaths of Huntingdon, Hunsdon and Knollys. In future his backers would be mostly younger men, like Rutland and Southampton, who packed little political punch. Essex's fall from favour over the next two years was tragic, but he was not an Icarus in free fall. Icarus had no enemies except his ambition and the sun. Essex had plenty. Some opposed him as a warmonger and power-seeker. They considered his anti-Spanish policy dangerous and expensive and they formed a peace party around the Cecils. Others, notably Ralegh, opposed him for more personal reasons.

Ralegh had been Essex's number two at sea on the "Islands Voyage" and they fell out badly when Essex missed the Spanish treasure fleet. But Ralegh's dislike went deeper. He had never been accepted as a five-star courtier and he found Essex's arrogance insufferable. Ralegh still harboured hopes of retrieving Elizabeth's affection and since Essex was sliding out of royal favour there was no harm in putting the boot in.

Henceforth Ralegh would be one of Essex's most dangerous enemies. And Bess Ralegh was no longer one of the close friends to whom Penelope would break the news of her new baby.

Probably at the end of November, Mountjoy's second son was born, again at Essex House. He was Penelope's ninth child. Of her five children by Lord Rich, four had survived, and by Mountjoy she now had four more. Her latest son, baptized on 8 December and recorded in the parish register of St Clement Danes, a few yards away, was called Scipio. His name reflected

Mountjoy's growing reputation as an army commander, yet the boy was still given the surname Rich. Nothing more is heard of Scipio and his name was not included in Mountjoy's will. Penelope had experienced only one previous infant death, Lord Rich's daughter Elizabeth. It would not be surprising if she suffered another, particularly as she was ill with smallpox soon after Scipio was conceived. But it is also possible that the baby came to be known as St John, the second son named in Mountjoy's will, for whom no baptismal record has been found.

Mountjoy's other children – Penelope, Isabella and Mountjoy – were flourishing at Leighs with Lord Rich's children. Robert and Henry were now ten and seven years old, and his daughters Lucy and Essex were young ladies in their teens.

∽

If Penelope had just lost her baby Scipio she would have been pleased by Lettice's visit to London that winter. It was a last-minute decision. Lettice had been expecting Essex to visit her in Staffordshire. He retired to Wanstead following the Azores debacle and told Lettice he would come to Drayton for the winter, turning "monk" as he sometimes put it. But when the queen mollified him with the title earl marshal of England he returned to Court. In November Lettice wrote to him wondering if Elizabeth might now be willing to receive her at Court. Sir Christopher had business in London and they could come together. Lettice, now in her fifty-fifth year, had given up riding everywhere and "a winter's journey" to London by coach would be slow, muddy and uncomfortable. Nonetheless she would do it, if he wished. There was Dorothy to see, too. The past year had been exceptionally sad for her.

At the beginning of the summer Dorothy's first son, a "goodly boy, Northumberland's heir, the little Lord Percy", died when he was just a year old. A few days later she gave birth again at Syon House and on 24 June Northumberland wrote happily to Essex that his sister was "very well" and had "recompensed her last loss and another nephew to you is born". In his haste, Northumberland forgot to ask Essex to be the boy's godfather, so he wrote again the following day, explaining: "Your sister is very desirous of it, and I should have much joy if you might have been present your self." In less than six months, however, the new baby, also named Henry, was dead. It put added strain on Dorothy's difficult relationship with "the Wizard Earl", but by the autumn she was pregnant again.

In December, Lettice asked Essex once more if he thought Elizabeth would receive her. On the whole, she wrote, "a country life is fittest for disgraced persons but if you find reason to wish my coming then you must presently send some coach horses to fetch me for my own will never be able to draw me out of the mire". She advised him to see if Lady Warwick (widow of Leicester's brother Ambrose) and Lady Leighton (Lettice's sister Elizabeth) thought it a good idea. They were both still among Elizabeth's ladies. "Let me hear accordingly from you," Lettice added, signing off as usual, "Your mother, infinitely loving you."

Lettice came; and spent weeks hanging around in London. In mid-February she was still waiting. Essex was using his persuasive powers, but not exclusively on the queen. The earl "is again fallen in love with his fairest B; it cannot choose but come to the Queen's ears, and then he is undone and all they that depend on his favour," wrote one regular gossip. "Fairest B" was Mistress Brydges, one of two maids to the queen who were in trouble earlier in the year for flirting with Essex. Elizabeth was said to have exchanged "words and blows of anger" with them and only allowed them back at Court when they promised not to repeat the offence. Fresh philandering with "Fairest B" would not be overlooked.

While Lettice waited for her chance to see Elizabeth there were feasts and entertainments in Essex House. On St Valentine's Day, Essex's steward Sir Gelly Meyrick organized "a very great supper at Essex house", with music, dancing and a full family turnout: Lettice, Penelope, Dorothy, Frances, Essex and Mountjoy, their friends Lady Bedford and Lord Rutland – but no sign of Lord Rich. After supper the players came in to perform two plays for them, and kept the party going until "one o'clock after midnight". And when the last lute songs and madrigals died away, and the fires burned low, Penelope and Mountjoy could retire to the large canopied bed with its black and gold hangings, in the chamber Lord Leicester set aside for her nearly twenty years before.

Despite female distractions, Essex was, in fact, trying to persuade Elizabeth to receive Lettice. His mother's disgrace was so well known around Court that he now made it a test of his own status with the queen. But every time Elizabeth agreed and Lettice was brought to the privy galleries, Elizabeth found an excuse not to be there. When she pulled out of a meeting at the last moment, on 27 February, Lettice was left waiting to give her "a fair jewel of £300". The slight was so public, "all the world expecting her Majesty's coming", that Essex went up the private stairs to Elizabeth's chamber, so the gossips said, "in his nightgown", to try and persuade her. Suddenly the next day "Lady Leicester was at Court, kissed the queen's hand and her breast, and embraced her, and the queen kissed her ladyship". It was the most perfunctory reunion possible. Lettice would have liked a repeat before she and Sir Christopher returned to the country, but Elizabeth refused.

At the St Valentine's "great supper" there was another absentee as well as Lord Rich. Henry Wriothesley, the Earl of Southampton, was missing. For the past three or four years his feet had been firmly under Essex's table and he joined Essex's campaigns. Early in February, however, the queen – as unreasonable as ever – refused his request to marry one of her maids, Elizabeth Vernon, Penelope's cousin. Mistress Vernon was the daughter of Earl Walter's sister, Elizabeth, and Sir John Vernon. She was beautiful, vivacious and determined, though perhaps not so gifted as Penelope at languages and music. Southampton had been openly flirting with her for years. In September 1595, Rowland Whyte noted, "My Lord of Southampton doth with too much familiarity court the fair Mistress Vernon." Instead of permission to marry, Elizabeth handed Southampton a licence to travel abroad for two years. It was more than a hint that he should get lost, and four days before the supper party he took leave of London and a tearful Mistress Vernon.

The tears were a giveaway. "His fair mistress doth wash her fairest face with too many tears," observed one courtier, speculating on the reason. He was right: Mistress Vernon was pregnant. Penelope and Essex settled her into Essex House and arranged for Southampton to sneak back into the country in August and marry her. Cousin Elizabeth was a Devereux in all but name and it was important to preserve her honour, or as much of it as was left. In addition, Southampton was a key ally in Essex's cause. Sooner or later the queen was bound to hear that Southampton had defied both her orders, not to marry and not to be in England, and Penelope and Essex were taking a calculated risk in helping him. Sure enough news spread that "Mistress Vernon is from the court and lies in Essex House. Some say she hath taken a venue under the girdle and swells upon it." Elizabeth was apoplectic. She had the new Countess of Southampton committed to one of the better apartments in the Fleet prison and ordered the earl to join her on his return from France.

The Southampton affair did not improve matters between Elizabeth and Essex, but their relationship had reached meltdown anyway. Tension between the war and peace parties was intense, and Burghley touched a tender spot when he sanctimoniously pushed Psalm 55, verse 23, across the table to Essex. It was an all too familiar text: "Men of blood shall not live out half their days." Earl Walter had died in Ireland in his mid-thirties, and in Ireland Tyrone's rebellion had escalated into full-scale war; before the autumn England would suffer a bloody and humiliating defeat at the battle of Yellow Ford.

Since his return from the Azores, Essex had been losing his grip on the queen's favour, his power and his temper. At the end of June a dispute in council over appointments to Ireland sent him spinning out of control. The way Cecil's historian Camden tells it, Essex turned his back on the queen in contempt, she boxed his ears, he put his hand to his sword, others stepped in to stop him drawing it and he swore "a great oath that he neither could nor would swallow so great an indignity". Before he was hustled out of the chamber he hurled another insult at her, claiming he would never have put up with that from her father, and left Court. A later report said he added one more unforgivable comment, "she was as crooked in her disposition as in her carcass".

Penelope was in Staffordshire during the summer, visiting her mother and Sir Christopher again. This time she took Lord Rich and three of their children. There had been talk of Lord Rich going to Ireland, but it was now unlikely and the problems of Ireland seemed a long, long way off as they enjoyed the Staffordshire countryside. On an impulse, Penelope decided to go to Chartley, taking everyone with her, and she sent her cook to warn the steward, William Trew, that they were coming the following day. The cook arrived when the Chartley staff were going to bed, Trew complained to Richard Bagot, and it threw his wife Margaret and the servants into a frenzy preparing rooms and beds "all that night". Trew sent to York for more food, "another firkin of salmon", and extra horses. By four o'clock in the afternoon everything was "in good order". But the house was thrown into confusion again by the arrival of a footman to say "the ladies" were staying another day at Drayton.

It was nothing to the consternation caused by news of Essex's showdown with Elizabeth, which reached the family with considerable speed. Lettice wrote: "I cannot be quiet till I know the true cause of your absence and discontent." If the problem was Ireland, she was confident he was wise and politic enough to deal with it. If it was "men's matters", he had sufficient courage to cope with them. And if it was "women's matters" he "should be skilful" enough in those sorts of problems by now. Above all, she entreated him: "have ever God and your own honour before your eyes." It was precisely Essex's sense of honour and ancestry that made it difficult to back down and offer Elizabeth the abject apology she wanted.

Essex was still skulking at Wanstead when Lord Burghley died early in August. Burghley had been the architect of Elizabeth's reign since she ascended the throne forty years ago, and her grief when one of her "old guard" passed away was extreme. This was not a time for Essex to be away from Court. "I fear the longer your lordship doth persist in this careless humour of her majesty the more will her heart be hardened," warned uncle William Knollys; "I pray god your contending with her in this manner do not breed such a hatred in her as will never be reclaimed." The same thought echoed through the family. "The Wizard Earl" wrote Essex a sharper, briefer note: "Noble brother I long to know whether we shall have you a countryman long, or a courtier shortly."

Essex returned as "a courtier shortly", and it *was* short. He and Penelope had genuine respect for Burghley, and Essex would not miss his funeral. "The Old Fox" had done his duty as Essex's guardian, and their differences were political, not personal. On 29 August the earl joined the 500 mourners who walked solemnly beside Burghley's coffin from the Strand to Westminster Abbey. Then Essex returned to Wanstead. He was disenchanted and frustrated with a life controlled by an elderly woman who refused to see the rightness of his policies. He'd grown tired of the shallowness and deceit.

If Essex didn't like Elizabeth's attitude, she certainly didn't like his. He was too arrogant by half, behaving as though he had a God-given right to challenge the crown. Yet when he collapsed with fever some days later, she began to relent. Uncle William made sure the queen knew he really was ill, but warned him she still "looketh for a better answer from you of submission", and urged him to "do it as soon as you may".

Lettice sent Sir Christopher to Essex and following his visit she wrote anxiously for more news of "the indisposition my friend left you in at his coming away". By the middle of September Essex gave in, admitted his gross error, apologized, and Elizabeth allowed him back to Court. Dorothy wrote with relief: "Dear Brother, I cannot but desire to know how the court air and humours agree with you. If both sort with your health and contentment, none shall be more glad [than] your most affectionate sister, D. Northumberland."

As one the family had backed him, closing ranks, adopting his cause with sympathy, urging him back into power; and it was Penelope, he claimed later, who wielded the strongest influence over him. Her diplomacy and popularity at Court gave her access to Elizabeth, and kept open a vital channel of cordial contact. And her care and loyalty to Essex were total. Summoned urgently by him, Penelope sent his messenger straight back to William Downhall, Essex's master of the horse, with a note:

> Good Mr Downhall, this bearer tells me my brother would have me come to the Court, in the morning early. I am here scarce well and in my night clothes, having nothing else here. But yet I will come and desire not to be seen by any but himself, wherefore I pray you come for me as early as you think good, and devise how I may come in very privately.

It sounds as though Essex's request caught her away from home and Essex House, but close enough to London to get to him quickly. In a postscript she explained that she would have preferred to visit Essex by night to avoid anyone seeing her. She had not replied directly to her brother "because I thought he would be asleep before the messenger came". Her own indisposition, her lack of clothes, her sleep, were of no consequence when he needed her.

By the end of October cousin Elizabeth also needed her. The Southamptons were out of jail and Penelope took Elizabeth to Leighs to lie in for her first baby. When the child arrived on 8 November she was, naturally, named Penelope, with Lady Rich as her godmother.

∼

Mountjoy, meanwhile, was continuing to climb the Court ladder. In mid-October he moved with the queen from Nonsuch Palace to Richmond for a month. Once again it was rumoured he would soon be a privy councillor. Once again he was not, but he *was* on a short list of two for the post of lord deputy of Ireland. After the massacre of English forces at Yellow Ford on the Blackwater in August, Elizabeth was facing total defeat in the province. The population was largely Catholic, hostile to England and potentially pro-Spain. The previously feuding Irish chiefs, O'Donnell and Tyrone (better known in Ireland as The O'Neill), had reached an agreement of sorts and their joint aim was to drive the English out, recognize Philip of Spain as king of Ireland, and rule the country themselves in his absence. Elizabeth needed to send one of her best military commanders, and Mountjoy's vigorous handling of the Spanish threat the previous autumn had not been forgotten. He was among her most senior and distinguished soldiers, and still in his thirties. The other nominee was uncle William Knollys, fifty-nine years old next Lent.

Essex vetoed both. Privately he did not want to lose a supportive elder statesman like William from the council. Publicly he claimed Mountjoy was a scholar not a soldier. He "had small experience in martial affairs, save what he had gained in the small time he served in the Low Countries", and he was "too bookish". Everyone knew Mountjoy was a bookworm, interested in theology, but he had proved his worth under fire for years. Clearly for reasons Essex was not explaining, he didn't want Mountjoy packed off to Ireland. Could it be for Penelope's sake? She and Essex had known since Earl Walter's death that a job in Ireland was a poisoned chalice, maybe literally. Mountjoy's health had never been really sound and the bogs and fogs of Ireland could break a stronger man than he. Penelope would not want her children's father sent there.

But in opposing both nominees, Essex allowed himself to be outmanoeuvred. If they were not good enough perhaps he should go. As Elizabeth moved to Whitehall for Accession Day, rumours swirled round Court thicker than an Irish mist: "Some think the Lord Mountjoy shall be sent thither deputy; others say the Earl of Essex means to take it upon him, and hopes by his countenance to quiet that country." Actually Elizabeth (and Cecil) had already decided: Essex should go, with another grand title, lord lieutenant. Cecil moved in subtle ways and Penelope could see that her brother had been presented with a chance he could not refuse: to redeem Earl Walter's reputation.

To help finance his campaign, Wanstead would have to be sold. But Wanstead was too precious to Penelope to let it go. It held so many memories, from the days when Leicester gave her rooms there in the early years of her marriage, to the spring when she realized the strength of Mountjoy's love for her. To please her, and to support Essex, Mountjoy bought it for £4,300. The deal was complex and Essex did not remove his goods for some three months. But by Christmas it was settled. At last, Mountjoy owned a property worthy of him; far enough from London for them to occupy it as a family, and usefully close to Leighs.

Christmastide and New Year 1599 should have been the happiest time for Penelope. Mountjoy's status was increasing, the children were growing and Lord Rich was not making unnecessary difficulties about access to them. But the icy-cold weather and Essex's impending departure cast a deep chill over the season. On mid-winter's night it had been so cold, for so long, that the Thames was almost frozen over. Two days after Christmas thick snow fell, softening the sounds of the city, settling in heavy folds over a thousand roofs and spires. In the palace stables horses stamped to keep warm, snorting thick white plumes into the cold air. In the yards servants swept the snow aside, clearing the way for huge logs to be hauled into the great hall. Maids hurried along unheated passageways, up and down the privy stairs, and the kitchen boys cracked ice for the cooks.

On New Year's Day Sir Edmund Tilney, master of the revels, could be found fussing around the palace, checking that the players would not say anything to offend her majesty. Shakespeare and the Lord Chamberlain's Men favoured Essex and they had come close to offending Elizabeth before with topical references. They knew they were on dangerous ground if they did it again.

Twelfth Night brought another feast, and this year's was in honour of the Danish ambassador. Those who watched would remember it well. It was a scene to tell their children and their children's children – how the queen stepped down from her chair and took the Earl of Essex's hand. She had chosen him to lead her out to dance. In the silent seconds before the musicians struck up a galliard for her, some sighed with relief. Others wondered how devious and dissembling Elizabeth could be. Perhaps it was a sign that Essex was still her chief favourite. Perhaps it wasn't. Would the queen keep him by her side, or was this a parting gift before she sent him to his fate?

Uncertainty and rumour spread faster than the melting snow, but Essex knew he was going. The days of his favour had finished. To the queen's "witty" godson, Sir John Harington, he boasted: "I have beaten Knollys and

Mountjoy in the council and by god I will beat Tyrone in the field." Penelope knew it was bravado and beneath it he viewed the project with gloom. But there was no backing out even though it was obvious Cecil and his cronies would make hay in the sunshine of Essex's absence.

The gloom deepened on 13 January 1599 with the death of Edmund Spenser, suddenly in Westminster. It was a sad day for everyone who cared about poetry, and it was especially poignant for the Devereux family. Who could forget his words "Sweet Thames, run softly, till I end my song" and his tribute to Essex as the hero of Cadiz? Three days later he was buried in Westminster Abbey. Other poets threw their quill pens into the grave in homage to him, and Essex picked up the bill for the funeral.

A few days later there was another, happier, ceremony for the Devereux. Essex's stepdaughter, Elizabeth Sidney, was married to Roger Manners, fifth Earl of Rutland. He was a twenty-two-year-old Essex loyalist and his choice of bride was hero worship. Elizabeth was still thirteen and the marriage may not have been consummated before he left with Essex for Ireland. Both men had been left fatherless and inherited an earldom before they were twelve. Both had grown up wedded to chivalry; and Rutland's marriage to Philip Sidney's daughter would prove as miserable as Essex's to Philip's widow. But Rutland was now bound to Essex by more than admiration and comradeship, and he would support his father-in-law for better or worse – mostly worse.

On 12 March Elizabeth signed letters patent to Essex to be lieutenant general and governor general of Ireland. Two days later he signed a new will. It was a standard precaution for commanders heading into battle, but it highlighted the dangers. The following day his belongings were removed from Wanstead to Essex House. It was a bittersweet day for Penelope. On 27 March, "about two o'clock in the afternoon, Robert Earl of Essex, took horse in Seething Lane and from thence, being accompanied with divers noblemen and many others, himself very plainly attired, rode through Grace-Street, Cornhill, Cheapside and other high streets". Thousands of Londoners came out on to the streets "crying 'God bless your lordship, God preserve your honour'", and for four miles they stood two-deep to cheer him on his way.

Penelope could picture him following the same route Earl Walter had taken on his last, fateful visit to Ireland, twenty-three years before. The old post road to Holyhead passed within a bowshot of both Drayton Bassett and Chartley, and on 3 April he was at Drayton, pausing with Sir Christopher to see Lettice before they set sail. It was a brief visit. In spite of delays due to contrary winds, Essex reached Dublin on 15 April. He took with him on his staff Southampton, Rutland, Sir George Carey and Gelly Merrick, as well as Sir Christopher. Few of his appointments pleased Elizabeth.

Penelope stayed long enough in London to pick up what was said of her brother around Court. Francis Bacon's opinion – "I did as plainly see his destiny chained to that journey" – though recorded later, was in many minds. Few doubted that the earl had as many enemies as friends. One hinted darkly, "He goeth not forth to serve the queen's realm, but to humour his own revenge." Another said bluntly that Essex was "crazed, but whether more in body or mind is doubtful".

Essex was still waiting to sail from Holyhead when Shakespeare's new play *Henry V* opened at the Curtain theatre in Shoreditch. It hailed him as "the General of our Gracious Empress". Before long, the Chorus told playgoers, Essex would return victorious from Ireland, "Bringing rebellion broached on his sword". Shakespeare was treading on dangerous ground again. His play openly compared Essex with "this Harry", King Henry V, the hero of Agincourt.

Penelope would have loved it, and the cheers from the audience. She knew how close her brother stood to the crown. Maybe Shakespeare had heard it too.

With Essex away, the Court took on a duller tone and Elizabeth decreed the Garter ceremonies at Windsor should be low key. Because of the Irish problems, she said. Cecil's crony Lord Cobham was one of the new knights admitted to the order, and in May Essex's position was weakened further when the plum job of master of the Court of Wards was given to Cecil. Burghley's death left it vacant and Elizabeth dangled it in front of Essex for months. It was potentially so lucrative that it would have solved his financial crisis at a stroke, and he was banking on it.

Penelope was in Staffordshire when that bomb dropped. On a Monday early in May she tidied up her affairs at Essex House, wrote to Dr Julius Caesar, the judge and lawyer, and asked him to continue acting for her in her absence. Then she left, taking cousin Elizabeth and baby Penelope with her. Their pace was more leisurely than Essex's, as they followed him along the post road, first to Drayton, where Lettice was on her own, and finally to Chartley. Lord Rich didn't come this year, nor did Mountjoy, but Penelope probably took some of their children, and soon they were settled into Penelope's old home. Her goddaughter was just six months old and she was not the only reason to make it a slow journey: cousin Elizabeth was already pregnant again.

Chartley in May was a haven of peace. On fine days hardly a ripple ran over the moat. Moorhens meandered in and out of the reeds and jackdaws nested in the ruins of the old castle. On 10 May Penelope wrote to Southampton in Ireland apologizing for neglecting to write to him, and assuring him his little daughter was "exceeding fair and well". As for his next child, Penelope was hoping to "win my wager" that it would be a boy. It was one of Penelope's typically short and direct letters, but her tone with the earl is confident and relaxed. She knew him well and thanked him for his "exceeding kindness" in writing to her so often. There was no need for the formal and exaggerated protestations of friendship she used to Robert Cecil.

After the tension of Court politics it was good to be away at Chartley, though they kept in touch with London news. In June the countess wrote to her husband to tell him her pregnancy had failed, but she passed on some gossip to "make you merry". She and Penelope had heard the racy news that Essex's enemy Lord Cobham, nicknamed Sir John Falstaff, "is by his Mistress Dame Pintpot made father of a goodly miller's thumb, a boy that is all head and very little body".

For two months Penelope and her cousin stayed at Chartley, looked after by Margaret and William Trew. But at the height of the summer, with swallows and martins wheeling overhead and poppies waving in the fields, they had to leave. The countess wrote to Southampton again, on 8 July, to tell him Penelope had been called back by Lord Rich: "Therefore go to him she needs must." The following day Penelope herself wrote: "My Lord Rich doth so importune me daily to return to my own house as I cannot stay here longer than Bartholomewtide." He wanted her back at Leighs soon after 24 August to help him settle a land dispute which was threatening to rob him of "the greatest part" of his estates.

Penelope's relationship with her husband was still strong enough for her to treat his request seriously, and Leighs was "my own house". Rich was evidently unhappy that she had been away so long and she did not want to upset him further. On the other hand, she wanted her cousin and baby Penelope with her, and she had worked out how to make Lord Rich agree. First she wrote to him saying she would come as soon as she knew where Southampton wanted his wife to go; and what her brother wanted, since they were technically his guests at Chartley. Next she appealed to Southampton to square it with Essex and write to her and to Lord Rich, saying that he and Essex wanted the countess to go to Leighs. At the request of two earls, Lord Rich was bound to be "well contented" with the plan. Having carefully organized things the way she wanted, and manipulated all three men, she went on to express her sorrow at the news of Sir Harry Danvers's injury. He had received a gunshot wound, and she hoped "it will not mar his good face". The accident had happened on 16 June and there was more bad news from Ireland. It was some relief to know Mountjoy was not there as well.

Mountjoy was in London, increasingly in demand for his expertise in military matters. He was also keeping an eye on Essex's best interests. His parting letter to Essex in March, before the earl sailed for Ireland, was a model of loaded, coded advice. Essex, he wrote, should remember to be on his guard "against all intended mischiefs". Without naming Cecil, he reminded Essex "who possesses the mind of her that rules", and begged him "to leave none of your provisions to the pleasure of your enemies". It would be folly to rely on "what the Estate promiseth". Promises from London would not necessarily be honoured. Had Cecil read it, Mountjoy's sentiments would not have pleased him, but for the moment it was Mountjoy's views on Spain that mattered most. Through the summer there was growing fear that another Spanish fleet was being prepared and London would be its target. By August the country was in panic mode. Mountjoy was appointed deputy general of the army and kept busy at Somerset House.

Rumours and strange stories spread like wildfire: King James was in arms ready to invade and support a Catholic uprising. In London, the night watch was doubled, chains were fastened across the city streets, and lanterns hung "at every man's door, there to burn all the night". Large numbers of soldiers were mustered, but the Spaniards did not appear. Keeping troops on standby was draining the exchequer, already stretched by Essex's demands for more supplies, and Elizabeth feared it would run dry. The rumours grew wilder. Maybe this crisis was invented "to show some that are absent" – who else but Essex? – that London could be defended. So he needn't think of bringing his army over from Ireland to topple his enemies at Court.

Early in September the army was stood down. Elizabeth was at Hampton Court. Penelope was back at Leighs with her cousin to help Lord Rich with his lawsuit. But there were other demands on her time and support. After Essex rode away from Seething Lane, Frances, pregnant again, stayed on at Walsingham House with their children: "Little Robin" and Penelope, another of Lady Rich's goddaughters. But early in the summer five-year-old Penelope died and on 27 June she was buried at All Hallows, beside her baby brothers, Walter and Henry.

As autumn began, Frances, increasingly stressed and fearful for Essex's safety, grew terrified of another miscarriage or stillbirth. Penelope arranged to be in London for her lying-in and came up to Essex House from Leighs. But while they waited, there was more disturbing news. Foolishly, Essex had returned from Ireland without Elizabeth's permission. Arriving at Nonsuch Palace early in the morning, he stormed into her bedchamber before she was dressed, without her wig and face paint in place. And he was under arrest.

Chapter Twenty-Two

SEPTEMBER 1599–DECEMBER 1600

"We that are not of the council do see no hope"
– Lord Mountjoy, 1599

*E*ssex had left Dublin with a handful of men and reached Nonsuch in little more than three days. Around 10 a.m. on Friday 28 September he "made all haste up to the presence so to the privy-chamber, and did not stop till he came to the queen's bed-chamber, where he found her majesty newly up, and the hair about her face". At first Elizabeth welcomed him, despite the shock, but when he returned to her after dinner his reception was cooler. By nightfall he was under arrest.

What had happened in Ireland that sent him rushing back regardless of her instruction "we absolutely command you to continue"? The situation there was alarming when Essex arrived in April 1599. His army was the greatest yet sent to Ireland, but he was outnumbered at least two to one. More than 20,000 Irishmen were in arms under Tyrone and Tyrconnel, and Essex could do little against their guerrilla tactics. An invasion from Spain was expected daily to support them, and by the summer, with his troops deserting in droves, he had achieved nothing. "Much time and excessive charges have been spent to little purpose," Elizabeth wrote to him. Furthermore, he had defied her orders by giving the Earl of Southampton and Sir Christopher Blount appointments on his staff. In September he held an unorthodox parley with Tyrone, conducted on horseback at a ford in a river, out of earshot of anyone else, and agreed a truce without exacting any concessions. Elizabeth regarded Tyrone as a traitor. To negotiate with him without witnesses was either stupid or devious. "We marvel you would carry it no better," Elizabeth wrote to Essex, "to have good testimony to your actions." It looked horribly like an English surrender, and no one could confirm what Essex had agreed.

Ireland had defeated him, as it had Earl Walter. But it was what was happening in London that brought Essex rushing back. While Essex and his followers had gone to Ireland, Cecil and his cautious peace party had remained at Court, controlling policy and, Essex believed, encouraging Elizabeth to refuse his requests for more money, men and horses. Even if Elizabeth *had* graciously agreed to Essex's demands he would still have felt threatened, knowing his enemies were grouped comfortably round the council table, keeping the home fires of criticism burning. And Elizabeth would *not* meet his demands. He had done nothing, she replied, to justify her outlay. Essex became desperate. The only solution he could see was to return as quickly as possible, take Cecil and his party by surprise, and re-exert control over the council.

A few hours after his first interview with Elizabeth at Nonsuch, Essex was joined at dinner by Lord Rich and Lord Mountjoy, the earls of Rutland and Worcester, "and many knights". Gathered around Cecil's private table sat the earls of Shrewsbury and Nottingham, and Essex's arch enemies Cobham and Ralegh. It was a formidable line-up, and Cecil's party carried more weight with Elizabeth. That night Essex was under arrest in his rooms. Four days later he was placed in detention with the lord keeper of the Great Seal, Sir Thomas Egerton, at York House (now the lord keeper's official residence), while Elizabeth prepared to move her Court to Whitehall.

Penelope was already in London awaiting the birth of Frances's baby at Walsingham House. She had come in good time to be with her sister-in-law, expecting her brother to be absent in Ireland when the baby was born, not under arrest in London. On Sunday 30 September Frances was "well delivered of a young lady". It was a relief to everyone; but it was no time for a grand family gathering and the child was baptized "without much ceremony", and named for her mother.

Penelope had cousin Elizabeth with her at Essex House but their stay was about to be cut short. Essex's transfer on 2 October to Egerton's custody meant that he was living under guard a few yards away along the Strand. With Penelope and the Countess of Southampton in residence, Essex House rapidly became a rallying ground for Essex's supporters, doubtless with Penelope's encouragement.

Elizabeth was not amused and she let it be known that Penelope's open-door policy was causing offence – and not a little alarm. Essex was the most popular aristocrat in London and Elizabeth could not sit by while his house became an HQ for everyone at odds with her government. The capital was still tense after the summer's rumours and there were soldiers returning from Ireland to join the malcontents living rough in the city. Penelope, realizing her presence was harming her brother's cause with Elizabeth, left London, taking the countess with her. By 11 October they had "gone to the country to shun the company that daily were wont to visit them in town".

~

It is unlikely that Penelope intended to back off for long, and the next few weeks found her variously in "the country", at Court and in London. On Monday 15 October, late at night, Dorothy arrived at Essex House "upon some difference between her and her husband"; and at the beginning of November Penelope and Dorothy both obtained permission to attend Court as "suitors" to plead Essex's case. "All men's eyes and ears are open to what it will please her majesty to determine," wrote Rowland Whyte.

While Elizabeth and her council considered Essex's future, the usual ceremonial rolled on, pretending it was business as usual. But when the Accession Day tilt took place without the man who had been its star for the past decade, Essex's absence looked ominous and rumours escalated. He was in solitary confinement. He was ill. He was about to be sent to the Tower.

Mountjoy, together with Southampton and Sir Christopher Blount, both back from Ireland, laid plans to prevent that. They would spring Essex from York House and smuggle him either "privately into France" or to Wales. Alternatively – and witnesses later confirmed Mountjoy was behind this more dangerous plan – they would use force and "by possessing the Court with his friends to bring himself again to her majesty's presence", they would make Elizabeth reinstate him. Essex, however, refused to flee. He was convinced he could answer any charges, whether insubordination, failure to carry out the queen's instructions, leaving his post without permission, or wasting Elizabeth's money. But while he remained in captivity his supporters' fears increased. Frances and Sir William Knollys were the only visitors allowed, and at night Frances had to return to her mother.

On 29 November William Trew, now managing Essex House, wrote to his wife Margaret: "Upon Monday and Tuesday last the rumour was all over that my lord was gone to the Tower. Yesterday being Wednesday all went well on our side. At four o'clock the queen, my lady Warwick and the Earl of Worcester went privately to York House to my lord. What is done this night I know not, but we hope well." Trew's hopes were misplaced. Essex had refused to attend the meeting in Star Chamber saying he was too ill, and he was heavily censured. In fact Essex *was* growing seriously ill, partly with despair and the "black dog" of depression that was never far from his moodiness. His supporters feared he would do something rash and Anthony Bacon wrote warning him against "somewhat that amounteth to a new error", and counselled him against "dire and peremptory despair".

Penelope could not stay away while her brother's safety and health deteriorated and she decided openly to reoccupy Essex House, whether the queen liked it or not. She told Trew to expect her and her companions on 1 December, claiming she was returning because she was "weary of the country".

Public sympathy for Essex was running dangerously high. Shakespeare's comparison between Henry V and Essex was not what Cecil wanted to hear and any lingering favour Elizabeth showed the earl needed to be checked. Early in December she "used some speech of favour towards him, which much troubled the contrary party", and Cecil must have grown increasingly alarmed when Lady Rich began putting pressure on Elizabeth. Early in December Penelope and Dorothy, both dramatically dressed in black, arrived at Court as "humble suitors" begging for Essex to be removed "to some better air and more convenient place". Frances was not permitted at Court, but she too was pleading with everyone she could for Essex's release.

On 19 December, perhaps partly thanks to Penelope's "mourning" dress, Essex was reported dead and "the bell tolled for him" at St Clement Danes. But while his friends put it about that "he cannot live out this month", others said he wasn't ill at all. Penelope hurried to Elizabeth, now at Richmond for Christmastide, claiming she needed to see him before he died to sort out some money matters. The queen "spoke with her and used her very graciously", but still refused her access to him.

Elizabeth celebrated Christmas with bravado, filling Richmond Palace with lords and ladies to show she could enjoy herself without Essex. On most evenings she watched the dancing, "old and new country dances, with tabor and pipe"; and she played cards, chiefly primero, with Lord North, Robert Cecil and Lord Buckhurst. On New Year's Day 1600 the usual ritual of gifts went ahead. Penelope, Lord Rich and Mountjoy were all in attendance, giving and receiving presents from the queen. So they were all still in her favour. But there was no gift for Essex and his offering to Elizabeth was not accepted. He had already been in custody at York House for three months, and even "Little Robin" had to return to Eton without seeing his father.

The poet John Donne, currently Egerton's secretary and watching the way the wind blew at Court over Christmas, thought Essex was "no more missed here than the angels which were cast down from heaven" – and had similarly little chance of being returned to high favour.

Penelope asked Cecil again and again to help her gain access to Essex. "I have been a very importunate suitor unto her majesty for leave to see my unfortunate sick brother," she told him; "and have received so much comfort of her, though she hath not granted it, as I may hope to obtain it." Since Elizabeth had not treated her unkindly, if Cecil would put in a good word for her, there was a good chance the queen would agree. Elizabeth, however, told Penelope she could not give her permission because she would then have to grant Dorothy access as well. Nothing deterred, Penelope wrote to Cecil pointing out it "need be no argument against me", because she had "humbly and earnestly" asked first.

Penelope made no secret of her lobbying. Rowland Whyte told the Sidneys: "The Lady Rich earnestly follows her desire to have leave to go see him; she writes to her majesty many letters, sends many jewels, many presents. Her letters are read, her presents received, but no leave granted."

Eventually, one of Penelope's letters unleashed Elizabeth's anger. It was unusually long and elaborate for Penelope and it began with conventional courtesies: "Early did I hope this morning to have had mine eyes blessed with your majesty's beauty." Passionately she pleaded the cause of her "unfortunate brother, whom all men have liberty to defame". But under a thick layer of classical and biblical allusions she pulled no punches, pointing out to Elizabeth that if the queen's "fair hands do not check the course of their unbridled hate", his enemies will pursue him to "his last breath". And having removed him they would make "preparation for greater mischiefs", and then "make war against heaven" – Elizabeth herself. It was a serious charge, obviously directed at Cecil. Finally, Penelope played the sympathy card, reminding Elizabeth that Earl Walter lost his life because of Ireland. It was unthinkable that Essex's children should grow up knowing two of their forefathers had perished "being employed in one country, where they would have done [the queen] loyal service, to the shedding of their last blood".

So far Elizabeth had treated Penelope kindly, and at first she accepted that the letter was motivated by loyalty and love for Essex; and Penelope continued to attend Court. Lettice had come to London to help obtain Essex's release and the New Year's gift she sent Elizabeth was "very well taken". On 19 January Penelope and Lettice went to Richmond and took lodgings while they tried to see the queen, but Elizabeth was busy, preparing to move on to Chelsea, and their trip was wasted. A week later, Penelope was still allowed to attend Court. But by 2 February, "My lady Rich was called before my lord treasurer", Lord Buckhurst, and questioned about her letter. Penelope put up a spirited defence, insisting she meant what she wrote. Yet she convinced her interrogators she was loyal to Elizabeth and they let her go. During the first week of February she wrote to Elizabeth again, "but in other language", and since the letter is lost one can only guess that it was conciliatory and repeated her loyalty.

Essex, meanwhile, was recovering well and was rescheduled to appear before Star Chamber. But the hearing was postponed after he wrote a submissive letter and his supporters "were in some heart again". Elizabeth, they believed, by "little and little will be won to give him the liberty of his own house".

Convinced he was about to be allowed home early in March, Penelope, Lettice, Dorothy and Southampton's wife Elizabeth assembled at Essex House. But their presence "hindered it". Elizabeth took umbrage at them forming a welcome committee and decided he must stay with Egerton at York House. But her attitude was softening and on 20 March he was allowed back to Essex House, though still under guard.

Penelope's position, conversely, was getting more serious. On 21 February friends believed she was "sick, sickly discontented". The following day she was called up by the council again about her letter and "excused herself by sickness". Four days later: "Lady Rich is commanded to keep her house, the cause thought to be that by her means certain copies of a letter she writ to the queen is published abroad; she denies it, it rests upon proofs."

Who leaked the letter to the printers is not known, but Elizabeth was incensed. Penelope was given a few weeks to recover, and ordered to keep quietly to her house, probably St Bartholomew's, before she was summoned again to explain the letter's publication. On 29 March word went round that Lady Rich "feigns sickness, and has stolen into the country". Rowland Whyte put it more tactfully: "My lady Rich and lady Southampton are got to Leighs in Essex."

There was no chance Mountjoy could join her and advise her. On 7 February Elizabeth had dispatched him to Ireland as Essex's replacement.

~

Within three weeks of Essex's surprise return, Elizabeth decided Mountjoy should be the new lord deputy of Ireland. He tried to get out of it, arguing the job was too difficult for him and his health was not up to it, but Elizabeth was adamant. In part his refusal was based on the hope that Essex might be freed to resume his duties in Ireland, though there was no chance of Essex being reinstated.

Mountjoy was the obvious choice to take over the difficult job of raising army morale and subduing the Irish rebels, and his successes were to make him the "greatest English soldier of the period". But little did Elizabeth realize she was placing the army in the hands of a man who had been plotting against her chief ministers for months, and who was prepared to use force to release Essex from captivity.

Mountjoy had, however, made it clear to Essex that it was not Elizabeth he wished to see an end to. It was the councillors who were ruining the country, and "we that are not of the council do see no hope to keep long together this state from assured ruin. I pray God the queen may with all prosperity out-live their negligence." To bring down the current regime, he believed it was vital to get support from King James of Scotland. Through summer 1599, while Essex was in Ireland, Mountjoy had been sending secret messengers to James assuring him that Essex would support his claim to succeed Elizabeth.

In October, with the army under his control, Mountjoy became the key figure among Essex's supporters. As Sir Charles Danvers put it: "When the government of Ireland was imposed upon my Lord Mountjoy" the dangers facing Essex, "whose case he [Mountjoy] seemed extraordinarily to tender", prompted Mountjoy to send more secret messengers urging James to commit himself to action now to release Essex and secure the throne of England for himself. "Lord Mountjoy would leave the kingdom of Ireland defensibly guarded and with four or five thousand men" come to England to join James's troops and Essex's supporters, Danvers explained.

Mountjoy was playing an extraordinarily dangerous double game. At Court over New Year he and Penelope were exchanging gifts with the queen, knowing he would soon depart for Ireland as Elizabeth's lord deputy. In private, he was waiting to hear if James accepted his offer to commit treason, leave his post without permission, march on London and force Elizabeth to acknowledge the Scottish king as her successor.

When Mountjoy set sail for Ireland early in February there was no word from James and Essex remained under guard in York House. As the months passed there was still no commitment from James, so Essex, now released to his own house, sent both Southampton and Sir Charles Danvers to Ireland to encourage Mountjoy to hold to the plan to take control of the Court even without Scottish back-up.

~

Penelope was now coming under increasing censure. There were signs that she had not been guilty of printing and circulating her letter, published with an old letter of Essex's opposing Cecil's peace policy with Spain. But her continual efforts to avoid questioning, by staying in the country, gave the impression she had more to hide. She would have to give in. On 26 May Sir Charles Danvers, now a regular go-between for Essex, Southampton and Mountjoy, travelled downriver to visit her and the Countess of Southampton, and Penelope was soon back in London.

Essex was due to face trial first, but one Court observer was certain "the poor lady [Rich] is like to have the worst of it, being sent for and come up to answer and interpret her riddles". On 5 June Essex was brought before a special commission in York House and savagely questioned by the attorney general Sir Edward Coke. Coke was assisted by Francis Bacon, Essex's former protégé, who later insisted it was only his job as queen's counsel to put the case together. It was Coke who fronted it and he was out to prove again, as he had with Dr Lopez, that he was a penetrating prosecutor. In fact, his tactics backfired. Essex ate a certain amount of humble pie, spent two hours on his knees during the twelve-hour hearing, and won a degree of sympathy. But his refusal to admit insubordination annoyed the commissioners. He was stripped of his offices and ordered to stay under house arrest, but in his own home.

Penelope's letter was held up in the trial as "an insolent, saucy, malapert action" and throughout July she was "not at liberty to go where she will". Near the end of the month, however, knowing she would soon be questioned, she again defied her detention order and left the city. When Cecil instructed Lord Buckhurst to interrogate her, it took him some time to find her.

"It was Tuesday before the Lady Rich came unto me," he explained to Cecil on 13 August; "for she was gone to Barn Elms and thither was I fain to send for her." Frances, pregnant again despite the night-time curfew on her visits to Essex, had retired to her mother's Thames-side home early in July, and there Penelope joined them. The delay in questioning her was not the only thing that irritated Cecil. Lord Buckhurst had been too easily won over by Penelope's answers in the spring, Cecil believed, and he briefed him to guard against being charmed again.

Cecil was wasting his time. "I took that course with her which your letters prescribed," Buckhurst told Cecil, briefly recounting his interview, but it is obvious Penelope ran rings round him. She "prayed me to give her majesty most humble thanks for her favour," he went on, "which she acknowledged with her follies and faults committed and assured that this should be a warning to her for ever not to commit the like; concluding still with her most humble desire to have the happiness to see her majesty, until which she should never enjoy a day of comfort to her heart".

It was another piece of humble pie, dished up with Devereux skill, but it didn't fool Cecil. Nonetheless, he forwarded Lady Rich's explanations to the queen, and with them a private letter Penelope had enclosed for Elizabeth.

In a simple move Penelope outsmarted Cecil as well as Buckhurst. Currently banished from Court, she created an opportunity to "speak" directly to Elizabeth in a letter for the queen's eyes only. She gave it to Buckhurst to enclose with her answers, rather than give it to Cecil herself, so that Buckhurst knew about it and there was less chance Cecil could "lose" it. Penelope understood Elizabeth well enough to know she always played one minister off against another, and sometimes curbed Cecil's power by excluding him from her confidence. A private letter between Lady Rich and Elizabeth would leave him permanently unsettled.

Having discussed Penelope's replies with Elizabeth, Cecil duly advised Buckhurst: "You may tell her ladyship that what she wrote in the enclosed hath passed the eyes of no other creature, and so it is true, I protest to God, for her majesty caused it to be burned." What exactly Penelope had written to Elizabeth he would never know, but he could guess some of it.

"I doubt not but I was and am in her ladyship's contemplation the person" principally referred to in her letters, Cecil told Buckhurst. Penelope had pointed at anonymous enemies who would turn their evil plans against the queen, in her original, long, offending letter to Elizabeth. Perhaps in her private letter she had added details. How could he be certain she had not denounced him by name, adding evidence? He couldn't. And the verbal answers Elizabeth had instructed him to relay to Lady Rich must have further unnerved him.

Her ladyship must understand that she had caused the queen considerable offence. Her ladyship's answers "showed a proud disposition, and not much better than a plain contempt of her majesty". Being "a lady to whom it did not appertain so to meddle in such matters", the queen considered Penelope's behaviour showed "stomach and presumption". Yet the queen would magnanimously accept that Lady Rich was *not* responsible for printing the letter. She was only guilty of being "so negligent that others might come by it".

A cold air of disapproval hung over Elizabeth's comments, yet she seemed determined not to raise a hand against her. Penelope was not welcome at Court, but she had royal "leave to dispose herself as may best agree with her own health". On 26 August both Penelope and Essex were given their freedom. Essex, under orders not to come to Court, retired to Ewelme, a few miles from Grey's Court.

Penelope went to Leighs, allegedly to care for Lord Rich who was "extreme sick and in danger". Really? Lord Rich's illness is always taken at face value, yet his only other known ailments are the seasickness that kept him out of the Cadiz and Azores expeditions. Was this also a sickness of convenience? So far the interrogations had not exposed any covert dealings with King James and Mountjoy. But it could not last long: at least one envoy to James had been picked up and was in the Tower. There were advantages to Lord Rich's "illness". If she was called again before the council, caring for her husband gave Penelope an alibi for staying well out of reach. And if things became too hot, she had an easy route to the Essex coast and the Continent – where Mountjoy planned to escape if he were summoned to London.

James was proving less responsive than Essex's supporters hoped, but the undercover negotiations went on. At Leighs in September, Penelope, Lord Rich and cousin Elizabeth were joined by Southampton. He had spent some time in Ireland with Mountjoy earlier in the year and recently he had been in the Netherlands. It is impossible to believe Lord Rich was unaware of Southampton's part in Essex's affairs. He may have distanced himself from the Devereux later, but he had been one of the first to join Essex when he arrived from Ireland at Nonsuch, and surely they now discussed the earl's fortunes as they sat round at dinner.

Essex's fortunes were, in fact, about to take a final turn that would spell disaster. After months of dithering, Elizabeth decided in October that she would not renew his monopoly on the sweet wines trade. Without that last prop to his perilous finances he was ruined. The next few months were some of the most dangerous Elizabeth ever faced. Essex was spinning out of control, driven desperate by financial ruin and his loss of royal favour and reputation. Some of his allies believed he was on the brink of madness, but his popularity was extraordinary. As well as the Londoners who loved him and cheered him in so many tournaments, there was a growing body of ex-soldiers in the capital, deserters from Ireland. They were unpaid, unemployed and as reckless as Essex himself.

Returning to London from the country he lay low for a little while and then threw open Essex House to everyone who would join him – "military men, bold fellows, men of cracked credit, malcontented persons". The house was also a hotbed of radical Protestants who preached seditious sermons, "to which the citizens flock apace". Now Essex made fresh overtures to James, and at Christmas he sent another emissary to Mountjoy to bring the army across from Ireland. Both of them held back.

Penelope, however, was solidly behind her brother and by December she was with him at Essex House. Two months later he insisted she had urged him on. There was no point in the claim unless it was believable; unless others had seen her influence over him and thought it significant. They had. In the official history of Elizabeth's reign, commissioned by the Cecils, William Camden recorded: "The Lady Rich the earl's sister (who having violated her husband's bed, was in the Queen's heavy displeasure) visiteth him daily." Elizabeth's answers to Lady Rich, her letters and Buckhurst's reports carry no criticism of Penelope's love life, yet Camden's comment fixed the way history would view her: the way Robert Cecil wanted it.

Chapter Twenty-Three

SPRING 1601

"He wore the crown in his heart"

– "The Wizard Earl" of Northumberland, 1603

*N*ew Year 1601 brought Penelope a brief respite from political tensions. On 8 January she was at Barn Elms with Frances and her mother and daughters. Lady Essex's new baby, Dorothy, was born a few days before Christmas, and her eldest daughter, fifteen-year-old Elizabeth, Countess of Rutland, was with them. Lady Margaret Hoby also paid a visit. Never expansive in her diary, Margaret merely listed the ladies present and noted: "after I came home I was pained in the toothache."

Elizabeth's husband, the Earl of Rutland, was back from the Netherlands, where he and Southampton had travelled the previous year, and both were once more involved in Essex's affairs. No less than five earls, three barons and sixteen knights were implicated in Essex's plans to destroy Cecil, and King James was now convinced an uprising was imminent. Having held back from committing troops before, he nonetheless replied encouragingly to Essex's latest appeal for help.

Stripped of offices, titles, income and his good name, Essex had no option now but to bid for power. If ever he and Penelope were to exact revenge for wrongs done to the Devereux, it was now. Bishop Goodman (not an Essex activist) believed Essex had personal reasons for his revolt: "the queen's harsh letters, and the mastership of the wards, which was promised him, being otherwise disposed, and his own father having spent himself and died in the service of Ireland." There were also two national problems that produced supporters for his cause: uncertainty over the succession and the unpopularity of the government. In the past two decades the economic divide had deepened. The poor were worse off than at any time for two centuries, food prices were rising, plague and apprentice riots were endemic. Essex's attempt to raise London on Sunday 8 February could, Cecil admitted, have turned out very differently.

Four days earlier Southampton held a planning meeting at Drury House, deliberately avoiding Essex House to allay suspicion. Without James's troops from Scotland or Mountjoy's from Ireland, should they first seize the Tower and its munitions, or the city, or the Court, now at Whitehall? Sir John Davies favoured securing the palace by arresting Ralegh, captain of the guards who stood by Elizabeth. Essex would then throw himself at Elizabeth's feet, demand the removal of his enemies and take control of the country. Ralegh's active dislike of Essex was common knowledge and rumour had it even "her majesty called him worse than cat and dog" because of his deeds against the earl. Essex was sure Ralegh, Cobham and Cecil were acting against him, and spread the idea they were plotting to make the Infanta of Spain Elizabeth's successor, instead of James.

The Drury House meeting broke up without agreement but they clearly intended to do something. Two days later Sir Gelly Meyrick, Essex's chief steward, aided by Lord Monteagle and "the Wizard Earl's" two brothers, Sir Charles and Sir Josceline Percy, came to an agreement with Shakespeare's company at the Globe playhouse. For forty shillings the players would present a special performance of Shakespeare's *Richard II* on Saturday 7 February. A play about a weak monarch deposed by a strong and crowd-pleasing subject was heady stuff and the parallels with present times were so strong that Elizabeth herself observed, "I am Richard the Second, know ye not that?" At his trial Essex would be charged with openly approving books about King Richard's downfall, and there is no doubt the players were bribed to present Shakespeare's play in order to whip up support for an anti-government demonstration. The power of the playhouses had soared since the opening of the Globe in 1599, and Shakespeare's political plays pulled in capacity audiences.

Essex, summoned again before the council, claimed he was too ill to attend but he was not too indisposed to entertain the ringleaders of his plot to dinner on the day of the play. Gathered with him in Essex House were "Southampton, Sir Christopher Blount, Sir Charles Danvers, Sir Robert Vernon and Lady Rich". By nightfall they had agreed an emergency plan and Penelope was fully involved in it. She sent a messenger to one of their supporters, Sir Henry Bromley, asking him to come to her immediately at Walsingham House, where she was staying; and when he reached her – having got out of bed – she told him the earl's life was in danger and warned him to be ready to act in the city the following day.

Early on Sunday morning the earl's supporters began gathering at Essex House. Elizabeth had had enough. She sent lord keeper Egerton, lord chief justice Popham, the Earl of Worcester and Sir William Knollys to tell him he must "speedily dissolve his company" and come to Court, where "his griefs should be graciously heard". Instead, Essex took the four lords hostage and some time after ten o'clock led his men out, down Fleet Street, up Ludgate Hill and through Cheapside. Brandishing their swords, they shouted, "For the queen, for the queen my masters", and claimed that "Essex that night should have been murdered by the Lord Cobham, Sir Walter Ralegh and others". But few Londoners stepped up to join them, and at most Essex's army numbered 300.

~

Penelope also left Essex House. Realizing they needed every heavyweight supporter they could muster, she ordered her carriage and grooms and drove fast to the Earl of Bedford's London home. It was after ten o'clock, Bedford recalled under interrogation, and "prayer being ended and a sermon begun, the Lady Rich came into my house desiring to speak with me speedily: which I did in the next room to the place where the sermon was, her ladyship then telling me the Earl of Essex would speak with me. Whereupon I went presently with her in her coach, none of my family following me out of the sermon room, and so departed with her unknown to my said family."

Bedford was desperate to shield his family and servants, and to stress his unwillingness to go with her. But Penelope's persuasiveness prevailed, as usual. When they returned and found Essex preparing to leave Essex House, Bedford insisted, he was not "acquainted with anything", and "desired to convey myself away". Bedford admitted he set off with Essex for the city, but left him "so soon as I might with safety, and to that end severed myself from him at a cross street end". Bedford was back home "about one of the clock".

Penelope was left in Essex House with Frances, a few of Essex's supporters and the hostages, now growing restless. Accounts vary on what happened next but they agree that the hostages requested Lady Rich and Lady Essex should "go to the chamber where the lords were, the better to pass the time". One observer recalled that Penelope declined and went into the courtyard and urged those guarding the hostages that "if they were true gentlemen they would throw her down the head of that old fellow", indicating Popham. It was an unfortunate taunt, as he would soon be sitting in judgment on her brother. Before anyone could do as she bid, one of Essex's supporters, Ferdinando Gorges, returned from the city and released the hostages. His kinsman, Ralegh, warned him earlier in the day that the revolt was doomed and Gorges slipped back to Essex House ahead of the earl, faked a message from him to free the hostages and went with them to Court.

Essex was only minutes behind him. He had failed to win support, most of his men had melted away and Sir Christopher Blount, "sore hurt in the head", was left behind. The city gates were locked, troops came from Court, and Essex and his few remaining rebels found themselves trapped at Ludgate. They retreated straight to the river at Queenhithe, grabbed as many boats as they could and rowed furiously back to Essex House stairs. It was disaster.

As dusk fell government forces surrounded the house. Yet rather than escape, Penelope remained inside, and with her stayed Frances and their gentlewomen. They barricaded the house with furniture and placed books in the windows. When soldiers broke down the outer gates to the Strand, entered the courtyard and began sniping into the chambers, they still stayed put. The ladies' presence and their servants' screams were off-putting to the soldiers, and without the hostages they were the only bargaining counter the rebels held.

Penelope was, in fact, buying time, and every second was vital. In his chamber Essex was hurriedly burning all his papers. Among them, it was said, were the contents of a little black pouch he used to wear round his neck: King James's letters.

Outside in the garden stood their old friend Sir Robert Sidney urging them to surrender. Southampton went out on the roof of the great hall and tried to make terms, but it was hopeless. The Earl of Nottingham, lord admiral, was in charge and he would accept no conditions. He was not an Essex supporter, despite being married to cousin Kate (the late Lord Hunsdon's daughter). Penelope could hear Sir Robert begging her brother and Southampton to give in, or to send the ladies to safety before the house was blown up. Nottingham had summoned two cannons from the Tower and they were trained on the house. At length one of Southampton's demands was agreed. The rebels could have two hours' grace to unblock the doors, let the ladies out and rebuild the blockade. Instead, at about 9 p.m. Essex admitted defeat. Penelope's courage had given him the time he needed.

Essex and Southampton "went down and opening the doors, each of them upon their knees surrendered their swords". Within an hour Essex was rowed across the river to spend the rest of the night a prisoner in Lambeth Palace. The next day he was taken to the Tower and his "followers went to their several places of commitment": the Tower, the Fleet, the Marshalsea and Newgate jail.

Penelope was taken prisoner to the home of Henry Sackford, keeper of the privy purse and a Cecil loyalist.

~

Lady Rich was the only woman in the house to be detained; the only woman named at dinner on the Saturday; the only one on the official list of rebels. And at number six, she was among the ringleaders with the earls of Essex,

Rutland, Southampton, Bedford and Sussex. Several barons were named beneath her, indicating that it was not rank that placed her high on the list: it was Cecil's certainty that she was one of the chief conspirators, and he was not going to risk her disappearing to the country again.

Rather than detain her at St Bartholomew's, she was held in a house where the servants were not under her control. But Penelope was not going quietly. Whether Sackford's staff refused to work for her, or she found them unsatisfactory, she was soon appealing to the privy council for "a cook to dress her meat" and "linen and other necessaries". Her request was passed on to Lord Rich on 17 February and five days later, since he had evidently done nothing, the council ordered him to send her bedding, hangings and whatever else she wanted.

There is some uncertainty about Lord Rich's whereabouts following the failed coup. He was not on the official roll of rebels, yet he appears sixth on "The names of those that were committed to the Tower for the Earl of Essex's cause". If he *was* arrested in the first feverish round-up, he was speedily released, otherwise the council could not have expected him to supply Penelope's needs.

Secretly Penelope must have been counting her blessings. Elizabeth was not squeamish about sending women to prison, though in more comfort than many of the rebels now crammed into stinking, rat-infested cells. Perhaps the sudden influx of traitors saved Penelope from a spell in jail, or the Tower. Perhaps it was the tolerance and affection Elizabeth always showed her. Whatever the reason, Lady Rich suffered nothing worse than detention in Sackford's household.

The charge against Essex, Rutland and Southampton was high treason, and Cecil was sure that before long they "shall have lost their heads". The verdict was a foregone conclusion. Like all state trials the object was to show that "justice" was done: the London crowds and Essex's former soldiers, still mooching dangerously round the capital, had to see that their hero was a traitor who'd had all the justice he was entitled to.

Secretary Cecil and the council called in the best legal brains in London. Sir Edward Coke, attorney general, was again chief prosecutor and Francis Bacon was in charge of examining witnesses. Three years later Bacon would write to Mountjoy (and publish) a lengthy self-defence arguing he was only doing his duty to the queen. Yet to many he would always be the man who betrayed his generous patron.

At the York House hearing the previous June, Sir Edward Coke had over-played his hand, accusing Essex of treason when the charge was only failure to carry out the queen's orders. Now Essex *was* up for treason and Coke could be relied on to do his worst. So could Ralegh. His evidence at the trial and alleged conduct at Essex's death racked up Ralegh's reputation as the earl's number-one enemy – and came back to haunt him at his own trial a few years later.

Against her brother's enemies Penelope, still imprisoned in Sackford's house, was now powerless; and more appeals from her to Elizabeth would probably be counter-productive. She had not yet been charged with any crimes, but that was surely only a matter of time.

~

On 19 February the trial of Robert Devereux, Earl of Essex, and Henry Wriothesley, Earl of Southampton, opened in Westminster Hall.

Among the twenty-five peers summoned to hear the case was Lord Rich. His grandfather had played the Judas role at the trial of Sir Thomas More in 1535 beneath this same smoke-blackened roof. Now Lord Rich wisely stayed silent. He had openly cultivated Essex's favour for twenty years and it would be unseemly to denounce him now. Besides, Lord Rich's part in the conspiracy would not bear scrutiny. He could only guess if Cecil knew about Richardo's part in Rialta's letters to James back in 1589. And only Cecil and Bacon knew exactly what Sir Charles Danvers, Sir John Davies, Henry Cuffe and the rest of the conspirators had said under interrogation. They had, in fact, begun to reveal the "Scotch intrigue" and the plots to release Essex from captivity. Yet none of that came out in court. The charges against Essex were his plot "to surprise the Court, his coming in arms into London to raise rebellion, and the defending [of] his house against the Queen's forces". It was not for lack of time. The trial went on all day and Cecil joined Coke in the attack.

"In this court I stand an upright man, and your lordship as a delinquent," Cecil sneered. Years of pent-up resentment poured out as he tore into the arrogant man who had lorded it over him since childhood. Essex's attempts at humility were "sheep's clothing", Cecil said; they fooled no one: "God be thanked we know you."

Then Cecil turned to Essex's religion and the succession. Listing the Catholics among the rebels – Sir Christopher Blount, Sir John Davies and Francis Tresham – Cecil continued: "Your religion appears by Blount, Davies and Tresham – your chiefest counsellors for the moment." He could have added the Percy brothers, Robert Catesby, Sir Charles Danvers, Lord Monteagle and Southampton himself, an "unsteady Catholic". The thick web of Catholic connections that surrounded the Devereux had not gone unnoticed. Others had privately accused Essex of being "corrupt in religion", but this was public.

"I stand for loyalty, you stand for treachery. You would depose the queen; you would be king of England," Cecil hissed. Others had reached the same conclusion. From Tuscany to Tralee it was whispered that Essex was aiming for the crown. At home the rumours were so strong that Mountjoy had reassured James "Essex was free from those ambitious conceits". Bishop Goodman wondered if Essex "might have possessed himself of the kingdom"; and "the Wizard Earl" later told James he knew that Essex "wore the crown of England in his heart these many years, and was far from setting it on your head".

Recent historians have dismissed Essex as an "upstart" claimant. But Essex's ancestry linked him to so many medieval kings that contemporaries took his bid for power seriously, even without his bar sinister – illegitimate – descent from Henry VIII. The *Baronage of England*, written within living memory of the events, noted "he might have replaced James".

The guilty verdict and Essex's death sentence were no surprise. John Chamberlain, watching the trial, was impressed with his dignity: "I never saw any go through with such boldness, and show of resolution, and contempt of death." But the following day, back in the Tower and under pressure from chaplains to clear his conscience before he met his "Maker", Essex "humbly desired her majesty would send some of the council to him", so that he could "deliver now the truth"; and Secretary Cecil and the Earl of Nottingham were duly sent to listen.

Essex proceeded to name and shame everyone he could, including Mountjoy and Penelope. Re-examined, the other conspirators testified to Mountjoy's involvement. Sir Charles Danvers referred to meetings in Mountjoy's house, admitted he had been a go-between to Ireland and claimed Mountjoy had undertaken the command of the army in Ireland with the intention of using part of it in England. After Essex's release from York House, however, Sir Charles said Mountjoy refused "to satisfy my lord of Essex's private ambition" and would not "enter into any enterprise of that nature". Henry Cuffe, who had written many of Essex's letters, confirmed that Danvers was sent to Mountjoy in Ireland and added: "only this I know, that Sir Charles found him very affectionate to the earl."

Essex's charge against Penelope did not lend itself to confirmation by others. It was too personal: "I must accuse one who is most nearest to me, my sister who did continually urge me on with telling how all my friends and followers thought me a coward, and that I had lost all my valour." And if that wasn't betrayal enough, he hinted that she should be pressed to tell more though it would not be easy. "She must be looked to, for she hath a proud spirit." It was the unkindest cut of all and a pointless betrayal. Penelope's loyalty to her brother had never wavered. Throwing her to the wolves could not help him.

Elizabeth cancelled the first warrant she signed for Essex's execution, but another was soon prepared. Frances was desperate. She wrote to Cecil imploring him not to press Elizabeth to sign it. Surely he would not wish his son, "your own same treasure [to] be made orphan by the untimely or unnatural death of his dear father". Her tear-stained letter lies in the British Library, achingly sad, awesomely simple in its final plea, "if it be once signed I shall never wish to breathe one hour after".

But the second warrant *was* signed. If Essex hoped the queen's old affection for him would come to his rescue, he was wrong. And if Elizabeth hoped he would crawl for forgiveness she too was mistaken. All Essex requested, and received, was a private execution instead of the public spectacle traitors normally suffered. On Ash Wednesday, 25 February, he was beheaded, while Ralegh stood watching. There was a chill wind over Tower Hill that morning, but no one saw Essex shiver as he removed his doublet. Quietly he knelt at the block in his fine linen shirt and waited for the first of the three strokes that it would take to sever his head. It was said he never felt anything after the first blow. It was also said that Ralegh blew tobacco smoke in his face – and that was not true.

Five days had passed since his trial. To Penelope it must have felt like eternity. Shut up in Sackford's house, she had yet to hear the details of her own indictment and trial. It seems she never wrote to Cecil as Frances did. Perhaps she knew the secretary of state too well to hope he would let her brother live. Essex had made it clear he believed Cecil and his henchmen were corrupt and profiteering from the Irish wars. Besides, while Essex lived there would be danger. Rumour had it the London apprentices were planning to raise a mob 5,000-strong to storm the Tower and release him. In Cecil's mind, Essex had to go.

Penelope's future was more problematic. There was no question about her involvement in the abortive coup. She had not been caught red-handed with a sword, but the dealings between Essex, James and Mountjoy had her pale, slim fingers all over them. When she was examined by the privy council, Penelope "used herself with that modesty and wisdom" they had come to know well. In contrast with Essex's confession, she gave nothing away, made no concessions and showed no sign of weakness. Far from being the one who led Essex on, inciting him to rebellion, she explained: "it is known that I have been more like a slave than a sister, which proceeded out of my exceeding love rather than his authority." It was a brilliant line of argument. Who could deny that she had been enslaved by loving him too well?

When the report of Lady Rich's interrogation was sent to Elizabeth, Penelope was "presently set at liberty and sent unto my lord her husband". That may have seemed to Penelope punishment enough, yet in essence she went scot-free.

Sir Christopher Blount, Sir Gelly Meyrick, Sir Charles Danvers and

Henry Cuffe followed Essex to the block. Southampton was held in the Tower under suspended sentence of death. Rutland, Monteagle, Catesby, Tresham and the Percy brothers were given swingeing fines. Yet Penelope was not put through a full treason trial. She was not returned to prison. She was not even fined.

Elizabeth's attitude to Penelope had always been one of affection and tolerance. She had turned a blind eye to her affair with Mountjoy for years, and had received her kindly at Court despite the various disgraces of her mother, brother and sister. She had accepted that Penelope was not to blame for circulating her letter. Elizabeth could hardly have treated Penelope more leniently if she had been her favourite granddaughter. Now she was letting her walk away when it was obvious she had been part of the conspiracy with James and Mountjoy.

Cecil must have been beside himself with frustration. What more might they have extracted from her with a little "gentle persuasion"? He was convinced there was "a further reach than appeareth" to this conspiracy and it soon transpired that the conspirators' dealings with King James – the relationship Rialta began a dozen years before – had come within a whisker of paying off.

Unaware that Essex was already dead, James's agents, the Earl of Mar and Edward Bruce, were on their way to London. James was certain that an uprising against Elizabeth and her unpopular ministers was pending and he had sent them to help plan it. When he realized they were too late, he instructed them to let it be known he was *not* involved in any actions against Elizabeth. James's incriminating letters had gone up in flames, with Essex's little black bag, while Penelope sat in Essex House surrounded by troops and cannons. But the conspirators' confessions told Cecil that James *had* been on the brink of intervening. And might still do so.

The Scottish king's power, and his friendship with Penelope, was one of her trumps. The other, of course, was Mountjoy. In Ireland Penelope's lover, the lord deputy, was delivering military successes that her father and brother only dreamed of.

Part IV

Triumph and Tragedy

1601–1607

Chapter Twenty-Four

SPRING 1601–JUNE 1603

"Finding the smoke of envy where affection should be clearest"

– Lady Penelope Rich, 1601

*I*n the twelve months since Lord Mountjoy landed at Dublin Bay he had proved himself the finest English general of the age. He secured the Pale – the English-controlled area – from Dublin to Dundalk. He established a fort on Lough Foyle, driving a wedge between Tyrone and O'Donnell's lands. And with his modesty and courteous manner Mountjoy won the confidence of his officers and restored army discipline and morale. But he ran up against the same problems as Essex. When he complained to Elizabeth that he was not getting adequate support from London and had no more authority than a "scullion", she sent the playful but useless response: "Mistress Kitchenmaid, comfort yourself in this, that neither your careful endeavour, nor dangerous travels, nor heedful regards to our service, could ever have been disposed upon a prince that more esteems them."

At the beginning of February 1601 he wanted to return from Ireland as "the reporter to her [majesty] of the state of that realm". He also wanted it understood that it was not an excuse to see Penelope. If Elizabeth would "have it so I will lie in the porch of her doors [at Court] and not see my wife" he promised, in a rare public admission that he and Penelope were an item. It provoked no criticism from Elizabeth, but she would not have it so. She wanted Mountjoy to stay put and consolidate his victories.

Besides, Mountjoy's request had crossed in the post with "a packet out of England, by which he understood that the Earl of Essex was committed to the Tower". The news "wrought strange alteration" in Mountjoy, according to his secretary. "In truth his lordship had good cause to be wary ... since by some confessions in England himself was tainted with privity to the earl's practices."

It looked bad for Mountjoy. Admittedly he had declined to take part in armed rebellion after Essex was released from captivity and James refused to commit his troops. Yet until the eleventh hour Mountjoy had been in it up to his neck. Cecil and Elizabeth must know by now that the rebellion was not a rash act in the heat of the moment. Months of smouldering discontent and discussion lay behind it. And in case he was called to London on suspicion of treason, Mountjoy had an exit strategy. He "was purposed with his said friends to sail into France, they having privately fitted themselves with may necessaries thereunto". Cecil's letters to him, however, showed that he was being accused of nothing except being Essex's friend.

"When you consider how near her majesty was to destruction and the kingdom to usurpation," Cecil wrote, it must surely cancel "all other good affections which long familiarity and confidence in the innocence of your friends have bred." Cecil was offering Mountjoy a chance to distance himself from the rebels, and he grabbed it.

"I dare assure you," Mountjoy replied, "the army is free from infection of this conspiracy." Choosing his words with coded care he went on: "nothing on earth neither an angel from heaven, shall make me deceive the trust [the queen] hath reposed in me." It was common knowledge he considered Penelope his angel; even Fr Gerard knew.

Elizabeth sent back her personal thanks to Mountjoy for his loyalty and love; offered to pardon anyone who was "seduced and blindly led" by Essex; and promised to recall her lord deputy the following winter. Nonetheless, Mountjoy rightly remained worried and there is a nervous edge to his follow-up letters to his "Sacred Sovereign".

It was vital to know how he, and Penelope, stood with those in power at Court, and no one was now more powerful than the Earl of Nottingham. For decades he had been the lord admiral, one of Elizabeth's most senior councillors, and his wife, cousin Kate, was still her closest companion. He had led the attack on Essex House, played a prominent part in Essex's trial, heard Essex's confession in the Tower, and with Cecil he questioned Penelope about her brother's accusations. It was Elizabeth who ordered her interrogation and decided to release her with no further trial, yet Penelope felt compelled to write to Nottingham thanking him for his help: "The obligations your favours have laid upon me are so great as they even burthen my soul with thankfulness ... your late kindnesses vouchsafed me so much comfort as the bond is more infinite than I can any way discharge."

She repeated her defence against "him that is gone". She had been a "slave" to Essex, Penelope explained, not because of his "authority", but out of love for him. It was an important point. No one would swallow the idea that her younger brother had "authority" over strong-willed Lady Rich. But her capacity for loving – her children, Mountjoy, Lettice – made it credible that she acted from "exceeding love" for Essex, whose courage, charm, vision and generosity were undeniable.

If Penelope realized that she had been too ambitious for him, she could not afford to admit it. Without her, he might *not* have risked so much to restore the honour of the Devereux. Had she, after all, expected too much of him? His ultimate weakness and betrayal, failing to shoulder responsibility for his own actions, seems genuinely to have puzzled her. "Yet so strangely have I been wronged," she wrote, "finding the smoke of envy where affection should be clearest." Essex had much to envy in his sister's strength of character. The self-doubt and depression that dogged him, the self-pity and paranoia that ruined his political judgement, were missing from Penelope's make-up. To her resolution and constancy came so naturally, she hadn't realized he did not share them.

As usual, much of the significance of Penelope's letter to Nottingham lay in her postscript. In the margin she added: "Your lordship's noble disposition forceth me to deliver my grief unto you, hearing a report that some of these malicious tongues hath sought to wrong a worthy friend of yours" – tactfully she left Mountjoy's name out of it. "I know the most of them did hate him, for the zealous following the service of her majesty, and beseech you to pardon my presuming thus much, though I hope his enemies can have no power to harm him."

She was right. Cecil, for one, was putting it about that Mountjoy "hath been a good while suspended" from Elizabeth's good opinion because he was "known to be more devoted to the late earl than became him". Mountjoy, meanwhile, had also written to Nottingham. Ostensibly he was asking the earl's advice and help in persuading Elizabeth to let him return to Court. The subtext said Mountjoy had no qualms about coming to London because he did not have a guilty conscience.

Nottingham's answer was affable, humorous and complimentary to Penelope. "I think her majesty would be most glad to look upon your black eyes here so [if] she was sure you would not look with too much respect on other black eyes. But for that if the admiral were but thirty years old I think he would not differ in opinions from the Lord Mountjoy." The queen wanted Mountjoy to remain in Ireland and the subtext this time said the matter was inseparable from Penelope. Mountjoy should be under no illusions: everything was known. Nottingham, writing to Mountjoy at the end of May, knew the lord deputy had officially "had the relation of it" already, but he proceeded to recount what Essex had told him and Cecil in the Tower, naming and blaming those chiefly responsible, and he listed those who had been executed: Essex, Sir Christopher Blount, Sir Charles Danvers, Sir Gelly

Meyrick and Henry Cuffe. Southampton, Nottingham believed, would be spared but kept in the Tower.

So there it was; almost everyone who knew the inside story had been silenced, and Elizabeth meant to be ignorant of what had passed because she wanted Mountjoy's services in Ireland. It was an unspoken pact. So long as Mountjoy kept his job he and Penelope stayed safe from further questioning. Their part in Essex's rebellion would be overlooked and further evidence suppressed.

∽

Elizabeth was visibly broken by Essex's death. Her depression was overwhelming. She told the French ambassador she would have spared the earl if he had asked her. Soon stories spread that he *had* asked, by sending back a ring she'd given him, as a token of submission, but it never reached her. Others said she gave no instructions for the death warrant to be used. It was the same old excuse she had used about Mary Queen of Scots. Whatever people said, Elizabeth knew – and Penelope knew – she could have saved him if she wished.

Sir John Harington, seeking an audience with her, received the tart response, "Go tell that witty fellow, my godson, to get home; it is no season now to fool it here."

Sometimes Elizabeth could rise to an occasion and dance a corranto, going through all its fast, complicated steps. Yet the prevailing mood at Court and in the capital was one of gloom and melancholy. Shakespeare caught it perfectly in the tragi-comedies he wrote around 1601–2. *All's Well That Ends Well* was a fervent prayer that all would end well at the end of Elizabeth's reign. The countess in the play rules her castle at Rossillion like a relic of the past. It is time for a new world order. Shakespeare, always topical, political and aware of what the Devereux were doing, states what Penelope and her brother had stood for. There is a new generation struggling to take the reins, destroy Cecil's power and cease fawning on the tyrannical, irascible old queen.

And when *Hamlet* was performed at the end of 1601, many would have linked the moody Dane with the dead earl who were their hero. The play was a triumph and it was doubly poignant to everyone who had seen the old tragedy of Hamlet by the late playwright Thomas Kyd. It was popular in the 1580s and its young hero bore an uncanny resemblance to Essex in his teens, when his widowed mother married the man who allegedly poisoned his father. Shakespeare had now updated the theme by developing Hamlet into a man of whom great things were expected, but whose indecision destroyed him. No wonder it was a good crowd-puller.

As the year drew to a close, Elizabeth held "such a small Court this Christmas that the guard were not troubled to keep doors at the plays and pastimes". Three times the players were called to perform for her, but it did not lift her spirits. She mourned Essex. Londoners mourned him.

There is no evidence that Penelope ever attended Elizabeth's Court again, and the impact of the rebellion continued to rumble on as Cecil tried to unearth all the "roots and offshoots of conspiracy". She was not, though, entirely alone and friendless. In December 1602 Rowland Whyte wrote to Sir Robert Sidney, who was staying with Sir John Harrington at Exton in Rutland: "The storm continues now and then, but all depends upon my Lady Rich's being, or not being amongst you." Penelope probably spent time with Lettice, who retired to Drayton under the double tragedy of the execution of her only surviving son and her third husband. As well as her mother, Penelope had Wanstead to see to, and Mountjoy's children. Little Penelope, Isabella, Mountjoy and St John were all under ten, and it seems most likely that Penelope gave birth to Mountjoy's youngest son, Charles, after he left for Dublin.

And money was a problem. The immediate effect of Essex's treason was to forfeit the family estates to the crown, cutting off Penelope's support from that source. Years later Mountjoy claimed Lord Rich abandoned her and refused to return her dowry. In reality, though he retained the capital he made her an allowance from it. Contrary to many accounts, however, he took no steps to divorce her. Yet naturally the distance between them had increased since she and Mountjoy made Wanstead their home. Her future security depended on Mountjoy, and while he remained in Ireland his life was constantly in danger.

~

Mountjoy was not a typical tough, weather-beaten warrior, but he never avoided danger. He pushed himself and his men to the limit with night raids and winter campaigning. His horse was shot under him and his hound was killed running at his stirrup. The lad carrying his helmet had it struck by a bullet. One chaplain, one secretary and one gentleman on his personal staff were killed. Two, including Moryson, were wounded and two more had their horses killed. His leadership and determination produced results, but at great cost to himself and anxiety to Penelope.

Spring 1600, when he arrived in Ireland, was unusually cold. There was snow on Easter Day and it continued so frosty and dry through April and May that the harvest was threatened. Some took it as an ill omen for the new century. Penelope had seen how life in camp in the bitter cold and damp of Ireland had aged her father, and she knew Mountjoy's health was not robust.

According to his secretary, who shared his tent and knew his habits better than anyone, Mountjoy took care to keep warm, eat as well as possible, rest every afternoon and "he took tobacco abundantly, and of the best, which I think preserved him from sickness, especially in Ireland". Possibly, but it has an ominous ring for modern minds.

When he was at Court, Mountjoy usually wore "two (yea, sometimes three) pairs of silk stockings". When he was "keeping the field in Ireland", on top of his "ordinary stockings of silk he wore under boots another pair of woollen or worsted, with a pair of high linen boot-hose". Plus a thick cloak "lined with velvet, and white beaver hats ... three waistcoats in cold weather, and a thick ruff, besides a russet scarf about his neck thrice folded under it. So as I never observed any of his age and strength to keep his body so warm."

Through the summer Penelope's fears grew with rumours that Spain planned to invade Ireland and assist the rebels, and in September the long-expected Spanish landing took place; not in the north as the Irish earls hoped, but at Kinsale in County Cork. Mountjoy had been pushing into Tyrone country, on the Armagh borders. Now he marched south fast. He reached Kinsale in mid-October, pinned down the Spanish troops in the walled town and began a long winter siege. Informers told him Irish forces were following him south under Tyrone and O'Donnell, and he could be trapped between his enemies. Through November conditions in his camp worsened. There was "intolerable cold, dreadful labour, and want of almost everything". As Christmas approached, so did a major encounter with the Irish outside Kinsale.

December was freezing cold. The new supplies and troops sent from England "were wholly wasted, either by death, sickness or running away", he reported. By Christmas Eve the weather was "dark, wild and thunderous". Some said lightning struck their weapons. Warned of a possible attack, Mountjoy stayed up all night and at dawn led a cavalry charge against the Irish and scattered them. It took several more attacks to finish the matter but after a while the Spaniards surrendered. O'Donnell sailed for Spain and Tyrone retreated to his Ulster stronghold.

Mountjoy had delivered Elizabeth her most important victory on Irish soil. It was as crucial as the 1588 Armada defeat and it changed history, for it brought an end to the power of the Gaelic chiefs and foreshadowed the Flight of the Earls six years later.

Cecil, of course, put it about that the Kinsale victory was the result of Irish cowardice and Spanish betrayals. If Mountjoy knew, he ignored it. He still had months of campaigning ahead, and no amount of waistcoats and stockings stopped him falling sick. Over New Year and into February "his lordship's sickness grew on him". Moryson attributed it to "his watching and cold taken during the hard winter siege at Kinsale". As they moved north Mountjoy was so ill that from Kilkenny he needed to be "carried in a horse-litter, and so all the journey, till he came to Dublin".

Back in London news went round that "the Lord Deputy came very sick of a cold and a flux to Dublin". His "distemper still continuing" through April, he could not take the field again until June. Elizabeth wanted Tyrone's head and Mountjoy pursued him with a scorched-earth policy right across Ulster, leaving famine and a terrible legacy of hatred behind him. What he wanted was to get back to Penelope and "the land of good meat and clean linen". At last Elizabeth agreed to accept Tyrone's surrender and on 30 March 1603 Mountjoy formally received his submission on behalf of the queen.

Tyrone didn't know Elizabeth was already dead. She had breathed her last in Richmond Palace six days earlier. It was evident for weeks that she was nearing the end. On Saturday the 19th she granted an audience to Robert Carey, youngest son of the late Lord Hunsdon, Henry Carey. When he said he was pleased she was "in safety and health", she took his hand, held it hard and answered: "No, Robin, I am not well!" The following day she heard Sunday service propped on cushions on the floor at the door to her chapel. By day and night she lay on them refusing to go to bed, take food or medicine. By Wednesday she was speechless and could only make signs to show that King James should succeed her.

When the last prayers of Archbishop Whitgift and Elizabeth's chaplains were over, they left her to her ladies. It was still "the Tribe of Dan" who surrounded her: the late Lord Hunsdon's daughter Lady Scrope, and two granddaughters; three generations of Penelope's Carey relatives. Lady Scrope was the keeper of a sapphire ring which King James had sent south with orders to return it to him the moment Elizabeth died. Defying the orders of Cecil and the privy council that no one must leave the palace, she threw it down to her brother Robert and he galloped away to Edinburgh. He wanted to ingratiate himself with James by delivering the welcome news and, unlike the ring that failed to save Essex's life, James's sapphire reached its rightful owner.

At midnight on Saturday, after an amazingly fast ride, Robert arrived at Holyrood and handed James his "blue ring". James now knew Elizabeth was dead; and after the privy council's official messengers arrived, James also knew he had been proclaimed king throughout the country. For most people James's accession was a huge relief – at least in the short term. Soon the king Penelope had plotted with and written to in secret years ago would be in London. It would change everything.

Some things had already changed during Elizabeth's dying months. Penelope's sister Dorothy and her "Wizard Earl" husband had been blessed with another son. Their disagreements and the deaths of two baby boys had prompted Northumberland to go abroad soldiering in 1601, but after his return Dorothy was soon pregnant again and their baby, born on 29 September 1602, was christened Algernon at Essex House. Queen Elizabeth was godmother by proxy and Robert Cecil noted: "The Earl of Northumberland is now a happy man." He was, in fact, so happy that he tipped Dorothy's footman £1 for bringing him the news. But harmony was short-lived. In November Dorothy was alone "at Syon with the child, being otherwise of a very melancholy spirit".

After Essex's execution Essex House had come under Nottingham's control. But before the year was out Essex's widow, Frances, and her mother, Lady Ursula Walsingham, were living there. The authorities were not being helpful and in November Frances had to appeal for the water supply to be restored for "two poor widows". Frances was trying to sort out Essex's debts and settle as much of his remaining estate as she could on "Little Robin" and her daughters, Frances and Dorothy. To help finance the deals she sold Walsingham House to the merchant and moneylender Peter Vanlore, and some time before Algernon's christening Northumberland took a lease on Essex House. In the spring of 1603, two years after Essex's execution, Frances was married again. Her third husband, Richard Burke, Earl of Clanricarde, was the young head of an Anglophile Irish family who had grown up in Essex's household and followed the earl to Ireland in 1599. He remained there fighting the Irish rebels, winning great praise and a knighthood from Mountjoy at Kinsale; and when he returned to England (ahead of Mountjoy) he rejoined the former Essex circle and married Frances.

The Earl of Southampton, meanwhile, had been held in the Tower, his death sentence commuted to life imprisonment, and one of James's first acts while still in Edinburgh was to order his release. It was one of many honours James handed out to the old Essex faction. For years he had regarded them as his only allies. But in the aftermath of Essex's coup he found Cecil prepared to treat him as heir apparent. The idea that Cecil backed the Infanta of Spain to succeed Elizabeth was largely an invention by Essex's party; and in the months before Elizabeth died Cecil worked hard to build bridges with James and ensure a smooth succession – for them both.

The new king travelled south quickly but his entry into London was delayed by Elizabeth's funeral. For two days her wrinkled old body, pathetically neglected, had lain at Richmond Palace waiting for its coffin while all eyes focused on the phoenix rising in the north. Badly embalmed and decomposing, it was taken by barge to Westminster to lie in state in

Whitehall Palace, before being moved to Westminster Hall. Finally, on 28 April, the coffin, with its life-size wax effigy of her on top, made its way to Westminster Abbey on a hearse drawn by four great horses draped in black velvet cloths, with red and black plumes and pennons at their heads and tails. Lord Rich was one of twelve barons who walked alongside, carrying tall lances with flags fluttering at the tip. More than 1,000 mourners, from peers to paupers, followed her, caped and hooded in black, and the crowds made "such a general crying, groaning and weeping as the like hath not been seen or known". If Penelope was among them, she probably shed few tears.

James waited at Theobalds with Cecil, hunting and handing out offices and honours. Mountjoy was made a privy councillor and raised from lord deputy to lord lieutenant of Ireland. The new king's entry to his capital was a somewhat muted event: the capital was gripped by plague. The rising death toll meant the playhouses were soon closed, coronation plans were kept low key and a triumphal royal procession through the city would have to wait. Nonetheless it was a splendid day for Penelope when James rode from Theobalds to London with Northumberland on his right, the Earl of Nottingham on his left and "Little Robin" Devereux in front of them carrying the king's sword. Northumberland was also made a privy councillor and commander of the sovereign's bodyguard, the gentlemen pensioners. Uncle William Knollys, Edward Wotton – Essex's secretary – and Sir Robert Sidney were made barons.

And Lady Rich was named one of six ladies-in-waiting to the queen, James's wife Anna. A new life was opening up for Penelope: after more than three years apart, Mountjoy should soon be on his way back to her. But he still had to arrange Tyrone's resubmission to King James, and deal with an outbreak of rioting. Across Ireland priests were openly celebrating mass, assuming James was pro-Catholic. Some towns claimed independence during the interregnum, and there were rumours of Spanish forces returning. It was June before Mountjoy sailed, bringing Tyrone with him, and there were still dangers ahead. In thick fog their ship ran among the treacherous Skerries rocks and had to put in to Beaumaris Bay. And as they rode to London the widows and orphans of soldiers who had died unpaid in Ireland lined the roads pelting the "arch traitor" Tyrone.

Mountjoy reached London, exhausted, on 6 June, but Penelope was not there to greet him.

Chapter Twenty-Five

MAY–DECEMBER 1603

"The place and rank of the ancientest Earl of Essex"

– King James I & VI, 1603

*E*arly in May Penelope had left London and travelled north to greet the new queen and accompany her to London. Anna was pregnant when Elizabeth died and, rather than hurry south with James, she decided to follow at her leisure, bringing their children. But her furious wrangling with the Earl of Mar over custody of her eldest son, Prince Henry, brought on a miscarriage, so Anna claimed, and weeks went by before she was ready to leave.

Cecil, meanwhile, authorized the six noble ladies and two maids of honour chosen for the queen's household to go and meet her. Among them, as well as Lady Rich, were two of Elizabeth's former gentlewomen: Lady Scrope and the Countess of Kildare (Nottingham's daughter and now Lord Cobham's wife), whom Essex had nicknamed "the spider of the Court". James had already sent some of Elizabeth's jewels and gowns to Edinburgh so that his wife would not enter England looking shabby, and her ladies-in-waiting now took a further supply. But Cecil was anxious not to risk more priceless English gems possibly disappearing into the Scottish heather, and Anna's official ladies were ordered to wait for her at Berwick, on the border. There was nothing, of course, to stop other ladies heading north to join Anna. So they did and some, not embargoed to stop at Berwick, raced on to Edinburgh to grab first place in the new queen's favour.

Penelope set off with no idea when Mountjoy would be free to leave Ireland and, even had she known it would be early June, she probably would not have passed up the chance to welcome the new queen. Despite the urgency, it was typical of Penelope to find time before she left to write to Robert Cecil recommending someone who needed a job.

On 1 June Anna left Edinburgh and when she reached Berwick she decided she wasn't very keen on some of her official English ladies-in-waiting. She had her own Scottish "first lady" of the bedchamber, Jane Drummond, her accomplice in secret Catholic worship; and she had a new English friend, Lucy, the young Countess of Bedford, one of those who had rushed all the way to Edinburgh. Lucy's husband was one of the old Essex party (despite his swift exit from the rebellion) and Lucy and Penelope quickly became Anna's closest companions.

Ten days later the queen's party reached York, to be received by the president of the Council of the North at King's Manor. It was familiar ground to Penelope, though the president was no longer her guardian. After Huntingdon's death the job went to Cecil's brother, who had welcomed James to York two months earlier and found him anxious about assassins. Anna, however, was happy to mix with people and stayed several days charming the citizens before she moved on to spend the night at Worksop Manor in Nottinghamshire. On 21 June she was at Woollaton Hall and the next day she and her party reached Ashby-de-la-Zouche. Formerly the seat of Penelope's guardian, it was another place that brought back memories, and by chance another "old girl" from the Huntingdons' school, Lady Margaret Hoby, arrived to pay her respects to the new queen. Margaret, once Penelope's sister-in-law, had been to London with her husband for Elizabeth's funeral, and finding that their path home to Yorkshire crossed with Anna's they stopped to kiss her hand. It was a coincidence Penelope could hardly have wished for: Margaret's brief marriage to Wat had not been a success and her rapid remarriage had caused upset in the family.

Wherever Anna stopped she was saluted by scores of titled ladies and country gentry, some petitioning her for more Catholic toleration. There was never enough room for all her attendants to share her resting place and it was a scramble for beds in nearby houses. On 23 June, while Anna stayed with Sir William Skipwith near Loughborough, others were sleeping over at Rockingham Castle, thirty miles away. The Countess of Cumberland and her daughter, Lady Anne Clifford, had driven there so fast from Kent that three coach horses dropped dead under them. In her diary, thirteen-year-old Anne noted: "Thither came my Lady of Bedford who was so great a woman with the queen that everyone respected her, she having attended the queen out of Scotland." The following day they joined Anna at "Mr Griffin of Dingley's which was the first time ever I saw the queen"; and to Anne's delight the queen "kissed us all and used us kindly". Dingley Hall, near Market Harborough, was the home of Sir Thomas Griffin and it did not pass unnoticed that Anna was staying with a well-known Catholic. At their next stop "an infinite number of lords and ladies" were present, but Anna's preferences were becoming marked.

Chapter Twenty-Five

The queen "showed no favour to the elderly ladies but to Lady Rich and such like company". Penelope had turned forty in January and Anna, not yet thirty, generally preferred younger people like Lucy. But Anna also liked brilliant, cultured, sophisticated people and Penelope fitted that frame perfectly.

As the queen's colourful cavalcade moved south, some in coaches, some on horseback, Anna and Penelope had time to discover how closely their tastes and upbringing mirrored each other's. In Denmark, Anna had a Protestant childhood and education and she was still nominally Lutheran. Since she arrived in Scotland in 1590, however, she had shown an increasing preference for Catholicism. At Dunfermline she surrounded herself with Catholic attendants and, though she had official Protestant chaplains, in private she worshipped as a Catholic.

"She likes enjoyment and is very fond of dancing and of fetes," observed the Venetian ambassador. She played the lute, virginals and several other instruments. She loved jewellery and clothes and her extravagance ran up huge debts for James. But the usual image of Anna as simply fun-loving and frivolous is wide of the mark. She spoke fluent French, soon acquired some Italian and her literary patronage became considerable. She shared Penelope's interest in foreign affairs and politics, claiming that her intrigues were "to help the king". She had a well-developed sense of her own position and prerogative, again like Penelope. And they both had a passion for plays and masques.

At Althorp House, in Northamptonshire, on Saturday evening, 25 June, they were in for a treat. As they drove through woods in the park they were waylaid by the sound of pipes playing a fanfare. A costumed Queen Mab and her faeries appeared before them and Anna's coach was hailed by a satyr sitting in a small tree. "Some solemnities are near," he cried and, climbing down to take a closer look at the queen and her party, he announced, "Sure they are of heavenly race." It was the start of a magical two days at the Spencer family home, and the first of many masques the playwright Ben Jonson would produce for the queen. Before the royal coach was allowed to drive on to the house, the faeries danced, Anna was presented with a jewel and two deer were released and hunted down in front of her. More music and plays followed and, as Jonson scornfully put it, "a morris of the clowns thereabout, who most officiously presented themselves". It would sound like the plot of *A Midsummer Night's Dream* – except that Shakespeare wasn't there.

On Monday, Anna's party moved on. They were due at Easton Neston later that day, where James would meet them and escort his family to Windsor. The journey had been an excellent investment of Penelope's time. It was the start of a royal friendship that brought her to the peak of her influence. And while Penelope was with the queen, Mountjoy had been reaping rewards from the king.

~

On 7 June, hours after he reached London, "the Lord Mountjoy, Lord Lieutenant of Ireland took the oath of a privy councillor at the council board". The following day James and his courtiers were entertained with great ceremony at Syon by "the Wizard Earl" and Penelope's sister. After months at Syon on her own, following the christening of their son Algernon, it seemed that Dorothy had patched up her quarrels with her husband, and in 1604 she would produce another son, Henry, though it was only a temporary truce.

Northumberland was difficult, but he was not stupid and beneath his show of deference to James he had reservations about the new king. James was a coarse man. Who else would have told elderly Archbishop Whitgift that the Church of England was like a man with syphilis? There was, James insisted, "no reason that because a man had been sick of the pox forty years, therefore he should not be cured at length". James was tactless, impatient and intolerant of views that differed from his own. He was bored by routine administration, especially if he wanted to get away and indulge his passions, which were chiefly hunting and handsome young men. He was at least bisexual and with age he became increasingly sentimental and drunk.

Yet James was also highly intellectual and scholarly. When he wasn't being boorish he could be erudite, and he shared with Mountjoy a real love of books and libraries. Both men were deeply interested in divinity (in James's case that included his own divine right to rule), and James held Mountjoy's opinions in great esteem. Soon Mountjoy was spending so much time with James that a group of Catholics plotting to kidnap the king were worried they might harm Mountjoy, Northumberland and Southampton in their attempt, all three being seen as Catholic sympathizers. But the "Bye" plotters, as they became known, were betrayed, and investigations revealed a more serious conspiracy to kill James and Prince Henry and put Arbella Stuart on the throne. And the "Main" plot involved Sir Walter Ralegh and Lord Cobham.

Cecil could not have invented a better chance to get rid of another personal rival. Ralegh had sided with him against Essex, yet Cecil regarded him as an enemy and his betrayal of Ralegh was cruel beyond belief. Arrested a month later, Ralegh made a half-hearted attempt at suicide and wrote of Cecil: "I thought he would never forsake me in extremity: I would not have done it him, God knows." Naively, Ralegh imagined Cecil's sense of personal honour might be relied upon.

Penelope never made that mistake. She knew Cecil would not let friendship stand in his way. If he saw someone falling he was more likely to put out his foot than his hand. She had Mountjoy's career to consider as well as her own, and she was punctilious in preserving a veneer of friendship with Cecil.

With the plotters under arrest, James carried on to collect Anna and her party and conduct them to Windsor, where the new Court was gathering.

At last Penelope and Mountjoy could be together again. So much had happened in the three and a half years since he rode off to Ireland. They had both reached forty after weathering extreme dangers, and Mountjoy had been seriously ill. His dark hair, always thin on top, was receding. But his unassuming manner, his gentle smile and his snub nose were the same. Penelope looked older too, yet her beautiful dark eyes still gleamed and she remained among the most glamorous, celebrated figures at Court.

"The queen had with her a Court of ladies and many very fair and goodly ones," Dudley Carleton wrote from Windsor; "but the ladies of Bedford, Rich and Essex [are] especially in favour." Everyone knew Lady Rich was Lord Mountjoy's mistress, but it was no bar to their place in high society. When the "great ladies and maids of honour" were sworn in as the queen's attendants, Lucy, Countess of Bedford, became one of Anna's top two ladies of the bedchamber, and Penelope was in the next most exclusive group, the six ladies of the drawing chamber.

Penelope's friendship with Anna, however, was enough to make Lucy jealous. "Now was my Lady Rich grown great with the queen," Anne Clifford wrote; "in so much as my Lady of Bedford was somewhat out with her [Penelope]." Despite Lucy's higher station in the pecking order, Anna seemed to be treating Lucy "even indifferently" compared with Lady Rich. Competition was intense. "The plotting and malice" among the ladies was so bad there was a danger they would "sting one another to death", sighed the Earl of Worcester.

There was no chance yet for Penelope and Mountjoy to get away to Wanstead. At Windsor Castle on 2 July, the knights of the Garter, Mountjoy included, were due to process to St George's ancient chapel and install new members of the order, one of whom was Southampton. To Cecil's annoyance, James insisted on keeping the earl with him since his release from the Tower. Southampton's almost feminine good looks and sweet voice were guaranteed to appeal to James, though his marriage to Penelope's cousin appears to have been a success. After their first child, Penelope's goddaughter and namesake, the countess gave birth to two sons and two more daughters.

As the Garter knights conducted their annual ceremony and feast, Penelope must have felt that fortune was smiling on her again. Mountjoy was recovering from his years in Ireland. Southampton and cousin Elizabeth were back at Court. Dorothy and "the Wizard Earl" were also enjoying royal favour. And Essex's disgrace was finally about to be erased. After the Court moved on from Windsor to Hampton Court, James issued a decree that Essex's three children, "Little Robin", Frances and Dorothy, should be reinstated "in noble blood". Out of "compassion and pity upon the said desolate infants", it was to be "as though the said earl had never been attainted". Short of bringing Essex back, it was the best thing James could do.

There were still more honours to come. On 21 July in the Great Hall at Hampton Court, with full pomp and pageantry, Mountjoy was made an earl. Resplendent in crimson velvet robes Mountjoy walked slowly into the royal presence and knelt before the king to hear the letters patent naming him Earl of Devonshire read out to the assembled Court. James placed the crimson and ermine cap and gleaming new coronet on his head, and the trumpets sounded. Mountjoy, now to be known as Devonshire, had done more than "rebuild the ancient house" of Blount. He had begun to amass considerable wealth and offices. Later in the year he was given the highest job in the army, master of the Ordnance. It was a post Essex had held, and it had been empty since his execution.

The coronation of James and Anna in Westminster Abbey on 25 July must have seemed to Penelope an anti-climax, and she was not alone. It was a low-key affair by Court standards. The plague epidemic was so bad that James was anxious "to prevent all occasions of dispersing the infection amongst our people". He was equally afraid of riots and assassins. Anyone not invited to the coronation was ordered to keep away, and those who were invited were allowed a limited number of retainers: earls fifteen, bishops and barons ten, knights five.

There were, however, some memorable moments: "Little Robin" again acting as James's sword-bearer; Penelope's sixteen-year-old son Robert receiving a knighthood from the king; and Anna, remaining seated, refusing to take communion according to the rites of the Church of England.

∼

The stench of death was everywhere in London that spring and early summer. It was the worst outbreak of bubonic plague since the terrible epidemic ten years ago. It started in February in the poorest areas along the south bank of the Thames, where ships from the Continent unloaded cargoes and infected rats. In the heat of summer it grew worse, festering among the filthy gutters and ditches that ran through the city like open sewers.

James couldn't wait to get away. By mid-August the Court was at Farnham in Surrey, and at Farnham it was Penelope's turn to be raised in the hierarchy. On 17 August James awarded her "the place and the rank of the ancientest Earl of Essex, called Bourchier". By her marriage Lady Rich was only one among many baronesses. Now, with the same ancestral rank her father and brother had enjoyed, Penelope took precedence over every baron's wife and over the daughters of all except four earls. It was a signal mark of favour.

From Farnham, James moved the Court and privy council on to Woodstock, trying to avoid the plague and almost certainly carrying it with them. Each house or castle they stopped at grew to look like some strange eastern caravanserai, with tents, baggage carts, coaches and horses spread around. Cecil, busy preparing the treason trial against Ralegh, wearily wondered if they would end up in York. But the next move took them south to Wilton, near Salisbury, home of Philip Sidney's sister Mary and her bachelor son, the Earl of Pembroke. He too had found favour with James.

Once the Court had settled in at Wilton, Ralegh was brought from London to stand trial at the bishop's palace in Winchester, and on 17 November the case opened with the newly created Earl of Devonshire among the commissioners appointed to hear it. The trial brought back memories of Essex. Sir Edward Coke, the attorney general, was again chief prosecutor, and again the verdict was a foregone conclusion. But unlike Penelope's brother, Ralegh was not popular with the crowds. They could not forgive his betrayal of Essex, and they hurled whatever they could at him as he was driven to the court.

Ralegh's defence was brilliant. "Never man spake so well in times past, nor would do in the time to come," one spectator said. Refusing to bow to Coke's bullying, innuendos and smears, Ralegh challenged every point, adding "what a mockery is this!" As the trials of the various conspirators unfolded, Coke and Cecil did everything to blacken their reputations, even parading Arbella as an innocent victim of the plot. Poor Arbella, now treated as a Stuart princess after years of house arrest under Elizabeth, was driven half scatty by her white-knuckle ride through life: one minute pampered, the next imprisoned because of her place in the succession. But her presence at the trial "proved" what scoundrels the conspirators were.

Ralegh was clearly disenchanted with the new king and had talked unflatteringly about him, but whether he was really involved in the plot is a mystery. Some said he intended all along to betray the others and show his loyalty to James. The jury, however, took a mere fifteen minutes to pronounce him guilty and Ralegh was condemned to be hung, drawn and quartered, his "privy members cut off, and thrown into the fire before your eyes".

If the trial made a mockery of justice, the execution of the sentences was worse. In a sickening charade, the four condemned men, Ralegh included, were twice led to the scaffold only to be taken back to prison as the happy recipients of James's temporary stay of execution. Whatever Ralegh had done to betray Penelope's brother, no one would have wished that on him, and at a stroke public opinion changed. Devonshire led the petitioners who begged James to revoke the death sentence and allow Ralegh to be held at his own

Sherborne Castle. Though they failed, Ralegh spent the next twelve years in the Tower in considerable comfort, with public sympathy as well as his books and chemical experiments.

No one knows what Penelope thought, but her heart must have ached for her old friend Bess and her boy Walter, conceived a few months after Damerei died. It was Bess who pawned her jewels to provide for the family; Bess who helped Ralegh build a new life in the Tower and bore him another son, Carew; and Bess who fought for years to keep hold of their Sherborne estate, only to see James hand it to his latest handsome inamorato.

With Ralegh's trial over, Wilton resumed its round of games and plays, drinking and flirting. Arbella, unhappy and unbalanced, watched with growing distaste. She disliked the way Anna's attendants talked of Elizabeth: "Our great and gracious ladies leave no gesture or fault of the late queen unremembered." Arbella had not spent years watching at first hand, as Penelope had, how Elizabeth destroyed people's lives and happiness. She also hated "to play the child again" in the light-hearted games that amused Anna and her ladies. And she strongly disapproved of the seemingly lax morals of the new Court. Daily, she claimed, "some even of the fairest" ladies were "misled and willingly and wittingly ensnared by the prince of darkness". Arbella was referring to the devil, not dark-haired Devonshire, but she was obviously thinking of Penelope. Cecil must have chuckled if her letter, like thousands of others, passed through his hands on the way to its rightful reader. Her friends and family kept warning Arbella to be careful what she wrote.

Others enjoyed Wilton even if she didn't. The best of London's writers and musicians – William Shakespeare and John Dowland – came down to entertain the new royal family and their friends. But as the year drew to a close, James and Anna decided to move their households to Hampton Court and spend their first Christmas as close to the capital as plague permitted. However much Penelope and Devonshire might wish to be elsewhere, they had no choice but to follow. Devonshire was a privy councillor, Penelope was on Anna's staff and they needed permission to be absent from Court. Besides, Anna was planning to put her mark on the Christmas revels with a season of plays and spectacular masques, and her plans involved Lady Rich.

～

In London "no one mentions the plague" and the place was "so full of people that it is hard to believe that about 60 thousand deaths have taken place", the Venetian ambassador reported to the doge. At Hampton Court the Christmastide revels were still in full swing long after Twelfth Night. Thanks to the plague there was a backlog of foreign ambassadors and envoys waiting to be received by the new king, and each one expected a banquet in his honour. From the Spanish ambassador's turn on St Stephen's Day, 26 December, until Candlemas on 2 February, when the Grand Duke of Tuscany's envoy had his feast and entertainment, it was almost non-stop. And then there was Anna's programme of plays and masques.

"We have had a merry Christmas and nothing to disquiet us save brabbles [petty disputes] amongst our ambassadors, and one or two poor companions that died of the plague," wrote Dudley Carleton. How could Penelope have disagreed? It was the first Christmas since Devonshire returned from Ireland. The whole Court was assembled, and she and her family were enjoying marked royal favour.

Every night there was "a public play in the great hall" at Hampton Court. Carleton thought James took "no extraordinary pleasure in them", but Anna and Prince Henry "were more the players' friends for on other nights they had them privately". Nonetheless James was happy to patronize Shakespeare and the Chamberlain's Men, now renamed the King's Men, and as one of their many royal command performances that Christmas they presented *A Midsummer Night's Dream*.

If anything delighted Anna more than plays, it was masques. The mixture of music, dancing, fantastic costumes and magical transformation scenes brought together all the arts she loved. Masques included speeches too, but it was the theme, the look and the music that mattered most; and during each show the masquers would move into the audience and take out partners to join in the dance. Disguisings had been popular for years, chiefly performed by men, though Penelope's great-grandmother Mary Boleyn had famously taken part in Henry VIII's masques. Now Anna, with the help of her ladies, raised the Court masque to new levels of sophistication, beauty – and cost.

On New Year's Night after "a play of Robin Goodfellow", eight young gallants performed "a masque brought in by a magician of China", who came down from "a heaven built at the lower end of the hall".

The hot ticket, however, was the Queen's Masque, *The Vision of the Twelve Goddesses*, specially written by poet Samuel Daniel and scheduled for Sunday 8 January. The foreign diplomats "were in so strong competition for place and precedence" that the French ambassador kicked up a fuss when he discovered he was not to be invited again. It made no difference. Anna was adamant: she had invited the Spanish ambassador, "and to have them both there could not well be without bloodshed". The Venetian ambassador, at least, was mollified by watching a play with James on Sunday afternoon; and the Florentine ambassador enjoyed supper in Lady Rich's chamber. Penelope was a political hostess, as well as one of Anna's masquers.

It was late that evening when the favoured audience filed into the great hall and found it transformed by a large rock with groups of "savages" arranged on it. From the top came "a winding stair of breadth for three to march" and on it stood a torch-lit procession of twelve goddesses, grouped "three by three". Each one wore a mask and a different coloured costume made of richly embroidered satins, cloth of silver and gold; and each had a headdress to show which goddess she represented. At the front was Anna, dressed as Pallas Athene, goddess of wisdom. Either side of her were the Countess of Suffolk, as Juno, goddess of women and marriage; and Penelope, playing Venus, the goddess of love. It said everything about Lady Rich's reputation. Each group of goddesses had their own torch-bearers, young pages in "white satin loose gowns", their robes and hair spangled with stars. And below the goddesses were three ladies dressed as the Three Graces in silver robes, holding bright white torches.

The effect was stunning – "being all seen on the stairs at once was the best presentation I have at any time seen", Carleton admitted. Anna had raided Elizabeth's wardrobe for costumes, cheerfully ignoring any symbolic value the sumptuous gowns might have. Not everyone approved of her chopping her own outfit at knee-length, "that we might see a woman had both feet and legs, which I never knew before", Carleton added. Half the fun was guessing who the masquers were, and there was meaning and symbolism in every position and move they made.

Slowly the procession descended. Each goddess glided to the side of the hall and placed a gift on the altar of the Temple of Peace, before joining hands to dance a stately measure. When they took out twelve men from the audience as their partners it looked like a gathering of Penelope's family and friends: Devonshire, William Knollys, Northumberland, Southampton, Robert Sidney, Pembroke and Lord Monteagle, another Essex rebel recently released from the Tower.

It was midnight before the goddesses retired in procession and returned unmasked, but still in costume, to enjoy a banquet with the king and ambassadors. The meal went off "with the accustomed confusion", according to Carleton, "and so ended … our Christmas gambols".

The cost of Anna's masque was astronomical, nearly £3,000, yet James encouraged her to plan another. It was not simply to keep her out of political intrigues. The Queen's Masque had instantly become part of the image of the Stuart Court. When James suggested the privy council fund Anna's next Christmas special, they balked at coughing up the necessary, saying that was his privilege. Anna was planning it anyway.

Chapter Twenty-Six

January 1604–November 1605

"Lascivious appetites of all sorts"

– Sir Simonds D'Ewes, c. 1620

Beneath the sparkle of Christmastide, James was holding talks on the two issues that concerned him most: peace with Spain and religion. And he wanted Devonshire's attendance at both.

On 12 January, James opened a four-day conference on reform and change in the Church of England. He had summoned the bishops, and four leading Puritans who rejected the bishops' authority and disagreed with them over the sacraments, the Book of Common Prayer and much more. In truth James was more interested in hearing himself speak than anyone else and there was little for Devonshire and the other councillors to do. The king managed to be ruder to the Puritans than he was to the bishops, and any hopes they nursed of concessions to their views withered fast. Despite his upbringing in Presbyterian Scotland, James was not going to support their reforms. Nor was he listening to the Catholics. The idea, once deliberately encouraged by James himself, that his regime would be Catholic-friendly because he was the son of Mary Queen of Scots, was moonshine. And after the "Bye" and "Main" plots were revealed, there was *no* chance he would allow concessions to the Catholics. By the time James closed the conference it was obvious he would bolster the established Church. He agreed with Cecil: toleration was out, crackdown was in.

Early in January, while the Court was still in festive mood, Devonshire was also delegated to be one of the five English lords who opened preliminary peace talks with the Spanish envoy at his house in Richmond. The main talks took place later at Somerset House in the Strand, but before then there was another great ceremony that Penelope and Devonshire had to attend. In mid-March James and Anna made their long-delayed triumphal procession through the city from the Tower to Whitehall. James rode a small white Spanish horse with a rich canopy of state held over him by his most senior noblemen. Anna and her ladies rode in open chariots, waving to the crowds. It was a six-hour pageant, with the entire Court slowly processing beneath specially built decorative arches and banners, pausing for music, speeches and presentations. James did not really "give a turd", to use his own expression, for the views of the man in the street; and he hated exposing his royal personage to the danger from assassins. Unlike Elizabeth and her predecessors, James was more inclined to spend on his private pleasures, and favourites, than state spectacles for public appreciation.

The king would, however, push the boat out – literally – for foreign diplomats. His courtiers welcomed the Spanish negotiators from a small fleet of gondolas as the visitors' barges approached Somerset House. The riverside mansion was usually Anna's personal palace, but she and her ladies moved into Whitehall for the period of the peace talks.

The negotiations took up most of the summer. Devonshire had destroyed Spanish hopes of dominating Ireland. Spain's power had declined, her national debt was escalating and famine and plague were decimating the population. Spain wanted peace even without toleration for English Catholics. England in return wanted trading rights with the Spanish-owned West Indies, and on 4 August the Treaty of London was signed. In theory at least it promised perpetual peace, and it ended twenty years of open warfare since Elizabeth let Leicester lead an army to the Netherlands.

Devonshire would rather have been at Wanstead than sitting in Somerset House, yet it was time well spent. He received a fat pension from King Philip of Spain, one of several handed out to leading privy councillors to thank them for their assistance in bringing an end to the war. In effect they were now in the pay of Spain, but Devonshire did not milk the situation as shamelessly as Cecil. There is reason to believe Cecil was taking bribes from the Dutch *not* to make peace, at the same time as pocketing his pension from Spain, which started at £1,000 a year, soon rose to £1,500 and – at his suggestion – soared to £12,500.

～

Once the peace was signed Devonshire was at last able to get away to Wanstead for a summer interlude. Here in the calm and quiet of Wanstead he could relax with Penelope and his children. Their eldest child, Penelope, was now twelve years old; Isabella had turned nine in January; and though none of their three sons, Mountjoy, St John and Charles, had yet reached eight, they were fine boys who would one day join him riding, hunting and hawking in the parks.

Devonshire "delighted in study, in gardens, a house richly furnished and delectable rooms of retreat", Fynes Moryson recalled. He also liked "playing at shovelboard or at cards, in reading play books for recreation, and especially in fishing and fishponds". The Wanstead estate suited him and Penelope down to the last inch of its walled grounds. Beyond the formal gardens were lakes and ponds fed by the River Roding, and a heronry. They had enjoyed it for barely a year before Devonshire was sent to Ireland. Now he could supervise stocking the fishponds and build up his library.

The earl's books were not "for ostentation but for use", and he employed the expert antiquarian Sir Robert Cotton to help him create a famous and valuable collection. He would sit for hours reading, discussing life and letters, ethics and religion. Soon after Philip Sidney's death, the satirist and playwright Thomas Nashe hailed him as Sidney's successor in all things, including literary patronage. It was overly flattering, designed to win favours, yet it held some truth. Devonshire fostered the careers of numerous writers and academics, including Nicholas Breton, Samuel Daniel and John Ford. They knew how much they owed to his help and intellectual support, and to his well-stocked library.

Devonshire's tastes in food and wine were equally costly, "at dinner and supper having the choicest and most nourishing meats, with the best wines, which he drank plentifully and never in great excess". The Spanish pension came in useful, and "As his means increased so his table was better served, so that in his latter time no lord in England might compare with him in that kind of bounty."

As the new reign progressed, Moryson noticed his master was beginning to tire of Court life and he was less and less willing to leave his country retreat. His usually cheerful, round face was growing thinner and his ruddy complexion had turned swarthy. He could hardly have been pleased when his summer idyll was interrupted by a surprise visit from the Spanish peace negotiators. After signing the treaty they had "made a merry journey" to stay with Cecil at Theobalds. Two days later "they made the like journey to Wanstead and made appointment with my lord Cecil, there to surprise my lord of Devonshire, but he had a night's warning". If the joke was to surprise the earl with his mistress in his rural retreat, it somehow fell flat. The records don't mention if Penelope appeared, only that Devonshire "crammed their stomachs with all manner of dainties" before sending them back to London.

Soon Devonshire and Penelope had to be back in London too, for a royal banquet and ball to celebrate the treaty and bid the Spaniards goodbye. Seated at the top table in Whitehall Palace, with James and Anna and the leading Spanish diplomats, were Devonshire, Northumberland and "Little Robin", restored to his father's titles as Earl of Essex. "There were present at this ball more than fifty ladies of honour, very richly and elegantly dressed, and extremely beautiful," wrote the Spanish ambassador. After the feasting and dancing came bear-baiting, tumblers, and acrobats on ropes and horseback.

The earls of Southampton and Pembroke officiated as gentlemen ushers, and when the merrymaking was over Devonshire led the guests to their coaches, where more than fifty halberdiers waited with torches to light them home.

Twice during the evening Southampton had the honour of dancing with the queen. But his days of royal favour were numbered. Still only thirty years old, Southampton was arguably the most cultured and gifted member of the first Stuart Court. He was also, in aristocratic terms, the most senior survivor of the Essex faction. To Cecil it looked as though King James would *never* stop honouring the former rebels who had been his enemies. Could Cecil ever sleep easily while they were at Court? One by one his old enemies and shaky supporters – Ralegh, Cobham, Sir John Perrot and Essex, to name a few – had been removed. Cecil was steadily gaining the king's confidence. Elizabeth's "Pygmy" had reinvented himself as James's "Little Beagle". Perhaps it was time to remove the rest of the former Essex faction.

A rumour was started that Southampton was plotting to slay several Scotsmen close to the king, and he was arrested. It was an easy smear. Plenty of English courtiers criticized the presence of so many Scotsmen. In addition, Southampton was known to be out of step with James about toleration for Catholics. Nothing was proved against Southampton, but it was enough to scupper his chances of moving higher in James's service. All Penelope could do, as in days gone by, was offer support for his wife, cousin Elizabeth and their children.

Lettice was relying on Penelope's support, too. She had come up to London to file a lawsuit in Star Chamber against Sir Robert Dudley, the late Lord Leicester's "base-born" son by Lady Douglas Sheffield. As soon as James was on the throne, Sir Robert had started a series of cases to prove his parents had been married before Leicester's union with Lettice, and he was therefore the earl's legitimate heir. It was a pointless plea while Elizabeth was alive, but it might succeed with James. If it did, Dudley would claim Lettice's marriage was bigamous and Essex House and Wanstead were rightly his. Lettice counter-claimed that he was guilty of defamation and threatening her ownership of the properties. Penelope's response was to go public with her opposition to Robert's suit, and her influence was formidable.

"My Lady Rich is violent against Sir Robert Dudley; yet I find her much esteemed," wrote one observer. Sir Robert Sidney, recently raised to the rank of Baron Sidney, Leicester's only legitimate heir, had long ago reached agreement with Lettice over Leicester's debts and her inheritance. Now he and Lettice had common cause in fighting Dudley's suit, but the case was long and complex, and the fighting got dirty. Lady Douglas, supporting her son, claimed the proof of her marriage lay with Leicester's letters which had been stolen, and with witnesses who were mostly dead. Many had sympathy with

Dudley's attempts to prove his legitimacy and, as Devonshire put it, to "seek his perfection". Yet the consensus was that he'd been ill-advised to try.

When James raised Baron Sidney to the rank of Viscount Lisle, it was evident the case had been settled out of court. Six days later, on 10 May 1605, the Star Chamber verdict was given against Dudley, who soon left the country in disgust. Cecil's encomium on Lettice, delivered with the court's judgment, paid glowing tribute to her life with Leicester, "notwithstanding all his humours"; and bemoaned how "she was long disgraced with the queen". It doubtless sounded hollow to Penelope and Lettice, but it was a triumph for the Devereux. And no matter what sniffy comments Arbella made about the morals of beautiful ladies, Penelope's influence kept growing.

~

With Christmas approaching, the Court calendar was packed with plays and entertainments. It was James and Anna's first full winter season in the capital and from November onward the King's Men and their playwright, Shakespeare, were kept busy with command performances. At Whitehall Palace on All Saints' Day they presented Shakespeare's newest play, *Othello*, and three days later it was one of his old favourites, *The Merry Wives of Windsor*. In December they acted another new play, *Measure for Measure*, then *The Comedy of Errors*, and on 7 January it was *Henry V.* For weeks before Christmas, however, the production everyone was gossiping about was not one of the Bard's, but Anna's Christmas special. James had agreed to pay after all.

"We have here great preparations for the queen's masque; wherein besides her majesty will be eleven ladies," one courtier wrote, mentioning Lucy Bedford and Penelope. Dorothy, he went on, was "excused by sickness, [and] Lady Hertford by the measles". There must have been an outbreak, for Arbella was also absent with measles; and she must have been glad to avoid seeing Anna and her friends make a spectacle of themselves.

Anna had commissioned Ben Jonson to write this year's production, and Inigo Jones, a budding stylist and architect, to do the sets and costumes. It was an inspired pairing. Jonson was resolved to script something more dramatic than the previous year's offering, and Jones wanted to prove his mastery of stage machinery and decor. The result, *The Masque of Blackness*, performed on Twelfth Night, was sensational.

Jones transformed one end of the great chamber at Whitehall with a landscape from which "an artificial sea was seen to shoot forth". Out of the sea danced six tritons (half-man, half-fish), several mermaids and two huge sea horses. It was a vision of blues and sea-greens, shells and seaweed. When two professional actors appeared they declared themselves to be Oceanus, god of the sea, and Niger, the black god of "the Aethiop's river", the great river of

Africa. As they talked, flares and torches revealed another actor sitting high up on a moon beneath yards of blue silk scattered with stars, draped from the ceiling like the heavens at night. Most stunning of all was the "great concave shell, like mother of pearl", with lights shimmering round the edge. It seemed to "move on the waters" and inside it were the queen and her ladies, blacked up as twelve identical nymphs, the "Aethiop" daughters of Niger.

No one had seen anything like it. The nymphs' costumes were not cut-downs from Elizabeth's wardrobe this time. They were specially made from luxurious, filmy fabrics in blues and silver, "best setting off from the black" paint on their arms and faces. Their jewels and ropes of pearls glistened in the light of torches carried by twelve little "daughters" of Oceanus. Two by two, Anna led the masquers on to the floor to dance, each carrying a fan that identified the nymph she represented.

Penelope was Ocyte, known for swift-footedness, and her symbol, a pair of naked feet in a river, implied purity and an act of cleansing. It was an odd choice, unless Anna was aware that Penelope was planning something which would radically change her life.

Without masks it was relatively easy to see who was who among the twelve ladies – Anna was six months pregnant anyway – and their blackened appearance left the audience speechless. Dudley Carleton gave up trying to describe it. "There is a pamphlet in press which will save me that pains," he wrote. But he added that the costumes, though rich, were "too light and courtesan-like. Their black faces and hands, which were painted and bare up the elbows, was a very loathsome sight and I am sorry that strangers should see our Court so strangely disguised."

The king's late-night banquet for the audience and the masquers, still blacked up, was equally embarrassing. The tables and trestles loaded with food were "so furiously assaulted" they collapsed almost before anything had been touched, and the party turned into a drunken orgy. "What losses there were of chains, jewels, purses" Carleton could hardly bring himself to mention; but he could not resist adding: "one woman amongst the rest lost her honesty ... being surprised at her business on the top of the terrace."

Looking back a few years later, the diarist Sir Simonds D'Ewes said James's courtiers considered marriage "but a may-game", and "even great persons [were] prostituting their bodies to the intent to satisfy and consume their substance in lascivious appetites of all sorts". D'Ewes, like Lady Anne Clifford, was persistently po-faced and pedantic; but there was a growing band of critics who agreed with Lady Clifford's verdict: "All the ladies about the Court had gotten such ill names that it was grown a scandalous place and the queen herself was much fallen from her former greatness and reputation."

James's unsavoury behaviour was also drawing criticism. The morning after the wedding of Sir Philip Herbert and Lady Susan de Vere, late in December, James visited them "in his shirt and his nightgown and spent a good hour with them in the bed or upon, choose which you will believe best". Philip was the younger brother of the Earl of Pembroke, godson and nephew to Sir Philip Sidney, and another of James's favourites. The king was exceptionally generous to the bridal pair, giving them lands worth more than £1,000 a year and a splendid Court wedding at Whitehall. They were "married in the chapel, feasted in the great chamber, and lodged in the council chamber"; and "none of our accustomed forms [were] omitted, of bride cakes, sops in wine, giving of gloves, laces and points".

Penelope, planning her eldest son's wedding in February, could be forgiven for wondering if a Court occasion, with James as guest of honour, was quite such a good idea. She had successfully played matchmaker for young Sir Robert. He was heir to Lord Rich's huge fortune and just eighteen years old when the wedding took place on Tuesday 26 February 1605. His future wealth and his mother's influence made him a highly eligible young bachelor, but there was stiff competition for the bride, too. Frances Hatton was the orphan daughter and sole heiress to her father, Sir William Hatton, and to her maternal grandfather, the wealthy judge Sir Francis Gawdy. Talks had already started to marry her to Lord Buckhurst's son, the future third Earl of Dorset; and the union had Judge Gawdy's blessing. He did not want her to marry a Puritan and though Penelope's son had inherited her love of plays and masques, he followed Lord Rich in religion.

Some said it was Frances's stepfather, the unpleasant attorney general Sir Edward Coke, who forced her to marry Robert Rich. Others told it differently: "the Lady Rich prevented" the marriage to Lord Buckhurst's son by winning Frances's "good will"; and she then "contracted her [Frances] secretly to her son". It has a ring of truth. Penelope was good at using charm to get her way. Judge Gawdy promptly broke off relations with his granddaughter, but failed to write a new will, and when he died of apoplexy ten months later Robert claimed his estate on Frances's behalf.

Next it was the turn of Essex's son, "Little Robin", and in June plans were drawn up to marry him to Lady Frances Howard. She was the daughter of the Countess of Suffolk, who had partnered Penelope as the third pair of nymphs in *The Masque of Blackness*. The marriage, celebrated at the turn of the year, proved a disaster, though at the time it looked a splendid match, and Lettice could be proud that both Penelope and Essex's children were making powerful alliances.

Dorothy and Northumberland also continued to do well under the new regime. On 5 May, when the baby who had been so obvious beneath Anna's filmy costume was christened, Dorothy was one of the godparents. It was a significant honour, for the others were the queen's brother and Arbella Stuart, and Dorothy walked with them beside the new princess, "the high and noble Lady Mary", as she was carried to her christening in Greenwich chapel beneath a great canopy held aloft by eight barons.

And so the glittering party went on, with ever more luxury and extravagance, and with all the royal favourites in attendance. James was determined to compensate for his Calvinistic upbringing and his lack of funds as king of Scotland. Now he had money to spend – and spend it he did.

But while the new Stuart Court sparkled and revelled in its unaccustomed wealth, elsewhere in London and around the country all was not well. James had led people to expect he would allow Catholics more liberty, and they felt betrayed. The day Elizabeth died James was writing to the Earl of Northumberland: "As for the Catholics, I will neither persecute any that will be quiet, and give but an outward obedience to the law; neither will I spare to advance any of them that will, by good service, worthily deserve it." It seemed his arrival in England had been a false dawn. James was obviously less interested in keeping faith with his people than in "endlessly hunting", wining and dining diplomats and making lavish gifts to his fellow Scotsmen and favourites.

In the autumn of 1605 resentment revealed itself in a plot that could have blown a large area of London sky-high, taking with it most of the royal family, the lords temporal and spiritual and every member of parliament.

~

Essex's death had cleared the way for Cecil to ingratiate himself with the future king, but Essex's abortive revolt left behind a group of Catholics whose grievances were redoubled by disappointment in James. Robert Catesby, Jack Wright, John Grant, Tom Wintour, Francis Tresham and Lord Monteagle had supported Essex less than five years ago and managed to get away with their lives, albeit with savage fines. Catesby's life cost him 4,000 marks (nearly £2,700) and he was forced to sell his Oxfordshire manor, Chastleton.

In May 1604, just a year after James entered London, Catesby joined Wright and Wintour at the Duck and Drake in the Strand, near Essex House, to meet two men. One was Wright's brother-in-law, Thomas Percy, a distant cousin and land agent to "the Wizard Earl". The other was a man named Guido Fawkes.

Fawkes was a Yorkshire-born mercenary who adopted the named Guido while soldiering abroad. He will probably always be named as the villain behind the plot to massacre James and hundreds of innocent bystanders. Fawkes was found with the smoking fuse in his hand when the Houses of Parliament were searched at midnight on 4 November 1605. But it was charismatic Catesby who devised the dastardly plot to blow up the buildings while James was opening parliament the following day.

"Robin" Catesby was linked by marriages and friendship to almost every leading recusant family in the Midlands: the Treshams, Wintours, Grants and several branches of the Throckmortons – Bess Ralegh's family. Bit by bit he drew them into his plan. How soon Cecil got wind of it no one knows; or whether Cecil helped it develop in order to "discover" a treason. Given the number of conspirators and Cecil's spy network, it seems unlikely he was ignorant of what was going on, though it is just possible the plotters' strong family and religious ties bound them to secrecy.

They certainly swore an oath of secrecy as they ended their meeting at the Duck and Drake and moved into a neighbouring room to hear mass. And the celebrant was Fr John Gerard. Since Gerard's roof-top escape from the Tower six years earlier he had been moving around the country under cover, helping the Jesuit Superior, Fr Henry Garnet, to aid and succour Catholics. His contacts among Midlands landowners were impeccable and he knew all the families involved in the conspiracy. He heard their confessions; he joined a "pilgrimage" that thirty of them made to North Wales at the end of August, thinly disguised as a hunting party; and he had been responsible for converting to Catholicism the last man who joined the plot.

If ever there was a gilded youth it was Sir Everard Digby, kinsman to the Digbys at Coleshill where Lettice and Penelope stayed after Earl Walter died. Sir Everard, still in his early twenties, had looks, property, charm, honour, passion, a devoted young wife and two sons. What the Powder Plotters wanted when they tragically drew him into their conspiracy was his wealth and several stables of good horses.

The names that would soon be on every tongue – Tresham, Digby, Gerard – hovered around Penelope's past and her brother's rebellion. But this time Penelope took no part in it. When Guido and the thirty-six barrels of gunpowder were discovered, Lady Rich was attending to a pressing matter of her own. It did not immediately involve Devonshire, which was fortunate, for in this new national emergency his cabinet-level posts kept him at the centre of power.

As a privy councillor Devonshire was busy interrogating suspects, including the Earl of Northumberland, who was swiftly put in custody at Lambeth Palace in case he had been involved. And as master of the Ordnance, Devonshire led an army out of London "to those countries where the Robin Hoods are assembled, to encourage the good and to terrify the bad". No one knew how much support, perhaps foreign forces, the plotters had lying in wait in the shires.

While panic and fears of terrorists swept the country, few people would have noticed the judgment handed down in the Bishop of London's consistory court, on 14 November, in the case of Lord and Lady Rich.

Chapter Twenty-Seven

NOVEMBER 1605–MARCH 1606

"A fair woman with a black soul"

– King James I, 1606

*L*ondon was still reeling from the Powder Treason when a minor courtier recorded: "My Lord Rich and my lady were divorced upon Friday was sennight, before the high commissioners."

After a week-long hearing in the ecclesiastical court of London, a divorce decree was passed on Penelope and her husband. Lord Rich had sued for it on the grounds that his wife had committed adultery with a stranger – a man she would not name – and Penelope had confessed. She provided the judges with all the proofs of years and places they needed to find her guilty. The disgrace for Penelope was enormous, and Lord Rich could hardly have relished being labelled a cuckold. Yet they had agreed to cooperate and go through with it.

On 14 November the judges decided that the marriage had been legally performed, it had lasted some twenty-two years, and it would now end with a divorce *a mensa et thoro* – a separation from board and hearth. It was not a full divorce *a vinculo matrimonii*. Lord Rich had not sued for that. Full divorce needed an act of parliament, was almost never granted and would have bastardized their children. Separation, however, did not permit either of them to marry again during the lifetime of the other, and the court warned them they must now live celibately. But Bancroft, recently appointed Archbishop of Canterbury, hadn't finished yet.

"My Lord Archbishop chid my Lord Rich very much and gave my lady great commendation, telling what an honourable house she was of, and how hardly my lord had used her." It was astonishing that the court should be so partial to Lady Rich. Or it would have been, except that Penelope always charmed her judges into submission, and Bancroft detested radical Protestants. He "bad my Lord Rich go amongst his Puritans: thanks be to

God his grace could not touch my lady with that heresy, for hers is error
venialis. This matter hath done her some little good any way," wrote Philip
Gawdy reporting the case, "and there's an end of that matter."

It wasn't the end of the matter. And Penelope never intended it should be.

Six weeks later, on 26 December, ignoring the terms of the divorce, she
and Devonshire were married. It was a quiet ceremony at Wanstead, different
in every way from the sleazy spectacles at Court that Devonshire had come
to dislike. In the lovely house that held so many happy memories, where their
love affair had flourished, where Lettice and Leicester married nearly thirty
years before, Penelope and Devonshire were pronounced man and wife by
the earl's private chaplain, William Laud.

They knew, and Laud knew, that the marriage was illegal. If they hoped
to get away with it, as many had during Elizabeth's reign, they underestimated James's pedantry. If they were hoping to bury bad news beneath the
smokescreen of the Powder Treason, they miscalculated badly.

Throughout November and December the government was on high alert
as it rounded up, interrogated and tortured the remaining plotters. One
might have thought James had weightier matters to deal with than Penelope
and Devonshire's marriage, but he could always find time to indulge his
prurient interest in others' private affairs. When James was told about it he
was appalled. For nearly three years he had been happy to shower them with
honours and wink at their "sinful" lives. Now, perversely, he reacted with
moral indignation, deeply offended by their breach of the law.

Penelope and Devonshire might have guessed there would be a sanctimo-
nious reaction from James if they had paused to reflect on his crusade against
tobacco. James genuinely hated it and he was shocked at how fashionable it
was among English courtiers. Some spent up to £300 a year on it, though
others like Bess Ralegh's brother kept it down to £1 a month. It was partly
popular because it was said to be "an antidote to the pox". James soon
published an anonymous *Counterblast to Tobacco*, deploring it as "a custom
loathsome to the eye, hateful to the nose, harmful to the brain, dangerous to
the lungs". No "learned man ought to taste it," James thundered. Its effect on
their "inward parts" was "soiling and infecting them with an unctuous and
oily kind of soot"; and it ruined "the sweetness of man's breath".

James could just about overlook Devonshire's tobacco habit because the
earl was not the only one addicted. But the earl's marriage was a different
matter. It involved broken vows, bonds and legal contracts. At first James
kept his comments private, but when they had no effect on Devonshire he
went public: "You have won a fair woman with a black soul," James told him.
It was a common enough concept. The contemporary play *Lust's Dominion*
contained the line: "The whitest faces have the blackest souls." But James was

obsessed by the symbolism of white and black, good and evil. He was also terrified of powerful women, especially witches, and his comment revealed his paranoid suspicion that Penelope was dominant and manipulative.

Devonshire's wise counsel was important to James. He was helping to investigate the Powder Treason (not until 13 January did "proof" emerge that Fr Garnet and Fr Gerard were involved); and he was one of the commissioners at the plotters' trials at Westminster Hall in January. Penelope, however, was dispensable and early in 1606 she was dropped from Anna's list of ladies-in-waiting. James made it clear she was not welcome at Court and everyone was aware of her disgrace.

~

Lord Rich is usually seen as the one who was driving the divorce, determined to distance himself from Penelope and Essex's rebellion. In that case, why wait four years? The damage was done while Elizabeth was on the throne. Under James it was a badge of honour to have links with Essex. If, as some say, Lord Rich tolerated three people in his marriage because it gave him access to Essex, why cut himself off from Penelope when her constant access to James and Anna made her so valuable?

Technically his lordship was the one who petitioned for divorce, but what did he gain? He had lived with the situation for years and anyone who mattered knew Penelope was living with her lover at Wanstead. All the divorce case did was expose him to ridicule. He was in no hurry to marry again, and he did not for almost a decade after Penelope died. He treated her badly following Essex's execution, and the divorce judges had no doubts that Rich was a disagreeable man whom Penelope disliked. Yet after the divorce Lord Rich appears to have done nothing. He did not attempt to file a civil suit in the Court of King's Bench or Common Pleas for damages against his wife's lover, as he was entitled to, though it might have been difficult.

It was Penelope who gained most from the separation, not Rich. It was handled on her terms – keeping Devonshire's name out of it – and she provided proof of her own adultery. The logical conclusion must be that she arranged for Lord Rich to bring the case. It was not in her nature to be a passive player in life, and James's verdict on her "black soul" suggests he believed her responsible for what happened.

Penelope and Devonshire had, in fact, been laying plans ever since he returned from Ireland. Employing the best legal brains he could find, Devonshire set up a complex trust so that Penelope and their children could inherit his enormous wealth. Without it everything, including the lucrative customs on French and Rhenish wines which James had granted him, would pass to his distant kinsmen. Yet the property deed, dated February 1604, which set up the trust also made provision for his future wife and children, in the hopes that one day he and Penelope would be able to marry.

Why then did they rush from the divorce into the marriage? Why, after fifteen years, didn't they wait until the divorce was old news before they flagrantly ignored the law? Perhaps Penelope was anxious to go ahead, regarding it as an act of purification, like her nymph character, Ocyte. Perhaps she was stung by rumours that Devonshire might marry someone else. He had been named as a possible husband for Arbella Stuart in the past, and she was at Court throughout 1604. But it was only Arbella, in her mad ravings years later (possibly brought on by porphyria) who believed Devonshire had been her lover.

There was a more pressing reason: Devonshire's health. Since his return he and Penelope had spent more gloriously happy days together than ever before, at Wanstead and at Court. Before her eyes, his health was declining. He was never really robust, being prone to fevers and migraine-type headaches that lasted for days. He had been desperately ill in Ireland, and three winters' campaigning on top of his heavy smoking had damaged his lungs. By autumn 1605 they knew he needed help.

In October, Richard Andrews, an Oxford academic, physician and poet, was "called away out of the university". The reason was not made public, but it seems the earl wanted him in his household, and only after Devonshire's death did Andrews return to the university. Like Fynes Moryson, Andrews would have noticed that the earl's fingers were "great in the end", a classic symptom of lung disease, or cancer. Devonshire's dearest wish was now that Penelope and their children should inherit his wealth and estates. When the divorce was passed it must have been obvious they could not delay the marriage ceremony. Time was running out for Devonshire.

Their marriage could not legitimize their existing children, but at least her next baby would be unquestionably Devonshire's heir, and the chances are they suspected Penelope was pregnant. It was not unusual for the women in Penelope's family to continue having babies after their children married. Both her mother and grandmother had done so and now, while Penelope and Devonshire were married at Wanstead, a few miles away at Leighs her son Robert was celebrating the birth of her granddaughter, named Anne for the queen.

It was vital to Devonshire and Penelope to get their marriage accepted, and at Wanstead the earl sat down and wrote at length to James explaining why he believed it legal. His defence invoked every possible legal, moral and religious argument. He also wrote a more personal plea describing how, in 1581, Penelope, "being in the power of her friends, was by them married against her will unto one against whom she did protest at the very solemnity and ever after". There was discord between them right from the start and instead of being her "comforter", Lord Rich "did study in all things to torment her". He refrained from "any open wrong" to her through "awe of her brother's powerfulness", and after Essex's death Rich "abandoned" her and cheated her out of her dowry. The divorce was all Rich's doing and he had used threats to make her confess.

It would be surprising if Devonshire had *not* exaggerated and distorted things: he was fighting for the future of his children and his adored wife. But he never went so far as to claim that he himself was already informally contracted to marry her, thus making her wedding to Lord Rich null and void. It was William Laud's biographer, Peter Heylyn, who dreamed up that argument later. Laud believed that performing the illegal ceremony for Devonshire was the worst career move he ever made and it delayed his appointment as Archbishop of Canterbury. He was right. James considered Laud was not fit for high office because he had "a flagrant crime upon him". The king still reminded him ten years later: "Was there not a certain lady that forsook her husband and married a lord that was her paramour? Who knit that knot?"

In Heylyn's life of Laud he repeated Laud's opinion of Penelope: "A lady in whom lodged all attractive graces of beauty, wit and sweetness of behaviour which might render her the absolute mistress of all eyes and hearts." But in order to preserve Laud's reputation Heylyn probably invented the story that when Penelope and Devonshire were teenagers "some assurances passed between them of a future marriage"; and that after her marriage to Rich "the old flames of her affection unto Blount began again to kindle". Alternatively, Heylyn could be confusing what he'd heard of Penelope and Philip Sidney. Either way, it was not part of the case Devonshire put to the king, who was not impressed by his arguments.

James remained adamant that the marriage was illegal. Yes, he was grateful to the old Essex party. They had risked everything for him, offering to help seize the throne while Elizabeth was still alive, and to "gather fruit before it is ripe". But he had been paying off that debt for three years. Penelope's remarriage was a threat to his authority. It challenged the ecclesiastical laws he had just re-enacted and his new Bigamy Act of 1604; and if Elizabeth was lax about enforcing them, he was not. Disobedience equalled sedition and wickedness. No amount of intellectualizing, subtle arguments from scripture or pathetic pleas would persuade James to tolerate nonconformity to *any* of his decrees. But in Penelope's case his insistence on the law went beyond even his usual pedantry.

It didn't take a genius to wonder if someone was encouraging him. And could that be the same someone trying to put "the Wizard Earl" away with the Powder Plotters?

∾

Chapter Twenty-Seven

There was no doubt in Dorothy's mind who was behind her husband's down-fall.

On 27 November, when most of the conspirators were in the Tower with Guido Fawkes, James signed a warrant to hold Northumberland there as well, until his trial. Four of the ringleaders, however, were missing. Catesby, the Wright brothers and Thomas Percy had died or been shot after their gunpowder blew up at Holbeach House in Staffordshire as they fled north. And Percy was the only man who might have cleared Northumberland of any involvement. Percy had spent a couple of hours with the earl at Syon on 4 November, before going on to Essex House, where Northumberland's brothers were living.

Again and again "the Wizard Earl" declared he was not in the plot, and not a practising Catholic. He had evidence that he was preparing to attend parliament himself on the fateful day; and that Percy had swindled him out of £3,000 in rents to pay for the plot. Moreover, he was not named by the surviving plotters, even under torture. Unfortunately, however, his fore-fathers had a history of Catholicism and treason, his brothers had supported Essex's rebellion and he was generally unpopular. He was also known to be fed up with James and his Scottish hangers-on, and he had been a possible successor to Elizabeth: ninth in line to the throne. It was all circumstantial and in public Cecil maintained the earl's possible innocence. But it would not be the first time Cecil had privately tried to poison the king's mind against him. Since Cecil started smoothing James's way to the throne, after Essex's death, he had used every opportunity to "warn" James about the "diabolical" trio: Northumberland, Ralegh and Cobham.

Boldly Dorothy told James he was the only person who could divert "the ill will of a certain great personage". She had too much sense to name names but it was Cecil she meant. It made no difference. Northumberland remained under lock and key, waiting to see if he would face a full state trial.

By the start of 1606 Cecil had effectively silenced all his old personal and political enemies – except Penelope and Devonshire. And they had just ruined their own position by their marriage. Cecil must have chuckled harder than ever. All he had to do now was encourage James to stick to his decision that their marriage was illegal. How actively he pursued his agenda no one knows, but there is evidence that he and Devonshire were rowing early in the year.

In January, the earl attended the trials of the remaining plotters, and their gruesome executions. During February he sat in the House of Lords, where four days were devoted to a new bill against recusants. "About the same time," wrote Lady Margaret Hoby's husband, Thomas, "[there] grew a difference between two lords of the Upper House, who met by chance together in the king's little chamber."

The two peers were Devonshire and Lord Rich. "Foul words were passed and the lie [was] given to Devon." It was humiliating beyond measure to be publicly branded a liar, especially by Lord Rich. If anyone took the earl's side in the argument, Sir Thomas did not record it. Devonshire was rapidly losing friends and influence. It was common knowledge around Court that "the world began to change the titles of honour into notes of infamy" about him. He seemed weary and melancholy, allegedly because of his "last most dishonourable and both unlawful and ungodly match". Fynes Moryson thought he had a "countenance sad and dejected", like a man broken by disappointments.

In March, with the country still nervy from the Powder Treason, London was suddenly submerged in fresh rumours that James was in danger, possibly of being killed by an assassin at Woking. Penelope and the earl spent some time in London and then returned to Wanstead. The subject on everyone's lips was the forthcoming trial of grey-haired Fr Garnet, one of the Jesuit priests incriminated in the Powder Treason. In fact, Garnet had pleaded with the plotters to pull back from violence. He knew their secrets but the confidentiality of the confessional forbade him disclosing to the authorities anything they told him.

Henry Garnet was a sensitive, scholarly man, a brilliant linguist and classicist, expert at Greek and Hebrew, a skilled musician, compassionate and kind-hearted. Everything Penelope heard about him would recall those other peace-loving priests from her past. There was Fr Campion, slaughtered during her first year at Court; Fr Southwell, whose death Devonshire had eased; Fr Bolt, whom she had helped into exile; and of course Fr John Gerard. He was also linked to the plotters and he was still on the run.

Sir Everard Digby, brave and honourable to the last, swore at his trial that Fr Garnet knew nothing (not that Digby knew much, having only been drawn in at the last minute, for his money). Nonetheless Garnet was hunted down. After eight days in a tiny, cramped priest's hole he crawled out and gave himself up. He was half-dead from starvation, swollen legs and the stench of his own faeces. Brought to London at the end of January, he was questioned by Devonshire and the rest of the council, and probably tortured later to reveal "the little that he knew". His trial was set for 28 March and Devonshire was due to be there, at the Guildhall in the city.

Three days beforehand, the earl left Wanstead for London. He summoned his coach, took Moryson with him and left Penelope and the children in the country.

Chapter Twenty-Eight

APRIL 1606–MAY 1607

"In darkness let me dwell"

– John Coprario, *Funeral Tears*, 1606

*T*he Earl of Devonshire was thought to be visiting Cecil, or sorting out some other business in London before attending Fr Garnet's trial. But when the hearing opened at 8 a.m. on the appointed day, Devonshire was not there.

He had left Wanstead feeling well enough, but a few hours later, reaching Cheapside, he began to feel ill. Before long he grew feverish and in his condition he knew it was a bad sign. He decided to summon his lawyer, Joseph Earth, and to remain in London. For some reason he chose to stay at the Savoy, a former bishops' residence in the Strand that now served as lodgings and apartments, with a hospital and parish church.

Lawyer Earth was one of the experts who had set up the property trust for the earl, and he knew exactly how to update the documents and prepare Devonshire's will. Penelope's divorce and remarriage had been a disaster for them. Devonshire could only pray that his earlier property plan would be watertight. He knew every clause would be challenged by his common-law heirs, squabbling for a share of his huge wealth.

Immediately news of his illness reached Wanstead, despite her pregnancy Penelope hurried to London with their eldest son, Mountjoy. Reaching the Savoy on the 26th, only a day after he had left Wanstead, she found Devonshire certain he had a fever and asking for Dr Turner. He told everyone present "he had ever by experience and presaging mind been taught to repute a burning fever his fatal enemy". In his weakened state, with diseased lungs or chest and probably pneumonia, Dr Turner's decision to "let blood" was not a good idea, though it probably only hastened the inevitable.

A procession of witnesses, lawyers and scribes arrived to prepare and validate his various papers, and soon word spread that the earl "is sick of a burning fever and in some danger". At one point it looked as though "he was on the mending hand". Then he fell into a relapse. Reactions to the news were mixed. John Chamberlain wrote callously: "The world thinks if he should go now it had been better for him he had gone a year or two sooner." His old friends were more sympathetic and hurried to the Savoy. Among them were Sir Harry Danvers, who had served him bravely in Ireland; the Earl of Southampton, stalwart member of the Essex circle; and Sir William Godolphin, who had named one of his daughters after Penelope.

On 2 April, a week after Penelope joined him, the earl's strength was failing fast, but there was still his will to sign and witness, and other papers to complete. Sir Matthew Carew, master of the court of chancery, came to the Savoy and thought the earl looked "very sick as his countenance". Still Devonshire remained courteous and calm and Sir Matthew, aged more than seventy-five, was touched that the earl should thank him and apologize for having "put him to such pains".

Devonshire's last hours were slipping away, taken up with business matters and interruptions. It left so little time to be alone quietly with Penelope, to say goodbye. They had been married only three months. Surely they might have had a while longer, at Wanstead, together? The earl was not yet forty-four and he was going. It was unbearable. When at last the moment came on Thursday night, 3 April, Penelope was with him.

"I never saw a brave spirit part more mildly," Moryson wrote. According to Fr Gerard: "With his last breath he invoked, not God, but his goddess, his 'angel' as he called her." Gerard was in hiding half a mile away at Blackfriars, but he soon heard the news from the Catholic grapevine. And if his account was romanticized, it was not very different from another report. Contemporary historian Robert Johnston described the earl dying in Penelope's arms while her tears flowed and she kissed his dear hands and face. Penelope was "consumed with pain and grief". For a day and a night, veiled and dressed in black, she lay on the floor in the corner of the chamber, weeping. She lost the baby she was carrying. It was as though the earl had taken the child's spirit with him; perhaps it was God's punishment for her "sinfulness".

Devonshire's body, wrapped in a winding sheet and strewn with sweet herbs, was taken back to Wanstead to await his funeral. The news went round that he "died of a burning fever and putrefaction of his lungs". At first there was some sympathy for his lady, "for so she is now generally held to be", wrote Chamberlain. On 17 April his friend Carleton replied: "It is thought she will find good friends, for she is visited daily by the greatest who profess much love to her for her earl's sake." And yet, Carleton went on, "amongst the meaner sort you may guess in what credit she is".

Soon one of Devonshire's cousins accused him of bringing shame on the whole Blount family. Chamberlain was also peddling unpleasant comments. The earl had died "soon and early for his years but late enough for himself"; it would have been much better if his life had ended "before the world was weary of him". Some critics were plain wrong, like the report "of the five children (that she fathered upon him at the parting from her former husband) I do not hear that he hath provided for more than three". There was no truth in it, but it helped sway opinion against her.

~

Devonshire's victories in Ireland had earned him a state funeral and a grand tomb in Westminster Abbey. He was a national hero until the last three months of his life, and there were numerous tributes to him. Poet Samuel Daniel, who probably owed him most, recounted his life and triumphs in a long and fulsome *Funeral Poem upon the Death of the Late Noble Earl of Devonshire*. But Daniel played it safe where Penelope was concerned and made no mention of her. Referring obliquely to the earl's love life, he merely put in a plea that since men are not perfect, he hoped Devonshire's critics "will never be unkind".

Others were more open and addressed their lamentations to Penelope. John Coprario, the most sought-after musician of the moment, wrote a song sequence, *Funeral Tears, for the death of the Right Honourable the Earl of Devonshire*, that was both a tribute to the earl and to Penelope's musical skill. Some of the seven exquisitely sad songs were intended for her to sing, to help her mourning. "Fairest of ladies," Coprario urged in his preface,

> … since these songs are thine,
> Now make them as thou art thyself, divine.

His words and melodies express all the pain of her loss and heartbreak: "O sweet flower too quickly fading"; "My joy is dead"; "Poor wretched life that only lives in name"; "Fled is my joy, and never may return"; and

> O how wondrous hadst thou been
> Had but the world thy whole life seen.

Subtly, Coprario stirred his listeners' memories of Essex by reprising a tune to one of Shakespeare's songs in *Hamlet*. The fourth funeral song begins with the opening bars of Ophelia's lament, "How should I your true love know?" played on a lute. And as the haunting notes die away, a treble voice, like Penelope's, sings the sad solo "In darkness let me dwell". It was an echo that every courtier and every playgoer in London would pick up, and it linked Penelope's lament for Devonshire with the death of Essex, whose story was indelibly printed on Hamlet's tragic figure.

Coprario's words made it clear that Devonshire was being slandered before he was cold in his grave. The preface to the songs pointed to envy, rumour and malice – "the busy ape, the envious bold wolf, and the spiteful snake" – who were destroying the earl's reputation. His only fault, Coprario claimed, was love, and even that fault was limited. Devonshire had loved "As if all beauty had for him been framed" in one beautiful woman: the woman he married –

> For beauty more adorned no age shall know
> Than hers whom he his own for ever named.

It was a bitter indictment of the "spiteful adder-tongued hypocrisy" that snaked its way through Court gossip, and it was repeated by playwright John Ford.

Ford, who would become one of the best Jacobean dramatists, was a young protégé of Devonshire and in a lengthy verse elegy, *Fame's Memorial, or The Earl of Devonshire Deceased*, he denounced the slanders that were beginning to circulate about his patron. He recounted the earl's victories when "Mountjoy – the mounting joy of heaven's perfection" was "far greater than his name"; and deplored the way his life was "unjustly termed disgraceful". In the end, Ford added, Devonshire had been "united to his heart's delight … who was that glorious star". And he dedicated the poem to "The Lady Penelope, Countess of Devonshire".

Others doubted if she could claim that title. "My lord of Devonshire's funeral will be performed in Westminster about three weeks hence," wrote Dudley Carleton on 17 April. "There is much dispute amongst the heralds whether his lady's arms shall be impaled with his, which brings in question the lawfulness of the marriage." By 2 May the funeral arrangements were settled. "My lord of Southampton is chief mourner; my lord of Suffolk and Northampton assistants, and three other earls. It is determined his arms shall be set up single without his wife's." For Penelope it was a humiliating decision. If she was his lawful wife, her family arms should be quartered with his. Those responsible for the funeral arrangements had doubtless taken their cue from James and decided the marriage was unlawful. Penelope, her power gone with her love, was an easy victim of shabby politics, estate-grabbing greed and self-righteous prudery.

On 7 May Devonshire was laid to rest in St Paul's Chapel, Westminster Abbey, with all the pomp and ceremony of a state funeral, but the arms placed over his hearse indicated he was a bachelor. It was a public symbol of the disgrace that would follow Penelope always. She was an outcast from high society and there was no one left in power to plead her cause.

Dorothy's husband, Northumberland, was in no position to help, even if he wished to.

He had been in the Tower nearly six months, admittedly in a comfortable apartment rather than the dark, dripping dungeons flooded by foul water that ordinary prisoners endured. But his prospects were not rosy. The Venetian ambassador Nicolò Molin spoke for many when he remarked: "It seems impossible that so vast a plot should have been hatched unless some great lord was interested in it, and there is not the smallest indication against anyone except this nobleman."

Reserved, sarcastic, unpopular and deaf, Northumberland had no chance of conducting his own defence well; and when his case came up in Star Chamber on 26 June he was fined the near-impossible sum of £30,000 and imprisoned for life.

Dorothy's affection for him was irrelevant. Her future, and her children's, was bound up with his and she used all her Devereux determination and force of character to lobby people in power for his release. Cecil self-right-eously informed the earl that he "forbore to return any one harsh word" to the countess in reply to her "sour dealing". But her efforts made no differ-ence. Northumberland's previous support for James counted for nothing. Despite his claims to be a Protestant "the Wizard Earl" was seen as a leader of the Catholics – and to James and Cecil they were the enemy.

∼

Father Garnet was inevitably found guilty at his trial in the Guildhall and early on Saturday morning, 3 May, four days before Devonshire's funeral, he was dragged from the Tower to his place of execution outside St Paul's – a hundred yards from Blackfriars Gatehouse where Fr Gerard had been hiding. In the face of death Garnet won the heart of the mob with his quiet dignity, his insistence on his innocence, and his steadfast Catholic faith. As the hangman stepped up to cut him down alive from the gibbet, they surged forward shouting and stopped him, determined to ensure Garnet was truly dead before he was hacked in pieces – just as Fr Southwell had been helped by Devonshire.

Father Gerard did not hear the crowd cry "Hold, hold". A few hours before Garnet's execution, he was spirited away from the Blackfriars safe house, which Shakespeare bought a few years later. When Fr Garnet was put to death, John Gerard was leaving England for the last time, to spend the rest of his life abroad, writing up the story of his English mission.

The king had also left London a few hours earlier. He was heading for Newmarket and a spot of hunting. At Court, pleasures and pastimes went on. It was as though, one courtier wrote, "The gunpowder fright is got out of all our heads and we are going on hereabouts as if the devil was contriving every man should blow himself up by wild riot, excess and devastation of time and temperance." The first performance of Shakespeare's new play *Macbeth*, in August, must have been a sobering moment, but not for long. It was presented during a state visit by Anna's brother, King Christian of Denmark, and the riotous round of feasting and drinking plumbed new depths. When Cecil, now the Earl of Salisbury, entertained the royal visitors at Theobalds some ladies were seen to "roll about in intoxication". Those who played Faith, Hope and Charity in the masque were so drunk they were "sick and spewing".

Penelope was miles away. She spent part of the summer with her mother at Drayton, and took some of her children. In Staffordshire she could find a measure of comfort in the familiar surroundings of her childhood. As well as her own children, Cecil's son William, fifteen-year-old Viscount Cranborne, paid a visit to Drayton. Cecil had never remarried after his wife's sudden death in 1597, and his children had grown up motherless. William was a few months younger than Penelope's second son, Harry Rich; and Cecil's daughter Frances was fourteen, the same age as young Penelope. Cecil's children had all Penelope's sympathy, no matter what she felt for their father; and her letter to him after the visit is remarkable in its care for his son.

William got on well with Harry and they had enjoyed hunting together, until Cecil sent a servant with orders for William to leave and spend a few days visiting other friends. "The young hunters," Penelope explained, were so "discontented for fear of parting three days, [it] made them all lose their suppers and they became extremely melancholy." When it was agreed they could go together "with two servants apiece" harmony was restored. "I fear nothing," Penelope went on, "but their riding so desperately, but your son is a perfect horseman and can neither be outridden nor matched any way." She writes as a mother, and a woman who knew the joy of riding fast with the wind in her hair. Politics are forgotten, if not forgiven.

Penelope had opened her letter with enquiries about Cecil's health, knowing he had been so ill in the summer that James visited him on his sickbed. She made no reference to her own situation or grief, and there is no hint of self-pity. It was not in her nature. Her thoughts and care were for others, most touchingly for her mother. Lettice would soon be sixty-three. She had buried three husbands and three sons. Having William and Harry to stay had raised her spirits.

"My mother I think will grow young with their company," Penelope wrote to Cecil. And wishing him "perfect health", she defiantly signed herself "P. Devonshire". In her eyes she was still the Countess of Devonshire. It is an extraordinary, spirited letter for a woman not yet six months a widow. In the weeks ahead she would need all the spirit and determination she could muster. Devonshire's will was about to be challenged as viciously as he had feared.

~

There was a lot at stake. Devonshire died an extremely wealthy man. He had built up a huge portfolio of properties and the distant members of his family were prepared to fight hard to get it. From his ancestors, Devonshire had inherited a number of West Country manors, including Canford in Dorset and Bere Ferrers on the Tamar in Devon. He had added lands in Somerset, Worcester, Leicester, Southampton, including the manor of Lyndhurst, the site of Fotheringhay Castle in Northamptonshire, and of course Wanstead.

The deed of trust and Devonshire's will, signed the day before he died, meant his properties should pass straight to his beneficiaries from his trustees, the earls of Southampton, Suffolk and Salisbury (Robert Cecil), Lord Knollys (Uncle William) and Lord Danvers. Only those properties left outside the trust should pass to his common-law heir, who would doubtless be one of his distant kinsmen. In the will, Penelope and their five children were carefully identified. "The Lady Penelope one of the daughters of the late right honourable Walter, late Earl of Essex deceased, my very dear and loving wife" was to have a life interest in all his property. On her death it would pass in turn to the sons and daughters "of the said lady". To make it watertight only their Christian names were used: Mountjoy, St John, Charles, Penelope and Isabella, and "such issue as the said lady now goeth withall". Meticulously Joseph Earth had drawn up the order of inheritance starting with the eldest male heir and continuing to the youngest daughter's youngest daughter, varying each clause in case Penelope's baby was a son or a daughter. There were annual maintenance payments for each child and large dowries for the girls, "five thousand pounds of lawful money of England" for Little Penelope and £3,000 for Isabella.

Devonshire's distant kinsmen would have none of it. They fought Penelope through every court open to them, challenging the legality of her marriage, her character, the will, the trust deed, the children's paternity, their right to inherit. And they fought among themselves over who was the earl's heir. Early in June Devonshire's lawyers, led by Joseph Earth, were granted probate after his will was proved in the Prerogative Court of Canterbury (known as the PCC), the usual office for wills of the wealthy with widespread property. Then one claimant, Henry Baker, registered his objection in the appropriate appeal court, the Court of Arches, and the will was re-examined.

Joseph Earth had anticipated that and no less than eight witnesses had stood beside Devonshire the day before he died to watch him sign his last will and testament. Now each of them came forward to support Penelope, and swore on oath that it was indeed the signature of "Charles, Earl of Devonshire, Lord Mountjoy, knight of the noble order of the Garter, one of the king's majesty's most honourable privy council and his majesty's lord lieutenant of the kingdom of Ireland". Furthermore, though the earl was "weak and sick" in his body, he was "God be thanked therefore of good and perfect memory". On 22 November the PCC upheld the will.

Penelope had won the first round. But others were joining the fray and the sheer number of ecclesiastical courts, with their overlapping jurisdiction, meant the opportunities to claim and counter-claim were endless. In the Court of Wards, early in November, another relation, Sir Richard Champernowne, asserted his right to be the common-law heir, and the court put an embargo on the properties. Nothing could be done that might be detrimental to the estates, such as harvesting timber, and the case was deferred until the other litigation had been settled. That included another case brought by Sir Richard, in the Court of King's Bench. Champernowne was suing Sir William Godolphin, one of Devonshire's trustees, on the grounds that the deed had been drawn up in error. That attempt also failed. Penelope had won again.

So far the cases had turned chiefly on points of law. In December, however, Champernowne launched criminal proceedings against Penelope and the earl's lawyers in the Court of Star Chamber.

It made an uneasy Christmas. A year ago Penelope had stood by Devonshire's side while Laud pronounced them man and wife. Now she was facing charges of forgery and fraud. If she lost she could be imprisoned for life and lose everything she owned. There was some comfort in knowing that Devonshire's lawyers were on trial as well. But each time she heard or read their answers to the convoluted questions it brought back too clearly those sad days at the Savoy.

Was it not true that "the said late Earl of Devonshire for near three months before his death ... was discontented and displeased with his ... cohabitation with the said Lady Rich"? Was he not "weary of the said lady her company"; and having got away from her, "did not the said earl seem much discontented and mislike of the said Lady Rich and her son Mountjoy's coming to him from Wanstead to the Savoy ... did he not turn his face from them as seemingly ill willing to see or speak with them"?

No, replied Joseph Earth. There was no question of Penelope pursuing Devonshire against his wishes. Earth himself "at the special request of the said earl did fetch the said lady to him in his sickness, whose coming to the said earl was very acceptable and welcome". Devonshire was always, Earth insisted, "very tender and careful of the said lady and of her children and his greatest care was for their advancement and preferment".

Was it not true that "the said Lady Rich could not be the said earl's lawful wife but an harlot, adulteress, concubine and whore", and "that the said lady could not either for herself or children obtain any lands or goods of the said earl but by devices and deceits"? Did she not "at the reading of the said deed use some words to importune the said earl to remember her and her children in his will"; and wasn't her pregnancy imaginary, "done of purpose to have the earl pity her and convey his land to her or her children"?

No, said the eight witnesses, who included Devonshire's chaplain, William Laud. Devonshire was under no pressure from anyone. Penelope was not present. The earl was seated at a small table and she was in a separate gallery, where he could see her talking to some friends, while he dealt with his papers and signed them.

Had not the earl seemed "crazed, feeble, incoherent, senseless" and thus unfit to make a will; and did he not "fail of his speech and memory and so continue until about two of the clock or nearabouts in the afternoon of the third day of April last past"?

No, answered Sir William Godolphin. Devonshire never made "any incoherent speeches importing that his memory and judgement was crazed, feeble or impaired"; and Godolphin refuted the idea that Penelope's pregnancy was a pretence.

Cruellest of all were the probing questions about the cause of Devonshire's ill health and claims that grief and regret about his illegal marriage had brought on his fatal sickness. Did he not "find and perceive that the same had dishonoured him with the king's majesty"; and was it not shame and melancholy that caused the fatal fever that shortened his life? Impossible to answer. No one could deny that in the king's eyes Devonshire *had* been dishonoured and the earl had been profoundly disturbed by James's reaction. His secretary and others nearest him had certainly noted a character change (which modern medicine might put down to the terminal stage of lung cancer).

Question followed question, slanderous allegations were piled on insults, scoring deeper into Penelope's mind the memory of Devonshire's distress. Again and again she relived the pain of those last days. As the anniversary of his death passed, she was preparing to be re-examined, and later in April she gave her answers. Ignoring the name Lady Rich, used in all the questions and allegations against her, she gave her responses in her full title, The Lady Penelope, Countess of Devonshire. And she denied absolutely every charge. Champernowne's suit was "contrived and prosecuted of malice, for vexation and not upon any just cause or ground of suit, the same being stuffed with slanderous imputations," she declared.

On 19 May her second round of answers was given. By this time Penelope had conceded a point. She and her son Mountjoy dropped their claims to Devonshire's titles. Under no circumstances, however, would she answer to Lady Rich; and since it would seem like a denial of her marriage to revert to Devereux, she would use no surname. In future she would be known only as The Lady Penelope. Apart from that concession, the Star Chamber case gave every indication of going her way.

In the London Consistory Court, meanwhile, judgment was given early in May on the appeals against the PCC decision to uphold the will as valid for a second time. Now for the third time it was declared sound. None of the accusations against the will or Penelope had succeeded: victory was in sight.

Chapter Twenty-Nine

MAY–JULY 1607

"Neither wife, widow nor maid"

– Anon, 1607

*O*ver the past six years Penelope had been interrogated and tried for treason, adultery, fraud and forgery. At each hearing she had swung her judges and examiners to her side and there was every sign she would succeed again in the Court of Star Chamber.

In the Court of King James, however, there was no question of her achieving a comeback. In May, while Penelope was dealing with further legal questions, James and Anna were being wined and dined at Theobalds again, this time as its new owners. James was dazzled by the house from the first day he saw it, on his way to London in 1603, and he drooled over its deer parks every time he was invited there to hunt. Wisely Cecil bowed to the inevitable, and to his king, and swapped his glorious, gilded mansion for the clapped-out, old-fashioned palace at Hatfield, and a few other royal properties. On 22 May he threw a spectacular handover party for the royal family, with a masque in the long gallery specially commissioned from Ben Jonson and Inigo Jones.

A few days later Anna paid a visit to Dorothy at Syon. "The Wizard Earl" was still in the Tower and Anna's visit to his wife was a show of support from one Catholic sympathizer to another. Before Northumberland's incarceration, Syon's riverside gardens and vineyards were his passion. He planted hundreds of rose trees, apricots and a three-acre cherry garden, and from the Tower he continued planning. In 1607 a "nightingale garden" was "new-made" among damp scrub and thickets, and in early summer the birds' moonlight serenades would be at their best. If Dorothy invited Penelope to join her and Anna, the usual gossips did not mention it. And there is no record that Anna visited Penelope at Wanstead, though others did.

The previous autumn, when Penelope returned to Wanstead from her summer stay with Lettice, Essex's widow, Frances, came to see her. Frances's new husband, Clanricarde, held large estates and considerable influence in Ireland, but most of his life was spent in England. The two women had been friends for more than twenty years and Penelope had stood by Frances through all her problems with Essex and her pregnancies. Now approaching forty, Frances had two married children, Philip Sidney's daughter Elizabeth and Essex's son Robin, and two younger daughters by Essex. Her third marriage produced another three children and, following her new husband's example, she became a Catholic. Clanricarde was one of Fr Gerard's converts, but despite his open Catholicism James found him useful, thanks to his Anglophile views and power in Irish affairs.

James's friendship and favour, "Who's in, who's out", as *King Lear* had recently put it, was no longer the centre of Penelope's life. Her family affairs were all-absorbing, and her family was expanding. She remained close to her four Rich children, and as well as arranging Sir Robert's marriage she had Lucy, Essex and Harry to consider. And there were Devonshire's five children to plan for. Little Penelope, now fifteen, might need her dowry before long, and Isabella had turned twelve in January. The three boys were younger, but they had the Earl of Southampton, Mountjoy's guardian, to guide them.

In June it looked almost certain that the Star Chamber case would go Penelope's way and secure the children's inheritance. She had been in London for much of the hearing and she was there again early in July when she was taken ill. It would not be surprising if her health at last gave way. She had endured months of public humiliation, as well as the heartbreak of Devonshire's death. Her name had been dragged through the courts in the vilest way, and her energies drained by bitter legal interrogations.

Her sickness was said to be "a fever", though what sort no one knows. She had suffered from serious summer colds before. In 1590, writing to Jeanne Hotman, she explained she had been silent because, "I find myself extremely ill again of the rheum" – probably streaming mucous from her eyes and nose. And while staying in Staffordshire in 1599, she sent apologies to Southampton that she was "so ill of a cold as she cannot now endure to write a word". She may have had a bronchial weakness, or a bout of pneumonia. She may, after years of child-bearing, have suffered complications from her last miscarriage, soon after Devonshire's death, though she was well enough for her trip to Staffordshire that summer.

It seems unlikely that Penelope simply lost the will to live. The future held so much: her dearly-loved children and grandchildren; Frances's and Dorothy's young families; and Lettice. But perhaps even Penelope's fighting spirit could not combat her grief. That terrible, aching sense of loss wa supposed to fade after a year. Yet a second spring had come and gone and still the same sad memories lingered. Perhaps her heart was indeed broken and she was left vulnerable to any ailments. Whatever the cause, The Lady Penelope died on 6 July 1607, aged forty-four.

There are no official records of where or how. The only sure detail is the date, recorded later in an *inquisitionem post mortem* for the continuing wrangle over Devonshire's estate. Three other contemporary references to her death survive, all hearsay, apparently conflicting, and probably exaggerated for religious reasons.

"The Lady Rich fell sick, sent for Doctor Layfield, disclaimed her last marriage sent to her first husband to ask forgiveness and died penitently," wrote one observer on 21 July. Layfield was rector of St Clement Danes, the church closest to Essex House. He would be the obvious person to summon if Penelope were lodging in her old chamber. He would also be the natural Protestant choice if her eldest son was with her at some point; and Layfield would be duty bound to urge reconciliation with Lord Rich.

Three years later, however, Fr Gerard claimed that Penelope converted to Catholicism on her deathbed. After Devonshire's death, "her thoughts often turned to her forgotten purpose" – her conversion – he wrote in his autobiography. "Frequently she would talk about me to one of her maids of honour who was a Catholic. And when about three years ago this girl crossed to Belgium to become a nun she told me this and suggested that I should write and see whether I could fan these embers into a flame. I was in fact composing a letter, when I got word that she [Penelope] had died of fever. Happily she had been reconciled to the Church on her death-bed by one of our fathers."

Naturally Fr Gerard wanted to claim a famous convert, and he-would-say-that-wouldn't-he. But part of his story is certainly true. On 15 April 1607 one of Cecil's foreign correspondents informed him, "Mistress Deacon that heretofore attended on the Lady Rich" was recently admitted to the English convent in Brussels. Among others close to Penelope in her last months, Frances and Clanricarde would also have encouraged her to turn to the Catholic Church. And if Penelope was using her old rooms in Essex House, it would not be the first time a Catholic priest had secretly made his way up the back stairs. "The Wizard Earl's" Catholic brothers had the run of the place for several years.

Essex House is the most likely place where Penelope died. Dorothy and Northumberland had taken it over as their town house after Essex's execution, and though the earl also bought Walsingham House in 1605 it was for his own use (and it was sold after he was sent to the Tower). Dorothy and her servants and family continued to occupy Essex House and she was still using it a couple of years before her death in 1619. Essex House was the logical, comfortable, friendly place for Penelope to stay when she needed to be in London during her legal battles. And she could easily have summoned "one of our fathers" there. It would have been foolish for Fr Gerard to invent the entire story if she had, instead, been fully reconciled to the arch-Puritan Lord Rich.

The third contemporary report also casts doubt on Penelope's abject remorse and conciliation. Robert Johnston, writing within thirty years of her death, said she commended her older children to Lord Rich and "entrusted her second family to someone else". It was Southampton, in fact, who became guardian to young Mountjoy, and probably had been since Devonshire's death. He was the ideal candidate. He'd been close to both Essex and Devonshire, his wife Elizabeth was more sister than cousin to Penelope and his own youngsters would be good companions for Penelope's little ones. As the head of an ancient Catholic family, he too would have been a helping hand when she wanted to speak to a priest.

There is probably some truth in each account and the chances are that Penelope *did* find consolation in the "old faith" during her dying days, that she did receive visits from Dr Layfield and Lord Rich, concerning her elder children's future, and that she made others, including Southampton, responsible for the younger ones. Two things about her were never disputed, and Johnston summed them up. The Lady Penelope had been "outstanding in beauty", and "outstandingly kind".

In Penelope's lifetime, volumes of compliments had come her way – from Philip Sidney, Henry Constable, John Florio, Bartholomew Yong, John Davies, Matthew Gwinne, John Ford and many others. But now a posthumous silence began to fall around her. Briefly it was broken by Thomas Campion, who named her in Latin "Stella Britanna, Penelope" – the star of Britain. Even Morpheus, god of dreams, stood still and marvelled at her beauty, he wrote.

More frequent were the ribald rhymes that circulated, some so contrived that the meaning almost disappears up inside its own pun:

> The devil men say is dead in Devonshire late.
> Of late did Devonshire live in Rich estate
> The which with toys did Devonshire bewitch
> That Devonshire died and left the devil Rich.

A mock epitaph beginning "Here lies fair Penelope or my lady Rich" cruelly underlined her loss of status and title:

> She shuffled, she cut, she dealt, she played,
> She died neither wife widow nor maid.

Who was behind them, who laughed loudest, was anyone's guess. It scarcely matters now. They achieved their aim and destroyed what was left of her reputation.

Before long the facts of her life were forgotten, including where she lies. There is no record of her burial at Dr Layfield's church, St Clement Danes. An entry in the parish records of All Hallows by the Tower, dated 7 October 1607, has been said to read "A Lady Devereux", and the delay in burial could be explained by the ongoing dispute over Devonshire's estate. But the entry is abbreviated and it could equally well mean "Alice Devereux".

It seems unlikely now that anyone will ever know where the greatest beauty of the Elizabethan age is buried. It would be pleasing to think that one dark night she was laid to rest, in secret, beside the Earl of Devonshire in Westminster Abbey. But it is not very likely. There was no one left in power to fix that sort of favour; no one to ride out as her champion and defend her honour.

Epilogue

The Lady Penelope left behind her nine children. They were Lord Rich's sons Robert and Harry, and daughters Lettice (Lucy) and Essex; and Devonshire's two girls and three boys, Penelope, Isabella, Mountjoy, St John and Charles. Her mother, Lettice, still known as the Countess of Leicester, remained at Drayton Bassett. Her sister Dorothy, Countess of Northumberland, survived her with five children – one by Sir Thomas Perrot, the rest by "the Wizard Earl". Her brother Essex's three children, Robin, Frances and Dorothy, lived on; and so did his widow Frances, with her new Clanricarde family.

On Penelope's death, under the terms of Devonshire's will their son Mountjoy inherited the chief interest in the earl's estates, and although two legal decisions were pending, in reality most of the property had already passed to Devonshire's beneficiaries. But along with the property the children inherited Penelope's disgrace. It did not prevent her three eldest sons coming to Court, but they were not yet powerful enough or old enough to confront her critics. They had their way to make in the world, and openly objecting to James's opinion of their mother was not a good career move.

A posthumous silence about Penelope protected her children, and no one else had a reason to step forward to rescue her reputation. It suited Cecil very well to see her vilified and all knowledge of the Devereux' royal connections forgotten. And it was not something that bothered Lord Rich. Years went by before he remarried. The gossips said he'd repeatedly tried to find a new wife, and when he eventually married the widowed Lady St Pol in December 1616, he was "little or nothing the better by her", and he was "crazed in brain, to see himself overreached by his new wife" in money matters. In August 1618 he bought the title Earl of Warwick for £10,000, but he was still sneeringly known at Court as a cuckold, and in March the following year he died at his new London home, Warwick House in Holborn.

Although Penelope's children kept quiet about her, they also kept loyally together. They had spent their earliest years at Leighs, except perhaps for

Charles, the youngest, who was born after Devonshire and Penelope made Wanstead their home. And they continued to behave as one family long after her death. Penelope would have been delighted to see young Charles included by his Rich half-brothers in their family gatherings. Lady Anne Clifford, distantly related to them all and best friends with Robert's wife, records several visits to Warwick House in 1619, when Robert and his wife Frances, and Harry and his wife Isobel, were joined by Charles. Lady Anne knew which of their Rich uncles were illegitimate, so she must have known Charles was Devonshire's son, yet she repeatedly refers to "Mr Charles Rich".

It is hardly surprising that Court gossips chewed over the paternity of Penelope's sons for years. John Chamberlain took a typically bitchy line in December 1617 when he wrote, "Young Blount, Rich, or Mountjoy heir to the Earl of Devonshire is shortly to be made a baron." In order to obtain his title, Chamberlain went on, "he parts with the house and land at Wanstead". As usual, rumour got it partly right and partly wrong. During Mountjoy's minority some of his estates had been "conveyed away … without one penny recompense", he complained to King James. To compensate him, Mountjoy was made a baron and under James's son, Charles I, he was given the title Earl of Newport; but he never got Wanstead back.

With the coming of Charles I's reign England moved steadily toward civil war and inevitably the conflict between king and parliament, cavaliers and roundheads, found the brothers – like so many families – divided. Yet their friendships continued. It was a tribute to the love Penelope had shown to all her "precious jewels".

Her eldest son, Sir Robert, inherited Lord Rich's Puritan faith as well as his new title, Earl of Warwick. If Penelope died a Catholic convert it was all the more reason for him to keep quiet about his mother. Warwick became a leader among the "godly party" and one of the founders of the Protestant colonies in Massachusetts and Connecticut. His daughter Anne, Penelope's eldest grandchild, married Edward Montagu, future Earl of Manchester, another leading parliamentarian; and his grandson, another Robert, would marry Oliver Cromwell's daughter.

When the Civil War began in 1642, Warwick became admiral of the fleet for the parliamentary forces. Montagu took charge of a large part of the army, and Warwick's cousin, "Little Robin", now better known as the third Earl of Essex, also became a leading army commander – though not with much success.

Warwick's brother Harry Rich, Penelope's second son, ended up on the royalist side. Harry had inherited every ounce of Penelope's charm and good looks, plus a penchant for political intrigue, passionate affairs and characterful women. There is a story that in his early days at Court he landed a

£3,000 windfall when he saw a heap of coins on its way to the privy purse office, and King James heard him mutter that he would love to get his hands on them. James, no doubt feeling the same about Harry, sent the coins to his room. And there the story ends, perhaps because Harry produced at least seven children with his heiress wife, Isobel Cope. Thanks to her he landed another windfall, roughly half of Kensington, then outside London, and in 1624 he was made Earl of Holland. His popularity at Court, particularly with Queen Henrietta Maria, Charles I's wife, made it difficult for the parliamentary party to take Harry seriously when he swapped sides and offered to mediate between them. They decided to execute him after they captured him in 1649, and no amount of pleading by his brother Warwick could prevent it.

Mountjoy, Penelope's eldest son by Devonshire, also wavered between the warring parties. Before the battles began he had been abroad with Warwick, and in 1627 when Mountjoy wanted time off from Court to marry a rich heiress, it was Warwick who supported his plea, arguing that such wealthy wives were not available very often. On the outbreak of war, however, Mountjoy, now Earl of Newport, parted company with Warwick. But when the fighting was done, the half-brothers were reunited. If Penelope could have watched the wedding of her great-grandson Robert to Frances Cromwell in 1657, she would have rejoiced to see her two boys, Robert Rich and Mountjoy Blount, attending the celebrations side by side, and Mountjoy dancing with the bride.

As for the girls, Penelope's daughters seem to have married for love rather than money. Her first child, Lettice, known as Lucy, married a seasoned campaigner, Sir George Carey (or Carew) of Cockington, who was "treasurer at wars" in Ireland while Devonshire was lord deputy. He was some years older than Lucy, and he and their two children did not survive long. It is possible Lucy already had a child by Sir Arthur Lake when she married him soon after Sir George's death in 1616; but she too died only three years later. Her sister Essex married Sir Thomas Cheke of Pirgo, had eight surviving children, and continued the tradition of naming one daughter Essex. By the time the younger Mistress Essex was ready to marry, her cousin Anne had died, Essex became the new wife of Edward Montagu, and the mother of eight children. So between them Penelope's granddaughters Anne Rich and Essex Cheke laid the foundations for the Earl of Manchester's grand dynasty.

Penelope's eldest daughter by Devonshire, Little Penelope, was perhaps the one victim of her father's wealth. The publicity and scandal surrounding her parents' marriage and Devonshire's will may have left her prey to fortune hunters. She was only fifteen when her mother died and the £5,000 Devonshire left her would not come through till she was eighteen. In 1608 she married Sir Gervase Clifton and probably fibbed about her age, adding a couple of years. With both parents dead it was not difficult. After the birth of one son, also named Gervase, she died on 26 October 1613. Her tombstone claimed she was twenty-three, instead of twenty-one; and her widower went on to several more wives with fortunes.

If anyone came close to Penelope in adoring her "precious jewels", it was her mother Lettice, who lived on to enjoy their company for another quarter of a century. Penelope's relatively early death robbed Lettice of her closest companion. For years she had paid her mother summer visits, kept her company in London, and invited her to Leighs or Wanstead. After the double execution of Sir Christopher and Essex, Lettice stayed in Staffordshire, and after Penelope's death she had only one surviving child, Dorothy, Countess of Northumberland.

Dorothy had battled on bravely to have "the Wizard Earl" released from the Tower and after Cecil's death in 1618 she managed to get his fine cut from £30,000 to £11,000. Her boys Algernon and Henry lived chiefly with their father in the Tower, where he lodged in grand style with his books and servants in a large suite of rooms, and took his exercise in the canvas-roofed bowling alley. He was said to have formed an attachment to another woman during his imprisonment, and Dorothy rarely visited him in her later years. Yet her death in August 1619 left him inconsolable and he buried her with full ceremony at Petworth in Sussex, ordering the register to be inscribed "Dorothy that thrice honourable and right virtuous lady the Countess of Northumberland her corps were interred in the chapel on the fourteenth of this month".

With Lettice's last child gone, it could have been a lonely existence at Drayton Bassett. But following Penelope's example, her grandchildren made a habit of travelling to see her. In 1618, when her granddaughter Frances (the baby born two days after Essex's wild ride back from Ireland to Nonsuch Palace) married William Seymour, future Duke of Somerset, the ceremony was held at Drayton so that Lettice, now aged seventy-three, could enjoy the celebrations.

It was Essex's son, "Little Robin", however, who was Lettice's chief delight. After the failure of his marriage he spent part of every winter with her, or nearby at Chartley, until she died "upon Christmas Day in the morning 1634". She was buried, as she wished, "at Warwick by my dear lord and husband the Earl of Leicester with whom I desire to be entombed", in St Mary's Church. No one knew quite how old she was and the inscription on the tomb claimed she was in her ninety-sixth year. In fact, as Sir Francis Knollys's Latin dictionary shows, she entered her ninety-second year the month before she died.

It was nonetheless a remarkable age and almost to the end she was in good health, able to walk a mile a day. Longevity had restored her to respectability and there was considerable mourning in London. She was the last of the great Elizabethans. She had known the Virgin Queen, the dashing Lord Leicester, Drake, and the heroes of the Armada. With Lettice died so many memories – and the secret joys and sorrows of The Lady Penelope.

The tragedy of Penelope's life was the stuff of popular drama, and within five years of her death John Webster included part of her story in his blood-chilling revenge play *The White Devil*. Many must have noted that the tragedy of "the Famous Venetian Courtesan", with its illicit love and intrigue, bore a certain similarity to the life of The Lady Penelope.

John Ford's masterpiece play *The Broken Heart*, about Calantha, a girl of "beauty, virtue, sweetness and singular perfections", was also inspired by Penelope's forced marriage and forbidden love. And if playgoers had any doubts, the prologue confirmed it was based on fact:

> What may be here thought fiction, when time's youth
> Wanted some riper years was known a truth.

Off stage, Penelope's name and the facts of her life were slipping into oblivion. She became a victim of the Protestant propaganda machine and the search for blameless heroes of the reformed faith. Two of them, Sir Philip Sidney and the Earl of Devonshire, needed whitewashing where Penelope was concerned, and the least said about her the better. Devonshire's devoted secretary may have had his own reasons – probably sexual jealousy – for airbrushing her from his master's life.

For others it was incredulity. Her role in Essex's rebellion was hushed up partly on Devonshire's account, but also by resistance to the idea that a woman was capable of political thought. Mary Queen of Scots had baffled Elizabeth's ministers when she wrote "great discourses in matters of state – more than woman's wit doth commonly reach unto". And Elizabeth reminded Penelope she was "a lady to whom it did not appertain so to meddle in such matters".

There were a few oblique references to her in histories and chronicles, and they took their cue from Camden's comment that she had "violated her husband's bed". The Earl of Clarendon, writing the history of the Civil War with first-hand knowledge and while some of Penelope's children were still alive, took care not to name her. He described her son Harry Rich as the "younger son of a noble house and very fruitful bed, which divided numerous issues between two great fathers ... The reputation of his family gave him no great advantage in the world." From then on all that anyone was interested in, if they mentioned her at all, was her sex life. And generations of historians have cast her in the role of shameless libertine, flaunting her beauty.

But The Lady Penelope does not fit that mould – nor any of the stereotypes that history loves. She was an adulteress and yet constancy marked her relationship with her husband for ten years, and subsequently with her lover. Her strong character and intellect made her powerful but not cruel or evil. She was devoted to her family, loved by her servants, praised for her kindness, charm and beauty, and she would probably have pointed to her children as her greatest achievement. Yet she was not content to be a domestic goddess. Nor was she a proto-feminist, a "radical", "the first of a new kind of woman", furthering her brother's ambitions "as a means of achieving power herself" – as some would claim. She was a traditionalist with a strong conservative streak that inclined her to the "old faith". The connecting threads through her life are devotion to her family, past and present, and to family honour. Like all Elizabethan aristocrats she was steeped in the stories of her ancestry and determined to see her family and its fortunes restored to greatness. Her search for power was not for herself but for the Devereux.

Her political significance is the biggest secret of her life. Her part in Essex's rise and fall, and hence the whole course of Elizabeth's last decade, was in fact crucial: her relationship with Essex and Devonshire gave her a pivotal role in the group that plotted the overthrow of Elizabeth's government. And if Essex had had half Penelope's strength of character, he could have changed the course of English history.

Instead, he went to his death, and Penelope became one of the "disappeared" of history. The evidence of her role and her life was suppressed and ignored. But just enough fragments remain to point to her political importance. And in poems, music, plays and paintings she lives on, the inspirational beauty behind some of the loveliest love sonnets ever written: "Perfection's heir", cherished for her "royal heart".

It is hard to believe that Sir Philip Sidney, master of wordplay and hidden meanings, did not know when he wrote those lines that his heroine was descended from Henry VIII, the most Perfect Prince in Europe.

TABLE 1: THE TUDOR DYNASTY & QUEEN ELIZABETH'S COUSINS

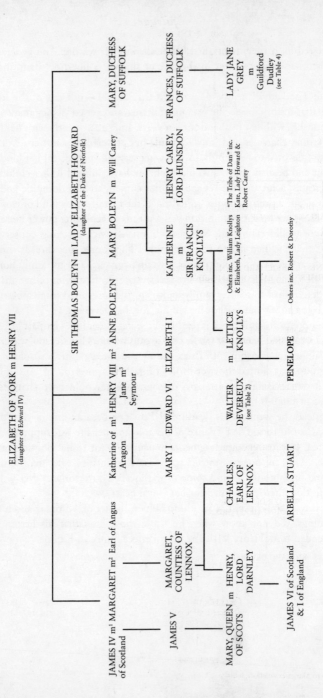

TABLE 2: THE DEVEREUX ROYAL ANCESTRY

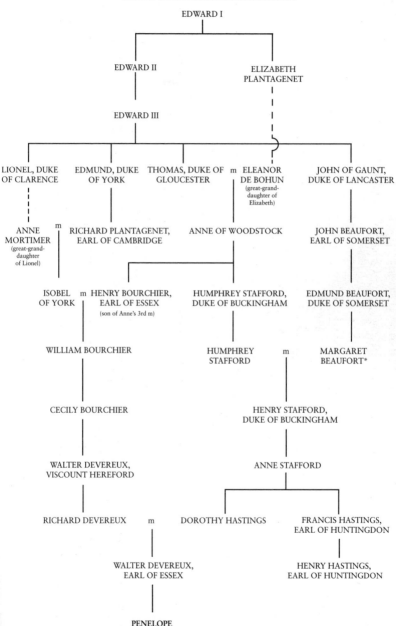

* cousin to Margaret Beaufort, mother of Henry VII

TABLE 3A: PENELOPE'S CHILDREN

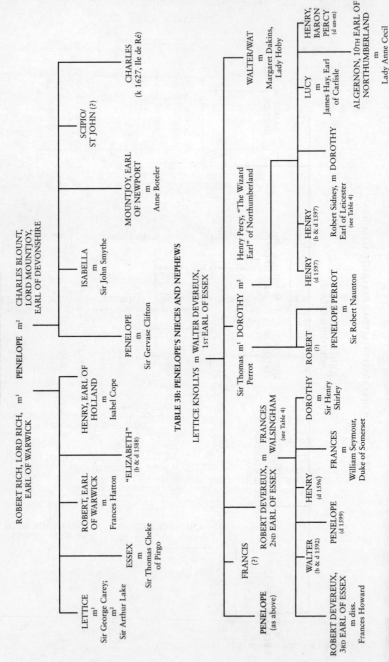

ROBERT RICH, LORD RICH, m¹ **PENELOPE** m² CHARLES BLOUNT, LORD MOUNTJOY, EARL OF WARWICK EARL OF DEVONSHIRE

LETTICE
m¹
Sir George Carey;
m²
Sir Arthur Lake

ROBERT, EARL OF WARWICK
m
Frances Hatton

HENRY, EARL OF HOLLAND
m
Isabel Cope

"ELIZABETH"
(b & d 1588)

ESSEX
m
Sir Thomas Cheke of Pirgo

ISABELLA
m
Sir John Smythe

PENELOPE
m
Sir Gervase Clifton

SCIPIO/ ST JOHN (?)

MOUNTJOY, EARL OF NEWPORT
m
Anne Boteler

CHARLES
(k 1627, Ile de Ré)

TABLE 3B: PENELOPE'S NIECES AND NEPHEWS

LETTICE KNOLLYS m WALTER DEVEREUX, 1ST EARL OF ESSEX

FRANCIS (?)

ROBERT DEVEREUX, 2ND EARL OF ESSEX
m
FRANCES WALSINGHAM
(see Table 4)

Sir Thomas m¹ DOROTHY m² Henry Percy, "The Wizard Earl" of Northumberland
Perrot

WALTER/WAT
m
Margaret Dakins, Lady Hoby

WALTER
(b & d 1592)

PENELOPE
(d 1599)

HENRY
(d 1596)

FRANCES
m
William Seymour, Duke of Somerset

DOROTHY
m
Sir Henry Shirley

ROBERT
(?)

PENELOPE PERROT
m
Sir Robert Naunton

HENRY
(d 1597)

HENRY
(b & d 1597)

Robert Sidney, m DOROTHY
Earl of Leicester
(see Table 4)

LUCY
m
James Hay, Earl of Carlisle

HENRY, BARON PERCY
(d un-m)

ALGERNON, 10TH EARL OF NORTHUMBERLAND
m
Lady Anne Cecil

ROBERT DEVEREUX, 3RD EARL OF ESSEX
m diss.
Frances Howard

PENELOPE
(as above)

TABLE 4: THE DUDLEY-SIDNEY-HASTINGS-DEVEREUX ALLIANCES

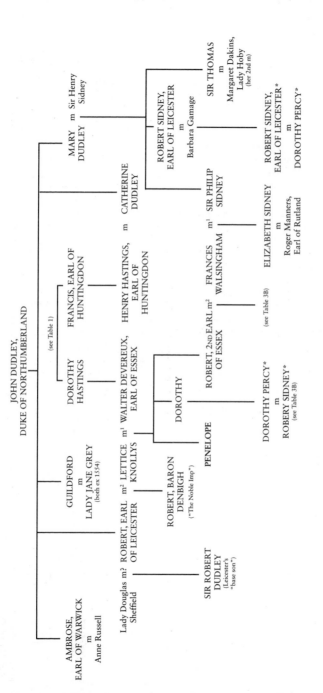

Who's Who

The main people in Penelope's life are shown below – using formal and informal forms of address – with some of the printed sources used in this study. For everyone the *Oxford Dictionary of National Biography* (*ODNB*) and G. E. Cockayne, *The Complete Peerage*, ed. V. Gibbs, 13 vols (1910–59), are basic sources:

Penelope Rich, née Devereux (1563–1607), Lady Rich, Countess of Devonshire: The first book to focus on Penelope was Maud Rawson's *Penelope Rich and Her Circle* (1911), mostly unannotated and including some inventions and inaccuracies, e.g. it missed a generation between Mary Boleyn and Penelope. Sylvia Freedman's *Poor Penelope, Penelope Rich* (1983) established birth dates for some of Penelope's children, squashing the claim that her two families overlapped; and used Freedman's legal expertise to analyse the divorce and law suits. Michele Margetts's unpublished Ph.D. thesis, "Stella Britanna: the early life of Penelope Devereux" (Yale, 1993), was based on exhaustive research, and with her published articles revealed considerable detail about the first twenty years of Penelope's life: "A christening date for Lady Rich", *Notes and Queries* (June 1993); "The birth date of Robert Devereux, Second Earl of Essex", *Notes and Queries* (March 1988); and "Lady Penelope Rich: Hilliard's lost miniatures and a surviving portrait", *Burlington Magazine*, vol. CXXX (October 1988), pp. 758–61.

Lettice Dudley (née Knollys) – her mother, Viscountess Hereford, Countess of Essex, Countess of Leicester (1543–1634): G. L. Craik, *The Romance of the Peerage*, 4 vols (1848–50), vol. 1, "Lettice Knollys, her marriages and her descendants"; and S. Adams, "The papers of Robert Dudley, III", *Archives*, vol. 94 (1996).

Walter Devereux – her father, Viscount Hereford, first Earl of Essex, "Earl Walter" (1539–76): W. B. Devereux, *Lives and Letters of the Devereux Earls of Essex, in the Reigns of Elizabeth, James I and Charles I*, 2 vols (1853); and C. Falls, *Elizabeth's Irish Wars* (1966 edn).

Robert Devereux – her brother, second Earl of Essex, "Essex" (1565–1601): P. J. Hammer, *The Polarisation of Elizabethan Politics: The Political Career of Robert Devereux, 2nd Earl of Essex, 1585–1597* (1999), is essential. See also R. Lacey, *Robert, Earl of Essex: An Elizabethan Icarus* (1971), and still worth reading is Lytton Strachey's *Elizabeth and Essex* (1928). The conspiracy and trial are dealt with in detail by J. Spedding, *The Letters and the Life of Francis Bacon*, 7 vols (1861–74), vol. II; and T. Salmon, *State Trials* (1738), vol. 1.

Robert Dudley – her stepfather, the Earl of Leicester, "Sweet Robin" (1532/3–88): S. Adams, *Leicester and the Court* (2000); "The household accounts and disbursement book of Robert Dudley, Earl of Leicester", *Camden Society*, 5th series, vol. 6

(1995); and "The Papers of Robert Dudley, I and II", *Archives*, vol. 20 (1992), and vol. 21 (1993); see also D. Wilson, *Sweet Robin* (1981).

Philip Sidney – her admirer, Sir Philip (1554–86), author of *Astrophil and Stella*, eldest son of Sir Henry and Lady Mary Sidney, brother of Sir Robert Sidney, and first husband of Frances Walsingham: K. Duncan-Jones's *Sir Philip Sidney: Courtier Poet* (1991) is the major recent work, together with her chapter, "Sidney, Stella and Lady Rich", *Sir Philip Sidney: 1586 and the Creation of a Legend*, eds J. van Dorsten, D. Baker-Smith and A. F. Kinney (1986). *The Poems of Sir Philip Sidney*, ed. W. A. Ringler (1962), and R. Howell, *Sir Philip Sidney the Shepherd Knight* (1968), are still important. And on contemporary identification of Stella see H. H. Hudson, "Penelope Devereux as Sidney's Stella", *The Huntington Library Bulletin*, 7 (April 1935); J. Robertson, "Sir Philip Sidney and Lady Penelope Rich", *Review of English Studies*, NS 15 (1964); and J. Roberts, "The imaginary epistles of Sir Philip Sidney and Lady Penelope Rich", *English Literary Renaissance*, 15 (1985).

Robert Rich – her first husband, Lord Rich, third Baron Rich of Leighs, first Earl of Warwick (1559/60–1619): C. F. D. Sperling, "Robert Rich, 1st Earl of Warwick", *Essex Review*, 42 (1933).

Charles Blount – her lover and second husband, Sir Charles, Lord Mountjoy, eighth Baron Mountjoy, Earl of Devonshire, "Mountjoy" (1563–1606): F. M. Jones, *Mountjoy: The Last Elizabethan Deputy* (1958); C. Falls, *Mountjoy: Elizabethan General* (1955) and *Irish Wars* (1996); A. Croke, *The Genealogical History of the Croke Family, Formerly Named Le Blount,* 2 vols (1823), vol. II; and the detailed accounts of his devoted secretary Fynes Moryson, *An Itinerary Containing His Ten Years Travel* etc, 4 vols (1907), vols 2 and 3.

Henry Hastings – her guardian, third Earl of Huntingdon, "Huntingdon" (c. 1536–95), cousin of Earl Walter: C. Cross, *The Puritan Earl* (1966).

Catherine Hastings (née Dudley) – her guardian, the Countess of Huntingdon (c. 1538–1620), sister to Lord Leicester and Lady Mary Sidney: *Puritan Earl*.

Dorothy Percy (née Devereux) – her sister, Lady Perrot, the Countess of Northumberland (1564–1619), wife of Sir Thomas Perrot (d. 1594) and the Earl of Northumberland: as below.

Henry Percy – her brother-in-law, ninth Earl of Northumberland, "the Wizard Earl" (1564–1632): G. Batho, "The household papers of Henry Percy", *Camden Society*, 3rd series, vol. xciii (1962); E. de Fontblanque, *Annals of the House of Percy*, 2 vols (1887); and G. Brenan, *A History of the House of Percy*, ed. W. A. Lindsay (1902).

Katherine Knollys (née Carey) – her grandmother, Lady Knollys (1523/4–69), daughter of Mary Boleyn and Henry VIII, and wife of Sir Francis Knollys: *ODNB*/Katherine Knollys (on line), and S. Varlow, "Sir Francis Knollys's Latin dictionary, new evidence for Katherine Carey", *Historical Research* Blackwell Publishing, Oxford (August 2007), vol. 80, 209, pp. 315–323.

The Lady Penelope

Francis Knollys – her grandfather, Sir Francis (1511/12–96), father of Lettice and William Knollys (and others) and a leading privy councillor: P. Collinson, *The Elizabethan Puritan Movement* (1967) and C. Garrett, *The Marian Exiles 1553–1559* (1938).

Henry Carey – her great-uncle, Lord Hunsdon (1526–96), son of Mary Boleyn, lord chamberlain to Elizabeth and father of **Robert Carey**: *The Memoirs of Robert Carey*, ed. F. H. Mares (1972).

Queen Elizabeth I – her godmother (1533–1603), half-sister to Lady Katherine Knollys: D. Starkey, *Elizabeth* (2001); *The Reign of Elizabeth*, ed. C. Haigh (1984); *Elizabethan Government and Society*, eds S. T. Bindoff, J. Hurstfield and C. H. Williams (1961), especially "The succession struggle" by Hurstfield; S. Doran, *Monarchy and Matrimony* (1996); and for pleasure, E. Sitwell, *The Queens and the Hive* (1962).

King James I, and VI of Scotland (1566–1625), Elizabeth's successor and married to Anna of Denmark: P. Croft, *King James* (2003); and "Correspondence of King James VI of Scotland with Sir Robert Cecil and others in England", ed. J. Bruce, *Camden Society*, LXXVIII (1861). On his mother, **Mary Queen of Scots (1542–87)**, Mary Stuart: J. Guy, *My Heart is My Own, the Life of Mary Queen of Scots* (2004); and on his cousin **Arbella Stuart (1575–1615)** see S. Gristwood, *Arbella, England's Lost Queen* (2003).

William Cecil, Lord Burghley (1520–98), Elizabeth's chief minister: A. G. R. Smith, *William Cecil, Lord Burghley* (1991), and E. Nares, *Memoirs of the Life and Administration of William Cecil*, 3 vols (1828).

Robert Cecil, Sir Robert, Viscount Cranborne, Earl of Salisbury, "Mr Secretary Cecil" (1563–1612), son of Lord Burghley: D. Starkey, *Rivals in Power* (1990), and P. Croft, "The reputation of Robert Cecil", *History Today* (November 1993).

Francis Walsingham, Sir Francis, "Elizabeth's spy-master" (1529–90), father of Essex's wife, **Frances**: C. Read, *Mr Secretary Walsingham*, 3 vols (1925); "The journal of Sir Francis Walsingham", ed. T. C. Martin, *Camden Society*, vol. 6 (1870–71); and A. Haynes, *The Elizabethan Secret Services* (2004).

Antonio Pérez, "the Wandering Spaniard", "Peregrino" (1539–1611), Essex's agent, foreign diplomat and spy: G. Ungerer, *A Spaniard in Elizabethan England: The Correspondence of Antonio Pérez's Exile*, 2 vols (1974); vol. I prints six letters to Penelope, and one to Lettice in Spanish. See also D. Green, *The Double Life of Doctor Lopez* (2003).

Fr John Gerard (1564–1637), Jesuit priest: *The Autobiography of an Elizabethan, by John Gerard*, trans. P. Caraman (1951); and A. Hogge, *God's Secret Agents* (2005).

William Shakespeare (1564–1616): on his connections with the Essex House circle and his use of contemporary politics, J. Shapiro, *1599 – A Year in the Life of William Shakespeare* (2005), is essential. See also P. Thomson, *Shakespeare's Professional Career* (1992); R. Wilson, *Secret Shakespeare* (2004); and M. Wood, *In Search of Shakespeare* (2004).

Documents

PENELOPE'S LETTERS

Her thirty-three extant letters, many of them brief recommendations for the bearers, are held by the following:

1. **Hatfield House, Hertfordshire**, has eighteen in the Cecil Papers, owned by the Marquess of Salisbury. Twelve of these, all addressed to Robert Cecil, are dated/endorsed and catalogued: vol. 30, f.96; vol. 32, f.87 and f.95; vol. 33, f.67; vol. 40, f.42; vol. 43, f.30; vol. 48, f.49; vol. 55, f.55; vol. 68, f.10; vol. 75, f.83; vol. 103, f.50; vol. 178, f.117. A further six do not show year dates and are conjecturally dated: vol. 109, f.24, to Essex's secretary Edward Reynolds [probably 1597/8]; vol. 206, f.95, to Essex's servant William Downhall [1597–January 1599, or end September 1599]; vol. 99, f.167, 10 May to the Earl of Southampton [probably 1599]; vol. 101, f.25, 9 July to the Earl of Southampton [probably 1599]; vol. 111, f.22, to Robert Cecil as Earl of Salisbury, 31 May [possibly later endorsed 1605]; vol. 193, f.15, to Robert Cecil as Earl of Salisbury [probably September 1606].

2. **Teylers Museum, Haarlem**, has six in the Hotman Letters, numbered 41–6, all without year dates. Three appear to post-date the Hotmans' departure from England, late summer 1590: no. 41, 10 September, to Jeanne; no. 42, 1 May, to Jean; and no. 43, 8 October, to Jeanne. No. 44, 11 September, to Jeanne, was probably written during the "Rialta" correspondence in 1589. Number 45, to Jeanne, probably dates from midsummer 1590, before the birth of Penelope's son Henry. Number 46, to Jean, may be earlier the same year. They were transcribed and translated from the French by Dr Margetts, "Stella Britanna", appendix C. Some are noted and published (in French) in *Correspondence inédite de Robert Dudley, comte de Leycester, et de François et Jean Hotman*, ed. P. J. Blok (Haarlem, 1911).

3. **Packington Old Hall, Warwickshire**, the Essex Letter Book, owned by the Earl of Aylesford, has three and one letter by Lord Rich amended by Penelope. Following a fire, the collection has yet to be recatalogued, but a microfilm of the originals and printed calendar are held by Warwickshire Record Office (WRO MI 229). Penelope's three letters of recommendation to Essex are: no. 48, June 1598; no. 49, March 1596; no. 50, undated. Number 51 is Lord Rich's letter to Essex, 23 December 1596.

4. **British Library**, London (BL) holds three: Lansdowne MS 57, f.118, to Burghley, 10 September 1588; Additional MS 12506, f.421, to Dr Julius Caesar, May 1599; and Stowe MS 150, f.140, one of several copies of Penelope's letter to Elizabeth, January 1600.

5. **Lambeth Palace Library**, London (LPL), has one: Bacon Papers, MS 657, f.61, to Anthony Bacon, 3 May 1596.

6. **Bodleian Library**, University of Oxford (BLO), has one: Tanner MS 114. f.139, to the Earl of Nottingham, undated but probably written March 1601.
7. **Henry E. Huntington Library**, California, has one: Hastings Papers HA 860, to the fifth Earl of Huntingdon, undated but probably 1606. The collection index also lists HM 102, "Copies of letters of Sir Walter Ralegh, Robert Devereux ... Penelope Rich ... and others" (but I have not been able to access the collection).

OTHER MANUSCRIPTS AND TRANSCRIPTS

Some of the principal collections of manuscripts relevant to Penelope can be searched on line via A2A (Access to Archives), though the Cecil Papers are not yet available. They can all be searched through published calendars including the Historic Manuscripts Commission (HMC) volumes. But many of the most pertinent letters have been transcribed, at least partially, and printed or published, as shown below.

Aylesford Papers/Essex Letter Book (as above, MI 229) has in total eighty-three letters: twelve by the second Earl of Essex and the remainder by the Earl and Countess of Northumberland, Lettice and Sir Christopher Blount, Penelope and Lord Rich, Lord Mountjoy and Sir William Knollys. Some also exist as transcripts taken in 1751 by Dr T. Birch, now BL Additional MS 4124.

Bacon Papers (as above LPL MSS 647–62) are the papers of Essex's secretary. There is a published *Index to the Papers of Anthony Bacon*, by E. G. W. Bill (1974); many are in *Memoirs of the Reign of Queen Elizabeth*, ed. T. Birch, 2 vols (1754).

Bagot Papers in the Folger Shakespeare Library, Washington (FSL MS L.a. 1–1076), contain much relevant correspondence which can be searched on line. Staffordshire Record Office holds microfilm copies of 128 letters to Richard Bagot and a printed transcript (SRO D 1721/3/290), unpaginated, which includes thirty-five letters by the second Earl of Essex (five, dated 1583–5 do not appear to be in the FSL collection), thirty-nine by Richard Broughton and eleven by Anthony Bagot. Approximately thirty letters to Richard Broughton were also published as "Richard Broughton's Devereux Papers", ed. H. E. Malden, *Camden Miscellany*, NS, XIII (1923). These include eyewitness accounts of Earl Walter's death and letters from the second Earl dated 1579–86. *Memorials of the Bagot Family* (1823) reproduces letters from all the above; and G. Wrothesley, "A history of the family of Bagot", *Staffordshire Historical Collection*, NS, XI (1908), relies heavily on them. NB. All of the Bagot Papers referenced FSL in this work are among the papers in SRO D/1721/3/290.

Bodleian Library (as above) collections include: Tanner MSS items on Irish affairs transcribed by C. McNeill and published as *The Tanner Letters* (1943), some of which are also in *The Court of King James the 1st by Dr G. Goodman*, ed. J. S. Brewer, 2 vols (1839). The BLO also holds one of two "fantastical" letters from the second Earl of Essex to Penelope: Misc. MS. Don.c.188 (the other is in the BL, see below) discussed by K. Duncan-Jones, "Notable accessions: western manuscripts", *Bodleian Library Record*, 15 (1996); and M. Margetts, "'The Ways of Mine own Heart': the dating and mind frame of Essex's 'fantastical' letter", *Bodleian Library Record*, 16 (April 1997). Both "fantastical" letters are transcribed by A. Freeman in "Essex to Stella: two letters from the Earl of Essex to Penelope Rich", *English Literary Renaissance*, 3 (1973); and

G. Ioppolo, "Reading Penelope Rich through her letters", *The Impact of Feminism*, ed. D. Callaghan (2006).

British Library (as above) naturally holds many relevant items, e.g. Additional MS 64081, one of the two "fantastical" letters noted above; and Additional MS 4149, f.306–19, the Earl of Devonshire's discourse on Penelope's second marriage.

Carew Manuscripts (as above, LPL MSS 596–638) were gathered by Sir George Carew who was with Mountjoy in Ireland. There is a published *Calendar of the Carew Manuscripts*, 6 vols (1867–73) by J. S. Brewer and W. Bullen.

Cecil Papers (also known as Salisbury and Hatfield, as above) are obviously a principal source and include many letters not addressed to Lord Burghley or Robert Cecil, either taken or copied when intercepted for surveillance (e.g. Penelope's letters to her brother's staff and the Earl of Southampton). The collection is calendared chiefly in HMC 9th Report, Cecil vols I–XXIV, but also in Reports 3–6. Many of the papers were published in: *A Collection of State Papers Left by William Cecil, 1558–1570*, ed. S. Haynes (1740) and a companion volume for *1571–1596*, ed. W. Murdin (1759).

De L'Isle Manuscripts: the private collection of Viscount De L'Isle, held at the Centre for Kentish Studies (CKS), Maidstone, include the Sidney correspondence KAO (U1475) and Kenilworth Game Book (U1475 E93). They were calendared HMC 77th Report, De L'Isle & Dudley vols I–VI. Many Sidney letters appear in *Letters and Memorials of State ... Written and Collected by Sir Henry Sidney, Sir Philip Sidney, Sir Robert Sidney*, ed. A. Collins, 2 vols (1746), and many other works.

Devereux Papers at Longleat House, owned by the Marquess of Bath, are the chief collection of family papers. Referenced DE, the relevant volumes are I–III, V–VII and X, and boxes I–VII. In addition, the Dudley Papers, ref. DU, have useful material. Both sets of papers are calendared in HMC Report 58, Bath Volume 5, Talbot, Dudley and Devereux Papers 1533–1659. The family history, *Devereux Lives* (as above), was compiled from these and other private and state papers, but not from the Cecil Papers.

Rich Papers, also in the Folger Shakespeare Library, relate chiefly to a junior branch of the family (descended from Lord Rich's younger brother). Rich family pedigrees exist in the BL Additional and Harley MSS collections.

State Papers used here are either held by National Archives (formerly the Public Record Office, PRO) or quoted from the calendars: *Letters and Papers Foreign and Domestic, Henry VIIIth* (LP Henry 8); *Calendar of State Papers Domestic, Elizabeth* (CSP Dom); *Calendar of State Papers Foreign* (CSP For); *Calendar of State Papers Simancas/Spain* (CSP Simancas); *Calendar of State Papers Venetian* (CSP Venetian); and *Acts of the Privy Council* (APC).

Miscellaneous papers, including Queen Elizabeth's Gift Rolls, were used by J. Nichols to compile *The Progresses and Public Processions of Queen Elizabeth ... and Remarkable Events*, 3 vols but they have variations between editions (1788, 1823, 1828), inconsistent pagination, and undeclared excisions from sources; some of which should become clear in a new edition being prepared by Warwick University.

NB. In quoting from the above, spelling, punctuation and dates have usually been modernized.

Notes, Quotes and Sources

Throughout this study the mixed use of originals and calendared documents, published and unpublished studies is deliberate. Repeated sources are referenced by short forms (using author, title or both). Dates given are new style, i.e. year-dating from 1 January, not 25 March, as on most contemporary documents.

Part I   Childhood and Ancestry 1563–1580

Chapter 1

"An harlot, adulteress, concubine and whore": Star Chamber papers; PRO STAC 8/108/10.

For the date of her death, see Chapter 29 notes.

A "black soul": Falls, *Mountjoy*, p. 180. "Here lies fair Penelope": Hudson, *Penelope as Stella*, quoting from BL Additional MS 15227, f.7. The "scandal of her age": R. Bagwell, *Ireland under the Tudors*, 3 vols (1885–90), vol. 2, p. 326. For "flaunted her beauty", "emotional cripple", "without love" and "philanderings" see: *Elizabethan Icarus*, pp. 15, 23, 313. Sitwell, *Queens and the Hive*: "false, sly, arrogant", p.418. She "bore her husband children": Falls, *Mountjoy*, p. 62. "Adultery seized the imagination": A. Haynes, *Sex in Elizabethan England* (1997), p. 6.

For "perhaps a main instigator": Craik, p. 265; "a politician": Falls, *Mountjoy*, preface; and. "was probably crucial": Duncan-Jones, "Sidney, Stella and Lady Rich", p. 188.

Chapter 2

"A perfect model of manly beauty", Venetian ambassador, 1529: CSP Venetian 1527–33, 386.

"Nature could not have done more": CSP Venetian 1509–1519, pp. 557–63. "His majesty is the handsomest": S. Giustinian, *Four Years at the Court of Henry VIII*, trans. R. Brown, 2 vols (1854), vol. 1, p. 85.

Bessie Blount's affair with Henry VIII: B. Murphy, *The Bastard Prince* (2001).

The reference in Italian to Mary was "*una grandissima ribalda et infame sopre tutte*": R. Warnicke, *The Rise and Fall of Anne Boleyn* (1989), pp. 45–6. It was made in 1536 following Mary's meeting four years earlier with the king of France, who allegedly called her the greatest and most infamous whore [at Court].

Carey's mother, Margaret Spencer, was a granddaughter of Edmund Beaufort, grandson of John of Gaunt's eldest son, John Beaufort (d. 1410): E. Reilly, *Historical Anecdotes of the Families of the Boleynes, Careys* etc. (1839); and LP Henry 8, vol. III/ii, p. 1539.

The discovery of Sir Francis Knollys's Latin dictionary with its fresh evidence for Katherine Carey's birth puts it beyond reasonable doubt that Mary's daughter, at least, was a royal bastard. For full details of the dictionary and its implications see Varlow, "Latin dictionary", and *ODNB*/Katherine Knollys. The main arguments for dating Henry VIII's affairs with Anne and Mary Boleyn are given in: J. Gairdner, "Mary and Anne Boleyn", *English Historical Review*, no. 8 (1893), pp. 53–66, and no. 10 (1895), p. 104; E. W. Ives, *The Life and Death of Anne Boleyn* (2004); Warnicke, as above; and A. Hoskins, "Mary Boleyn's Carey children and offspring of Henry VIII", *Genealogists' Magazine*, vol. 25 (March 1997).

Will Carey died 22 June 1528: *Original Letters Illustrative of English History*, ed. H. Ellis (1824) vol. 1, p. 295. "Love overcame" and the "*cor rotto*" letter: M. A. E. Wood, *Letters of Royal and Illustrious Ladies* (1846), vol. 2, p. 193, and vol. 3, p. 279. Lettice's date of birth (November 1543) is fixed by the Latin dictionary (see above). Lettice as a maid of the privy chamber: BL Lansdowne MS 3/89, f.193, detailed in C. Merton, "The Women who Served Queen Mary and Queen Elizabeth", unpublished D.Phil. thesis (Trinity College, Cambridge, 1992).

Chapter 3
"The Christening of Viscount Hereford his child", New Year's Gift Roll 1562–3; PRO C 47/3/38.

Devereux Lives is the chief source of family history, but the birth date of Walter, first Earl of Essex, has been queried. Cockayne, vol. V, p. 3, 29ff, states he was born at Carmarthen Castle, 16 September, and baptized in the church there 18 September 1539; repeated in V. Lowe, *Some Pembrokeshire Devereux* (1976), and subsequently Margetts, *Birth of Robert Devereux*. But a family tree in *Broughton–Devereux Papers* gives 1540; and Craik, vol. 1, p. 25, interprets a Latin epitaph to mean 1541; *ODNB* says he was born at Chartley.

On Walter senior's private army and offices: H. Miller, *Henry VIII and the English Nobility* (1986), pp.142, 150, 202. Richard's marriage settlement: HMC 58, Bath V, p. 229.
"Trickle": A. Fraser, *The Gunpowder Plot* (1996), p. 6.

Walter's arrival at Court, expenditure and marriage date are deduced from his accounts: DE vol. III, f.14–25 (Margetts, "Stella Britanna", p. 35, noted the indication of his departure to Pembrokeshire) and box I, 34. See also *ODNB*/Lettice Dudley.

The website measuringworth.com calculates £158.9s.9d. was worth £32,299.37p in present value.

Penelope's choice of name: from the International Genealogical Index it now appears that a Penelope Devereux was born at "Devereux" Castle, Carmarthenshire, to Richard Devereux and Dorothy Hastings, c. 1546 (the year before Richard died), though she is not named by Lowe with sisters Mary, Elizabeth and Anne, and presumably died young.

On Chartley: W. White, *History, Gazetteer and Directory of Staffordshire* (Sheffield, 1851); *Erdeswick's Survey of Staffordshire*, ed. T. Harwood (1844), pp. 55–9; DE box V, 79, is Chartley Manor survey 1595/6; Nichols (1823), vol. 1, p. 532. In 1781 the first of two fires destroyed the house.

For Penelope's date of birth see: Margetts, "Penelope's christening date", pp. 152–4. Baptismal records for the parish of Stowe-by-Chartley do not begin until 1574, hence the place of birth is unrecorded, but tradition and *Devereux Lives* say Lettice and Walter retired to Chartley and Penelope was born there. Walter's absence from parliament (see T. E. Hartley, *Proceedings in the Parliaments of Elizabeth I*, vol. I, 1558–1581, p. 67), may confirm this. On Robert's birth date: T. Milles, *The Catalogue of Honour* (1610), p. 863, A. Kippis, *Biographia Britannica*, 5 vols (1780), vol. 4, p. 131, and *Devereux Lives*, vol. 1, p. 7, state Robert was born 1567 at Netherwood in Herefordshire, and *Elizabethan Icarus*, p. 9, repeats the date 10 November 1567. But according to DE box V, 68, the year was 1565, and I am indebted to Dr Kate Harris for full details of the document, which is also discussed in Margetts/*Birth of Robert Devereux*.

For the Bagot family see Bagot Papers above. They give Richard Bagot's children as Margaret, Anne, Walter and Anthony, born 1552–8. Richard Broughton, born 1534, married Anne in July 1577.

On Thomas White, son of Nicholas White, Master of the Rolls in Ireland; Gabriel, son of the Count Montgomery; and Robert's tutors Ashton and Wright, see *Polarisation*, pp. 18, 23, 25. Holmes as Penelope's tutor: BL Lansdowne MS 24, f.208. For Penelope's musicianship see Chapter 19.

~

Lamphey: *Lamphey Bishop's Palace* (2000), CADW; inventory LP Henry 8, vol. X, p. 173; and Maurice Howard, *The Early Tudor Country House* (1987), p. 112.

For Dudley Knollys see Chapter 2; and his death, June 1562, is recorded in BL Additional MS 48023, published as "A Journal of Matters of State", eds S. Adams, I. W. Archer and G. Bernard, *Camden Society*, 5th series, XXII (December 2003).

On Henry Knollys's wedding to Margaret, daughter of Sir Ambrose Cave: A. Young, *Tudor and Jacobean Tournaments* (1987), p. 201; Merton, "Women who served", p. 116; CSP Simancas 1558–1567, pp. 451–2. "The queen's majesty is fallen": J. Ross, *The Men Who Would be King* (2005), p. 119. For "one of the best looking": CSP Simancas 1558–1567, p. 472; and Ross, pp. 102–3.

On Elizabeth's Hatfield "old flock" see Adams, "Eliza enthroned", Haigh, *Reign of Elizabeth*, p. 64.

Chapter 4

"The Queen of Love", Edmund Spenser, *The Faerie Queen*, Book 4, verse 4, 1590.

Hampton Court is described by the Duke of Wirtemberg, 1592: *England as Seen by Foreigners*, ed. W. B. Rye (1865).

Accession Day, 17 November, and London in late Elizabethan England: Shapiro, *1599*, prologue and pp. 186–9; also R. Strong, *The Cult of Elizabeth* (1977).

Leicester's accounts are typical of courtiers' costs: HMC 58, Bath V, pp. 136–8, and pp. 148–51; and L. Stone, *The Crisis of the Aristocracy* (1965). Burghley's one hundred people: Nicolson, p. 112.

Elizabeth's household: D. Loades, *The Tudor Court* (1992), pp. 57–9, states there were eleven waged posts for women, plus unpaid, extraordinary ladies-in-waiting. S. Frye and K. Robertson, *Maids and Mistresses, Cousin and Queens – Women's Alliances in Early Modern England* (1999), p. 132, puts it at sixteen paid female posts, which were held by only twenty-eight different women during the forty-four-year reign.

~

Lady Margaret Douglas, Countess of Lennox (d. 1578), and Lady Frances Grey, Duchess of Suffolk (d. 1559), see Chapter 6.

Katherine Ashley (also know as Astley), see *ODNB*. New Year gifts 1562 are listed in Nichols (1823), vol. I, p.120ff. Elizabeth Knollys (later Lady Leighton) is often wrongly named Cecilia, see Varlow, "Latin dictionary". She was a waged gentle-woman of the privy chamber from 1566 and served the queen until 1583, despite her marriage in May 1579, aged thirty, to Sir Thomas Leighton of Guernsey: FSL L.a. 188. She continued as an extra lady of the bedchamber for many years.

"The Tribe of Dan" nickname for Hunsdon's large family is recorded by Robert Naunton in *Fragmenta Regalia* (written c. 1626), ed. F. H. Mares (1972). C. Lee, *1603* (2003), p. 129, suggests it was taken from the Old Testament (Book of Judges, chapter XVIII, v.1) because the tribe had lands in the north. It is more significant that Dan was the son of Jacob and his wife's handmaid Bilhah, as Hunsdon was the son of the queen's former maid Mary Boleyn. Additionally, the Tribe of Dan sent more men to war than any of the other tribes of Israel yet did not receive their rightful inheritance; just as Hunsdon's many sons were angered that he did not receive greater recognition from Elizabeth. Naunton knew the inside story of Hunsdon's family because his wife (married 1619) was Penelope's niece, Penelope Perrot.

On Lord Leicester and Amy Robsart see Wilson, *Sweet Robin*, chapter 7, and many others; and diplomatic reports, e.g. CSP Simancas 1558–1567, p. 175.

~

Sir Francis's correspondence "I would to God I were so dispatched" etc. is repro-duced in "Papers relating to Mary Queen of Scots, communicated by General Sir William Knollys", *Philobiblon Society Miscellanies*, XIV–V (1872–6). For "distracted with sorrow": CSP Scotland 1563–1569, vol. ii, pp. 606, 612. On the relative burial costs see Varlow, "Latin dictionary"; and Thomson, *Shakespeare's Career*, p. 153, notes that Hunsdon's will provided £1,000 for his ornate monu-ment.

Elizabeth was "forgetful of her own health": Haynes, *State Papers*, p. 505.

~

Lettice's presence at Court alone is sometimes deduced from New Year gift lists (e.g. 1564, FSL Z.d.12 and 1567, BL Additional MS 9772) showing gifts presented by Lettice but not by her husband. But the lists are not totally reliable or complete. There is evidence (e.g. Sir Francis Knollys's correspondence, as above) that gifts might be presented on behalf of courtiers by other family members.

Devereux Lives (and others) confuse the events of the Norfolk marriage plan, Mary's arrival at Tutbury and the Northern Earls' uprising. In fact, Mary was taken to Tutbury in February 1569; the Norfolk marriage plan (hatched in 1568) was exposed during the summer; and in November the northern uprising began; see C. Haigh, *English Reformations* (1993), p. 257. Walter writes from Chartley accepting the commission on 27 November 1569: CSP Dom 1547–80, p.348. Wat's birth date: Chapter 3.

Chapter 5

"Beware of the Gypsy, for he will be too hard for you all", Thomas Radcliffe, third Earl of Sussex, 1583; Wilson, *Sweet Robin*, p. 249.

The commissions of lieutenancy: HMC 9, Cecil, vol. 1, p. 443.

"I never saw nobleman": CSP Dom 1547–1580, p. 350.

"There is less danger": Francis Walsingham, and see Read, *Walsingham*, vol. 1, pp. 53–63, for the Northern Earls and Mary Queen of Scots.

Walter's movements in the years 1572–6, his use of Durham House, London, and periods at Chartley can be traced from the Bagot Papers, Devereux Papers, *Devereux Lives* and State Papers; e.g.: FSL L.a. 479 at Chartley, 22 July 1572; FSL L.a. 187 his riding accident December 1572; HMC 58, Bath V, p. 233, show Lettice also in London, November 1572. His investitures are in: DE box II, 38–40, and III, 45; *Catalogue of Honour*, p. 38; and *Biographia Britannica*, vol. 4, pp. 125–31.

The possibility of children attending Court is evidenced by Barbara Sidney's visit to Court (see Chapter 18); and their presence during Elizabeth's progresses is discussed below.

On Ireland: Falls, *Irish Wars*, chapter 8 and p.114, for "ridiculous" assessment. Earl Walter's negotiations with Elizabeth and appointment as governor are in: *Devereux Lives*, vol. 1, pp. 30–32; DE vols I and II; DE box III, 47 (24 July 1573).

His wills (30 November 1572 and 3 August 1573): DE box III, 44 and 49. His letter to Burghley proposing marriage for Robert is BL Lansdowne MS 17 f.47; and "his mother's wing" is *Devereux Lives*, vol. 1, p. 67.

Privy council discussions, 1574: "The Journal of Sir Francis Walsingham", ed. T. C. Martin, *Camden Society*, VI (1870–71), pp. 15–16.

On Walter's relationship with Leicester see *Devereux Lives*, vol. 1, pp. 72–6; and "by the advice" is W. Dugdale, *The Baronage of England* (1676), p. 178.

New Year gift lists (see also Chapter 4 notes) are scattered in: FSL; BL Additional MSS, e.g. 5751, 4827, 38857; National Archives, e.g. PRO C47/3/39; and elsewhere. Some are reproduced (partially) in Nichols, e.g. (1823) vol. II, pp. 65–90, and 249–275. See also A. J. Collins, *Jewels and Plate of Queen Elizabeth I* (1955), pp. 249–52.

Kenilworth: for information from the Game Book (see De L'Isle Manuscripts above) I am obliged to Dr Adams; on Robert Dudley and Amy Robsart see Chapter 4; and on Lady Douglas Sheffield see "Memorials of the Holles family by Gervase Holles", ed. A. C. Wood, *Camden Society*, 3rd series, vol. LV (1937). For "*giovane bellissimo*" and "generally detested": CSP Venetian 1558–1580, pp. 81, 492. George Gascoigne, *The princely pleasures at ... Kenilworth* (1575) are in Nichols (1823), vol. I, pp. 426–523.

A meeting between Penelope and Philip at Chartley in 1575 is usually dismissed (e.g. *Shepherd Knight*, p. 28) following Ringler's judgement (p. 437) using the advice given to one of Elizabeth's hosts to remove his family from his house. But the advice relates to vacating bedchambers, and even though the host's family were billeted with neighbours, they would be welcome to attend the queen. The purpose of a Progress was to make friends, see and be seen. In addition, Barbara Sidney's visit to Court (see Chapter 18) shows the queen was not averse to children attending. J. M. Osborn, *Young Philip Sidney* (1972), pp. 344–7, proves the

Sidney family was travelling with the royal party before and after the visit to Chartley; and Osborn concedes that Lettice "may have welcomed the chance to have the members of the Court see her daughter's budding beauty".

Chapter 6

"Some evil received in my drink", Earl Walter, 13 September 1576: *Broughton Devereux Papers*, item 6.

"As the thing is publicly": CSP Simancas 1568–1579, p. 511.

"Because I know this Christmas time"; "I am come to that pass"; and "The master of my ship": *Devereux Lives*, vol. 1, pp. 125, 129–30, 135. Earl Walter's gift, presented at Hampton Court: BL Additional MS 4827. His departure from Court, journey to Chartley and Dublin can be pieced together from the same sources as noted in Chapter 5, plus Collins, *Sidney*, vol. 1. His new will, 14 June 1576: DE box IV, 59; and his letter to Broughton, 22 July: DE vol. V, f.18.

The idea that Philip travelled with Walter: *Courtier Poet*, p. 108.

"The physicians have fully resolved": *Memoirs of William Cecil*, vol. 3, p. 74.

∼

Earl Walter's last letters, investigation into his death and eyewitness accounts by his secretary Edward Waterhouse and chaplains are reproduced in *Broughton Devereux Papers*, e.g. "a disease took me", item 6.

Waterhouse's letter to Dr Peny: DE vol. V, f.20.

Evidence that Walter believed he had been poisoned is also in Nicholas White's letter (30 September) with autopsy details: BL Lansdowne MS 21, f.66. Walter's letter to Elizabeth: Murdin, *State Papers*, p. 300.

On Naunton and *Fragmenta Regalia* see Chapter 4 notes.

Funeral procession, costs, and payments to servants: DE vol. V, f.22–7; HMC 58, Bath V, pp. 247–8; and *Devereux Lives*, vol. I, p. 150, and vol. II, pp. 481–2.

∼

Waterhouse's letter, "what will come of the treaty": Collins, *Sidney*, vol. 1, p. 147. Robert's letter, "my lord and father the last service": BL Lansdowne MS 22, f.200; and Waterhouse's "this extreme cold weather": BL Lansdowne MS 23, f.190.

∼

Robert's "leave to tarry here": BL Lansdowne MS 22, f.204; and his visit to Court: DE vol. V, f.17.

Robert's life with the Cecils: *Polarisation*, p. 24.

On Lettice's dower: DE vol. V, f.24; and her letters to Burghley: BL Lansdowne MS 24, f.26, 28 and 208 – which includes: "one that teacheth my daughters." The Bennington estate, Hertfordshire, had been mentioned in Earl Walter's proposal for Robert to marry Burghley's daughter. It was confirmed as Lettice's in 1590, later passed to Robert and was sold by his widow: DE box II, vol. III, f.172, and vol. IX, f.29.

On George Digby see *Leicester and the Court*, p. 206.

Lettice's visits to Coleshill were referred to in the libel *Leicester's Commonwealth*, see Chapter 11. Details of hunting and gifts of venison: Kenilworth Game Book (see Chapter 5 notes). For visits to Buxton see *ODNB*/Lettice and Robert Dudley. Anne Bagot's wedding: FSL L.a. 241 and Wrothesley, p. 83.

"My lady of Essex came to Hackney", and "to be bold to trouble him": FSL L.a. 249.

It is provisionally year-dated by FSL to 1580, but the reference to disturbances in Wales indicates it can be dated to 1577.

On the Countess of Lennox and Arbella Stuart, see *Arbella*, pp. 35–50.

Chapter 7

"How to breed and govern young gentlewomen", Countess of Huntingdon, 1618; BL Lansdowne MS 162, f.132.

Huntingdon "useth not such flattering": HMC 58, Bath V, p. 139.

York and King's Manor were the Huntingdons' home from 1572 (*Puritan Earl*, p. 26) throughout the time Penelope was in their care. See: J. Stuart Syme, "The King's Manor, York", *Yorkshire Archaeological Journal*, 36 (1944–6). It is difficult to be certain how much time Penelope and Dorothy spent with them between February 1578 and January 1581, when Penelope came to Court. The Devereux accounts (1576–1586, DE vol. V, f.22–66) show that the girls' maintenance money went to Lettice (only Wat's went to the Huntingdons), perhaps indicating they spent much time with Lettice. But there is no supporting evidence and the Huntingdons had been entrusted by Earl Walter with his children's upbringing, hence it may be assumed they spent the three years chiefly at York. It has been suggested the Huntingdons were at Court from Christmas 1578 to spring 1579 and brought Penelope and Dorothy with them, possibly to stay at Leicester House. Again there is no supporting evidence and the Bagot correspondence which mentions Robert in London (see below) does not refer to Penelope or Dorothy.

On Margaret's early life: J. Moody, *The Private Life of an Elizabethan Lady: The Diary of Lady Margaret Hoby* (2001), pp. xvi–xix.

～

Essex's expenses are in DE vol. V, f.34 (see also Chapter 13). Anthony Bagot's letter "This first of February", FSL L.a. 37 and further correspondence, including FSL L.a. 235, show Essex remained in London till late February.

On Anjou and Simier see: Read, *Walsingham*, vol. 2; and Ross, chapters 7 and 8.

～

Depositions (3 March 1581) concerning the marriage in 1578: CSP Dom 1581–1590, p. 11; and Tyndall's statement is HMC 58, Bath V, pp. 205–6.

For Elizabeth's progresses 1578 see Z. Dovey, *An Elizabethan Progress* (1996); and "to see my lord of Leicester": HMC 58 Bath V, p. 90.

Wanstead was granted to Will Carey: LP Henry 8 vol. IV/i, p. 464. Elizabeth's visits, hosted by the Rich family, and subsequently Leicester, are noted by Nichols (1788), vol. 1, pp. 1, 5, 7; and vol. 3, pp. 19, 36. On Leicester's ownership see Adams, "Household accounts". Philip Sidney's *The Lady of May* is in K. Duncan-Jones's edition of his work in the Oxford Poetry Library series (1994), p. 145. Given that Penelope was only with the Huntingdons three years, not five as previously thought, it is less likely she was present at Wanstead during *The May Lady*.

The "second marriage" claim was made in *Leicester's Commonwealth*, see Chapter 11.

Mary Queen of Scots's letter (4 July 1579): S. Doran, *Monarchy and Matrimony* (1996), p. 162. William Camden, *The History of the Most Renowned and Victorious Princess Elizabeth, late Queen of England*, 4 vols (1630), vol. 2, p. 95, first claimed that Simier broke the news. The "central enigma": *ODNB*/Lettice Dudley.

Huntingdon's letter, "to put her highness in mind": BL Lansdowne MS 31, f.105.

Essex and his studies: "much grieved thereat" is in FSL L.a. 248; and "I think I shall be in Cambridge" is FSL L.a. 456.

Part II Marriage and Politics 1581–1590

Chapter 8

"Towards Aurora's Court", Sir Philip Sidney, *Astrophil and Stella*, 1582/3.

Walsingham's letter, "very graciously received": Huntington HA 13057, is dated 31 January and says the audience with Elizabeth took place the preceding day.

For Whitehall Palace and the tournaments see Shapiro, pp. 27–37; *Courtier Poet*, p. 202; and A. R. Young, *The English Tournament Impresse* (1988), p. 171. The New Year gifts are in Nichols (1823), vol. II, p. 300ff. The banqueting house: Read, *Walsingham*, vol. II, p. 47, calls it new, following Nichols; but it was built in 1572 and Margetts, "Stella Britanna", p. 186, points out it was probably refurbished.

"Her beauty great": William Byrd, *Weeping Full Sore*, see Chapter 19.

"Perfection's heir" and "When nature made her chief work": *Astrophil and Stella*, sonnets 71 and 7.

"A lute of senseless wood": *The Poems of Henry Constable*, ed. J. Grundy (1960), p. 125.

Anne Vavasour "was brought to bed": Huntington MS HA 13066.

Penelope is usually called a maid of honour and, though there is no record that she was sworn in to the queen's household, she was referred to as one of "our maids" by Richard Brackinbury, see Chapter 9.

~

Elizabeth Knollys, Lady Leighton, see Chapter 4 notes. The "spider of the Court": *Polarisation*, p. 387.

Penelope's rooms at Leicester House are recorded in inventories taken between 1585 and 1586 and November 1590, HMC 58, Bath V, Dudley Papers, pp. 208, 219, 221, 224. Some are published by C. L. Kingsford, "Essex House, formerly Leicester House", *Archaeologia* (1923), pp. 31, 48. The November 1590 inventory shows that the original furnishings were replaced by black and gold hangings.

The idea that Lettice was currently "living in Staffordshire and cut off from the Court" (*Poor Penelope*, p. 46) is not correct: her son was born at Leicester House, June 1581.

Penelope's portraits: several are listed in the inventories of Leicester's properties. The only one believed to survive is the double portrait with Dorothy, now at Longleat House (see page 6 of Illustrations). It is assumed to be "The picture of two young ladies" in the 1583 Kenilworth inventory, HMC 77, De L'Isle and Dudley, vol. 1, p. 291; and listed again in November 1590 as "two ladies in one picture". Although it was at one time incorrectly catalogued at Longleat (Margetts, "Hilliard's lost miniatures") its significance was not lost on the curators. It shows signs of over-painting and there is doubt about the respective identities of the sitters, but the likelihood is that Penelope is on the right. Its listing in the 1583 inventory supports the idea that Dorothy was also in London during 1581/2. A portrait at Lambeth Palace which carries the later inscription "A Countess of Devon Shire" has sometimes (e.g. *Poor Penelope*) been identified as Penelope, and

I am obliged to Karen Hearn of Tate Britain for the opinion that this is unlikely. See Chapter 13 for Nicholas Hilliard's miniatures of Penelope.

On Drake: "I know not the secret points" is Collins, *Sidney*, vol. 1, p. 283. Elizabeth's Deptford visit is detailed in Ross, p. 154; and the French visitors' schedule is in Walsingham's Journal.

Essex's new clothes are: *Polarisation*, p. 30. For *The Four Foster Children of Desire* see *Courtier Poet*, pp. 205–10; *Tournament Impresse*, pp. 14, 171; and A. R. Young, *Tudor and Jacobean Tournaments* (1987), pp. 155–8.

~

Greenwich Palace: C. Aslet, *The Story of Greenwich* (1999), p. 62.

"Mr Stonar's": Walsingham's Journal, p. 43. Nichols (1788) names Loughton Hall, Havering and Luxborough Hall, Chigwell, as belonging to Mr Stoner.

The plague: P. Hughes and J. Larkin, *Tudor Royal Proclamations*, 3 vols (1969), vol. II, p. 486.

Leicester at Kenilworth: CSP Dom 1581–90, p. 26.

Elizabeth would "befool the world": CSP Venetian 1558–80, p. 448.

Chapter 9

"In years very fit for my Lady Penelope", Henry Hastings, Earl of Huntingdon, 1581; BL Lansdowne MS 31, f.105.

Baroness Rich's gift to Elizabeth: Nichols (1823), vol. II, p. 300.

On the Rich family see Who's Who and W. G. Hoskins, *The Age of Plunder* (1976), p. 132. "He is full of dissimulation", quoted from Miller, p. 226; and "the legal murderer" is quoted in W. D. Montague, *Court and Society from Elizabeth to Anne*, 2 vols (1864), pp. 291–302. Lord Rich's presence in Ireland: HMC 58, Bath V, p. 240. On Elizabeth's visits to Wanstead and Leighs see Chapter 7.

~

The value of the Devereux estates: *Devereux Lives*, vol. II, pp. 483–5; and Baron Rich's burial, 4 April 1581: Felsted parish register, Essex Record Office D/P 99/1/1.

"A poor man of no language": Essex Letter Book no. 51.

Bishop Aylmer: J. Strype, *The Life and Acts of … John Aylmer, Bishop of London* (1821), p. 55.

The £500 payment to Lord Rich is DE vol. V, f.52.

~

Sir Henry Sidney: "I assure you before God" is Collins, *Sidney*, vol. 1, p. 256; and "I left her a full fair lady" is in *Courtier Poet*, p. 4.

On Philip's Catholic interests see: *Courtier Poet*, pp. 124–7, 166, 198; and J. Bossy, *Giordano Bruno and the Embassy Affair* (1991).

The marriage testimonies are in Chapter 7 notes. The French ambassador's references to Lettice's pregnancies: *ODNB*/Lettice Dudley. Baron Denbigh's birth, 6 June 1581, was first noted by Adams, "Papers of Robert Dudley, III".

~

Essex's spending on clothes for Penelope's wedding: DE vol. V, f.53–4. His letter regarding "*voluptatis honestae*" with Lord Rich (BL Lansdowne MS 33, f.20) has been translated both as a request for permission to leave Cambridge (e.g. M. W. Wallace, *The Life of Sir Philip Sidney* [1915], p. 247) and as a post-trip apology (e.g. *Poor Penelope*, p. 45). Either way, it was followed by a trip to Kenilworth, where Leicester was in residence on 28 September: CSP Dom 1581–90, p. 26. The gelding gift: DE vol. V, f.54.

On Penelope's wedding and Brakinbury's letter, "will be married about Allhallow tide", see: L. C. John, "The date of the marriage of Penelope Devereux", *Publications of the Modern Language Association* [*PMLA*], 49 (1943), pp. 961–2; and J. M. Purcell, "A cup for my Lady Penelope", *Modern Language Notes*, vol. XLV (1930), p. 310. Though the date is often stated as 1 November, it could be any day in early November. The month is confirmed by Devereux accounts HMC 58, Bath V, p. 248; and Sir Francis's payment is DE vol. V, f.52.

The countess's visit to Wilton: Ringler, p. 442; and Mary's baby was born on 15 October: *Courtier Poet*, p. 218. Philip's absence: his letter to Burghley, Murdin, *State Papers*, p. 364, states he has taken leave of Elizabeth; his letter to her (10 November) is written from Gravesend; and he is not known to be in London, at Baynard's Castle, until 14 November: *Courtier Poet*, p. 218.

Chapter 10

"You teach my tongue with one sweet kiss", Philip Sidney, *Astrophil and Stella*, 1582–3.

Essex's spending on the wedding: DE vol. V, f.53. The plan for his future control: DE vol. V, f.24.

The date of Denbigh's birth (6 June 1581, see Chapter 9) has settled the date of Sidney's tournament motto "*Speravi*". William Camden's surmise that Philip's dashed hopes related to his lost inheritance (see *Courtier Poet*, p. 194) remains dubious. Tilting was bound up with chivalry and courtly love and it would be mean spirited to express public jealousy about money when Leicester had the good fortune to have a son. Philip's dashed hopes surely relate to a lady, Elizabeth or Penelope. He had hoped to persuade Elizabeth against the French marriage and failed; or he had fallen in love with Penelope.

Anjou's £10,000: J. B. Black, *The Reign of Elizabeth* (1959), p. 355. Philip's return to Wilton: Collins, *Sidney*, vol. 1, p. 392.

⁓

For contemporary identifications of Stella see Who's Who above, and *Shepherd Knight*, pp. 181–3. Ringler dates the poems to 1582. Robertson suggests Penelope must have liked the identification. Most critics conclude *Astrophil and Stella* was an elaborate "conceit" inspired by Penelope, and possibly read by her, yet not strictly autobiographical. Many, however, accept that some romantic attachment existed and for Philip at least it may have been deeply emotional. But there is no external evidence, except Philip's deathbed "confession" (see Chapter 12), and no justification for claims that they had an affair: "openly to cuckold", *Elizabethan Icarus*, p. 23. Indeed, *Courtier Poet* points to Philip's stronger relationships with men.

Quotations from *Astrophil and Stella*: "Rich in all beauties" – sonnet 37; "aught so fair" – sonnet 21; "That whereas black" – sonnet 7; "Where roses gules" – sonnet 13; Sidney's arrow – sonnet 65; "that rich fool" – sonnet 24; "rich, meaning my Stella's name" – sonnet 35; "with how sad steps" – sonnet 31; "Stella looked on" – sonnet 41; "coachman" – sonnet 105; the river trip – sonnet 103; "I saw and liked"

– sonnet 2; "Oh sweet kiss" – song II; "I never more will bite" – sonnet 82; "wants horns" – sonnet 78.

A first meeting between Philip and Penelope is possible not only in 1575 at Chartley (see Chapter 5), but following Philip's return from Europe in June 1577 (*Courtier Poet*, p. 133), when Penelope and Lettice were hunting at Kenilworth, since Philip is also mentioned in the game book that year.

Various musical settings are noted by Hudson, *Penelope as Stella*, p. 566.

~

For Mountjoy's assertions regarding Penelope's forced marriage see Chapter 27.

Lord Rich as "rough and uncourtly": *Devereux Lives*, vol. I, p. 153; "a little man": *Shepherd Knight*, p. 191; and "did not make his mark": *Poor Penelope*, p. 42.

Privy council actions against Lord Rich: APC 1581–2, pp. 297, 298; and APC 1588 pp. 318–9.

Lord Rich's attendance as a JP is shown in J. S. Cockburn, *Calendar of Assize Records Essex Indictments Elizabeth I* (1978) and *Essex Record Office Q/SR 100/2*. "Lady Rich widow" is named in the Michaelmas quarter sessions, 26 September 1588.

Leighs (also named Leez, and still referred to as a priory): Nichols (1823), vol. 1, p. 99; Maurice Howard, *The Early Tudor Country House* (1987), pp. 148–51; A. W. Clapham, "The Augustinian Priory of Little Leez and Mansion of Leez Priory", *Transactions of the Essex Archaeological Society*, NS 13 (1915), pp. 200–217; and A. L. Rowse, *Ralegh and the Throckmortons* (1962), p. 125.

Penelope's letter: "Since I first knew you" is Hotman Letters no. 43, to her "*très chère servante*" Jeanne de Saint-Martin. For the Hotmans and the Hotman Letters see p. 281; Chapter 11 notes; and Margetts, "Hilliard's lost miniatures".

The accusation "emotional cripples" is in *Elizabethan Icarus*, p. 23.

Penelope's rooms at Wanstead: see inventories listed in Chapter 8 notes.

~

The births of Penelope's first two children are unrecorded, and presumably occurred at Leighs.

Lettice's comment, "if you had come this night": Essex Letter Book no. 33. For John Florio's dedication to her see Chapter 19.

The January 1584 gift list: BL Egerton MS 3052.

Count Laski: *Ralegh and the Throckmortons*, chapter VI; and Arthur's marriage, p. 98.

Chapter 11

"Your sister that most infinitely loves you", Penelope Rich, Essex Letter Book no. 50 (undated); quoted from BL Additional MS 4124, f.89.

On Dorothy's marriage: Strype, p.130 and Addition 8; *Courtier Poet*, pp. 227–8; and BL Lansdowne MS 72, f.10–11. Thomas Perrot's "service, zeal and love": CSP Dom 1581–1590, p. 114. On Sir John see *Bastard Prince*, p. xi, and Chapter 16 below.

Leicester's will: Adams, "Papers of Robert Dudley, III", p. 3; and *Courtier Poet*, p. 227.

Broxbourne was the home of Sir Henry Cock, Sheriff of Hertfordshire. *Brenan's House of Percy*, vol. II, p. 52, states Dorothy was banished there by Leicester for refusing his marriage plans for her. Her letters on Thomas's imprisonment and money are BL Lansdowne MS 39, f.172 and 181.

Philip's marriage settlement: HMC 77, De L'Isle and Dudley MS, vol. I, p. 273.
Mary Queen of Scots's comment, "beyond all reason": Guy, p. 454.

~

Essex's movements (York, Lamphey, Chartley) can be pieced together from his accounts and letters: DE vol. V; FSL Bagot Papers; *Broughton Devereux Papers*; and "£45.7.9" is HMC 58, Bath V, p. 251.
Baron Denbigh: the portrait "quite defaced": HMC 58, Bath V, p. 22; his death: Adams, "Papers of Robert Dudley, III", p. 3, note 11; and his illness is dealt with in *Leicester's Commonwealth*, ed. D. C. Peck (1985), p. 89. *ODNB*/Lettice Dudley deals with the question of his stature; and "a noble imp of great virtue" is in *A Tract on the Succession to the Crown, by Sir John Harington, 1602*, ed. C. R. Markham (1880), p. 41
Leicester's letter, "to comfort my sorrowful wife": Wilson, *Sweet Robin*, p. 245; and H. Nicolas, *Memoirs of the Life and Times of Sir Christopher Hatton* (1845). For "upon the late death" see CSP Dom 1581–90, pp. 190–91. Leicester's letter "I do thank you" is HMC 58, Bath V, Talbot Papers, p. 50; and "that it pleased you so friendly" is CSP Dom 1581–90, p. 192.
Leicester's wills are itemized above, and I am grateful to Dr Simon Adams for pointing out that while in 1582 Philip was named heir (in the event of Denbigh's death), the July 1584 settlement dealt only with Lettice's jointure; the 1586 settlement was in favour of his "base" son; and his final will was made 1587.

~

Essex's visits to York, Lamphey and Chartley are deduced as above; and his letter "careless of mine own estate" is BL Additional MS 32092, f.48. Lettice's "Your sister threatens revenge" is Essex Letter Book no. 40 (undated). For the "fantastical" letters see Other Documents: Bodleian Library and British Library.

~

Lord Rich's gift at New Year 1585: detailed by Margetts, "Stella Britanna", p. 271, from Folger MS Z.d.16.
Visit to Kenilworth by Leicester and Lettice: *ODNB*/Robert Dudley.
Essex's arrival at Court: *Polarisation*, p. 37. "Your father hath not left you": FSL L.a. 566.
Elizabeth Sidney's date of baptism is usually given as 20 November (*Courtier Poet*, p. 279 and others) but *The Registers of St Olave Hart Street, London, 1563–1700*, ed. W. B. Bannerman, Harleian Society Registers, vol. 46 (1916), p. 12, states: "15 November, Elizabeth, daughter of Sir Philip Sidney."
Lord Rich's command of a troop of fifty lances: *ODNB*/Robert Rich.
On Jean Hotman see: Ringler, p. 441, and D. Baird Smith, "Jean de Villiers Hotman", *Scottish Historical Review*, 14 (1917). Born 1552, Jean was the Huguenot son of the famous jurist and author François Hotman. He came under Calvin's influence on the Continent and studied law before arriving at Oxford in 1581. He soon became a secretary to Leicester and one of the highly intellectual circle around William Camden. After his marriage to Penelope's lady companion, Jeanne, and Leicester's death in 1588, he became Penelope's emissary to King James (see Chapter 13) and returned to France with Jeanne late in 1590. Speculation surrounds the identity of "ma clarté", my light, in a few of Penelope's letters to the Hotmans. Some suggest it is Charles Blount, others King James, but the references are too slight to be revealing.

Chapter 12

"The world was never so dangerous", Lord Leicester to Elizabeth, 21 November 1587; Murdin, *State Papers*, p. 591.

Anne Bagot's marriage: see Chapter 6.

Essex's instruction to "remove all bedding", and Sir Francis's response: *Devereux Lives*, vol. 1, p. 172ff.

On the Babington Plot, Robert Poley, Gilbert Gifford, etc., see Haynes, *Secret Services*, and Read, *Walsingham*, vol. 2. The Bagot–Phelippes letters, "hunting afoot": FSL L.a.. 691–698.

~

Leicester's comment, "There is never a man here": is CSP Foreign 1585–6, p. 53.

For the lengthy correspondence, "You may assure yourself" and "servant to Sir Philip", etc., see Murdin, *State Papers*, pp. 439–528.

On Philip Sidney's death and "confession": see Robertson, "Philip Sidney and Lady Penelope Rich"; and Duncan-Jones, "Sidney, Stella and Lady Rich", note 9.

~

Poor Penelope, p. 63, gives 19 March 1587 as the birth date for Robert Rich, though the *ODNB* gives May or June. Essex's New Year gift, January 1587, is detailed by Nichols (1823), vol. II, p. 498.

On Elizabeth's relationship with Essex see "When she is abroad", FSL L.a. 39; "lewd cravings": Smith, *William Cecil*, p. 242; and "Essex intruded himself": Loades, *Tudor Court*, p. 165.

The North Hall episode, "this disgrace both to me and my sister", is told by Essex: BLO Tanner MS 76, f.29; reprinted in *Goodman's Court of King James*, vol. 2, p. 1.

New Year gift roll for January 1588: usually cited as BL Additional MS 8159 but queried by Margetts, "Stella Britanna", p.305.

~

One of the most recent Armada accounts is J. Barratt, *Armada 1588* (2005). Leicester's request for Lord Rich's cooperation, "Though he be no man of war": CSP Dom 1581–90, p. 511.

"The queen being at dinner": HMC 58, Bath V, p. 213; and Wilson, *Sweet Robin*, p. 300.

On Elizabeth's lodgings see M. Christy, "Queen Elizabeth's visit to Tilbury in 1588", *English Historical Review*, 34 (1919); suggesting she used Belhouse (also known as Belhus), home of the Barrett family, at Aveley on the second night. Edward Barrett I (d. 1585, leaving a second wife) was succeeded by his grandson, Edward II, whose widowed mother Christian (née Mildmay) was Walsingham's niece. I am obliged to Dr Margetts for information that it seems to have been used by Edward I's widow. For Penelope at Belhouse see Chapter 20.

"I am come amongst you": quoted from J. E. Neale, *Queen Elizabeth I* (1934), p. 302.

~

Leicester's letter, "a great bellied lady", is BL Lansdowne MS 57, f.108; and "your poor old servant" is in Wilson, *Sweet Robin*, pp. 301–2.

"I would have been glad" is BL Lansdowne MS 57, f.118. Essex was granted York House early 1588 (*Polarisation*, p. 72) and Penelope was clearly using it by September. Her letter to Jeanne a year later shows she used it rather than the Richs'

town house at St Bartholomew's. Elizabeth's takeover of Leicester House is sometimes dated immediately after Leicester's death, but Kingsford, "Essex House",
suggests it was seized early 1590, when the April inventory was taken; a contents'
sale was held in June; and in November (HMC 58, Bath V, p. 224) it was returned
to Lettice.

The brief life and christening of Penelope's third daughter is evidenced by Elizabeth's
christening gift: Nichols (1788), vol. II, p. 115; and by two poems, "A calculation
of the nativity of the Lady's Rich's daughter born upon Friday in the year 1588",
and "Of the death of my Lady Rich's daughter", see *Poems of Henry Constable*, p.
157 and 170. There is no note of the baby's name, but with the queen as
godmother she was likely to be named Elizabeth. See also Chapters 13 and 19.

Penelope's letter "*amorous no more*": Hotman Letters no. 46.

Chapter 13

"The fineness of her wit, the invention, and well writing", Thomas Fowler reporting
King James VI of Scotland's comments on Penelope's letters, 1589; Cecil Papers,
vol. 18, pp. 50–60.

The date of Lettice's marriage is uncertain: *ODNB*/Christopher Blount cites gossip
in Paris in May which indicates it took place in March, before the expedition to
Portugal, though it has often been dated later.

"There is a good deal": Craik, vol. 1, pp. 127–47. Craik, and Falls, *Irish Wars*, p. 281,
correctly identified Christopher as the son of Sir Thomas Blount, not a younger
brother of Charles Blount (eighth Baron Mountjoy). See more on the Blount
family in Chapter 14.

ODNB/Lettice Dudley deals with rumours of poison. The claim that Sir Christopher
sold off Lettice's jewels – "a clock of diamonds ... a great table diamond ... How
he bestoweth them God knows" – is in Croke, p. 250; but Lettice was playing the
sympathy card and it may not be reliable. Nor is "unhappy choice": *Polarisation*,
p. 34.

Thomas Fowler's theft and flight: HMC 58, Bath V, p. 220.

Poley was "no fool": Haynes, *Secret Services*, p. 115. Haynes casts doubt on Poley's
Catholicism, despite Margaret Poley (Christopher's mother) being a well-known
Catholic. Poley's part in Marlowe's murder is examined in numerous studies.

~

Essex's letter, "unconstancy", etc., is one of his "fantastical" letters: BLO Misc. MSS
Don.c.188.

He "took horse in St James's Park": FSL L.a. 40.

Sir Roger Williams and the *Swiftsure* are detailed in *Polarisation*, pp. 93, 148; and on
Williams's will see Collins, *Sidney*, vol. 1, p. 377.

Henry Wotton's comment "strangled almost in the cradle": is in his *Reliquiae
Wottonianae* (1651).

~

The warrant to search "the house at Bishopsgate of Thomas Fowler": HMC 58, Bath
V, p. 220.

A "nickname for everyone": Cecil Papers, vol. 18, pp. 50–60; HMC 9, Cecil, vol.
III, pp. 434–43.

Penelope's letter "*une responce pour le prince*": Hotman Letters no. 44.

On Nicholas Hilliard's portraits: see: K. Coombs, *The Portrait Miniature in England* (2005); and Margetts, "Hilliard's lost miniatures". The miniature *Portrait of a Lady, Possibly Lady Rich c. 1590* (in Her Majesty The Queen's Collection, Windsor) suggests at least one has survived, and Karen Hearn of Tate Britain sees no reason to doubt the identification. On Hilliard's connection with the Knollys and Dudley families: N. Blakiston, "Nicholas Hilliard and the Court", *Burlington Magazine*, 96 (1954), and M. Edmond, *Hilliard and Oliver* (1983). Hilliard's children Lettice, Penelope and Robert (b. 1579–88) are believed to be the godchildren of Lady Leicester, Penelope and Essex.

"To Mr Hilliard upon occasion": *Poems of Henry Constable*, p. 158. On Constable see also: L. I. Guiney, *Recusant Poets* (1938), and A. Haynes, *The Gunpowder Plot* (1994), pp. 12–18.

There is no reason to think the Rialta letters were inconsequential (*Poor Penelope*, p. 83, and others). "There were many things ... vindictively": Craik, p. 260.

On efforts to link Essex to the Catholic "Dacre Plot": P. Reid, *The King's Council in the North* (1975), pp. 226–30. James's reference to the trouble the Rialta letters caused Essex is in *Polarisation*, p. 91.

~

Essex's marriage is usually dated early 1590 (*Polarisation*, pp. 54, 86–7, 89–90), since Elizabeth's anger at it appeared to erupt in autumn 1590 and his first child was born in January 1591 (FSL L.a. 258). But there are arguments for an earlier date: Read, *Walsingham*, vol. 3, p. 170, suggested it was soon after Philip's funeral (1587). In addition, DE box V, 68, dated May 1587 (see Chapter 3 notes) is Essex's discharge from any fine (past or future) for marrying as a minor, on the grounds that his knighthood (September 1586) had raised him to his majority. And, as Dr Margetts has pointed out, PRO WARD 9/221 f.217 (November 1588) is Frances's first payment for a licence "to marry at her pleasure". Thus by the end of 1588 both had taken steps to free themselves for marriage, and the date of their wedding may be 1589.

On Essex as Philip's political heir and the marriage that "disparaged the dignity of the house" see *Polarisation*, p. 54. For Philip's Catholic sympathies see Chapter 9. Frances's willingness to "live very retired": *Illustrations of British History*, ed. E. Lodge, 3 vols (1838), vol. II, p. 422.

~

Wat's marriage: *Lady Hoby's Diary*, pp. xix–xxi; and *Puritan Earl*, p. 55.

"I have never been so cross with him": Hotman Letters no. 44; dated to 1589 by reference to King James, "*le prince câché*".

Lettice at Leicester House, March 1590, and Essex's letters to her: HMC 58, Bath V, p. 223.

The description of Elizabeth, "wrinkled, her eyes small", is by Paul Hentzner (1598), *England as Seen by Foreigners*, p. 103.

Penelope's greetings to Buzanval: Hotman Letters no. 46; and her instructions to Jean: Hotman Letters no. 45.

For Henry Rich's baptism, 19 August 1590, at St Mary's, Stratford-le-Bow: Cockayne, vol. VI, p. 538; and Penelope was "churched": *Ralegh and the Throckmortons*, p. 125.

Notes, Quotes and Sources

Part III Love at Last 1590–1601

Chapter 14

"Comes Sir Charles Blount, Rich in his colours", George Peele, *Polyhymnia* (1590); *The Life and Minor Works of George Peele*, ed. C. T. Prouty (1952), vol. I, p. 231.

On Accession Day: Loades, *Tudor Court*, p. 102ff ; Young, *Tudor and Jacobean Tournaments*; and *Polarisation*, pp. 144–6.

Peele's poem (echoing Philip Sidney's sonnet 37, see Chapter 10) is usually taken to mean that Charles wore Penelope's colours, owing to the punning use of "Rich". But it is simplistic to read the pun into the first line as well as the repetitions; and neither the Rich nor Devereux colours were blue (azure) and gold (or). Burke's *Heraldry and Genealogy of the Extinct and Dormant Peerage* shows both included red (gules). The Sidney crest, however, was a gold arrowhead on a blue ground and Philip frequently appeared in blue and gold. Charles's declaration was more subtle than wearing Penelope's colours. In the multi-layered language of the tilt, by wearing colours commonly associated with Philip, whose poetry declared him to be Penelope's admirer, Charles was assuming the role of her champion. It is unlikely he would have made a public declaration that Penelope was at that time committing adultery.

∽

Blount family background: Jones, *Mountjoy*; Croke; and *Bastard Prince*.

The "philosopher's stone", and "untimely prodigality": *Fragmenta Regalia*, pp. 281–7; and CSP Dom 1581–90, pp. 58, 378. Some family records show Sir Walter of Barton Blount (d. 1403) as the son not of Isolda but of Sir John's second wife, Eleanor Beauchamp. Croke relies heavily on Naunton and on Moryson's *Itinerary*. On the legal dispute see *Puritan Earl*, pp. 86–7; and CSP Dom 1581–90, p. 26. Charles's birth place is assumed to be Canford Manor, inherited by his father from Gertrude, Marchioness of Exeter.

Personal details, e.g. "brown hair, sweet face": Moryson and Naunton.

The "bullets are taken out": CSP For 1583–8, pp. 84–5. His presence on Drake's ship: H. Kelsey, *Sir Francis Drake* (1998), p. 336. The date of the chess-piece quarrel is uncertain and is sometimes placed earlier in the 1580s, but it cannot pre-date 1587, as the two men did not overlap at Court until after Charles's return from the Netherlands, except briefly in autumn 1585 when Essex was only nineteen.

Charles as "a mirror image of Essex": Ioppolo.

∽

On Frances's "slight infertility" see *Courtier Poet*, p. 253. Penelope and the Walsinghams' staff: Collins, *Sidney*, vol. I, p. 390. "The Countess of Essex doth within eight days": FSL L.a. 258. The birth place, date and baptism are noted in Bannerman, *Registers of St Olave*, p. 14.

"When birds do sing": Shakespeare, *As You Like It* (1599).

Charles at Dover: Cockayne, vol. IX, p. 344.

Wanstead: see Chapters 7 and 13. The transactions Essex initiated with Lettice (1590) finally resulted in a transfer in 1593. Entertainment costs at Wanstead: HMC 58, Bath V, p. 254.

Chapter 15

"O mistress mine! Where are you roaming?" Shakespeare, *Twelfth Night*, c. 1599.

Lord Rich at Quarter Sessions: see Chapter 10 and Cockburn. The case of William Chapman, 7 December 1590: Q/SR 115/33; and the couple "together at one time": Q/SR 98/80.

For Charles's account of Penelope's marriage see Chapter 27.

"Captain General of the English forces": DE box V, 74.

Wat's marriage: see Chapter 13; and V. A. Wilson, *Society Women of Shakespeare's Time* (1924), pp. 78–9.

Frances's letter: "your going away" is HMC 9, Cecil, vol. IV, p. 169.

For Elizabeth Southwell, see below.

Arthur Throckmorton's visit to Leighs: pp. 124–7 of *Ralegh and the Throckmortons*, based on *The Diary of Arthur Throckmorton 1578–1613*, 3 vols, Canterbury Cathedral Archives CCA-U85/38/14.

Bess's "unmeetness yet to marry": A. Beer, *Bess: The Life of Lady Ralegh* (2004), p. 43.

Wat's death: *Carey's Memoirs*, pp. 25–6, and *Devereux Lives*, vol. 1, p. 231. The "late accident" and Elizabeth's letters: Murdin, *State Papers*, p. 651. Margaret's remarriage: FSL L.a. 265, and *Lady Hoby's Diary*, pp. xxii–xxiii.

~

Arthur's diary entry "*le jour quand je savoye*": *Ralegh and the Throckmortons*, p. 160. On Damerei, see Beer, pp. 56–66, and R. Lacey, *Sir Walter Ralegh* (1973), p. 167.

Burial of Lady Rich: FSL V.b. 194.

"I infinitely long to hear": Essex Letter Book no. 17.

Elizabeth Southwell: *Polarisation*, pp. 95, 320; and Chapter 20 below. Baptism of Frances's son Walter: *Polarisation*, p. 105, note 179, and p. 284, note 88.

Penelope's rooms at Leicester House see Chapter 8. Her daughter Penelope's date of birth: St Clement Danes parish registers (Westminster City Archives), vol. I, f.26, first noted in *Poor Penelope*, p. 86.

Ralegh's letter, "before any man living": Murdin, *State Papers*, pp. 663–4.

Anne Broughton's letter: FSL L.a. 224.

~

Essex as "a new man": FSL L.a. 45 and L.a. 267. The "plague increaseth": FSL L.a. 272. For the birth of Frances's baby, Penelope: *Polarisation*, p. 284.

Wanstead entertainment costs for the Vidame, May 1593: HMC 58, Bath V, p. 254.

Chapter 16

"Your Ladyship's flayed dog", Antonio Pérez, c. 1593; G. Ungerer, *A Spaniard in Elizabethan England: The Correspondence of Antonio Pérez's Exile*, 2 vols (1974), vol. 1, p. 80. I am indebted to Mara Prengler Hogg for translating the letters Pérez addressed to Penelope and Lettice, published in the original Spanish by Ungerer.

"Don Armado": Ungerer, vol. 2, argues he is a parody of Pérez, not of Ralegh; and *Love's Labour's Lost*, with its hunt scene, is partly based on Essex's politics and entertainment at Wanstead.

For Jorge de Montemayor's *Diana* see Chapter 19.

~

Essex came under pressure to vacate York House in 1592, see *Polarisation*, p. 131; and in 1593 had set up his secretariat in Essex House, see *Devereux Lives*, vol. 1, p. 307; and Adams, "Papers of Robert Dudley, III".

"I would you were well rid": LPL, Bacon MS 653, quoted from *Double Life of Dr Lopez*, p. 177.

Standen's letter: Ungerer, vol. 1, pp. 232–3.

Nicholas Clifford was the son of Earl Walter's sister Anne, and Henry Clifford, brother to the Earl of Cumberland. Nicholas was thus cousin to Cumberland's diarist daughter, Lady Anne Clifford, and to Penelope and Essex (who stayed with the Cliffords at Keyston when he was a student: *Polarisation*, p. 29).

Essex's summons to Dr Giffard: HMC 58, Bath V, p. 260.

~

"I have discovered": *Devereux Lives*, vol. 1, pp. 307–8.

The state of London: G. B. Harrison, *Elizabethan Journals*, 3 vols (1928–33), vol. I, p. 289; C. Haigh intro. to A. L. Rowse, *The England of Elizabeth* (2003), p. xix; Loades, *Tudor Court*, p. 87; *Polarisation*, p. 162, on anti-Semitism; Shapiro, pp. 8–9, 195 and p. 206 on authoritarianism and bad harvests.

~

Essex's expenses, debts, gambling and bills from Vanlore: HMC 58, Bath V, pp. 252, 257, 262. Also on gambling see Loades, *Tudor Court*, pp. 96, 190.

James's letter to Essex, "this long time": Birch, *Memoirs of Elizabeth*, vol. 1, p. 175.

See *Polarisation*, pp. 165–71, for "the whole nobility" and growing contact between Essex and James. Haynes, *Secret Services*, p. 117, details James's animosity to the Cecils. But the claim that the Cecils preferred other successors is refuted in Hurstfield, "Succession struggle".

~

On the Cecils' finances: L. Stone, *Family and Fortune* (1973), pp. 22, 40–41; Loades, *Tudor Court*, pp. 145–6; and *Polarisation*, p. 354, note 72, for Burghley's failure to correct corruption.

"Whether you have mistaken the queen": Murdin, *State Papers*, p. 655. "If we lived not in a cunning world": Essex Letter Book no. 45.

Lord Derby's illness, "like soot or rusty iron": L. De Lisle, *After Elizabeth* (2005), p. 30; and Thomson, *Shakespeare's Career*, p. 41. For Sir John Perrot, see *ODNB*.

On the vogue for Catholicism and Essex's connections: Haynes, *Gunpowder Plot*, p. 11; C. Haigh, *English Reformations* (1993), pp. 264–6; Wood, *Search of Shakespeare*, pp. 151–6. For Fr Alabaster see *Recusant Poets*; for Bushell see Wilson, *Secret Shakespeare*, p. 49; for Sir Griffin Markham see *After Elizabeth*, p. 177; and Chapters 19 and 26 below.

Chapter 17

"To lay bare what was deepest in her heart", Fr John Gerard, *The Autobiography of an Elizabethan*, trans. P. Caraman (1951), pp. 34–6.

"The queen and I will provide": quoted from Hogge, p. 66.

~

Father Gerard did not date his meetings with Penelope, but they must have occurred between December 1591 and April 1594. The most likely date is early 1594, when Hogge details the North End raid, pp. 212–21. See also: Haigh, *English Reformations*, and Thomson, *Shakespeare's Career*, pp. 18–20.

William Wiseman as a JP: Essex Record Office, Q/SR, 21 October 1592.

A "mischievous escapade": *Poor Penelope*, p. 109. To "receive, relieve, comfort": Hogge, p. 114.

For Shakespeare in Lancashire see E. Honigmann, *Shakespeare: The Lost Years* (1998).

Charles's assistance to Fr Southwell: Hogge, p. 190; and Wilson, *Secret Shakespeare*, p. 140. Wilson describes Charles as a Catholic "fellow-traveller", p. 159. On Sidney's Catholic sympathies: see Chapter 13.

For Mistress Deacon see Chapter 29.

~

"My Lady Rich hath not gone out her time": HMC De L'Isle and Dudley, vol. II, p. 152.

Charles's brother "hastened his death by debauchery": Falls, *Mountjoy*, p. 19. Mountjoy's inheritance: Cockayne, vol. IX, pp. 341–3; and Birch, *Memoirs of Elizabeth*, vol. II, p. 189. "'I confess I am poor": Jones, *Mountjoy*, p. 30.

~

Sir Thomas's will and death, February 1594: *Poor Penelope*, p. 94. Penelope Perrot grew up to be the wife of Robert Naunton.

For the Percy family see Who's Who above.

Chapter 18

"No man is more high and eminent", "R. Doleman", *A Conference about the Next Succession to the Crown of England* (printed in Antwerp, 1594).

For the Gray's Inn revels see *Gesta Grayorum 1688*, ed. W. W. Greg, Malone Society Reprints (1914); and Harrison, *Elizabethan Journals*, vol. II, p. 1. Penelope's attendance: *Poor Penelope*, p. 87.

Payment to the players at Dorothy's wedding: HMC 58, Bath V, p. 262.

~

Isabella's christening: St Clement Danes parish register (Westminster City Archives) vol. I, f.29, first noted by Margetts, "Stella Britanna", p. 406.

The visit to Cambridge: *Polarisation*, pp. 304–5.

Barbara Sidney's growing family included, in 1595, at least two sons and three daughters. Another son, Robert, was born in December 1595 and another daughter, Bridget, in January 1597. Barbara then joined Robert in Flushing for a year; but before and afterwards her friendship with Penelope flourished.

Essex's third son, Henry: Bannerman, *Registers of St Olave*, p. 17.

"Worthy Sir Robert": Cecil Papers, vol. 32, f.87 and others, as noted above.

Pérez's farewell dinner: HMC 58, Bath V, p. 262.

Mountjoy in Portsmouth and "your letters into Staffordshire": Essex Letter Book nos 55 and 53.

Penelope's visit to Lettice and the selection of the tapestries: Collins, *Sidney*, vol. I, pp. 347–86.

~

On the "Doleman" book: Hurstfield, "Succession struggle"; *Polarisation*, pp. 139–41, 145; *After Elizabeth*, pp. 31–4. Fraser, *Gunpowder Plot*, p. 6, assessed Essex as one of the nobles "in whose veins flowed a trickle of royal blood from previous dynasties". But that is an underestimate (see Chapter 3) and ignores their connection through Mary Boleyn. It has not always been ignored: David Hume, *History of England* (1822), vol. 5, p. 357: "Essex was descended by females [i.e. not his

Devereux ancestry] from the royal family; and some of his partisans had been so imprudent as to mention his name among those of other pretenders to the crown."

Accession Day: "Upstaging the Queen: the Earl of Essex, Francis Bacon and the Accession Day celebrations of 1595", in *The Politics of the Stuart Court Masque*, eds D. Bevington and P. Holbrook (1998).

~

Barbara's visit to Court: Collins, *Sidney*, vol. I, p. 366, and the christening arrangements, pp. 371–86.

Harington's *Tract on the Succession to the Crown*, p. 41, said Essex was upset by Huntingdon's death.

Chapter 19

"Sweet Thames, run softly, till I end my song", Edmund Spenser, *Prothalamion*, 1596.

On Essex/Leicester House see Kingsford and Adams, "Papers of Robert Dudley". For the double wedding: *Polarisation*, p. 286.

On Barnfield see T. W. N. Parker, *Proportional Form in the Sonnets of the Sidney Circle: Loving in Truth* (1998), pp. 205–6, note 33.

Musical sources: *My Lady Rich – Her Tears and Joy*, recorded by Emily Van Evera and Christopher Morrongiello, Heartsease Productions (2005) includes: *Corranto Lady Rich* (*Fitzwilliam Virginal Book*) and *A la volta Mistress Lettice Rich* (*Margaret Board Lute Book*).

See also: L. M. Ruff and D. Arnold Wilson, "The madrigal, the lute song and Elizabethan politics", *Past and Present*, 44 (August 1969); and J. L. Smith, "Music and late Elizabethan politics: the identification of Oriana and Diana", *Journal of the American Musicological Society* (December 2005), naming Penelope as Thomas Morley's "Diana" in his "Oriana" madrigals.

On Byrd, who "made music with Jesuits": Bossy, *Giordano Bruno*, p. 121; and on Tessier see Duncan-Jones, "Sidney, Stella and Lady Rich", pp. 184–9.

John Dowland's work is detailed by Ruff and Wilson, and by Smith, as above; see also *ODNB*.

John Florio: *The Essays of Michael de Montaigne as translated by John Florio*, 3 vols (1908). Volume 2 dedication was jointly to her niece (Philip Sidney's daughter Elizabeth) and to "truly richest Lady Rich".

For Bartholomew Yong see *Montemayor's Diana etc. Translated by Yong*, ed. J. M. Kennedy (1968). Yong's translation remained in MSS until 1598, when it was printed with a lengthy dedication to Penelope.

Henry Constable: see Chapters 12 and 13. Penelope's message for Constable, in her letter to Jean Hotman (Hotman Letters no. 46) that he should be "amorous no more", has prompted the idea that he was in love with her; but Parker, *Proportional Form*, p. 151, denies it was genuine passion. Constable went abroad under suspicion of treason, shortly after his mission with the Rialta letters, and converted to the "old faith".

On Nicholas Hilliard: see Chapter 13; and on John Coprario, John Ford and Samuel Daniel see Chapter 28.

"the star of Britain, Penelope" is quoted from Falls, *Mountjoy*, p. 224; and "To descant on thy name" from *Poor Penelope*, p. 201.

"Who is it that says most": William Shakespeare, *Sonnets to Mr W. H.*, number 84. On the playhouse as a forum for political comment see Thomson, *Shakespeare's Career*, p. 32; and on Shakespeare siding with Essex, including the Falstaff episode, see Shapiro, pp. 19–21. Shakespeare's character Sir John Oldcastle (*Henry IV/i*) offended Lord Cobham because an earlier Lord Cobham was named Oldcastle. In his next play, *The Merry Wives of Windsor*, Shakespeare renamed the character Falstaff.

Southampton's move into the Essex House circle is often put around 1598; but Collins, *Sidney*, vol. 1, p. 348, shows his relationship with Penelope's and Essex's cousin, Elizabeth Vernon, dates from 1595.

Love's Labour's Lost: see Ungerer, vol. 2, p. 377ff.

Chapter 20

"With best forewinds", Elizabeth I, 1596, quoted from Strachey, *Elizabeth and Essex*, p. 104.

Penelope's letter, "my brother's own troubles": Cecil Papers, vol. 33, f.67.

Rumours of "a mighty army the King of Spain made": *List and Analysis of State Papers Foreign, 1596*, ed. R. B. Wernham (2000), p. 222.

Commissions to Essex: DE box V, 80, and box 81 for Calais.

Drake "slung atween the roundshot": *Drake's Drum*, Sir Henry Newbolt (1897).

Mountjoy did not go on the Cadiz trip: Jones, *Mountjoy*, pp. 204–5, explains how the confusion arose. Lord Rich did not go either, though he advanced £1,000 towards it and intended to go: *ODNB*/Robert Rich.

"I must yield you many thanks": Cecil Papers, vol. 40, f42; and "while I am in this solitary place": LPL Bacon MS 657, f.61. Penelope was probably at Leighs or Wanstead, to where Lord Rich had returned by July.

Pérez's return to England and "three sisters and goddesses": Ungerer, *Pérez*, vol. 1, pp. 90–91.

"If this force were going to France": Essex Letter Book no. 82.

On Elizabeth's anger (May 1595), at learning Southwell's bastard was Essex's son: *Polarisation*, pp. 95–6 and pp. 319–20. Frances's son Henry buried at All Hallows, 7 May 1596: *Polarisation*, p. 284, note 88.

~

"There is not a braver man": quoted from Strachey, *Elizabeth and Essex*, p. 106.

Penelope's letters, "when you hear any more news", and "the happy news": Cecil Papers, vol. 43, f.30, and vol. 48, f.49.

For details of the Knollys tomb: Varlow, "Latin dictionary" (and see Illustrations). Churchyard's epitaph, "A Sad and Solemn Funeral of the right Hon. Sir Francis Knowles" (1596): *Frondes Canucae* (repr. 1816).

The changing officers are listed: Loades, *Tudor Court*, appendix II. The treasurership, vacated in July 1596 by the death of Sir Francis Knollys, went to Lord North for a year, and Sir Francis's son William became comptroller of the household and a member of the council (in 1602 he finally became treasurer). The job of chamberlain, vacated in July 1596 by the death of Lord Hunsdon, went to William Brooke/Lord Cobham, instead of to Hunsdon's son, George Carey. But Brooke's death, March 1597, vacated the post again and George (now Lord Hunsdon) got it. Brooke's son Henry (now Lord Cobham) got Lord Warden of the Cinque Ports, which Essex wanted for himself or Robert Sidney.

The "most complete and dramatic victory": *ODNB*/Robert Devereux. "Great England's glory": Edmund Spenser, *Prothalamion*, 1596.

"I commend my duty unto you": Birch, *Memoirs of Elizabeth*, vol. II, pp. 50–51.

Essex: "hath with the bright beams of his valour": Black, *Reign of Elizabeth*, p. 423.

His "courtship to the common people": William Shakespeare, *Julius Caesar*, 1599.

Mountjoy's orders and warnings: APC 1586–1600, pp. 122, 141, 282, 287.

Mountjoy "Rich": in the absence of birth records for the three sons named in Lord Mountjoy's will – Mountjoy (his heir, later Earl of Newport), St John and Charles – the dates must be speculative. Falls, *Mountjoy*, pp. 229–31, suggested young Mountjoy was born before the end of 1596, and was about ten when his father died in April 1606, and there seems no reason to disagree, given that Pérez knew Penelope was pregnant in March, and there is no evidence the pregnancy failed. The latest date for his birth would be November 1596 and the earliest, as Dr Margetts has pointed out, is 2 July, because he was still under twenty-one on 1 July 1617 (evidenced by PRO: STAC 8/47/13). See also Chapter 21, concerning the birth of Scipio.

∽

Lord Rich in France, see: Wernham, *State Papers Foreign 1596*, pp. 198–9; Ungerer, vol. 1, p. 294, for his letter from Rouen; and Essex Letter Book no. 51 for his letter to Essex from Belhouse, where he and Penelope were staying in December, and Penelope stayed again September 1597.

∽

Lady Bacon's letter, "a nobleman's wife": Birch, *Memoirs of Elizabeth*, vol. II, p. 218. Essex's reply: LPL Bacon MS 660, f.281. The lady is believed to be Lady Derby: *Polarisation*, pp. 320–21.

Edward Jones, "a saucy fellow": Shapiro, p. 36.

Chapter 21

"The General of our Gracious Empress", William Shakespeare, *Henry V*, 1599.

Yong's description of Penelope attending revels at Middle Temple: Kennedy, *Montemeyor's Diana*, p. 3. The rest of the events of 1597–8 are drawn from previous principal sources, particularly Shapiro for the political implications of Shakespeare's plays, e.g. *Henry V*, and the dedication of Hayward's *History of Henry IV* to Essex. For Essex's illness see G. B. Harrison, *The Life and Death of Robert Devereux, Earl of Essex* (1937); and *The Letters of John Chamberlain*, ed. N. E. McClure, 2 vols (1939).

"Worthy brother" and "This banishment": Essex Letter Book nos 49 and 52.

∽

Penelope's letter, "a lady and friend of yours": Cecil Papers, vol. 55, f.55.

"You can hardly imagine my dear sweet son": BL Additional MS 4124, f.80.

For the baptism of Scipio (first noted in *Poor Penelope*, p. 80) see St Clement Danes parish register (Westminster City Archives). As there are no further references to him, he may have died young. Alternatively, as Margetts, "Stella Britanna", p. 406, speculates, Scipio may have been another name for one of the three sons named in Mountjoy's will; and Margetts suggests it was Mountjoy. The name Scipio was occasionally used for both Essex and Lord Mountjoy, but more commonly for Essex (e.g. Thomas Churchyard's *Fortunate Farewell* to Essex – "Now Scipio sails" to Ireland, printed in Nichols, vol. II). It is understandable that a boy would drop the name after Essex's execution (1601); but since young Mountjoy was more likely to have been born in 1596, if Scipio was one of the three sons it is probably St John.

~

Lettice's letters, "a winter's journey" and "a country life is fittest"; and "the Wizard Earl's" "recompensed her last lost": Essex Letter Book nos 39, 24, 8 and 9.

Penelope's visit to Chartley: FSL L.a. 911.

"I cannot be quiet till I know"; "I fear the longer your lordship doth persist"; "Noble brother I long to know", and "Dear Brother": Essex Letter Book nos 38, 43, 10 and 16.

Penelope's letter to "Good Mr Downhall": Cecil Papers, vol. 206, f.95.

~

Wanstead was sold to Mountjoy in December (*Polarisation*, p. 130) and on 15 March Essex removed his goods to Essex House: FSL G.b.4 inventory.

Essex's new will: DE box VI, 92. His departure is described in Falls, *Irish Wars*, p. 229; and his stop at Drayton, 3 April, is *Devereux Lives*, vol. II, pp. 18–19.

"I did as plainly see": Strachey, *Elizabeth and Essex*, p. 198.

Penelope to Dr Julius Caesar: BL Additional MS 12506, f.406.

See Cecil Papers for: "exceeding fair and well", vol. 99, f.167; "to make you merry", vol. 100, f.91; "therefore go to him she needs must", vol. 101, f.16; and "Lord Rich doth so importune me", vol. 101, f.25.

Mountjoy's warning "against all intended mischiefs": Jones, *Mountjoy*, p. 46.

The death of young Penelope: Ungerer, vol. 1, p. 88.

Chapter 22

"We that are not of the council do see no hope", Lord Mountjoy, 1599; *Cabala, sive Scrinia Sacra, Mysteries of State and Government* (1654).

Essex in Ireland: J. Bardon, *A History of Ulster* (2005) as well as Falls, *Irish Wars*. Elizabeth's instructions, criticism and arguments with him: Brewer and Bullen, *Carew MSS*, 1589–1600, pp. 314–25. Essex's return to Nonsuch, followed by the birth of Frances's baby: Collins, *Sidney*, vol. II, pp. 127, 130, 133–4. Many of Essex's letters are in DE vol. VII, f.101–147. His audience with Elizabeth at Nonsuch was not his last (as often claimed); see Trew's letter 29 November: FSL L.a. 912.

~

S. Brigden, *New Worlds, Lost Worlds: The Rule of the Tudors* (2000), pp. 347–50, is a useful summary of the events of October 1599–February 1601, including Donne's "no more missed here than the angels". For contemporary accounts: Collins, *Sidney*, vol. II, includes Elizabeth's Christmas, p. 154. Birch, *Memoirs of Elizabeth*, vol. II, has Essex's refusal to attend council and Penelope's visit to Court, pp. 440–41. HMC 58, Bath V, pp. 266–82, has Anthony Bacon's letter to Essex. CSP Dom 1598–1601, p. 365, notes the tolling of St Clement Danes bell. Nichols (1823), vol. III, p. 461, lists Elizabeth's New Year gifts.

Penelope's letters: Cecil Papers, vol. 75, f.83; vol. 68, f.10; and vol. 178, f.117. Her letter to Elizabeth exists in many copies. One (BL Stowe MS 150, f.140) is dated 1 January 1599 (old style, i.e. 1600), but other evidence places it later in the month, and Ioppolo, "Reading Penelope Rich", suggests it was written by Essex.

On Penelope's interrogations (January–March 1600): Rawson, p. 228, is the only source for "what I meant I wrote", but gives no reference. Ringler, p. 443, cites Huntington MS HM 102, f.15 as source for her spirited defence (see Other Documents, above). Penelope's movements and escape "to Leighs": Collins, *Sidney*, vol. II, pp. 161–82; *Chamberlain's Letters*, vol. I, p. 86; and Dudley Carleton's letters: CSP Dom 1598–1601, pp. 392, 414.

~

The "greatest English soldier of the period": Falls, *Irish Wars*, p. 7. The plot to release Essex from captivity, and Mountjoy's involvement in Essex's plans were revealed during interrogations in February 1601, outlined in Jones, *Mountjoy*, p. 96; and Falls, *Irish Wars*, including Mountjoy's promise to bring the army over from Ireland, p. 279.

~

Charles Danvers's visit to Penelope (May) is in Collins, *Sidney*, II, p. 197; and "interpret her riddles" is in *Chamberlain's Letters*, vol. I, pp. 95–6.

Essex's hearing at York House (June), including Penelope's "saucy, malapert" letter (described by Moryson, *Itinerary*, vol. 2, p. 314) is in HMC 58, Bath V, pp. 269–76. Buckhurst's report to Cecil: CSP Ireland 1600, p. 346; and Cecil's response "You may tell her ladyship": HMC 9, Cecil, vol. X, pp. 167–8, from a much amended draft, Cecil Papers, vol. 181, f.62.

Essex and Penelope "given their freedom" and Essex's return to Essex House: *Devereux Lives*, vol. 2, pp. 116, 134. Lord Rich's illness is only evidenced by Whyte's letter: Collins, *Sidney*, vol. II, p. 215.

The envoy to James who was put in the Tower was Henry Lee: Shapiro, pp. 316–17. Southampton's visit to Leighs is noted by G. P. V. Akrigg, *Shakespeare and the Earl of Southampton* (1968), p. 107.

Penelope "violated her husband's bed": Camden, vol. 4, p. 171.

Chapter 23

"He wore the crown in his heart", Henry Percy, ninth Earl of Northumberland, 1602–3; "Correspondence of King James VI of Scotland with Sir Robert Cecil and others in England", ed. J. Bruce, *Camden Society* (1861), p. 66.

Lady Hoby's Diary, 8 January 1601, p. 135. For "the queen's harsh letters" see *The Court of King James the First by Dr G. Goodman*, ed. J. S. Brewer, 2 vols (1839), vol. I, p. 157.

Elizabeth calls Ralegh "worse than cat and dog": FSL L.a. 6.

The Drury House meeting and performance of *Richard II*: Wood, *Search of Shakespeare*, p. 233ff; and Shapiro, p. 135ff, for political relevance of the play.

Statements by Essex's fellow conspirators are published in several sources: Spedding, *Bacon*, vol. II, pp. 167–336; Bruce, "Correspondence of King James", appendix; CSP Dom 1598–1601, p. 548ff; and CSP Dom 1601–3, pp. 1–19. HMC 58, Bath V, pp. 277–82, is an account of 8 February.

The conspirators named at Essex House: CSP Dom 1598–1601, p. 572, included Sir Robert Vernon (brother of Penelope's cousin Elizabeth). Sir Henry Bromley's summons by Penelope is CSP Dom 1601–3, p. 4; which indicates she spent the night at Walsingham House and returned to Essex House on Sunday morning.

The Earl of Bedford's evidence: HMC 9, Cecil, vol. XI, p. 51. Sir John Davies, left at Essex House with Penelope and the hostages: CSP Dom 1598–1601, p. 548. For Georges's meeting with Ralegh: *Ralegh and the Throckmortons*, p. 220. And L. Stone, *The Crisis of the Aristocracy*, pp. 438–6, on the rebels' financial problems.

~

The list of rebels, HMC 9, Cecil, vol. XI, p. 44, does not include Lord Rich, but the list of those imprisoned, HMC 58 Bath V, p. 281, names him in the position Lady Rich occupies in the former list. I am obliged to Dr Harris for confirming that the original (DE vol. II, f.329) concurs with the calendar. Since there is no other evidence for Lord Rich's involvement, the second list may be in error.

Penelope's detention at Sackford's: APC 1600–1601, pp. 166–7, 176.

~

"God be thanked we know you"; and "you would be king of England": Salmon, *State Trials*, vol. 1, pp.164, 170. The Percy brothers and Lord Monteagle were known Catholics like Tresham and Southampton, an "unsteady Catholic": Haynes, *Gunpowder Plot*.

Lady Russell called Essex "corrupt in religion" in 1596: *Devereux Lives*, vol. 1, p. 318.

Essex's ambitions for the crown: "upstart" claimant is Shapiro, p. 286. See *The Baronage of England*, W. Dugdale (1676), pp. 178–9. "I never saw any go through": *Chamberlain's Letters*, vol. 1, pp. 119–20. Essex's "confession" was reported to Mountjoy by the Earl of Nottingham, with the reassurance that Penelope was "set at liberty": McNeill, *Tanner Letters*, pp. 35–7.

Frances's letter, "If it be once signed I shall never wish": BL Lansdowne MS 88, f.14.

The London apprentices: *New Worlds, Lost Worlds*, p. 349.

Penelope's defence, "more like a slave than a sister": *Goodman's Court of King James*, vol. II, pp. 18–19, from the original BLO Tanner MS 114, f.139.

Cecil, "a further reach than appeareth": CSP Dom 1601–3, pp. 152, 154.

James's agents on their way to London: *After Elizabeth*, pp. 71–2.

Part IV Triumph and Tragedy 1601–1607

Chapter 24

"Finding the smoke of envy where affection should be clearest", Lady Penelope Rich, 1601; BLO Tanner MS 114, f.139.

Elizabeth's letter to "mistress kitchenmaid": Brewer and Bullen, *Carew MSS*, vol. III, p. 481.

Mountjoy in Ireland: Moryson, *Itinerary*, vol. 2. His letter "and not see my wife": CSP Ireland 1600–1601, pp. 173–4. Cecil's "when you consider how near": CSP Dom 1598–1601, p. 547. "I dare assure you": CSP Ireland 1600–1601, p. 198. "I think her majesty would be most glad": McNeill, *Tanner Letters*, pp. 35–7.

~

For Christmas 1601 see Shapiro, Thomson, *Shakespeare's Career*, *Chamberlain's Letters*, and Sir John Harington's *Nugae Antiquae*, ed. T. Park, 2 vols (1804). On Hamlet see Shapiro, pp. 318–31; and Haynes, *Secret Services*, pp. 187–8. The story of Essex's ring is dealt with in *After Elizabeth*, p. 145.

There are no known details of Penelope's movements in the aftermath of the trial.

For her finances: *Poor Penelope*, p. 151. She was not entirely friendless since she was thought to be with Harrington (father of the Countess of Bedford, and cousin to John Harington, Elizabeth's godson): Collins, *Sidney*, vol. II, p. 262.

~

On Mountjoy's campaigning and health: Moryson, Falls and Bardon, plus *Chamberlain's Letters*, vol. I, pp. 132–3, 139; *Memorials of State … Collected from the Papers of Ralph Winwood*, ed. E. Sawyer, 3 vols (1725), vol. I. And *New Worlds, Lost Worlds*, p. 353, on conditions in Kinsale camp.

Elizabeth's death: *Carey's Memoirs*, pp. 116–26, and *After Elizabeth*, pp. 114–27.

~

On the birth of Algernon Percy: G. Batho, "The finances of an Elizabethan nobleman: Henry Percy, Ninth Earl of Northumberland", *Economic History Review* (1957), pp. 433–49. Dudley Carleton's letter describing Dorothy "at Syon with the child" is quoted by Batho.

On Essex House: Kingsford, "Essex House", for Frances's occupation; Adams, "Papers of Robert Dudley, III"; DE vol. III has "bills and dealings" of Vanlore with Essex and Frances, 1589–1607; and Batho, as before, p. 448. The date of Frances's marriage to Richard Burke (or de Burgh), fourth Earl of Clanricarde, is uncertain (probably before April 1603; their son Ulrick was born 1604). Since Burke did not become a member of the English peerage until 1624 (later Earl of St Albans) Frances retained her title Countess of Essex.

Elizabeth's funeral: *After Elizabeth*, p. 188; and *Arbella*, p. 256, quoting "such a general crying" from John Stow's eyewitness *Annales of England* (1605).

Penelope becomes a lady in waiting to Anna: HMC 9, Cecil vol. XV, p. 56.

Chapter 25

"The place and rank of the ancientest Earl of Essex", King James I & VI, 1603; CSP Dom 1603–10, p. 32.

Penelope as one of Anna's ladies: see the Earl of Worcester's list in E. Lodge, *Illustrations of British History*, 3 vols (1838), vol. III, p. 88. And L. Barroll, "Inventing the Stuart Court masque", *Politics of the Stuart Court Masque*, pp. 121–43, note 16. For "the spider": *Polarisation*, p. 387, note 250.

Penelope's letter to Cecil before leaving London: Cecil Papers, vol. 103, f.50.

Anna's journey south: HMC 9, Cecil, vol. XV, p. 126; *After Elizabeth*, pp. 234–42; *The Diaries of Lady Anne Clifford,* ed. D. J. H. Clifford (1990), pp. 21–5; and *Lady Hoby's Diary*, p. 190. Penelope was an exception to Anna's aversion to her official ladies. Lucy Russell, Countess of Bedford (daughter of Sir John Harrington of Exton), was born 1581, died 1627.

"She likes enjoyment": Nicolo Molin, CSP Venetian 1603–7, p. 513.

Ben Jonson's masque at Althorp: Thomson, *Shakespeare's Career*, p. 162.

~

James: "sick of the pox" is quoted from A. Nicolson, *Power and Glory* (2003), p. 50.

For Ralegh's plotting see Lacey, *Walter Ralegh*, chapter 7; and *Ralegh and the Throckmortons*, pp. 237–8. "The queen had with her": *Dudley Carleton to John Chamberlain*, ed. M. Lee (1972), p. 35.

The "plotting and malice": Lodge, *Illustrations*, vol. III, p. 88.

Order for the ennoblement of Essex's children is PRO C 89/9/11.

Ralegh's trial: Lacey, *Walter Ralegh*, pp. 295–307, and *Arbella*, pp. 273–6. For the remainder of Bess's life see Beer, *Bess*, and Lacey, *Walter Ralegh*, pp. 313–21.

"Our great and gracious ladies", and Arbella's other views: *Arbella*, pp. 289–9.

~

The Venetian ambassador: CSP Venetian 1603–1607, p. 128.

"We have had a merry Christmas": *Dudley Carleton*, pp. 53–9. For the *Vision of the Twelve Goddesses*, see Barroll, "Inventing the Stuart masque". The Florentine ambassador's supper with Lady Rich was observed by the Earl of Worcester: Lodge, *Illustrations*, vol. III, p. 87.

Chapter 26

"Lascivious appetites of all sorts", Sir Simonds D'Ewes, c. 1620; *The Autobiography and Correspondence of Sir Simonds D'Ewes*, ed. J. O. Halliwell, 2 vols. (1845), vol. 2, pp. 325–6.

The Hampton Court conference: *Power and Glory*, pp. 41–52; and J. R. Tanner, *Constitutional Documents of the Reign of James I* (1930), pp. 60–69, includes extracts from W. Barlow's *Sum and Substance of the Conference* (1604).

The triumphal procession: A. G. P. V. Akrigg, *A Jacobean Pageant* (1962), p. 30. Arrival of the Spanish embassy: Wilson, *Secret Shakespeare*, p. 159; and Stone, *Family and Fortune*, p. 17 on Spanish pensions.

~

The ages of some of the children (named in Devonshire's will) are necessarily speculative: Penelope, bapt. 30 March 1592; Isabella, bapt. 30 January 1595; Mountjoy, probably born early autumn 1596; Scipio/St John, bapt. 8 December 1597, and Charles. It is possible Charles was conceived after his father returned from Ireland; but Penelope was then over forty and it is more likely Charles was at least conceived by early 1600. Fynes Moryson, living at Wanstead from 1603, is the source for Devonshire's life, yet he does not give details of the children. Moryson, who never married, also avoids mentioning Penelope. He refers to Devonshire's "grief of unsuccessful love brought him to his last end" (*Itinerary*, vol. 2, p. 267); and recalls that during Essex's trial "the Lady Rich her letter to the queen was pressed with very bitter and hard terms" (p. 314). Devonshire's few personal letters (e.g. BL Additional MS 12506) also give some details about his hawking, shooting rabbits and fishing.

Visit of the Spanish diplomats: *Dudley Carleton*, pp. 61–3; and the Whitehall banquet is described by Spanish ambassador Juan Fernandez de Velasco in Rye, *England as Seen by Foreigners*, pp. 117–28.

For Lettice's lawsuits against Sir Robert Dudley: *ODNB* and Adams, "Papers of Robert Dudley, III".

~

The King's Men's performances: Thomson, *Shakespeare's Career*, pp. 169–70. See also A. Gurr, *Playgoing in Shakespeare's London* (1987).

"We have here great preparations": *Winwood*, vol. II, p. 39. For *The Masque of Blackness* see Barroll, "Creating the Stuart Court Masque", pp. 131–6. "There is a pamphlet", and Philip Herbert's wedding: *Dudley Carleton*, pp. 66–8. "All the ladies about the Court": *Lady Anne Clifford's Diaries*, p. 28.

"Lady Rich prevented": *Winwood*, vol. II, p. 49.

The baptism of Princess Mary: *Lady Hoby's Diary*, p. 216; and Fraser, *Gunpowder Plot*, p. 117.
"As for the Catholics": quoted from Fontblanque, *Percy Annals*, vol. II, pp. 240–41.

~

Details of the plot are drawn from Haynes, *Gunpowder Plot*; Fraser, *Gunpowder Plot* and *Power and Glory*. For "where the Robin Hoods are assembled" see *Winwood*, vol. II, p. 173.

Chapter 27

"A fair woman with a black soul", King James I, 1606; quoted from Jones, *Mountjoy*, p. 180.
"My lord Rich and my lady were divorced": *The Letters of Philip Gawdy, 1579–1616*, ed. I. H. Jeayes (1906). A summarized copy of court findings is BL Additional MS 38170, f.82–4. On the legality of remarriage see: L. Stone, *The Road to Divorce 1530–1987* (1995). Under Elizabeth remarriage was not unusual: Craik, vol. 1, pp. 416, 418–19. But James's new laws included a draconian Bigamy Act (1604).
Spending on tobacco: *After Elizabeth*, p. 306; *Ralegh and the Throckmortons*, pp. 119, 191, 259; and Lacey, *Walter Ralegh*, p. 315.
Lust's Dominion, by John Marston, Thomas Dekker, William Houghton and John Day (c. 1599).
The royal household, HMC 9, Cecil, vol. XXIV, p. 67, listed by 18 March 1606, does not include Penelope.

~

On Devonshire's property trusts: *Poor Penelope*, p. 175ff, and PRO C 142/306/146.
Devonshire's relationship with Arbella: *Arbella*, pp. 193, 430. His health, see: *ODNB*/Richard Andrews; Moryson's comment on the fingers was noted by Margetts, "Stella Britanna", p. 385.
The wording of Devonshire's will and Penelope's failed pregnancy (see below) invite the assumption she was pregnant in December.
Devonshire's defence of the marriage and his letter to King James exist in many copies, e.g. BL Additional MS 4149, f.306–319, and BL Lansdowne MS 885, f.86–7.
Some "assurances passed between them": P. Heylyn, *Cyprianus Anglicus, or the History of the Life and Death of ... William Laud* (1719), p. 36. Laud, later Archbishop of Canterbury, was said to have held 26 December as a day of penitence for the rest of his life (partly giving rise to the identification of a portrait at Lambeth Palace as Penelope, see Chapter 8 notes).
"Was there not a certain lady", quoted by Jones, *Mountjoy*, p. 181, note 34. To "gather fruit": Bruce, "Correspondence of King James", p. 62. On Cecil's part in Penelope's downfall, Jones (p. 181) adds: "One cannot but surmise what sinister part Cecil had played."

~

On Cecil's betrayal of Northumberland, see Fontblanque, *Percy Annals*, vol. II, pp. 226–8, and Batho, as before.
See Haynes, *Gunpowder Plot*, p. 131, for Northumberland's place in the succession; p. 115 for Dorothy's letter, "the ill will of a certain great personage"; and p. 110 for rumours of James's assassination.
The "diabolical" trio: quoted from *Arbella*, p. 306.

"Foul words were passed": T. Birch, *The Court and Times of James the First*, 2 vols (1848), vol. I, p. 59.

On Fr Garnet, see Fraser, *Gunpowder Plot*, pp. 250–51; and Nicolson, *Power and Glory*, pp. 112–16.

Chapter 28

"In darkness let me dwell", John Coprario, *Funeral Tears, for the Death of the Right Honourable the Earl of Devonshire*, 1606.

The quarrel with Cecil's and Devonshire's visit to London: CSP Dom 1603–10, pp. 234, 278, 304. Details of Devonshire's last days are from Moryson, including "his fatal enemy". For the Savoy: Nichols (1788), vol. II. Contemporary gossip: Dudley Carleton, John Chamberlain and Ralph Winwood. Fr Gerard's account: *Autobiography of an Elizabethan*, p. 35.

Robert Johnston, *Historia Rerum Britannicarum 1572–1628* (1655), described Penelope lying on the floor of the chamber; quoted from Falls, *Mountjoy*, p. 234.

Samuel Daniel (see *ODNB*), author of Anna's masque, *The Vision of the 12 Goddesses*, had already found himself in trouble with his tragedy *Philotas*, which linked Devonshire closely to Essex's career.

On John Ford: K. Duncan-Jones, "Ford and the Earl of Devonshire", *Review of English Studies*, XXIX (1978), pp. 447–52. For Coprario see *ODNB* and Van Evera, *My Lady Rich* (see Chapter 19).

Devonshire's burial: Westminster Abbey Muniments, WAM 41809.

"It seems impossible that so vast a plot": CSP Venetian 1603–7, p. 293. See also Haynes, *State Papers*, p. 86, and pp. 115–16 for "sour dealing"; and Fontblanque, *Percy Annals*, vol. II, p. 239.

Father Garnet: Wilson, *Secret Shakespeare*, p. 296; and Fraser, *Gunpowder Plot*, pp. 263–7.

"The gunpowder fright", and the scenes at Theobalds: *Nugae Antiquae*, vol. I, pp. 348–53. On *Macbeth* see Wilson, *Secret Shakespeare*, p. 18.

Penelope's letter, "The young hunters": Cecil Papers, vol. 193, f.15. A contemporary report that "Harry Devereux", brother to the young Earl of Essex, was present is mistaken: young Essex had only two sisters.

Devonshire's will: PROB 11/108, re-examined 11/109/322; the *inquisitionem post mortem*: PRO C 142/306/146 to establish his estate; and the Star Chamber court case is STAC 8/108/10.

Chapter 29

"Neither wife, widow nor maid", Anon, 1607; BL Additional MS 15227, f.7.

On Theobalds: *Power and Glory*, pp. 137–8. On Syon: G. Batho, *Syon House: The First 200 Years*, p. 14.

"I find myself extremely ill again": Hotman Letters no. 45; and "so ill of a cold": HMC 9, Cecil, vol. XV, p. 113. The three reports of her death are: Thomas Coke's letter is HMC 12th Report, Appendix I, Coke MSS p. 63; Fr Gerard's account in *Autobiography of an Elizabethan*; and "outstanding in beauty", from Johnston, *Historia Rerum Britannicarum*.

Southampton's role as guardian is confirmed by: PRO STAC 8/47/13, 1 July 1617, issued on behalf of Mountjoy Blount, as a minor.

~

Thomas Campion's "Umbra" (1619): *The Works of Thomas Campion*, ed. W. R. Davis (1969).

For contemporary ribald comments: Hudson, "Penelope Devereux as Stella", pp.110–14.

There has been confusion over the date of her death and place of burial. The date, given in the postmortem PRO C 142/306/146, was formerly transcribed as 7 July and published in Falls, *Mountjoy*, p. 243 (and others). But Dr Margetts's revised reading ("Stella Britanna", p. 410) indicates the correct date is 6 July. The suggestion in *Poor Penelope*, p. 195, that an entry in All Hallows church register relates to Penelope has also been challenged, and I am indebted to Dr Margetts for details of her rereading of the entry, which casts doubt on the identification. There is no entry for Penelope in St Clement Danes register, or in Felsted records, which are extant for the period, and where one might have expected her to be buried if she had been reconciled to Lord Rich. Her last resting place remains, therefore, unknown.

Epilogue

Lord Rich's remarriage: *Letters of John Chamberlain*, vol. II, pp. 44, 101. He died at Warwick House in Holborn, 24 March 1619, and was buried a fortnight later at Felsted church, near Leighs.

Robert Rich (Penelope's eldest son), later second Earl of Warwick: *Lady Anne Clifford's Diaries*, e.g. p. 76, evidence the brothers being together.

Sir Harry Rich (Penelope's second son), later Earl of Holland: see *Power and Glory*, p. 119, for his £3,000 from King James; see also Cockayne, vol. VI, p. 538; executed in March 1649, a few weeks after Charles I.

Mountjoy Blount (Penelope's eldest son by Charles Blount), later Earl of Newport: see *Letters of John Chamberlain*, vol. II, p. 122; loss of Wanstead, CSP Dom 1611–1618, p. 504; at Robert and Frances Cromwell's wedding, *Dudley Carleton*, p. 175.

Penelope's daughters: Lucy and Arthur Lake, see Craik, vol. 1; young Penelope and Gervase Clifton, see *Poor Penelope*, p. 86, for the discovery of her correct age; and Isabella's marriage to Sir John Smythe, Collins, *Sidney*, vol. I, p. 147.

Lettice at Drayton: *Polarisation*, pp. 95–6, note 115, says Essex's illegitimate son, Walter, by Elizabeth Southwell was sent to live at Drayton. Her regular visits from "Little Robin", third Earl of Essex, followed the breakdown of his marriage to Frances Howard.

For "great discourses in matters of state": ODNB/Mary Queen of Scots.

The "younger son … fruitful bed": Clarendon's *History of the Rebellion*, vol. I, p. 37, and vol. VI, pp. 404–5.

The Broken Heart, whose plot is triggered by a forced marriage, has been called an "elegy on the tainted nobility of the last years of the Elizabethan Court, as well as of two of its most striking luminaries, Charles Blount and Penelope Rich": Duncan-Jones, *Ford and the Earl of Devonshire*. See also S. P. Sherman, "Stella and *The Broken Heart*", *PMLA* (1909).

"Perfection's heir": *Astrophil and Stella*, sonnet 71.

Index

London, Treaty of (1604) 238, 239
Lopez, Dr Roderigo 141-2, 143, 205
Lord Chamberlain's Men 170, 178, 181, 193, 235
Loyola, Ignatius 148
Lucas, Sir Thomas 87
Luxborough Hall, Chigwell, Essex 59, 70-71

macPhelim, Sir Brian 42
"Main" plot 230, 237
Mar, Earl of 216, 227
Margaret Tudor 34
Marlowe, Christopher 110, 171
Mary, Queen 22, 24, 26, 34, 54, 122, 147, 149
Mary Stuart, Queen of Scots 16, 35-8, 54, 60, 90, 91, 93, 97-100, 102, 109, 116, 237, 272, 280
Mary Tudor, Duchess of Suffolk 34, 36
Mauvissière, Seigneur de 116
Meyrick, Sir Gelly 61, 188, 194, 209, 215-16, 220-21
Middle Temple, London 125, 168, 182
Monteagle, Lord 209, 213, 216, 236, 244
Montagu, Anne, Lady Mandeville (née Rich; P's granddaughter) 249, 269, 270
Montagu, Edward, Viscount Mandeville later Earl of Manchester 269, 270
Montagu, Essex, Lady Mandeville (née Cheke; P's granddaughter) 270
Montemayor, Jorge de: *Diana* 139
Montgomery, Gabriel 29, 119
More, Sir Thomas 73, 125
Morgan, Thomas 98
Morley, Thomas 167
Moryson, Fynes 126-7, 154, 222, 223-4, 238-9, 249, 252, 254
Mountjoy, Charles Blount, Lord *see* Devonshire
Mountjoy, James Blount, sixth Baron Mountjoy 39, 124
Mountjoy, William Blount, seventh Baron Mountjoy 96, 124, 125, 132, 155

Naunton, Penelope (née Perrot; P's niece) 49, 118, 156
Naunton, Sir Robert 49

Nonsuch Palace, Ewell, Surrey 32, 71, 78, 91, 95, 102, 137, 192, 197, 198, 199, 207, 271
Norfolk, Duke of 38, 40
Norris, Sir John 96, 111, 126, 129, 132
North, Roger, Lord 59, 66, 78, 102, 176, 201
North, Winifred, Lady (née Rich) 72
North End, Essex 150, 151
North Hall, Hertfordshire 103, 111
Northern Earls, rebellion of 38, 39-40, 41
Northumberland, Dorothy Percy, Lady Perrot, Countess of (née Devereux; P's sister) 28, 40, 41, 47, 52-4, 55, 56-7, 67, 68, 118, 132, 151, 169, 175, 231, 239, 241, 243-4, 263-6, 271
  marriage to Sir Thomas Perrot 23, 88, 89, 93, 103, 117, 155-6, 279
  marriage to "the Wizard Earl" 16, 154, 158, 187, 200, 225, 230, 257, 271
Northumberland, Henry Percy, ninth Earl of ("the Wizard Earl"; P's brother-in-law) 54, 111, 126, 225, 226, 230, 231, 236, 239, 250, 251, 257, 263, 265, 279
  marriage to Dorothy 16, 154, 156, 158, 187, 200, 230
Nottingham, Catherine Howard, Countess of ("Kate"; née Carey; Lettice's cousin) 34, 59, 67, 69, 78, 211, 219
Nottingham, Charles Howard, Earl of 67, 69, 105, 162, 173, 175, 176, 211, 219-21, 225

O'Donnell, Rory *see* Tyrconnel, Earl of
Oxford, Earl of 64, 66

Parma, Duke of 104, 105
Peele, George 122, 123, 124
Pembroke 27, 30
Pembroke, Henry Herbert, second Earl of 59, 74, 75, 78, 159
Pembroke, Mary, Countess of (née Sidney) 44, 59, 74, 75, 78, 104, 159, 166, 233
Pembroke, Philip Herbert, fourth Earl of 233, 236, 240, 243

Peny, Dr 49
Percy, Algernon (P's nephew) 225, 230, 271
Percy, Sir Charles 209, 213, 216
Percy, Henry *see* Northumberland
Percy, Henry (P's nephews) 230, 271
Percy, Sir Josceline 209, 213, 216
Percy, Thomas 244, 251
Percy family 39, 156
Pérez, Antonio ("the Wandering Spaniard"; "Peregrino") 137-42, 144, 147, 158-9, 168, 170, 172, 174, 175, 180, 280
Perrot, Sir John 88, 146, 155, 240
Perrot, Lady Dorothy *see* Northumberland
Perrot, Penelope *see* Naunton
Perrot, Robert 155
Perrot, Sir Thomas 30, 88, 89, 93, 95, 96, 101, 102, 109, 135, 155-6, 268
Phelippes, Thomas 98, 99, 100
Philip II, King of Spain 104, 138, 139, 172, 173, 179, 192
Poley, Margaret (Marjery) 109
Poley, Robert 98-101, 110-111
Popham, lord chief justice 209-210
Portsmouth 155, 158, 160, 173, 175, 178, 179, 184
Portuguese expedition (1589) 111-12, 116, 117
Powder Treason (Gunpowder Plot) 147, 244-8, 252, 258
Prerogative Court of Canterbury (PCC) 259, 260, 262

Ralegh, Bess (née Throckmorton) 133, 186, 234, 245
Ralegh, Damerei 136, 234
Ralegh, Sir Walter 13, 60, 95, 102, 103, 108, 110, 133, 136, 156, 170, 172, 175, 185, 186, 199, 209, 212-13, 215, 230, 233, 234, 240, 251
Regnans in excelsis (papal bull) 40
Reynolds, Edward (Ned) 140, 174
Rialta affair 112-16, 144, 168, 213, 216
Rich, Anne (P's granddaughter) *see* Montagu
Rich, Charles (P's son by Mountjoy) 222, 238, 259, 268, 269

Index